Organization Practice

A Guide to Understanding Human Services

Second Edition

Mary Katherine O'Connor

F. Ellen Netting

WILEY

John Wiley & Sons, Inc.

Copyright © 2009 by John Wiley & Sons, Inc. All rights reserved.

Published by John Wiley & Sons, Inc., Hoboken, New Jersey.
Published simultaneously in Canada.

Library of Congress Cataloging-in-Publication Data:

O'Connor, Mary Katherine.

   Organization practice : a guide to understanding human services / Mary Katherine O'Connor, F. Ellen Netting. – 2nd ed.
      p. cm.
     Rev. ed. of : Organization practice / F. Ellen Netting, Mary Katherine O'Connor.
     Includes bibliographical references and index.
     ISBN 978-0-470-25285-7 (pbk.)
  1. Human services. I. Netting, F. Ellen.   II. Netting, F. Ellen. Organization practice.   III. Title.
    HV40.O33 2009
    361–dc22
                                                                             2008033285

Printed in the United States of America

10 9 8 7 6 5 4 3 2 1

Organization
Practice

This is for Lisa Gebo, a great intellect and an even greater woman.

Contents

Preface   ix

Acknowledgments   xv

ORIENTATION AND OVERVIEW

1   Human Service Practice in a Diverse Organizational Landscape   3
2   Frameworks for the Organization Practitioner   41

PART I   STRUCTURE AND CONTROL

3   Traditional Organizations   91
4   Practice in Traditional Organizations   119

PART II   CONSCIOUSNESS RAISING FOR CHANGE

5   Social Change Organizations   153
6   Practice in Social Change Organizations   179

PART III   CONNECTION AND COLLABORATION

7   Serendipitous Organizations   213
8   Practice in Serendipitous Organizations   239

PART IV   INDIVIDUAL EMPOWERMENT

9   Entrepreneurial Organizations   273
10   Practice in Entrepreneurial Organizations   299

CONCLUSION

11   Multiparadigmatic Practice   327

Appendix A: Organization Assessment   365

Glossary   375

References   385

Author Index   401

Subject Index   409

Preface

THERE HAVE BEEN some very interesting developments in organization practice since we wrote the first edition to this text. There is more empirical evidence to support the existence and viability of alternative ways of organizing and practicing within human service agencies. Therefore, we have included more material related to the empirical research undertaken by us and others regarding a multiparadigmatic approach to understanding human service organizations. The various frameworks have been included as a way to corral the chatter that gets created when one comes to understand the complexity of the issues involved in dealing with multiple, respectable ways of organizing practice within organizational structures.

We have become a bit more savvy about our perspective and the accompanying challenges therein, as well as understanding better the clarity needed to allow space for alternative practices. In this edition, more attention is given to the paradoxes practitioners encounter when units or programs within an organization do not match the predominant identity, cultural assumptions, or goals of the larger organization. More attention is given to the role of advocacy and change objectives within each organizational perspective. We also examine personal challenges with lack of fit between preferences (comfort zones) and reality encountered in everyday survival within complex human service organizations.

This second edition of *Organization Practice* truly represents the culmination of multiple layers of collaborative thinking and work. The ideas remain essentially the same; however, the presentation has been substantially modified in order to make the information much more practical and user friendly. Former readers will notice expanded practice examples, including four extensive case studies to illustrate concepts and ideas intended to enrich the reading and learning experience. End-of-chapter discussion questions have also been developed. New readers will encounter an attempt on our part to recognize and manage the complexity of organization practice that, while relying on philosophy and theory, is very much tethered to the lived experience of professionals practicing in organizations guided by the values of the helping professions. Although much of our thinking is based in postmodern thought, we have been particularly attentive to our language usage and have provided an extended glossary to help. In addition, we hope we have been transparent and avoided vagueness as much as possible. Sometimes, however, it is impossible to keep it simple, so we encourage those using the text to "keep on keeping on." Our students tell us that this approach to organizations becomes understandable over time. Once it is understandable, it serves as an invaluable tool for practice.

Much more about organization practice, beyond merely understanding culture and structure, has been developed for this edition. It continues to be built on multiple perspectives, with the four major parts of the text outlining types of organizations derived from different assumptions about what constitutes reality and guided by very different organizational goals. The idea is that with an understanding of the undergirding assumptions, one can understand the logic of the decisions that go into creating the organization and the expectations for practice within these different types of organizations. It is not our intention to determine what is best overall, but for readers to develop the capacity to use a variety of approaches to organization practice, depending on the need.

The major content of the text is divided into parts covering four types of organizations (Traditional, Social Change, Serendipitous, and Entrepreneurial) with additional introductory and concluding chapters. Each of the four content parts details the theories that can be used to guide each type of organization in a chapter that focuses on understanding that organization's primary identity and goals. This more theoretical chapter is followed by a chapter on practice and standards within that type of organization. The four major parts of the book are designed to clarify the fundamental differences among organizations when worldview, organizational culture, and goals are joined. The multiple perspectives as detailed in the works of Burrell and Morgan (1979) and Cameron and Quinn (1999; 2006) guide the entire text.

Chapters 1 and 2 set the stage for the material that follows. Chapter 1 is rather definitional in nature, establishing various dimensions of the organizational world, its practice arenas, and programs and services, as well as human service organizational types and relationships. Here the reader will get a quick overview of the current organizational landscape, including a historical accounting of the major theories involved in organizational structure and practice. Discussion will include how the various theoretical approaches have developed over time, outlining the resultant assumptions about organizations, employees, managers, and leaders. It is our belief that a good historical grounding is necessary to understand the logic of the contemporary decisions. We also follow the adage that those who do not understand their history will be forced to repeat it. Because this is such an analytical text aimed at managing complexity, information regarding critical thinking, self-awareness, and leadership will be surfaced in the context of multiculturalism and diversity.

Chapter 2 introduces the frameworks that will be used throughout the text to connect theory to practice in human services. Discussed separately and then integrated into the scaffolding of the remainder of the text, paradigms (Burrell & Morgan, 1979), competing values and cultures (Cameron & Quinn, 2006), Myers-Briggs (Myers, 1998), and strategic management (Mintzberg, Ahlstrand & Lampel, 1998) will be described briefly and then brought together by introducing the four types of organizations that will be the focus of the remainder of the text.

We believe this integration is a useful vehicle for the sort of organizational and practice responsiveness necessary in the complex, multicultural world of the 21st century. Discussion questions at the end of these chapters will deepen students' basic conceptual understandings prior to embarking on the more theoretical and practical considerations in the next four parts of the text.

Parts I, II, III, and IV are written in a parallel format, with two chapters each. Each part contains an introduction that covers the major goals of the type of organization that is the focus of that part. Also included is an extensive case intended to provide an exemplar of the lived experience in the type of organization that will be further interrogated in the rest of that part of the text. The case example should begin the thinking about organizational perspectives. These cases are also intended to provide a basis for comparison of how different sets of assumptions drive organizational structure and influence the development of different cultures and practices within human service organizations.

In the first chapter of each part, we will examine important structural characteristics of a human service organization with goals that fit within the specified perspective on organizing. Theories and assumptions about structure and behavior will also be introduced that fit with the particular perspective. In the second chapter of each part, we will focus on standards for practice in an organization congruent with the goals and perspectives outlined in the earlier chapter. The derived characteristics covering values, mission/philosophy, organizational structure, and programs and services will set the stage for the expectations related to roles and relationships, leadership, and practice. Between the two chapters, a full picture of a specific type of organization will be offered in order to surface the differences that accrue within organizations that reflect differing assumptions. Particular attention will be given to the social justice implications of the values, preferences, and decision-making strategies relevant to the organization's goals, so that eventually the reader will come to understand the paradoxes that are naturally part of human service organizations, regardless of type. The four parts of the text capturing differing organizational goals are: (1) Structure and Control, (2) Consciousness Raising for Change, (3) Connection and Collaboration, and (4) Individual Empowerment.

Part I: Structure and Control covers the organizational perspective most traditional and familiar to readers. Chapter 3 details the Traditional Organization and its commonly accepted ways of organizing. Both the theories and the cultural identities supporting this approach are detailed, along with real-life examples showing how concepts actually operate in practice. In Chapter 4, we examine the practice expectations derived from this approach to organizing. The strengths and challenges of planned change will be detailed with examples. End-of-chapter discussion questions have been designed to enhance the reader's critical thinking about understanding and practicing in traditional, bureaucratic human service organizations with established and legitimized identities and reputation. The idea is to begin to challenge the thinking about Traditional Organizations so that a space is created for alternative, new, or emergent organizational arrangements.

Part II: Consciousness Raising for Change begins the construction of that space for the development of new roles and relationships between management, practitioners, and clients. In Chapter 5, we focus on Social Change Organizations that have social reform and large-scale advocacy at their core. Theories guiding structure and practice calling for transformative, perhaps revolutionary, change, including power and politics and postmodern traditions, are investigated. The consequences of clear declaration of radical change goals at the class level are detailed as a transition to Chapter 6. In this chapter, the dialectical nature of practice, the ways in which power and politics are operationalized, along with the risks that may be involved are covered with examples drawn from more progressive current practices. In this chapter we also introduce the themes of paradoxes that will be seen throughout the rest of the text. Here, the paradoxes of radical units within more traditional types of organizations or those of internally ordered organizations with radical social goals will be explored, through both the case narrative at the beginning of Part II and the end-of-chapter discussion questions. The idea here is to help the reader consider how to bring empowerment and more radical change into society, also demonstrating how to risk transformation from within traditional organizational structures.

Part III: Connection and Collaboration takes a more consensus- and context-based approach to organizing, following the more interpretive perspectives of the Serendipitous Organization. Chapter 7 emphasizes those organizational theories focusing on meaning making and context. More modern theories such as organizational culture and sense making are highlighted to help the reader understand how in Chapter 8 practice norms in these organizations are often unstated and difficult for outsiders to understand. Practice in Serendipitous Organizations can both complement and compete with other approaches. Treatment of Part III's case example in both chapters is intended to show both commonalities and differences between this type of organization and expected practices in more traditional and radical organizations. The challenges as well as the paradoxes that emerge with an orientation to process are addressed and further developed in the end-of-chapter discussion questions. The expectation is that the reader will not be naïve about the difficulties imbedded in appreciating difference while also seeking consensus.

We have left the most challenging alternative perspective until last. *Part IV: Individual Empowerment* appears at first to be antithetical to organization practice. In fact, it would seem that the Entrepreneurial Organization is antithetical to any sort of structure. In Chapter 9, from a theoretical perspective, comparison will be made with radical change entities in order to highlight how individual empowerment organizations are tied to power and politics theories, critical theory, certain branches of feminist theory, and postmodern theories, as are organizations with larger-scale transformative change goals. The difference will be illustrated through the antiadministration approach to theory. Part IV's case example will, we trust, provide a provocative backdrop for exploring the nature and consequences of this emerging approach to organizing. Chapter 10 is all about paradox. The issues of organizing without organizational structures and creating organizations that empower individuals and respect differences at all costs are explored. This exploration continues in the end-of-chapter discussion questions on the challenges of transforming individuals within highly flexible organizational boundaries or within organizations having no traditional boundaries whatsoever.

A final effort at helping the reader compare and contrast the material is found in the concluding Chapter 11, Multiparadigmatic Practice. This final chapter is provided to offer extensive details to be used with critical analysis that should allow for evenhanded consideration of the costs and benefits of structuring organizations from the four different perspectives presented. Strengths and challenges of organization practice from each perspective are offered in order to straightforwardly look at the paradoxical consequences in the absence of pure organizational types.

The appendix that follows Chapter 11 is composed of an organization assessment tool that should enable the reader to identify and assess the congruence and paradoxes between and among perceptions of the ideal organization, the work unit in which one spends the most time, and the overall organization in which practice occurs. This is offered as both an assessment and a planning tool for future practice.

From this entire discussion it should be clear that throughout the text a great deal of attention is given to the existence and management of paradoxes that one encounters when units or programs within an organization do not match the predominant identity, cultural assumptions, or goals of the larger organization. Our goal is also to raise readers' consciousness of the potential personal paradoxes that can accrue when there is lack of fit between organizational preferences and organizational reality. Our intention is not simply to raise the possibilities, but also to help the manager and the practitioner realize when there is a problem requiring some sort of change in organizational structure, practice, or status. In short, we hope that more of your attention will be directed beyond appropriate practice within a given organization to an enhanced vision of the role of advocacy and change objectives within each organizational perspective. In that way, the role of practitioner as advocate can in fact be appropriately activated when necessary, regardless of the organization's goals, structures, or expectations. We sincerely hope that this book can serve as a launching platform for future human service leaders to engage in thoughtful and competent organization practice that develops in response to changing contexts, needs, and expectations. From our vantage point of multiple perspectives, we have learned more and more every day. As a result of your engaging with the material here, we trust that options and possibilities will open for you, as well.

Acknowledgments

OUR STUDENTS AND community colleagues have been instrumental in bringing us along and we are indebted to them for that. We especially thank a decade of Planning and Administration students (even those who thought theory was "way boring") for their willingness to play with these ideas even when they were not so well developed. We are also grateful for their insightful and practical feedback to various versions of the first edition. If other students think this edition speaks to them, it is because of the conversations we have had with our own students. Many of our students have become our professional colleagues in the community as they have graduated to become leaders in the field. Others have gone on to become social work educators. Thankfully, they continue to be our helpful critics for these ideas. We are very appreciative of two special social service agencies that allowed us to empirically test the ideas herein. If this edition is particularly useful, we are decidedly indebted to those collaborations.

We are indescribably grateful to the academics who have given us constructive feedback about the challenges and opportunities that our first edition represented for them in the classroom. That feedback and the suggestions by reviewers of this edition have come together to help us create a new and, hopefully, improved version of our original work. We are particularly grateful to our practitioner colleagues, who not only have found our approach useful but have given us insights into its usefulness. The naming of the organizational types is based on a collaboration with Nancy Macduff, who came up with the words to describe each paradigmatic type so that volunteer managers could use our work. "Thank you" is also in order to Paul McWhinney, John Purnell, and Karen Legato, who were open to collaborations for empirical testing of our ideas.

Nothing could have made this second edition a reality without Lisa Gebo, who always believed in us and encouraged our creativity. The editorial staff at Wiley, especially Sweta Gupta, Stevie Belchak, and Rose Sullivan, have always been responsive and helpful to us in every aspect of the writing process.

Finally, we are grateful to Dean Frank R. Baskind and the faculty of the Virginia Commonwealth University School of Social Work for supporting our research so that we could further extend our ideas. Special thanks go to our collaborator, Humberto Fabelo, who enthusiastically joined with us in testing the Burrell and Morgan framework. Particular appreciation is due to our friend and colleague, David Fauri. David's generosity of spirit and respectful, yet critical, feedback have been instrumental in the growth and further development of the ideas contained herein.

ORIENTATION AND OVERVIEW

CHAPTER 1

Human Service Practice in a Diverse Organizational Landscape

I N THIS BOOK, we focus on the knowledge and skills practitioners rely on to professionally work and survive in organizations. *All* human service practitioners engage in organization practice, regardless of their focus. In this chapter, we want to impress upon the reader the importance of competent organization practice because most practitioners will work within, and with, many different organizations throughout their professional careers. We define **organization practice** as *working and surviving in organizational arenas by making changes that address the needs of multiple stakeholders and constituencies, strongly grounded in professional values, critical thinking, and self-awareness.*

One can find as many definitions of organizations as there are writers on organizations. Shafritz, Ott, and Lang (2005) define **organizations** as "social unit[s] with some particular purpose" (p. 1). They contend that "the basic elements of organizations have remained relatively constant throughout history: Organizations (or their important constituencies) have purposes (which may be explicit or implicit), attract participants, acquire and allocate resources to accomplish goals, use some form of structure to divide and coordinate activities, and rely on certain members to lead or manage others" (p. 2). These characteristics vary, depending on the environment in which an organization operates. We find Shafritz, Ott, and Lang's (2005) definition to be to the point and we agree with their assumption that there is something "social" about this unit or arena by the very nature of multiple people being involved. They also assume there is "some particular purpose" for this social unit to come together. *Purpose* is a broad, inclusive word that could include goals and objectives, but does not have to do so. And there may be multiple purposes, depending on the organization.

In this chapter, we provide a brief overview of the human service organizational landscape, including the arenas in which professional practice occurs. We make explicit our assumptions and biases, followed by a focus on programs and services as well as types of human service organizations and their relationships. A brief historical review of organizational theory development is provided to whet the reader's appetite for a more specific focus on selected theories in subsequent chapters. Included in this section are theoretical assumptions held about different units of analysis in organizational settings—the organization itself, employees, and persons in formal managerial and leadership roles. The use of critical thinking and self-awareness for leadership in organization practice follows with special attention to the student or employee who is clinically, rather than organizationally, oriented. We end this chapter with attention to the kind of complexity and **diversity** that is found in multicultural settings, which leads to our second chapter, in which established frameworks for understanding the complexity of organizing human services are introduced.

AN ORGANIZATIONAL WORLD

To understand the role of organizations in professional life, it may be helpful for readers to think about how they view work. Many years ago, a worker in an agency might have aspired to remain in the same organization for years and to "move up" in that agency. Today's employment expectations are much different. It is more typical for people to change jobs frequently. It is also more typical for agencies and services to go into and out of existence, as well as to perform their functions across political, economic, societal, and ideological boundaries. Examining organizations as practice arenas must be placed within the broader global context of changing expectations of what one looks for in a position and how employees define themselves within the contemporary world of work.

Since the world is often viewed through inter- and intraorganizational contexts, composed of many different organizations that perform various functions within and across international boundaries, few persons are untouched by multiple organizations. Organizations are an integral part of a contemporary lifestyle, and they are arenas in which the exchange of resources occurs on a regular basis. They may be situated in defined geographical communities or they may transcend geography, connected by technological innovation, as with **virtual organizations**. Their purposes and structures are as varied as their numbers.

In addition, there are organizations that deliver no human services directly but perform support functions such as providing funding, planning for and oversight of human service providers, **advocacy** for special population groups, and/or education and training for those persons who do provide services. These organizations often have staff who review grant applications and determine who will be funded, contract for services with providers, set priorities among competing human service needs, formulate and interpret policy, advocate for change, and influence technologies used in service delivery. They are very much a part of the human service landscape, even though they are not direct providers of human services.

We take an expansive view of human service work, encouraging professionals to recognize that there are no clear-cut, separate sectors in which human service work is conducted. Thus, we expose one of our many assumptions in writing this book that contemporary human service work occurs through traditional, alternative, and emerging auspices and that many organizations are involved in the formulation and interpretation of policy, in influencing provider agencies, and in the daily delivery of human services. Given the ever-changing landscape of human service delivery, mapping it is a challenge.

ORGANIZATIONAL PRACTICE ARENAS

Rothman, Erlich, and Tropman (2008) identify three large system **practice arenas**: communities, organizations, and small task groups. These arenas are anything but mutually exclusive. Communities, organizations, and groups overlap and interact and all are organized for a purpose. To add to the complexity, more and more organizations are operating across communities, states, nations, and international boundaries. When the world is one's practice arena, to be effective, it becomes a challenge for practitioners to be respectful of different cultures and contexts when enacting organizational work.

Practitioners, in both their personal and professional lives, by virtue of being a part of these complex arenas, are tied to numerous organizations that relate to and even formally affiliate with various communities and groups. Practitioners are professionally affiliated with an organizational structure or structures, whether they are private practitioners within the confines of a small group practice or public officials within a complex web of bureaucratically entangled relationships. Few professionals are free agents who can afford to practice without the support of an organizational base. The few who operate as independent consultants or solo practitioners create their own organizations that interact with and depend on a multitude of organizations for survival. Organizations may even be the object of their **interventions**. Even if an organization is not located in another part of the world, each organization will have distinctive cultures, requiring the use of multicultural skills for effective practice.

Organizations have been viewed by some theorists as situated in uncertain, turbulent environments in which they are constantly responding to **constraints** (things they can not change) and **contingencies** (things about which they have to compromise and negotiate). Yet, it is not just the environments in which organizations operate that are uncertain and turbulent. Organizations face internal uncertainties and turbulence as well. Organizations are dynamic, changing entities that are situated in dynamic and changing communities. Given the nature of these settings, to be successful, practitioners must understand as much as possible about these dynamics.

Adding to complexity, organizations that support and deliver human services vary in how they are structured. It is important for practitioners to know the architecture of the organizations within which they practice. One often hears the term *formal* used to describe an organization. This implies that there are also *informal* organizations. It is not always easy to define clear boundaries between a formal and an informal organization. For example, a group of committed citizens may organize to provide services to persons in need. In the process of organizing they may develop a statement of purpose, rally the support of volunteers, and develop a process for their services. They are technically an informal group. But what happens when they decide to form a nonprofit corporation so that they can receive funding from outside sources? If they are incorporated, they are formally recognized as a nonprofit organization. They may still have the same purpose, continue to use volunteers, and deliver their services in the same way. Yet, they are no longer just a "group"; they are an *organization*. Perhaps there are degrees of formality. We cannot tell you clearly when a group becomes a formal organization or when service delivery becomes formalized. Both the challenge and the opportunity in organization practice is that boundaries between organizational practice arenas are not always clear and distinctive.

SOME BEGINNING COMMENTS

Before we thoroughly examine the concept of organization and focus on those that engage in human service delivery, we would like to release the reader from some of the constraints of order, finality, and logic. You might be hoping that you will find some universals that you can apply to all organizations so that human service delivery systems will make sense once you've studied organizations. You might hope that practicing in organizations will be easier having read our material. If any of these thoughts sound familiar, we offer some alternatives to consider.

First, we, and others, will frequently refer to organizations as *systems* and to human service delivery *systems*. Do not be fooled by these references to *systems*. The word *system* may lead you to think of something that is logical, consistent, and definable as it works; however, you will encounter many organizations (perhaps most) that seem very unsystematic. This may not be because you "just don't get it." It could be that these systems don't make sense without understanding the full context in which they operate. It could even be that they don't perform like systems at all. It could be that your assumptions about how things should work are so different from the assumptions held about the organization by others, that you are experiencing a clash in cultures. Do not despair, for this presents an opportunity to learn about different cultures. Some organizations will have similar characteristics, but every organization will have its own uniqueness. Some will be so unique that they will be different from those you have previously experienced and unlike others you will know. Do not jump to any conclusions about what you are experiencing until you can fully understand the major aspects of the cultural context of that organization. Only then is appropriate assessment possible.

Second, we find that some people approach the study of human service organizations with the assumption (or hope) that the reason they don't quickly see how the whole service system works is because they haven't yet learned enough about how individual organizations work. As they learn more, they might discover that the human service system seems fragmented or hard to understand. Frustration occurs because there is a deep-seated assumption that someone, somewhere, conceptualized the system and understands the "master plan." Let us assure you: There is no one overriding master plan. Sometimes there are few, if any, overriding plans at all. Other times there are multiple plans of how a system should work, plans that have not been coordinated or even articulated, plans that may even contradict one another. Some plans are rigidly scientific and others emerge (Netting, O'Connor, & Fauri, 2008). If you can't make sense of the delivery system, it is possible that the delivery system doesn't make sense. This is understandable when one thinks historically about how numerous organizations and groups emerged to address diverse needs in local communities. They did not arise simultaneously in a rational, concentrated effort to provide care. Some actually arose in protest of others that did not respond to the needs of invisible community groups. The landscape of human service delivery, therefore, is rich in diversity, offering you an assortment of perspectives. It is the exceptional situation that has a unified jointly held vision of human service delivery in a local community where organizations, though differing in structure and culture, mesh together to accomplish common goals in an apparently seamless responsive process. When organizations go global, the challenge of sense making grows exponentially. Imagine how potentially unattainable it is to find a jointly held vision across the borders of culture and geography. Without great care, some sort of superimposition of culture and norms about aspects of organization practice are inevitable. For us, mutual sensitivity and competence across cultures (whether those are local or international) is essential.

Third, no matter what we say, there will be exceptions to every rule. Any attempts to define, categorize, or classify organizations are only that: attempts. If you know of an organization that does not conform to what we say throughout this text, then it is because you know of an organization that does not fit. It is probably not that you "don't get it" or that the organization in question should be made to conform in order to do it "right." Let us be clear in our message: We are attempting to provide some manageability in examining this landscape when in actuality we know that disorder and chaos are the way many of our systems creatively solve the problems associated with human service work. Organization practice, therefore, requires one to constantly be assessing and reassessing situations. This is why you are here: to learn about organizations so that you will become knowledgeable and skilled in a highly complex arena of practice. Our goal is that you learn about and respect the many dimensions of difference in organizations in order to professionally survive and thrive.

ORGANIZATIONS AS COLLECTIONS OF PROGRAMS AND SERVICES

Organizations that support and deliver human services address concerns about people and their needs, making them somewhat different from organizations in general, yet most of the organizational literature is not directed to these type organizations. We recognize that not *all* organizations delivering human services are full-time human service agencies, nor is *everything* a human service organization does focused on direct service delivery to clients. In our view, organizations that fund, plan, advocate, and/or educate are in the human service business, even though they are not direct providers of services. If such organizations are social units that come together for a purpose, then these organizations often find ways to pursue that purpose in the form of programs.

Programs

We are defining **programs** as structural containers for long-term commitments, services, and/or activities designed to directly or indirectly address human needs—a set of activities designed to fulfill a social purpose (Netting, O'Connor, & Fauri, 2008). Direct human service programs focus their activities on addressing specific client needs, whereas indirect programs support these human service efforts, focusing on such areas as fundraising, public relations, or advocacy. Sometimes, entire organizations will be devoted to these support functions. For example, a state human service department may be an oversight and planning agency for those providers who deliver services locally. Similarly, a foundation that funds a program initiative to provide case management for troubled youth is supporting direct service grantees who implement its program.

In order to fully support direct client-serving programs, human service providers may have a variety of other types of programs. For example, a human service agency could have **direct service programs** to assist clients, usually attempting to make their situations better in some way, and **staff**

development and training programs that focus on staff, the intention being that if staff have additional knowledge and skills they will be able to do better direct service provision. The agency could have **support programs** that may be program-, organizational- or community-based, with the intention being that their activities are processes that will lead to higher quality programming.

Obviously, there are organizations that do not deliver direct human services but still have programs and still hire practitioners. Roles that practitioners play in these organizations are reflected in titles such as *advocate, trainer, planner, policy analyst, administrator, monitor, evaluator,* and *program officer.* Other organizations, called **provider agencies**, hire practitioners in direct practice roles to implement programs through the provision of services.

SERVICES

A **service** is a specific intervention. For example, a service could be counseling or receiving a mobile meal. Both are human services because they directly impact individuals in need. While one is less concrete (counseling) than the other (a meal), both services might be linked in a senior citizens' program designed to address the psychological and nutritional needs of older persons. Programs tend to be comprised of multiple services. Although organizations do not always conceptualize their activities as programs composed of services, it is helpful to use this framework in looking at how human services are delivered.

This conceptualization is also useful in separating what is occurring in a human service organizational context as it attempts to meet clients' needs. At times within the service system, funding sources and other persons in power do not immediately recognize the need for new programs and services. Even well-designed programs and innovative service technologies may require piloting within an organization before they will be embraced. Sometimes there are unpopular causes or population groups who are not served at all. In these cases, hopefully, programs, services, or even new agencies emerge in response to these unmet needs.

TYPES OF ORGANIZATIONS THAT PLAN AND DELIVER HUMAN SERVICES

PUBLIC AGENCIES

Public or governmental agencies are mandated by law at some level of government. A **public agency** in the U.S. context is established through a local, a state, or the federal system with the purpose of that agency contained in legal statutes. Examples of public agencies are local, state, or federal departments of human or social services, health, education, and aging. Public agencies are created through legislation and are charged with implementing public social policies. Since social policies are formulated, developed, debated, and eventually approved and enacted by public policy makers, public agencies inherit the controversies sometimes surrounding the social policies that mandate their programs and services. Their destinies as service entities are deeply imbedded in current and past political ideology.

Public agencies that deliver human services vary in how they are structured. For example, Ezell and Patti (1990) examined state-level human service agencies in Delaware, Florida, Minnesota, Oregon, South Carolina, and Utah. These six states were selected because they represented diversity in comprehensiveness (how many different services they provide), integration (how connected or interrelated their services are with one another), and centralization of services and decision making. Even though these researchers hoped to find "what is best" in terms of how public human services are structured, they reported that every state had something to offer and that each state's agency had strengths and limitations. In each state, various constituencies had different expectations, some of which conflicted. The design of state and local agencies represented compromises among diverse constituencies and the outcomes they would accept.

Public agencies are often large in size for reasons of efficiency because they are mandated to serve numerous population groups with multiple problems. However, this does not mean that they will look the same. In fact, given differences in regional and local resources and needs, it is questionable that they should look the same. We disagree when people say that if you have seen one public bureaucracy, you have seen them all. They may appear hierarchical in structure, but there are many different ways to design an effective public agency, just as there are different ways to determine effectiveness. Because of the political context of the public agency, it is the political process of consensus building that determines public agency design and the scope of its services. Therefore, there will be much diversity in terms of what and how many programs an agency will have from state to state. This is also the case for what services each program will contain, how its programs will relate to one another, how centralized or decentralized its decision-making and authority structures will be, and how many branch offices it will have.

PRIVATE AGENCIES

Private agencies are a broad category of organizations, including those that are called *nonprofit* and *for-profit*. Both nonprofit and for-profit organizations are part of the human service enterprise and are different from public agencies. Recently in the United States and elsewhere, new approaches are developing that in some ways combine non-profit and for-profit. Called social entrepreneurs and social businesses, they often blur the lines in creative ways.

Nonprofit Organizations Nonprofit organizations are referred to as *nongovernmental, third sector, voluntary, charitable,* or *tax exempt agencies* depending on the nation in which they are located. They typically have uncompensated, voluntary boards of directors who cannot benefit financially from the organization's profits. Any profit made must be reinvested in the organization.

Lohmann (1989) points out that using the prefix *non* to describe an entire group of organizations is not particularly helpful. He compares naming a sector *nonprofit* or *nongovernmental* to defining lettuce as a mammal. "Lettuce is a non-fur-bearing, non-milk-producing, non-child bearing, and non-warm blooded nonanimal. Further, as a mammal, lettuce is highly ineffective, being sedentary and not warm-blooded. All other mammals are much faster. Lettuce is also remarkably non-agile and fails to protect its young. On the whole, lettuce is a miserable excuse for a mammal!" (p. 369). Lohmann's wit reveals the challenges posed by defining one sector (nonprofit) in light of another (for-profit).

Nonprofit agencies have been described over the years in numerous ways: as representative organizations of a defined body of the citizenry; as nonstatutory organizations; as nongovernmental organizations with an elected board of directors; as organizations supported by voluntary (nontax) dollars; and even as organizations that "feel" voluntary. We add to this laundry list the possibility that some voluntary agencies today do not feel voluntary at all. They are struggling to become more businesslike and in the process are having identity crises over what they really are. For us, what probably makes a nonprofit agency voluntary is that their board of directors must serve without compensation and, therefore, are volunteers.

As part of the complexity of the nonprofit landscape, and contrary to popular belief, nonprofit organizations can make profits. In fact, if they do not make profits, they may have little chance at stability and growth. The defining characteristic of a **nonprofit organization** is that it is barred from distributing profits, or net earnings, to individuals who exercise control over it. These individuals might be directors, officers, or members. Net incomes, if any, must be retained and devoted to the purposes for which the organization was formed (Hansmann, 1981). This means that any funds left over at the end of a fiscal year must be reinvested in the organization, not distributed to any constituency.

Another element that muddies the distinction between types of agencies in human services is the highly interdependent nature of the service delivery system. This interdependence is particularly notable between the governmental and the nonprofit environments. It is the rare nonprofit human service organization that does not count on a portion (sometimes a large portion) of its funding from governmental sources. Whether an agency depends on food subsidies to keep its day care costs low or on social service contracts to provide foster care, the independent, community-based, voluntary nature of nonprofits is somewhat of a myth. Because of this apparent interdependence, services in the private sector seem to be almost as political as those in the government sector, just in different ways.

For-Profit Organizations   For-profits are businesses, sometimes called *corporations*. They are part of the commercial or market economy. They must pay taxes. They have boards of directors who generally are compensated and they may have investors or stockholders, all of whom can benefit financially from the organization's profits.

For-profit organizations have always been part of the human service landscape, but have become more involved in service delivery since the 1960s. For example, "between 1965 and 1985, for-profit centers and chains emerged as the fastest growing source of child care in the United States," increasing from 7% to 24% of the market niche serving the child care needs of employed parents (Tuominen, 1991, pp. 450–451). Another example is the nursing home industry, which is predominantly run by for-profit businesses. With privatization of human services, which has emerged as a cost-saving scheme at the national and state levels, the once-assumed distinctions between profit and nonprofit, governmental, and non-governmental entities are blurring. Many for-profit agencies are competing against nonprofits for governmental service contracts. In addition, non-profit organizations may even create for-profit agencies to generate income that can be contributed to their causes. For example, for-profit thrift stores are often a stable source of income for nonprofit groups that are highly involved in human service delivery.

Social Entrepreneurs and Social Businesses   Starting with Muhammad Yunus, the Bangladeshi economist and winner of the 2006 Nobel Peace Prize, who started the Grameen Bank (see *Banker to the poor*, 2003), which provides microcredits to the poor, a newly developing human service approach focusing on social change is being established worldwide. **Social entrepreneurs**, using the ideas and methods of business entrepreneurs, are revamping the nonprofit sector around the world so that the nonprofit sector has become the fastest-growing segment of society (Bornstein, 2004). Using innovative ideas and determination, social entrepreneurs from the United States to Brazil and from Hungary to Africa are breaking established rules about how to enact human services. Social entrepreneurs use their own expertise, social and political connections, and sometimes their own money to leverage action toward positive change, ranging from tackling poverty, pollution, and inadequate health care, to lack of education. What seems to hold the organizing structures of the social entrepreneurs together worldwide is a vision of what might be possible through the power of ideas, and the belief that through many means it is possible to make changes for the better. It appears that each social entrepreneur approaches the solution to the problem differently, so each organization that has been created is also very different.

Muhammad Yunus has moved beyond his role as a social entrepreneur to develop the concept of a social business. The idea is to use the power of free enterprise to solve the great social problems of poverty, hunger, and inequality (Yunus, 2007). Along with Danone, the French corporation, makers of Dannon yogurt, he has launched a purposefully designed social business whose purpose is to provide affordable yogurt for children in Bangladesh. From this effort has developed what Yunus calls a more humane form of capitalism, one that looks at human consequences, rather than the bottom line of profit. His idea goes beyond the idea of corporate social responsibility, where corporations modify their policies to benefit others as they do business, to the creation of "another kind of business— one that recognizes the multi-dimensional nature of human beings . . . set up . . . not to achieve limited personal gain but to pursue specific social goals" (p. 21). Several models have emerged that include social investors providing funds for social enterprises ranging from eye care hospitals to transportation infrastructures. The investors expect the return *of* their money at some specified point, while not expecting a return *on* their money. What profits are made after the return of the investments are reinvested into the enterprise, much like in the nonprofit world.

With all this diversity, a full picture of the human service landscape must include the linkages among and between organizations. To remain vibrant and relevant, for-profits, like nonprofit and public agencies, must make connections with various groups and communities. This network of relationships is probably most clear with the emerging social entrepreneurs and social businesses, but it is a necessary backdrop throughout the human service environment. We now turn to some of the ways in which organizations interrelate.

ORGANIZATIONAL RELATIONSHIPS

Whether they are public, nonprofit, or for-profit, organizations are often committed to or have allegiances with other organizations and with other arenas—groups, communities, and even nation-states. These organizations may represent or be affiliated with economically and politically disadvantaged populations who are not served or are underserved by other human service providers. **Affiliations** may be formed around ideologies, belief systems, values, or population groups. They may be formed when a particular group agrees to provide funding to a cause. Some of these relationships are more explicit or more formalized than others. For example, a public agency's mandate may be very specific in defining the population group to be served, and the special-interest groups that advocated for the social policy that created the agency will likely have strong feelings about how the organization carries out its mandate. A nonprofit agency may have evolved out of an advocacy group that wants to address the needs of homeless people and has become a more formalized organization committed to continuing its cause. A for-profit organization with a high commitment to social responsibility may contribute to service delivery by donating a portion of its profits to a charitable agency with which an affiliation is formed.

Whatever the type of agency, some organizations are explicit in espousing their relationships for ideological, religious, legal, economic, and/or political reasons. It is impossible here to fully explore the many forms these connections can take or even all the terms used to describe them. Terms like *association, affiliation, linkage, coalition, alliance, allegiance, federation*, and a host of others are heard in organizational corridors as practitioners dialogue about interorganizational, group, community, and international relationships.

To illustrate the diverse external connections organizations can have, we briefly examine some typical ways of connecting through: (1) association, (2) ideological community, (3) franchising, and (4) host relationship. It is important to note that like much of the blurring related to organizations, these are not mutually exclusive categories, and are only examples of many of the ways organizations relate to other entities. Organizations may have multiple connections of different sorts with various groups and communities. We do not intend for these examples to be all-inclusive, but we want to spark the reader's interest in how diverse an organization's relationships can be.

ASSOCIATIONS

Kramer (1981) defines **voluntary associations** as "membership organizations which usually have a social purpose—a 'cause'—and usually seek to benefit their constituency" (p. 9). Billis (1993) called voluntary associations "groups of people who draw a boundary between themselves and others in order together to meet some problem, to 'do something'" (p. 160). This definition sounds very similar to the definition we gave earlier for an organization: There is a structure, participants, and a purpose. The difference is that the boundary in a formal organization may be recognized by a charter and bylaws approved by a public body. A voluntary association can technically exist without being legally formalized. On the other hand, voluntary associations can be highly formalized, such as the National Association of Social Workers (NASW), the Child Welfare League of America (CWLA), the American Association of Retired Persons (AARP), or the American Association of Homes and Services for the Aged (AAHSA). It can be argued that voluntary associations are so widespread that they are the "authentic roots or core of the nonprofit sector" (Harris, 1998, p. 144).

Voluntary associations may have individual or organizational members, sometimes they have both, and these members may pay dues. For example, NASW members are individual practitioners who identify with the social work profession. AARP members are older persons who wish to affiliate with one of the largest lobbying groups in the United States.

Umbrella associations are "nonprofit associations whose members are themselves nonprofit organizations and it is estimated that one out of every five nonprofit organizations belongs to an umbrella association" (Young, 2001, p. 290). For example, CWLA and AAHSA have organizational members. CWLA attracts organizations that provide services to children, whereas AAHSA's affiliates are an assortment of nonprofit long-term-care facilities and service providers for elders and others needing chronic care. These associations often have national meetings at which their members come together for professional enhancement, political action, or socialization.

It would be impossible to fully explore the nature of organizational associations in one chapter. However, it is important to note that multiple writers have developed typologies of **interorganizational relationships**: those situations in which more than one organization works in some way with others, thus cutting across formal organizational boundaries. For example, Bailey and Koney (2000) provide a continuum of associational types beginning with the concept of: (1) affiliation; followed by (2) federations, associations, and coalitions; (3) consortium, networks, joint ventures; and ending in (4) mergers, acquisitions, and consolidations. Bailey and Koney view affiliations as the loosest form of connection, in which two organizations relate with both maintaining total autonomy. Federations, associations, and coalitions are moderately autonomous relationships in which both individual organizational goals and the goals of the member organizations are important. Consortia, networks, and joint ventures assume minimal organizational autonomy, whereas mergers, acquisitions, and consolidations require the organization entirely to relinquish its autonomy.

Research on associational structure is found in the globalization literature as attempts are made to understand the emergence of **nongovernmental organizations (NGOs)** in developing countries and international nongovernmental organizations (INGOs) (Brown & Moore, 2001). For example, Lindenberg (1999) reports the results of an international practitioner conference in which five associational structures are identified: (1) separate independent organizations, plus coalitions; (2) weak umbrella coordinating mechanisms; (3) confederations; (4) federations; and (5) unitary corporate models. In this typology, independent organizations function on their own, but may choose to loosely collaborate with others when it is convenient. These types of associations are transitory and normally focus on fleeting advocacy issues. Independent organizations with weak umbrella coordinating mechanisms are usually aligned with a central organization that has minimal power over the associated organization, whereas the confederation is one in which organizational members have ceded some degree of power to the central organization. **Federations** hold more centralized power, with the central unit actually making resource and other important decisions for subsidiaries as is the case in the unitary corporate model. Further exploring the federation concept, Foreman (1999) compares two U.S.-based organizations, World Vision International and Habitat for Humanity International. Both provide global relief services and both could be labeled as federations, yet Foreman illustrates how federations differ in their associational form. World Vision International is a donor-member-dominated federation, while Habitat is what she calls a "global bumblebee federation" because of differences in Habitat governance structures worldwide.

Many agencies are local representatives of national organizations. Prevent Child Abuse and The Alzheimer's Association, for example, operate in various relationships with national offices. It is important to explore just how strong these associations are and how much autonomy local chapters or groups have from central or national offices. Other organizations are associated with local groups, and may not be associated with a state, regional, national, or international body.

One often hears the term *grassroots* to refer to a movement or effort occurring in a local geographical area. Grassroots associations are one type of voluntary association, a type that is highly dependent on volunteers. Smith defines **grassroots associations (GAs)** as "locally based, significantly autonomous, volunteer-run, formal nonprofit groups that manifest significant voluntary altruism as a group; they use the associational form of organization and thus have an official membership of volunteers who perform all or nearly all of the work done in and by the nonprofits" (1999, p. 443). While the focus of much nonprofit activity has been on larger, more formal organizations having a wide scope of service, the grassroots association is comprised of local members who come together for a specific cause and are tied to a geographical community.

Never make assumptions about associations and what they mean, because no two organizations are exactly alike in their relationships with others. In many cases, it is the nature of the relationship that establishes not only the quality of the association, but also the structure of the organization that precedes or results from the association. We now turn to relationships that illustrate various ways and reasons organizations choose to connect or identify with a particular group for ideological, cultural, or religious reasons. Notice that in many cases there seems to be a communal rather than architectural understanding of organization in what follows.

IDEOLOGICAL COMMUNITIES

Relationships with ideological communities may be more or less loosely constituted, but they add to the cultural identity of the organization and its reason for being. We now briefly explore three types of communities with which organizations might relate. Note that these types of communities are not always geographical or place related, but may be related to "non-place" communities (Fellin, 1995, p. 4).

Religious or Faith Communities **Religious affiliates** are social service organizations that publicly acknowledge a relationship with a religious group or faith community. Typically, they are separately incorporated as nonprofit organizations and have names like Lutheran Social Ministries or Catholic Charities. Nonprofits with religious affiliations proliferated during the late 1800s and early 1900s and are still very much a part of the traditional human service network. Over the years, these organizations have been called *sectarian agencies, church agencies, church-related agencies, church affiliates*, and more recently *faith-based agencies*. Few assumptions can be made about the meaning of religious affiliation, for it will vary by agency. Few religious affiliates today serve persons only from the faith groups with which they affiliate and many denominations have always served persons from any faith tradition. These affiliates often receive public dollars to carry out their mission and it is often hard to distinguish what makes them "religious" (Ellor, Netting, & Thibault, 1999). Yet they maintain an affiliation with a religious group, an ideological symbol that may hold different meanings for administrators, staff, and consumers (Netting, O'Connor, & Yancey, 2006).

Although faith-based groups have provided human services for hundreds of years in many countries, the debate over what constitutes a faith-based organization in the United States escalated in 2001 with the Bush administration's establishment of the White House Office of Faith-based and Community Initiatives. This initiative underscored the "Charitable Choice" provision in the Personal Responsibility and Work Opportunity Reconciliation Act of 1996 (often called "Welfare Reform"), which sought to reduce barriers to faith-based groups interested in accessing public funds to provide human services. It is important to recognize that with these policy changes, the concept of a faith-based organization expanded beyond traditional nonprofit religious affiliates to include community-based congregations and groups, many of which are not formally incorporated as nonprofit organizations (see, for example, Cnaan, 1999, 2002; Wineburg, 2001; Wood, 2002; Wuthnow, 2004).

Ethnic Communities Some agencies are related to ethnic communities. Thirty years ago, Jenkins (1980) began studying the ethnic agency as a special form of social organization. She defined the **ethnic agency** as having the following characteristics: (1) serving primarily ethnic clients; (2) predominately staffed by persons who have the same ethnicity as the clients served; (3) having a majority of its board from the ethnic group served; (4) having an ethnic community and/or ethnic power structure to support it; (5) integrating ethnic content into its programs; (6) desiring to strengthen the family as a primary goal; and (7) maintaining an ideology that promotes ethnic identity and participation in the decision-making process.

Research on ethnic agencies continues, as illustrated by Cortes' (1998) study of Latino nonprofit agencies. He defines Latino nonprofits in the United States as those "whose missions focus on Latino community members" (p. 439). He adds that they are usually tax-exempt corporations with Latino boards of directors, led by Latino chief executives, or they are voluntary associations dominated by Latino constituencies.

Feminist Communities Ideological relationships may be based on a feminist perspective of service delivery. A **feminist organization**, according to Martin (1990), "meets any of the following criteria: (a) has a feminist ideology; (b) has feminist guiding values; (c) has feminist goals; (d) produces feminist outcomes; (e) was founded during the women's movement as part of the women's movement (including one or more of its submovements, e.g., the feminist self-help health movement [or] the violence against women movement)" (p. 815). Feminist organizations emerge in various sectors. They can be nonprofit or profit making, their structures can vary, and they can be local or national in their domain (Martin, 1990). Feminist organizations use paid and volunteer staff in different ways (Metzendorf & Cnaan, 1992).

Organizations that affiliate with a feminist group or ideology are often alternative agencies that have emerged because traditional service providers have not been sensitive to gender differences. Hyde (2000) elaborates on the nature of feminist social movement organizations (FSMOs), asserting that "FSMOs are the embodiments of feminist theory and practice, and reflect varied missions, structures, issues, strategies and products. Examples include peace encampments, lesbian-rights networks, economic development and micro-lending institutions, cultural centers, displaced homemaker leagues, reproductive rights groups and credit unions" (p. 49). She identifies three major ideological streams with which feminist organizations may identify: liberation (socialist or radical), liberal (women's rights), and cultural (woman-controlled) (Hyde, 2000, p. 50), underscoring the recognition that there are multiple feminist ideologies.

Having introduced multiple communities with their own ideologies with which organizations may relate, we now turn to another type of relationship: the franchise. Though this concept is long established in for-profit circles, it now has relevance for both nonprofit and for-profit human service organizations.

FRANCHISES

Many agencies are local representatives of regional, national, or even international organizations. Oster has defined such a connection as a **franchise** relationship in which local agencies or chapters conform to the following traits: "(1) The franchiser transfers to the franchisee the exclusive right to use a trademark or sell a particular product. Often though not always, this right is given over a particular territory. (2) In exchange, the franchisee pays the franchiser and may have to agree to purchase supplies or new materials from the franchiser. Typically, the fee involves some initial lump sum and then ongoing fees keyed to the level of business. (3) The franchiser provides some assistance to the franchisee, typically on technical, operating matters, and maintains some control of the way in which the business is operated. (4) Any residual profits and losses from the business go to the franchisee," which means it can go into providing more service (1992, p. 224).

Nursing homes (e.g., Manor Care), assisted-living facilities (e.g., Sunrise), and day care facilities (e.g., KinderCare) are recognized trademark names of franchised for-profit agencies. They are also deliverers of human services. Consumers expect standard quality from franchised operations, just as they anticipate that hamburgers or milkshakes from a franchised company in any city in the world will be the same. Although nonprofit agencies may not think of themselves as franchises, there are numerous long-established exemplars where the franchised concept applies. Oster contends that "more than half of the top 100 charitable nonprofits are franchise organizations" (1992, p. 226). Goodwill Industries and Planned Parenthood, for example, operate in franchise relationships with national offices. Goodwill Industries has 179 affiliates in the United States, whereas Planned Parenthood has 171 (Oster, 1992, p. 225). Local affiliates may pay their national organizations a percentage of their operating budgets in exchange for the use of the logo and name, technical support, and various activities such as lobbying at the national level for policies relevant to agency needs. Some local chapters may engage in shared fundraising with national bodies, in which funds are distributed by a formula to local and national groups. Restrictions placed on franchisees vary greatly.

HOST RELATIONSHIPS

Human services may be delivered by departments, programs, or individuals housed within host organizations. **Host organizations** are typically large agencies that deliver human services or employ helping professionals as part of what they do, but whose primary purpose is not the delivery of human services. Therefore, host organizations can be health-care systems, school settings, the military, commercial enterprises, or various other organizations in which a unit or component delivers human services. In host organizations, practitioners are viewed as "institutional guests" (Auslander, 1996, p. 15). Clients do not generally come to a host organization for the purpose of obtaining human services since that is not the primary function of the organization. However, in the process of providing what clients need, host organizations may engage practitioners or social service units to assist in meeting needs.

Examples of host organizations cut across sectors. Large health-care systems host multiple helping professionals such as social workers and chaplains who work on interdisciplinary teams. Public utility companies may hire practitioners to assist low-income clients with billing issues. For-profit businesses may establish employment-assistance programs (EAPs) to provide support for employees who are dealing with child and elder care issues. Religious congregations may hire parish nurses or social workers to provide services to persons within their local community. Military bases may have family service programs designed to address psychosocial needs of military families. Legislators may hire practitioners to assist with constituency services. With the diversity that has been showcased here, it should be clear that a good portion of professionals are likely to find themselves practicing in organizations that do not always define themselves as human service agencies, but that definitely provide human services. Table 1.1 summarizes the types of relationships we have just highlighted.

THE ONGOING SEARCH TO UNDERSTAND COMPLEX ORGANIZATIONS

A growing literature is focused on trying to better understand how different assumptions play out in organizational practice (see, for example, Netting & O'Connor, 2003) and in management (Preston, 2005; Quinn, Faerman, Thompson, & McGrath, 2003). Evidence of this quest is found in recent studies, particularly in organizations dedicated to social change and radical reform that view themselves as having advocacy goals. For example, Minkoff (2002) talks about the hybrid organizational form in a study of national women's and racial and ethnic minority organizations since 1955. This hybrid occurs when a social change organization houses both direct service and advocacy programs. The direct service programs are typically more traditional in that they are geared toward finding ways to serve immediate needs within the existing system, all the while collecting information that will inform advocacy for structural change. Lewis

Table 1.1
Selected Types of Organizational Relationships

Types	Descriptions	Examples
Associations	People or organizations that voluntarily associate for a defined purpose; includes membership organizations and grassroots associations	National Association of Social Workers (NASW) Child Welfare League of America (CWLA) American Association of Homes & Services for the Aged (AAHSA)
Ideological Communities	Organizations that align with the ideologies and values of religious, ethnic, feminist, or other communities	Catholic Charities (religious affiliation) Latino Nonprofit (ethnic affiliation) Women's Shelter (feminist affiliation)
Franchises	Organizations that have a relationship with regional or national organizations and seek to carry out the same goals locally	Prevent Child Abuse America The Alzheimer's Association The United Way American Red Cross YMCA
Host	Organizations that house programs and services, but do not view social services as their only or primary mission	Social Services in Hospitals School Social Work Services Parish Social Work Programs EAP Programs Family Assistance Programs (Military)

(2002) discusses how there have been two streams of thinking about nonprofit organizations—one pushing them toward becoming more traditional and the other stream saying they can't become like for-profits or they lose their identity. Researchers are asking questions about how organizations that hold different assumptions survive in a very traditional funding environment (see, for example, Bordt, 1997; Gibelman & Kraft, 1996; Koroloff & Briggs, 1996; Lune, 2002).

By now, we hope you have a glimpse of the structural and sectoral variation that is possible in organizations involved in human service advocacy, planning, oversight, and delivery. This diversity makes generalizations and expectations about human service organizations challenging. **Diversity** (differences that represent fundamental and instrumental variations) has long been a challenge for those interested in understanding the best ways to structure organizations and to manage human behavior within them. This text joins in that effort.

Earlier in this chapter, we gave the reader permission to recognize that just because she or he "doesn't get it" does not mean that there is a logical order just waiting to be discovered. One of the authors is reminded of when she graduated from her master's program in social work with a concentration in planning and administration. She kept waiting to be "found out" because the service delivery system just didn't make sense and somehow she knew it must fit together in some logical manner. She discovered that she held deep-seated assumptions, based on organizational theories she had learned, theories that had espoused sets of universal rules to guide organization practice. For example, there *should* always be just one supervisor to whom a person reports. Didn't everyone know that? There *should* always be an organizational chart with clear lines of authority. How could an organization exist without a visible structure? She was perplexed and discomforted when she encountered organizations with matrix supervisory structures and agencies in which no organizational charts had been developed. She couldn't figure out why people didn't just fix these obvious flaws in their agencies when she pointed them out. Logic, based on her set of assumptions, just didn't always click with others who didn't seem to need this same kind of order. But from where did her need for order come? The assumptions that she brought to organization practice were literally tied to her view of the world and to the organizational theories she had embraced. She felt comfort in these theories because they supported her assumptions (or perhaps she got her assumptions from being taught the theories). Either way, the problem came when she saw effective real-world practice that contradicted all of what she had learned to expect, practice in which differences were rampant.

Almost since the inception of organization studies, the goal has been to minimize difference in order to create predictable performance. Daly (1998) asserts that the "philosophical underpinnings of Western thought have resulted in . . . [seeking] order to end chaos and uncertainty, suppress contradictions, and find the one perfect truth" (p. xiv). This drive for sameness and predictability viewed difference as a problem and standardization as necessary for an effective and efficient operation. There was a push to find the one best way to design organizations and to prescribe how people should act within them. Ironically, early organizations may not have been structured similarly (Netting & O'Connor, 2005), and even if they developed that way, people were highly diverse. The result of ignoring those human differences as our knowledge grew meant that some staff people were able to "fit" and others did not, that some people were viewed as deserving clients and others were not.

Assumptions about organizations, about the employees within them, and about strategies about how to manage and/or lead these complex situations are embedded in the practical and scholarly literature. It is important to know what these assumptions might be because they are rarely stated, but are often part of the organization's culture. In the sections that follow, we quickly go over a few of those assumptions as illustrations of how they might influence thinking and acting within human service organizations.

ASSUMPTIONS ABOUT ORGANIZATIONS

For many years, theorists have searched for ways to understand and to order organizations. Organizational scholars have even attempted to order and categorize the theories that have emerged. In 1961, both Scott and Koontz classified organizational theories, referring to a "management theory jungle." Hutchinson (1967) categorized theories according to scientific management, environmental and human relations school, man (*sic*) as decision maker, and current theories of management. A bit later, Scott and Mitchell (1972) added neoclassical theory, systems concept, organization processes, and organization change. Bolman and Deal (1997) made sense of organization theories by categorizing them into the structural frame, the human resource frame, the political frame, and the symbolic frame. Farazmand (1994), on the other hand, cited three categories: instrumental rationality that includes classical and neoclassical theories; systems theories; and critical and interpretive theories. Shafritz, Ott, and Lang (2005) identify nine "major perspectives" on organization theory: classical organization theory, neoclassical organization theory, human resource theory or the organizational behavior perspective, "modern" structural organization theory, organizational economics theory, power and politics organization theory, organizational culture theory, reforms through changes in organizational culture, and theories of organizations and environments. Hatch and Cunliffe (2006) delineate modern, symbolic, and postmodern perspectives in their readable text.

In 1997, Morgan published the second edition of *Images of Organization*, the first version of which had sold extremely well because it touched a cord with readers attempting to define and understand organizations. Morgan demystified what was often seen as "a kind of magical power to understand and transform the situations [successful managers and problem solvers] encounter" (p. 3). His premise was "that all theories of organization and management are based on implicit images or metaphors that lead us to see, understand, and manage organizations in distinctive yet practical ways" (p. 4). Defining **metaphors** as "attempt[s] to understand one element of experience in terms of another" (p. 4), he proceeded to elaborate on the metaphorical images most frequently used when people try to define and understand organizations. Morgan's list of metaphors include: Organizations as Machines, Organizations as Organisms, Organizations as Brains, Organizations as Cultures, Organizations as Political Systems, Organizations as Psychic Prisons, Organizations as Flux and Transformation, Organizations as Domination. Morgan details each metaphor, identifies theories that reflect each metaphor, and examines the strengths and limitations of each.

All of the typologies discussed here attempted to order very complex ways of approaching organizations. Sources such as Hatch and Cunliffe (2006), Shafritz, Ott, and Lang (2005), and Morgan (1997) are readily available if the reader is interested in pursuing their various theoretical perspectives. Our intent here is simply to plant the seed that there are many traditional assumptions and concepts that have dominated thinking about organizations in the previous century as well as more contemporary conceptualizations of organizational life. In subsequent chapters, we will be tracing efforts to understand organizational structure, organizational goals, and behaviors. The major theories and assumptions about organization will be placed within the frameworks that guide the book so that the reader can see how philosophical and theoretical assumptions are based within deeply held worldviews.

Table 1.2 summarizes some of the important contributions made by influential organization theoretical perspectives, most of which developed from a post-industrial business model. Keep in mind that each perspective

Table 1.2

Primary Contributions by Organizational Theoretical Perspectives

Theoretical Perspective	Primary Contribution
Classical Theory	Recognized the importance of formal organizational structure and productivity
Human Resource/Organizational Behavior Theory	Recognized the importance of individuals and groups, the informal "system," and their relationship to the organization
Neoclassical Theory	Acknowledged organizational complexity
Modern Structuralist Theory	Transcended traditional, naive approaches to formal structure and provided a more comprehensive, balanced perspective of multiple sets of factors that relate within organizations
Systems Theories	Viewed organizations as open systems within changing environments
Power and Politics Theory	Acknowledged the importance of influence, politics, and informal power within organizations, beyond traditional views of authority as legitimized power
Organization Culture Theory	Recognized that organizations develop their own beliefs, grounded in deeply held assumptions and values
Sense-making Theory	Pointed out the ways in which organizational players reconstruct or "make sense" out of what happens

reflects certain assumptions that may contradict others. The point is that with the development of both classical and modern organization theories that reflect the complexity of post-industrial and technological societies, understanding organizations also becomes increasingly complex. Added to the global nature of many organizations and the multicultural profile of most American work environments, the old ways of categorizing organizations may feel insufficient (even oppressive) to persons in organizations intent on creating a more socially just work environment in a more just society. Honoring difference requires honoring diverse ways of understanding, communicating, thinking, and doing. It is our assumption that categorizing perspectives into ways of thinking about organizations is only a beginning step. To fully engage in organization practice, one must get beyond recognizing different perspectives or worldviews (sensitivity) to actually being able to use different ways of understanding in one's work (competence).

Each perspective brings with it certain insights and emphasizes particular aspects of organizational life while overlooking other essential elements. Even though these insights are only possible as a result of applying a particular perspective, much has been left unexamined. To date, no one approach has been able to fully capture the complexity of organizational life. Organizational diversity includes elements like purpose, structure, type, affiliation, and location as well as values, beliefs, and assumptions undergirding agency culture. Staff and client diversity includes gender, race, nationality, sexual orientation, attitudes, religion, values, and cultural diversity. Staff members are often diverse in terms of the professions they represent. Individuals also reflect diversity within groups, including differences represented and covered by the Americans with Disabilities Act or the Age Discrimination Act. These multiple, and often overlapping, aspects of diversity are related to organizational behaviors and outcomes. It is no surprise that Cox (1994) makes the provocative assumption, "**managing diversity** is among the most important management challenges of this decade" (p. x).

ASSUMPTIONS ABOUT EMPLOYEES

Behavior of the people comprising organizations has also been categorized, particularly since the development of the human relations theories of organizational behavior. Historically, managers have been told to understand their subordinates by categorizing either their behavior or their attitudes. The idea is that through understanding, the manager can better plan, specialize, and use authority and leadership for organizing, controlling, and managing (Hutchison, 1967).

An alternative to this controlling approach is the very popular Myers-Briggs test (Myers, 1998), built on Jungian theory and developed by

Katharine Cook Briggs and Isabel Briggs Myers to allow "the constructive use of difference" (as cited in Martin, 1997). The Myers-Briggs model of personality is said to provide insight into how and why people understand and approach the world in different ways. It is based on the assumption that there are four dimensions of personality preferences. The first is how one directs energy (**extroversion** vs. **introversion**). The second is how one prefers to take in information (**sensing** vs. **intuition**). The third is how one prefers to make decisions (**thinking** vs. **feeling**). And the fourth is how one is oriented to the outer world (**judging** vs. **perceiving**). These preferences are combined into 16 different types, combining *I* for *introvert* or *E* for *extrovert* with *S* for *sensing* or *N* for *intuitive* and either *T* for thinking or *F* for *feeling* and *J* for *judging* or *P* for *perceiving*. A particular combination of the four purportedly describes how one sees the world (Myers, 1998). A paper-and-pencil questionnaire is used to assess type, where there is no right or wrong answer or right or wrong types. The idea is that all types are good, just different.

The valid and reliable instrument seems to identify how the mind is used, and how the individual feels most comfortable, natural and, thus, confident. It shows how people have different interests, ways of behaving, and ways of viewing strengths and needs for growth. Isabel Myers believed understanding of differences is "useful whenever one person must communicate with another or live with another or make decisions that affect another's life" (Myers as cited in Myers & Kirby, 1994, p. 16). Since the 1980s, there has been a general public acceptance of the Myers-Briggs characterization of ways we perceive and relate to the outside world, leading to a level of acceptance that there is no one "best style." It seems there is a growing acceptance that uniqueness brings strength, different styles are useful, and differing perceptions are assets. These attitudes are entering the organizational field with the recognition that personality type is related to career satisfaction and organizational competence (Tieger & Barron-Tieger, 1992), team members' types affect team building (Hirsh, 1992), and ways of describing and analyzing organizational situations set the stage for organizational change (Lawrence, 1993).

Although the Myers-Briggs is designed to respect differences, the tool has not always been used for that purpose. Management trainers have used the Myers-Briggs over the years to point out why different employees had different needs, but the message was often interpreted by managers as a way to understand why things were not working and to try to corral or manipulate employees to "get with the program." Thus, the Myers-Briggs instrument can be used to control the behavior of subordinates, even though that was not necessarily its intent. Until recent developments by postmodern theorists (see, for example, Fox & Miller, 1995; Hassard & Parker, 1993), there was an assumption (or at least a hope) that there was a one best way of doing the business of organizing. Differences were recognized, but they were viewed as liabilities rather than strengths. Some managers searched for order and conformity among subordinates, rather than focusing on the strengths that exist amid diversity.

ASSUMPTIONS ABOUT MANAGERS AND LEADERS

It has long been recognized that managers can hold, and act on, different assumptions about employees. For example, according to McGregor (1960), Theory X managers assume that workers inherently dislike work and have to be closely supervised. Conversely, Theory Y managers see followers as eager to work and capable of participating in decision making. Tannebaum and Schmidt (1958) identify a continuum between what they call the *autocratic* (boss-centered) and the *democratic* (subordinate-centered) leader, who hold different assumptions about managing employees. The idea underlying these categories is that managers and leaders tend to be consistent in how they interact with supervisees and that this approach is based on personal philosophy and assumptions about human behavior (Lewis, Packard, Lewis, & Souflee, 2001).

Using Koontz, Hutchinson outlines six schools of management thought (Hutchinson, 1967, p. 10): operational school, empirical school, human behavior school, social systems school, decision theory school, and the mathematical school. Pfeffer (1981), having a great interest in power within the organization, suggests four models of management theory: rational, bureaucratic, decision process/organized anarchy, and political power. Bolman and Deal (1991) suggest that theorists of leadership and management can be sorted into rational system theorists, human resource theorists, political theorists, and symbolic theorists.

Four leading schools of research on leadership emerged during the 20th century: "trait, style, contingency, and the new leadership paradigm" (Bargal, 2000, p. 305). Each approach was intended to explain the concept of leadership, and each had its accompanying assumptions. The *trait approach*, which predominated from the 1930s through 1950s, assumes that leaders are born rather than made. Leaders are assumed to have certain personal characteristics such as a need for power or achievement and these traits are viewed as making them successful. The style approach emerged as early as the Ohio State studies on leadership in the 1940s (Stogdill & Coons, 1957). Various scholars focused on leadership style and their work continues to influence contemporary views of leadership (Bales, 1954; Likert, 1961). The *style approach* assumes that leaders can be categorized according to patterns of behavior, such as how they show consideration for their employees, define tasks to be done, and monitor employees in carrying out responsibilities (Bowers & Seashore, 1966).

Later, Blake and Mouton (1978) categorized management styles according to the attitudes displayed by leaders, attempting to categorize leadership behaviors on a grid rather than along only one continuum. Their widely cited managerial grid categorizes five types of leaders along two axes: concern for people and concern for production. Blake and Mouton believed that a leader who had high concern both for people and production was the ideal type for which managers should strive. Other writers used the terms *task* versus *relationship* for *production* and *people* (Reddin, 1970), and suggested that leadership is more situational than being one ideal type for all occasions.

The *contingency approach* to organizational leadership emerged during the 1960s. Theorists such as Fiedler (1967) emphasized the importance of context in determining what would work in any given situation. The assumption that context has to be taken into consideration is an important contribution. As theorists attempted to understand assumptions about leadership and its practical application to managing people within an organization, the concept of **situational leadership** emerged (Hersey & Blanchard, 1977), in which the fit between leader and follower has to be carefully assessed and then style has to be adapted.

We remember participating in the 1970s in very popular training exercises in which everyone tried to categorize one's assumptions about leadership. It was very typical for a trainer to come in, administer a tool, and then have everyone categorize themselves. In this particular event, the trainees were either vanilla, chocolate, or strawberry. As it was explained, vanillas had certain assumptions, chocolates had others, and strawberries had others, yet all were equally important and valued (some people might like different flavors more than others, but there was no one right way). The point was to recognize that the assumptions held are different and that individuals tend to lead with their preferred assumptions.

We use this example to illustrate that there is nothing new about recognizing that people bring different assumptions to organizational leadership and management. This has been in the management literature for years. The difference now is that some managers/leaders are beginning to seek ways to take advantage of these differences rather than seeing them as barriers to productivity. This changing perspective is reflected in the new leadership approach. The new leadership approach contrasts with the trait, style, and contingency perspectives, all of which are grounded in a social psychological tradition (Bargal, 2000). One of the framers of the **new leadership approach**, Burns (1978) views leaders as creators of vision, culture, and strategy. Terms such as *transformational* and *transactional leader* are used to portray an approach to leadership in which old assumptions are challenged and organizational cultures are created and changed. The overriding assumption in the new leadership approach is that change is inevitable and that a visionary leader can transform the workplace into a meaningful arena (Bargal, 2000).

LEADERSHIP IN COMPLEX HUMAN SERVICE ORGANIZATIONS

Practitioners in human service organizations (whatever roles they play) must think critically about their own and others' assumptions about organizations and organizational behavior. This includes recognizing major theories that have influenced and continue to influence their thinking about organizations. Critical thinking about organizations will inevitably lead to disagreement, because no two people will hold the exact same assumptions. Being aware of the potential for clashes of assumptions and the need to clarify one's own perspectives is key to future organization practice.

For those readers who just relaxed because they do not plan to be an organizational *leader* and who think the contents of this book do not apply to them, we have a clear message to convey. We assume that every professional has leadership responsibilities within any organization in which he or she works, because leadership is not just a title or position like manager or administrator, or something only full-time macropractitioners do. **Leadership** is an attitude about responsibilities in an organization based on professional skills and a set of values that compel an individual to act. Leadership may come from any organizational member, regardless of the formal authority and power structure in that organization. The clinician who knows what happens to clients on a daily basis has a responsibility to provide that information to others for targeting further service development. These actions demonstrate leadership skills. The line worker who visits clients in their home environments will know more about what really happens to the agency's clientele than will managers who may have ultimate programmatic decision-making responsibility. Sharing the information will shape the program. The line worker demonstrates leadership skills by carefully documenting what she is learning and is responsible for clearly conveying this information to others who have ultimate program or legal responsibility. The program director who is aware of low staff morale and who needs to find ways to promote teamwork will be a leader for her staff team even if it is primarily the agency director's responsibility to establish the staff tenor for the whole agency.

Leadership requires having vision about what information is important to share and when to share it so that change can happen in organizations. Leaders do not merely identify and assess a problem, but plan for and facilitate successful problem resolution. Problem identification and solution are skills and responsibilities of all practitioners. For us, this means that organizational leadership is a professional responsibility of every practitioner, no matter what position one holds. This approach to leadership and the change that can result is not new (Brager & Holloway, 1978; Kettner, Daley & Nichols, 1985; Netting, Kettner, & McMurtry, 2008; Resnick & Patti, 1980).

We are committed to this long-established tradition that every professional can be a leader in initiating change, regardless of organizational role. Our hope is that readers will see the importance of both direct practice skills and accompanying understandings of human behavior, and the specifics of organizational skills from which to develop successful leadership for change. Professional leaders must develop the skills necessary to flourish in the chaos that accrues with multiple perspectives that produce different ways of doing the work of delivering human services in a multicultural environment. Foundational organization practice skills include critical thinking and self-awareness.

The Role of Critical Thinking in Organization Practice

Gibbs and Gambrill say that "**critical thinking** involves a careful appraisal of claims, a fair-minded consideration of alternative views, and a willingness to change your mind in light of evidence that refutes a cherished position" (1996, p. 23). For us, critical thinking has some important dimensions, starting with the examination of assumptions, goals, questions, and evidence involved in the phenomenon under scrutiny. It requires the use of reasonable (nonreactive) and reflective thinking focused on what to believe and what not to believe (Ennis, 1989). Critical thinking is actually part of problem solving in that it is not just an appraisal of claims or arguments; it is not just a way of discovering the mistakes in thinking of others. Instead, when fully engaged, it allows for deep understanding of issues. At its best, critical thinking is dialogic. It requires reflective/analytic listening along with active pursuit of clarity of expression. To truly engage in critical analysis one must understand what is intended in order to actively pursue the evidence and reasons supportive and contrary to the position being studied. This means that alternative points of view must be elicited and fully considered.

Regardless of the writer about critical thinking (see, for example, Gibbs & Gambrill, 1996; Kroeger & Thuesen, 1988; Paul & Elder, 2002; Ruggiero, 2001), their thoughts on the important tasks in critical thinking appear similar. The critical thinker must deal with the differing opinions of experts and how those contradict or support one's own opinion. The critical thinker must generate multiple perspectives in order to evenhandedly assess costs and benefits even when the thinker holds little belief in the alternatives. Finally, and most important, the critical thinker must be willing to shift personal opinions and patterns of thinking. In Box 1.1 we have provided some straightforward guides for engaging in critical thinking.

In thinking critically, one's assumptions and those of others are examined carefully and could be changed, based on new or alternative information. The process is not an easy one if these assumptions are cherished, or tightly held, almost as immutable truths. Groups within organizations,

Box 1.1

BASIC QUESTIONS OF A CRITICAL THINKER

- What is the *reason* for my thinking? Why am I doing this (purpose/goal/ objective)?
- What precise *question* (problem/issue) am I trying to answer?
- Within what *paradigm* (perspective/ideology/point of view) am I thinking?
- What *assumptions* am I making? What am I taking for granted (concepts/ variables/ideas)?
- What *information* (data/facts/observations) am I using? What might I be overlooking? What is missing for a complex picture?
- How am I *interpreting* the information? What are alternative interpretations (from different paradigms/perspectives/ideologies/points of view)?
- What *conclusions* am I making? Given alternative conclusions, why do I prefer these?
- If I accept the conclusions, what are the *implications*? What might be the positive and negative consequences if I put my position into action?

Source: Adapted from Paul (1993).

even entire organizations, can cherish assumptions. Schein (1992) calls this pattern of shared basic assumptions the basis of organizational culture. When consensus is so great as to create a perspective resembling a culture, the assumptions of that consensus are tenaciously held. Basic assumptions in organizations can come to be so taken for granted that one finds little variation in thinking or performance within a cultural unit. In fact, if a basic assumption is strongly held in a group, members will find behavior based on any other premise inconceivable. If, for example, the culture in a foster care unit is one of blaming biological parents, it is unlikely that anyone within the unit would actively consider the parents' strengths. Regardless of data, it would not be part of the assessment considerations because it would not occur to anyone to even think about strengths.

People in organizations may discover that their cherished assumptions are not congruent with what they are observing. Recognizing this discrepancy poses a dilemma—suffer the anxiety of moving to another assumption or hang on tenaciously to avoid the pain that accompanies change. Either choice is uncomfortable in its own way.

Some of the challenges to self-awareness can be overcome through clear, critical assessment. In writing this book, we hold numerous *cherished* assumptions. We assume that professionals have no choice but to think critically; otherwise, clients will not receive the best services one can provide. We assume that human service practice will be fraught with conflicts, some intentional and others totally unexpected. We know disagreements occur when different cherished assumptions collide.

Box 1.2

BEGINNING QUESTIONS ABOUT ASSUMPTIONS

1. What are your assumptions about organizations and organizational behavior?
2. When, where, and how did you develop these assumptions?
3. If you think about an organization with which you are familiar, do all your assumptions hold up? If not, which ones don't and why?
4. Think about an organization with which you are familiar. What basic assumptions do you think drive this organization's culture?

Depending on one's personality and style, conflicts may be tempered or ignited, but they will not be avoided. We also assume that organizations are arenas in which the potential for assumptions to clash will be accentuated by the sheer numbers of people who interact. But we also assume that this sets the stage for the practitioner to engage in a challenging and stimulating work environment that will stretch one's ability to use professional judgment based on well-reasoned thought. In addition, we assume that all this stretching and reasoning is based on one's desire to do the best possible work one can offer clients. This may mean struggling with (and possibly even changing) some cherished assumptions along the way. We know this is not easy, but see if you can begin to address the questions in Box 1.2.

No critical thinking process will produce effective results without the self-discipline necessary to achieve a consciousness about how one uses oneself in the organizational context. Once conscious use of self is part of a practice vocabulary, then real critical thinking can begin.

The Role of Self-Awareness in Organization Practice

Just as in direct practice, **self-awareness** within an organizational context requires an honest appraisal of oneself. There are many worthwhile discussions of self-awareness in relation to direct work with clients (see, for example, Hepworth, Rooney, Rooney, Strom-Gottfried & Larsen, 2006), but few speak specifically to the need for this same level of self-consciousness within the organizational setting. We agree with Falck (1988), who believes that interpersonal patterns and perceptions within an organization are key to understanding organizational behavior.

The same level of scrutiny of reactions within the organization is necessary as with an individual client. The organizational leader must be aware of personal biases, habitual distortions, and personal behavior that might contribute to the organization problem being addressed. These personal or internal elements may be contributing to the problem assessment or its solution.

Another area requiring honest scrutiny is personal style. It is necessary to know that the style in use is the appropriate one for the selected problem-solving strategy. If the organizational leader is naturally domineering, it must be clear that this dominance will produce the desired results. If one's style is naturally more shy or passive, will that type of communication pattern create the level of attention in others needed for problem resolution? Is natural assertiveness, confrontation, defensiveness, or a withdrawn pattern of communication warranted? The point of this assessment is the realization that what is natural in one's style might not be effective in each situation. With consciousness of the preferred style, and critical analysis regarding what is necessary with the people involved, the practitioner desiring change can strategically choose a style that is more likely to succeed. If more assertive discussion is necessary in order to be heard, even if a more quiet approach is preferred, the more effective strategy can be implemented because of introspection and critical thinking, and with appropriate skill development.

In addition, the organizational leader cannot assume that anyone's life experiences have been left at the door of the agency. A frank assessment of how one's life experiences might influence perceptions and judgments is essential for drawing valid conclusions regarding personal reactions to organizational experiences. The goal is to achieve personal reaction and reality congruence, but this is not possible until and unless the people involved are clear about how personal history shapes the lens with which they attempt to understand a situation. For example, experience of personal pain from abuse or neglect as a child might cause overidentification with a client or colleague in pain, to the degree that accurate appraisal of a situation is impossible. If a worker has had a history with controlling and critical parents, then critical feedback from those whose role it is to evaluate may not be received in the spirit it is intended. Similarly, if an employee has had a bad care giving experience with an older relative, she may have difficulty working with older persons who remind her of that relative. An active effort to disentangle personal reactions from the current reality is essential not only for sense making in the organization, but also for effectiveness.

For Kondrat (1999), there are at least five types of self-awareness involving successively higher orders of consciousness skills and complex thinking skills. Though her work is linked to direct practice, it is also very relevant for organization practice. Our students suggest that there may actually be seven types of awareness, including pre-conscious and contextual types. Therefore, we combine these two types with the five identified by Kondrat.

Pre-conscious self-awareness is a transitional phase, in which a person may recognize that she is not self-aware. This pre-conscious type is important because it is the beginning of the insight that something needs to happen differently. It is a triggering stage, in which one accepts the possibility that something needs to change in the way one looks at oneself. One recognizes that self-awareness is not present.

To be self-aware in an organization, a worker must first clearly experience awareness, and this is what Kondrat (1999, p. 459) calls *simple conscious awareness*. This type of self-awareness is when a light bulb goes on. *Reflective awareness*, a third type, requires distancing from the contents of an experience for observation and critique. It involves getting beyond the light-bulb experience and beginning to analyze why one has felt a certain way or acted in certain ways. A fourth type, *reflexive awareness*, requires attention to and understanding of how personal history and the actual personhood of the practitioner impact the situation under consideration. The fifth type, a more social constructivist version of reflexivity, is called *social constructive awareness*, and requires awareness of the mutual shaping that goes into meaning making within the organizational setting. The sixth level, essential for organizational leadership, is *critical reflectivity*. This requires asking reflective questions about bias and intolerance. For example, one might examine the biases that "center on the relationship between seemingly unproblematic, everyday behavior and racially structured outcomes" (Kondrat, 1999, p. 468). The idea in this type of self-awareness is to accept the responsibility and the power to act to change the structures that support and sustain unequal outcomes in vulnerable groups inside and outside of the organization. This type of awareness accepts the notion that organizational participants are not just passive recipients upon whom the organization acts, but also are active agents with responsibilities to challenge the status quo. This sounds remarkably similar to earlier visions of social work leadership within organizations (Brager & Holloway, 1978; Kettner, Daley, & Nichols, 1985; Resnick & Patti, 1980).

A critical reflectivity is essential in assessing not only personal beliefs and attitudes, but also how the social/structural environment of the organization may be continuing or extending majority power and privilege to the detriment of the more vulnerable. Therefore, there is likely a seventh type of self-awareness in which the full implications of one's reflective questions and actions are assessed. We call this *contextual awareness*, where self-awareness meets the reactions, resistance, and consequences of change, understanding and accepting the external results of articulation of individual consciousness. Table 1.3 summarizes the types of self-awareness.

Critical Thinking and Self-Awareness in Multicultural Organizations

As agencies become more diverse in populations served, in approaches to service delivery, and in addressing political, economic, and cultural challenges—there may be no resolutions or "real" answers about what constitutes the best structure or practice within organization. Consider,

Table 1.3
Types of Self-Awareness

Level of Self-Awareness	Characteristics
1. Pre-Conscious Awareness	The person begins to recognize that she or he is not self-aware.
2. Simple Conscious Awareness	The person clearly experiences awareness.
3. Reflective Awareness	The person is reflective, taking some distance from the experience so that he or she can observe and critique.
4. Reflexive Awareness	The person must pay attention to and understand how personal history and the actual personhood of the practitioner impact the situation.
5. Social Constructive Awareness	The person must be aware of the mutual shaping that goes into meaning making within the organization.
6. Critical Reflectivity	The person must ask reflective questions about bias and intolerance, accepting responsibility and the power to act to change oppressive organizational structures.
7. Contextual Awareness	The person recognizes the consequences of critical reflexivity and how her or his raising questions impacts others, and sees self in the context of others.

instead, that there may just be informed ways of acting without the expectation of closure, definitive analysis, and guarantees. Organizational leaders must, therefore, be open to considering multiple perspectives in which possibilities and opportunities can emerge from the chaos of uncertainty based on honoring differences.

From this standpoint, working in multicultural environments in ways that are *socially just* may mean that chaos and uncertainty will be the norm. We are giving you permission, as a future organizational leader, to stop fighting the chaos and instead relish the challenges it offers to use your best critical thinking skills to work toward needed change. We hope that the approach offered in these chapters will begin to equip you to practice in complexity and ambiguity, recognizing possibilities, accepting challenges, and overcoming obstacles.

As Resnick and Patti (1980) made clear, organizations are not just collections of personalities; they are much more complex phenomena. Imagine, then, that one enters an organization in which persons from diverse groups with different values and assumptions come together to achieve a purpose or purposes. Think about how the group and subgroup cultures will interact within an organizational culture to create their own set of values and assumptions. Consider that we have not even mentioned the clients one serves and how they fit into this multicultural interaction, though it is for the purpose of serving clients that the human service organizational culture is established in the first place. Even if the teams and groups within this organization work well together and share certain values and assumptions, clients will bring their own values and assumptions to the interaction. Cox refers to the concept of cultural fit as "the degree of alignment between two or more cultural configurations" (1994, p. 170). Practitioners have to develop skills in assessing cultural fit in order to work toward organizational change when client diversity is not compatible with established organizational culture.

Self-awareness is essential in working with the complexities of a multicultural environment. Without awareness of prejudices and stereotypes regarding those different from oneself, organizational members may be deceived into thinking that biases and stereotypes are absent from their thinking and behaviors. Workers in a multicultural environment should have the honesty and humility to admit the limits in their openness to difference. With this admission comes the recognition of the level of care necessary in communication and judgments so that personal prejudices do not cloud the picture or alienate those with whom solutions must be forged. Self-awareness is a key to moving away from prejudices and stereotypical perceptions, but until full liberation from discrimination and oppression is possible, it is also the major tool for managing organizational diversity.

The multicultural competency for which self-aware practitioners should strive has been labeled in the direct practice literature as *ethnic-sensitive* (Devore & Schlesinger, 1991; Lum, 1992) or *cross-cultural* (Harper & Lantz, 1996) competence. Helpful guidance for practice with the multiple cultures within and outside of an organization can be found in this literature. However, even more precise guidance is provided regarding direct practice. Lum defines this practice as minority practice, "the art and science of developing a helping relationship with an individual, family, group, and/or community whose distinctive physical or cultural characteristics and discriminatory experiences require approaches that are sensitive to ethnic and cultural environments" (p. 6). For direct practice, most theorists suggest that practice must be shaped with a sensitivity to experiences of racism, prejudice, and discrimination as well as attention to the specific cultural belief systems and behaviors that might influence individuals' views of themselves, their world, and their possibilities. This same sensitivity is important to organization practice. But sensitivity is not enough.

Many more details about competent multicultural practice will emerge throughout the rest of this book. For now, it is important to develop some elements of the type of respect that comprises effective multicultural practice. For us, the first element of respect is self-respect. In order to risk the hard work of cross-cultural communication central to respect, it is necessary to feel good about oneself. It is impossible to respect the "other"

Box 1.3

ELEMENTS OF COMPETENT MULTICULTURAL PRACTICE

1. Self-respect
2. Dialogue
3. Curiosity
4. Sense of safety
5. Recognition of worthiness

---

until people respect themselves. The second element of respect comes through dialogue. Real understanding, just like real critical thinking, is impossible without real communication. One can move beyond misunderstanding and anger through dialogue. Dialogue is possible only if all parties are fully present in the conversation. Attention to the conversation is essential. This attention sometimes will require vigorous conversation, sometimes called *dialectical conversation*. At other times, respect occurs through silently bearing witness to the personal narrative of a colleague or client. A third important element of respect is curiosity and being humble about one's knowledge. Paul and Elder (2002) call intellectual humility an important trait of the disciplined mind.

Multicultural practice requires true interest in the stories, experiences, and perceptions of others. Genuine respect is possible only when one knows people's real thoughts, feelings, and fears. The authentic communication of these basic aspects of human experience comes through a fourth element—sense of safety. Safety is created when one communicates a sense of the other's worthiness, which is the fifth element. Box 1.3 lists the elements of competent multicultural practice.

Lawrence-Lightfoot (1999) says that from these expressions of respect demonstrated through competent multicultural practice comes empowerment. We agree. Crossing the borders of difference through genuine understanding and respect allows everyone involved to gain more knowledge. This knowledge can be used to make decisions that will nurture self-confidence and self-reliance in organizations and social environments.

CONCLUSION

Organization leaders with the power and skills to effect needed changes in human service organizations must critically think about their own and others' assumptions about organizations and organizational behavior. Critical thinking in an organizational context will inevitably lead to conflict because no two people will hold the exact same assumptions. Being aware of the potential for assumptions to clash, managing the discomfort of lack of agreement, and clarifying one's own perspectives are key to organization practice, particularly as one works in increasingly **multicultural organizations**.

We link leadership with critical thinking and self-awareness, encouraging readers to be mindful of their assumptions about types of organizations, approaches to working in increasingly complex organizations, and the compatibility of their work with professional values. Practitioners within human service organizations must examine fit between organizational and professional values and look for ways to link the two. This responsibility is equally important for the line worker and the manager whose practice is either enhanced or impeded by the capacity for reflexive, complex, critically analytical thinking in the organizational context. Critical thinking is needed to engage chaos, sustain creativity, and maintain and construct effective and just multicultural organizations.

In this first chapter, we have emphasized diversity as a major theme in contemporary organizations, reinforced in different sets of assumptions that different people bring to organization practice at all levels. In the following chapters, with the help of several practical and philosophical frameworks for identifying and understanding diverse organizational assumptions, we will interrogate why they may be embraced with such fervor. We will also look at how these assumptions impact organization practice.

DISCUSSION QUESTIONS

1. Constraints are those things that an organization cannot control, whereas contingencies are negotiable. Sometimes it is hard to tell the difference between the two, and what might constrain one type of organization may be a contingency for another. Think about the landscape of human service organizations and identify situations in which constraints and contingencies might vary in relation to public and private agencies, distinguishing between nonprofits, for-profits, and social entrepreneurs and social businesses.

2. In this chapter, we defined programs as containing services of various types. In some smaller organizations, programs and services may be hard to distinguish. Identify a small organization and a large bureaucracy with which you are familiar. How are the concepts of program and service useful (or not) in explaining what these organizations do? Are there alternative concepts to programs and services (or even a metaphor) that you think would be useful in describing the way in which these organizations are structured?

3. Three types of programs (direct service, staff development and training, and support) were defined in this chapter. Can you think of examples of these three types? How do they differ in their goals? Do

you think they have equal value in human service organizations? Why or why not?

4. Associations come in many different forms. What are the differences between umbrella associations and grassroot associations? What would be the advantages and challenges faced by each?

5. Ideological communities may or may not be geographically bound. How would you define community beyond neighborhood for non-place-based ideological communities? Next, examine what religious/faith, ethnic, and feminist communities might have in common and how each might shape different types of agencies.

6. Franchise and host organizations may or may not be considered human service organizations, even if portions of their responsibilities include service provision. What special constraints and contingencies do these type organizations have? What are the advantages and challenges of working in these settings?

7. Write your assumptions about the "right" structure of an organization and the expected behavior of management and employees. How do your assumptions vary from those of your peers? (Keep this list handy as you read the rest of this book and see if they change in process).

8. Consider critical thinking and how you think it relates to leadership. Start a journey in self-awareness with a journal. As you read the text, make notes in your journal when you have reactions. Then analyze your reactions by trying to understand what the reaction is, why you are having it, where this came from, and what it might mean for you as a developing organizational leader.

9. Identify your comfort zone regarding different cultures. Where are you most comfortable and what makes you uncomfortable? What do you want to work on in your personal and professional life in order to be competent in multicultural environments?

CHAPTER 2

Frameworks for the Organization Practitioner

IN THE PREVIOUS chapter, we introduced critical thinking and self-awareness as essential characteristics of leaders in human service organizations. Organization practice excellence is possible only when one understands what is being undertaken and why. Understanding organization practice from both the context of the organization and the behavior within it can be enhanced by using insights from the organization and management field. In this chapter, we introduce a number of frameworks that when taken together can provide a basis for understanding diverse approaches to organizing. We believe these frameworks will also support and enable organization leaders at any level to withstand and perhaps even embrace the paradoxes that naturally accrue in complex organizations.

In this chapter, we first introduce theories as they relate to human service organizations because we suspect that theoretical approaches to guide practice may be the most familiar aspect of large system practice. To enhance the capacity to manage the diversity of assumptions in organizations, we extend the theoretical lens with both a paradigmatic and values framework for understanding organizations and the people within them. Finally, to bring the complexity full circle to managing behavior within organizational contexts, we conclude our integrative approach with the consideration of a framework for strategic management. The frameworks introduced in this chapter should serve as the stage for the details about organization assessment and practice that fill out the remainder of the text.

CONNECTING ORGANIZATIONAL THEORIES TO HUMAN SERVICE ORGANIZATIONS

Organizational theories were not developed by persons in the field of human service planning and service provision. Organizational theories have focused on the work of business corporations. While organizational theories based on business values may be useful, corporate goals and human service goals will differ at least slightly. Even when both business and human services focus on working with consumers, what brings the consumer into interaction with both organization types will differ. Therefore, sometimes appropriately connecting organizational theories to human service organizations is not easy. Later, you will see that this challenge increases markedly when one is attentive to multiple perspectives and multiple understandings about what constitutes a theory. For now, it is sufficient to grasp the challenges of transferring theory for practice from a business environment to a social service one.

Hasenfeld (1983, pp. 9–10) identified six unique characteristics of human service agencies that made them different from other organizations. First, the fact that their "raw material" consisting of people vested with moral values affects most organizational activities. For him, service technologies must be morally justified, because every activity related to clients has significant moral consequences. A second important distinction is goals. The goals of human service organizations are vague, ambiguous, and problematic, at least from the standpoint of controlled measurement. This is not due to incompetence, but because it is far more difficult to agree about what constitutes achieving desired "welfare" and responding to "well-being" needs of people than it is to construct or transform inanimate objects. Third, the moral ambiguity surrounding human services also implies that they operate in a turbulent sociopolitical environment. There are many interest groups with many perspectives and agendas, each attempting to achieve their values and aims through the organization. In business in a capitalistic society, the profit mandate clearly trumps alternative perspectives. Fourth, human service organizations must operate with indeterminate service technologies that do not provide complete directives about how to attain desired outcomes. Human nature is never as controllable or predictable as many of the elements in business or in the natural sciences. Fifth, the core activities in human service organizations consist of relations between staff and clients. It is within relationship that change occurs. Change is the product of the human service enterprise, a much different product than in most businesses. Finally, according to Hasenfeld, human service organizations lack reliable and valid measures of effectiveness, and, therefore, may be more resistant to change and innovation. We would take a more critical stance on this sixth element and suggest that the expectation of achieving valid and reliable measures of effectiveness itself fails to recognize how human service agencies differ from other organizations. Our integrated approach in this text would suggest that additional alternative measures are needed to capture this very uniqueness. Box 2.1 summarizes Hasenfeld's characteristics, all of which will be important later when considering the usefulness of particular theories in organization practice.

Box 2.1

HASENFELD'S SIX UNIQUE CHARACTERISTICS OF HUMAN
SERVICE ORGANIZATIONS

1. Consumers are raw material, consisting of people vested with moral values that affect most of their activities.
2. Goals are vague, ambiguous, and problematic. Moral ambiguity surrounds human services.
3. Indeterminate technologies do not provide complete knowledge about how to attain desired outcomes.
4. Core activities consist of relations between staff and clients.
5. Reliable and valid measures of effectiveness are lacking, making these organizations resistant to change and innovation.

Source: Hasenfeld (2000).

Hasenfeld (2000) continues to write about human service management and administration, stressing the importance of locating theories that take into account the nature of human service agencies. He warns (2000) that appropriate theories and tools for business organizations will not always work for human service agencies and that social work administration practices "must be anchored in organizational theories that take into account . . . attributes [of human service agencies . . . and] they must be empirically verifiable" (p. 90). Again, we agree with Hasenfeld, but think that much more discussion is necessary about what constitutes empirical verifiability, especially when working in diverse organizations in diverse environments (Netting & O'Connor, 2008). What is clear at this point is that the nature of human service organizations requires persons who are skilled in thinking critically and acting competently in the face of competing values and expectations from various constituencies, regardless of the theoretical guidance.

Later we will look closely at what constitutes theory in diverse organization practice, but for now do not overlook the possibility that the hunches people use to make decisions in practice are actually theories built on either explicit or implicit assumptions about the organization and its practices. Most times such basic assumptions become like theories-in-use, which tend to be neither confronted, debated, nor tested and, thus, are extremely difficult to change. To learn something new that might allow change in practice in this realm of hunches, hypotheses, and theories-in-use requires practitioners to resurrect, reexamine, and possibly change some of the more stable portions of their cognitive structures, because what is guiding the thinking that constructs such theories generally are value-driven preferences and biases. This is so close to beliefs that critical analysis and learning from this almost-unconscious position is intrinsically difficult, because the reexamination of basic assumptions temporarily destabilizes one's cognitive and interpersonal world, which can release large quantities of basic anxiety (Schein, 1992, p. 22). In the already-chaotic world of complex organizations, there is a tendency to avoid more destabilization, so theories-in-use remain uninterrogated.

From a more traditional approach to theories, the theories that focus on power and politics and culture and sense making may be helpful in recognizing conflict as a normal part of life in human service organizations. These theories may also be helpful in understanding alternative agencies. The search for order in organizational theory has become a search for understanding in a world in which organizations do not always make sense in traditional ways. In addition, in later chapters, it should become clear that the emergence of theories that go beyond purely rational ways of controlling people within organizations offers additional possibilities in critically thinking about organization practice.

What we do know is that working in multicultural organizations in ways that are socially just and respectful of difference may mean that some degree of chaos and uncertainty will be the norm. We are giving you permission, as a future organizational leader, to stop fighting the chaos and instead relish the challenges it offers to use your best critical thinking skills to work toward needed change with or without a traditional theory to guide you. We hope that the approach offered in this chapter will begin to equip you to practice in complexity and ambiguity, recognizing possibilities, accepting challenges, and overcoming obstacles.

THE IMPORTANCE OF FRAMEWORKS

The comforting thing about the use of traditional theories to guide practice is that once a theory is chosen, only the variables and their connections within the theory are of interest. All other information is extraneous, as it is not related to the assumptions of how the theory is thought to work in the real world. In some ways, this makes practice simpler, because less information is seen to be relevant. Rigidly applying a particular theoretical lens may, however, allow you to overlook essential elements in a unique organizational environment. Theories calm the chaos, but can also lull the practitioner into a false sense of clarity and certainty.

A **framework**, on the other hand, can provide additional room to maneuver without the blinders that might be part of unitary theoretical practice, while also establishing mechanisms to reduce the amount of information needing to be considered. A framework can be understood in architectural terms as the basic supporting part of a structure. It holds parts of something together and is basic to the structure. For us a framework is the conceptual and theoretical structure that allows an order or a system to be constructed, identified, and understood. The parts of a framework can be fitted and joined together to support and strengthen a holistic concept. From a cognitive perspective, frameworks are **heuristics**, like theories, that allow for a reduction of information in order to process meaning.

We think frameworks are more useful in the complexity of current organization practice because they allow one to establish order or a systematic approach without the level of reduction that occurs when unitary or even multiple theories are guiding understanding and practice. Frameworks have the advantage of giving form to one's approach to understanding without necessarily discounting potentially important elements. Frameworks provide the holistic skeletal structures for critical thinking.

PARADIGMATIC PERSPECTIVES AS A FRAMEWORK

People have different views of the world, embedded in assumptions that are important to them, whether they recognize them or not. Assumptions are set in diverse views of the world and in how people act within it. The term *paradigm* has been popularized in recent years and is loosely used in daily conversation to describe diverse worldviews or new ways of doing things. The concept of *paradigm* provides clues to why people believe there are certain ways in which an organization should do its work, including such things as what one person expects from another on a daily basis. A **paradigm** is defined as the general organizing principles governing perceptions, including beliefs, values, and techniques that describe what exists, where to look, and what the person can expect to discover (Ritzer, 1980). In keeping with this definition, we use *paradigm* to mean a worldview that contains a set of deep-seated assumptions that are so much a part of the person that it is often hard to step back and even know what those assumptions are. Paradigms, then, reflect the basic assumptions that order a person's world. These assumptions emerge in the context of the individual's experiences with others, organizations, communities, and the larger society. These assumptions create a framework to understand how one approaches self-awareness, critical thinking, and leadership.

A MULTIPARADIGMATIC FRAMEWORK

A variety of scholars over time have tackled the idea of what is real and how one comes to know it. Readers interested in the philosophy of science aspects of this might want to read philosophers of natural science and social science, and the postmodernists. More recently, scholars recognizing multiple ways of knowing have developed a variety of frameworks aimed at making sense of such multiple perspectives. Each framework looks at a multiplicity of approaches that consider whether reality is outside the individual or a matter of conscious construction (see, for example, Fay, 1996; Guba, 1990; Hagen, 1995; Laudan, 1996; Margolis, 1993). We have investigated a number of these frameworks and believe that the one developed by Burrell and Morgan (1979) offers the most flexible and also the most comprehensive approach to managing multiple perspectives in organizations.

BASIC ASSUMPTIONS OF DIFFERENT PARADIGMS

Burrell and Morgan (1979) begin by identifying four different perspectives that become the axes of a four-cell framework in which each paradigm is located. The first axis is formed by what they label *subjectivist–objectivist perspectives*, and the second is formed by *regulation–radical change perspectives*. Figure 2.1 illustrates how the perspectives could be visualized in a matrix. Keeping this framework in mind, both sets of perspectives are defined in the following.

The Subjectivist—Objectivist Continuum   Burrell and Morgan start with basic assumptions about the nature of social science in order to identify different paradigms. They begin by asking four basic questions:

1. What is human/social reality like?
2. How can, or do, we know this and how is knowledge about it transmitted?

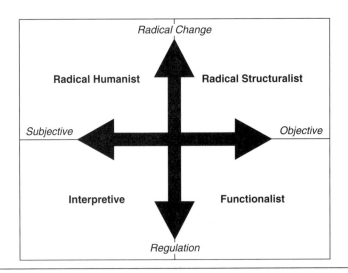

Figure 2.1   Burrell and Morgan's Paradigmatic Framework. *Source:* Adapted from Burrell and Morgan (1979). *Sociological paradigms and organizational analysis.* Aldershot, England: Ashgate. Figure 3.1, p. 22. Used by permission.

3. What is human nature basically like?
4. What methodology do we employ to study or observe human/social reality? (1979, p. 3)

In responding to these questions, most organizational theories can be seen as either subjectivist or objectivist in that the theories could be placed somewhere along the continuum representing either a more subjectivist or objectivist perspective:

Subjectivist ←——————→ Objectivist

Theories based on a **subjectivist perspective** assume that social reality exists primarily in the human consciousness (a product of one's mind). The subjectivist would say the answer to the first question is **nominalism**—human reality exists within the mind. In responding to the second question, a subjectivist would say that knowledge about reality is soft, subjective, and natural **(antipositivism).** From a subjectivist perspective, question three would be answered that human nature is based in **voluntarism**; people can be proactive in creating their own realities. Free human beings participate actively in the creation and construction of social reality and reality must be experienced to be transmitted and understood. Finally, a subjectivist perspective on question four would be **ideographic**, meaning that concern should not be focused on universal principles or an absolutist view. Instead, subjectivists emphasize what is unique and relative to the individual and the ways in which individuals create, change, and interpret the world. Asked what methods would be used to study organizations, subjectivists would prefer qualitative approaches, because words are the basis of shared meaning, but quantitative approaches could also serve to help understand the context in which meaning was constructed.

Think about a person who might be described as subjectivist. From a values and ethics standpoint, that person would be a **relativist.** A relativist does not abide universalism in which there is "one best way," thinking, instead that what is best depends on the time and the circumstance. Imagine an organization that might be subjectivist. This organization would be considered an "alternative" organization. It would be structured differently from traditional ways of organizing because traditional organizing seeks order through locating the best way to do the work of the organization. The subjectivist approach to organizing chooses flexibility in structure and communication, depending on the needs and resources of the context. The organization's communication patterns and expected behavior would change to be responsive to the needs of the particular situation, with no one expecting one way to work in all cases.

Theories based on an **objectivist perspective** would address the four questions quite differently. In response to "What is human/social reality like?" an objectivist embraces **realism**, placing reality above and beyond individual knowledge. Question two would be answered by the objectivist as **positivism**, in which knowledge about social reality is hard and concrete. From this perspective, social reality exists outside the individual. The objectivist response to question three would be that reality shapes action and perception, which is defined as **determinism**. In determinism, people are not shapers of their own realities, but are products of their environments. Asked what methods would be used to understand this perspective, natural science methods with quantitative data collection preferred over qualitative approaches would be applied to the study and understanding of social reality, a **nomothetic** stance. Generalizability would be the goal, with either qualitative or quantitative data.

Again, think about persons or organizations that hold objectivist perspectives. Not only is there one best way, but Truth with a capital *T* exists regardless of time or circumstance. Persons with this perspective would be **absolutists**, believing that there is only one appropriate value or ethical position that should hold regardless of the situation. Objectivist individuals believe in universal Truth over which they have no control. They are the searchers who seek the *right* answers. They would never be accused of saying that everything is relative, and when they work with subjectivists, they will often be frustrated by their colleagues' flexibility regarding perspectives and positions. An organization operating from this perspective would be traditionally organized in a bureaucratic and hierarchical structure. Rules of communication and behavior would be prescribed, predictable, and expected to occur in all cases.

Table 2.1 provides an overview of subjective–objective approaches and how they differ.

Regulation/Radical Change Continuum   In additional to their four questions about the nature of social science, Burrell and Morgan are also concerned

Table 2.1
Subjective–Objective Approaches to the Social Sciences

Subjectivist Perspective	Objectivist Perspective
Nominalism (in the mind)	Realism (external)
Antipositivism (soft, subjective, must be experienced)	Positivism (hard, real, tangible)
Voluntarism (people create their environments)	Determinism (people are products of their environments)
Ideographic (analyze subjective accounts that one generates by "getting inside" situations of everyday life)	Nomothetic (use methods of natural science to test hypotheses in accord with scientific rigor)

Source: Adapted from Burrell and Morgan (1979). *Sociological paradigms and organizational analysis.* Aldershot, England: Ashgate. Figure 1.1, p. 3. Used by permission.

about the nature of human society—the patterned associations between people over time. What assumptions influence how people come together or associate? Two distinct perspectives about society dominant in the literature create a continuum between regulation and radical change:

Regulation ←——————→ Radical Change

Theories built on **regulation** assume that society is characterized by social order and equilibrium. Reality is ordered, if not rule-governed, and knowledge for knowledge's sake is an acceptable result of rigorous, scientific inquiry. A regulation perspective is held by persons who embrace the status quo, seeking consensus rather than focusing on conflict.

On the other hand, theories grounded in **radical change** assumptions focus on deep-seated structural conflict, modes of domination, and even contradiction (change, conflict, and coercion in social structures). This perspective views reality as conflict-ridden, if not chaotic, and assumes that change happens only through chaos and/or conflict. According to this perspective, knowledge for change or action should be the goal of scientific inquiry.

Table 2.2 provides a list of concerns held by the regulation versus radical change perspectives.

Taking the two continua just described, Burrell and Morgan construct a framework by using the subjectivist–objectivist continuum to form the horizontal axis and the regulation–radical change continuum to form the vertical axis. Figure 2.1 provides the complete view of the four-cell typology in which assumptions held by different perspectives come together into four paradigms: Functionalist, Radical Structuralist, Interpretive, and Radical Humanist. Each paradigm represents a fundamentally distinct set of perspectives for analyzing organizations.

Burrell and Morgan assume that all organizations can be located within the context of the four paradigms according to the assumptions that are

Table 2.2
Concerns of Regulation–Radical Change Perspectives

Regulations Concerns	Radical Change Concerns
1. Status quo	1. Radical change
2. Social order	2. Structural conflict
3. Consensus	3. Modes of domination
4. Social integration and cohesion	4. Contradiction
5. Solidarity	5. Emancipation
6. Need satisfaction	6. Deprivation
7. Actuality	7. Potentiality

Source: Adapted from Burrell and Morgan (1979). *Sociological paradigms and organizational analysis.* Aldershot, England: Ashgate. Table 2.2, p. 18. Used by permission.

reflected in the organization's work. Burrell and Morgan's paradigms represent competing points of view with clearly defined boundaries, with different consequences for practice. We offer them as a way to move beyond the paralysis of cognitive dissonance into a comfort zone of paradox made possible by critical analysis and acceptance of ambiguity. We think that to practice appropriately in human services and to effect lasting change for clients one must understand the constraints and opportunities of each paradigm. This understanding will provide the flexibility to respond to very different expectations about what constitutes good organization practice based on different sets of assumptions about the role of organizations and the persons who associate within them.

Later in the book, full chapters will be devoted to each of these paradigms and to the various other frameworks that emerge from each set of assumptions that result in different approaches to organization practice. For now, we will provide an introductory view of each of the four paradigms.

Functionalist Paradigm   We begin here because it is from the assumptions within this paradigm that the majority of classical organizational theories emerged and evolved into "modern" structuralist thinking. Perspectives in this paradigm have influenced theorists who sought to describe (or even prescribe) a rational, orderly approach to work. The Functionalist Paradigm contains the dominant assumptions from which most organizations tried to function in the 20th century.

In the Functionalist Paradigm, objectivism meets regulation. Therefore, realist, positivist, determinist, and nomothetic perspectives about social science are combined with a concern for the status quo, social order, consensus, social integration, solidarity, need satisfaction, and actuality. In its overall approach, the Functionalist Paradigm seeks to provide essentially rational explanations of social affairs. It is pragmatic and problem-oriented, seeking to apply the models and methods of the natural sciences to the study of human affairs. It tends to assume that the social world is composed of relatively concrete empirical artifacts and relationships that can be identified, studied, and measured through approaches derived from the natural sciences.

Most traditional positivists and post-positivists subscribe to this perspective, which has been well defined by persons such as August Compte, Herbert Spencer, Emile Durkheim, Vilfredo Pareto, John Stuart Mill, George Herbert Mead, and William James. According to Burrell and Morgan (1979), the Functionalist Paradigm owes much to Marxist theory, German idealism, and sociological positivism.

For social work direct practice, Martin and O'Connor (1989, p. 78) analyzed the predominant practice theories according to the paradigms from which they were derived. They suggest that psychosocial casework,

---

Box 2.2

ASSUMPTIONS OF THE FUNCTIONALIST PARADIGM

From the Objectivist Perspective

1. Reality is above and beyond individual knowledge.
2. Knowledge about social reality is hard and concrete.
3. People are products of their environments; they are shaped.
4. Natural science methods can be applied to the study and understanding of social reality.

From the Regulation Perspective

5. Society is characterized by social order and equilibrium.
6. Knowledge for knowledge's sake is acceptable.
7. Consensus, rather than conflict, is important.

Source: Adapted from Burrell and Morgan (1979), Chapter 1.

---

transactional analysis, family systems therapy, structural family therapy, conjoint family therapy, cognitive-behavioral approaches, problem-solving therapy, behavior modification, and reciprocal group work models all fit comfortably within the Functionalist Paradigm. In community practice, they place the social planning model there as well. In a later section of the text, we will more fully describe the basic assumptions of the major theories of organization and organizational behavior. At this point, it is sufficient to say that Burrell and Morgan (1979) would place a majority of organizational theories within the Functionalist Paradigm. Box 2.2 summarizes the assumptions of this paradigm.

Radical Structuralist Paradigm This paradigm shares an objectivist approach to science similar to that of the Functionalist Paradigm, but it is directed at fundamentally different ends. Both paradigms are objectivist, but in the Radical Structuralist Paradigm a commitment to radical change intersects with objectivism. The Radical Structuralist Paradigm holds objectivism in common with the Functionalist Paradigm, but contrasts with functionalists by embracing a radical change perspective. Radical change focuses on modes of domination, contradiction, and deprivation. Objectivists assume that there is universal, rules-based knowledge, and in this paradigm that knowledge is gained for the purposes of radical change, emancipation, and potentiality. This perspective is realist, but concentrates on structural relationships to understand and generate fundamental conflicts on which will be based radical change at the class level. Radical structuralists focus on these structural relationships within a social world assumed to be realist, seeking to provide explanations of the basic interrelationships within social formations. In this paradigm, contemporary society is characterized by structural oppression based on fundamental conflicts that require radical change generated through political and economic crises.

Generally, philosophers who take the position that science should serve to critique the status quo of social affairs fit within this worldview. Their interest is in class conflict leading to a revolutionary overthrow of hierarchy, power, and authority. Such thinkers as Weber, the mature Marx, Engels, Lenin, Bukharin, Coletti, Dehrendorf, Rex, and Miliband are radical structuralists, according to Burrell and Morgan (1979). Kantian and Hegelian influences are also present. Burrell and Morgan suggest that there is very little American or British organizational theory development in this paradigm. Rather, organizational theorists taking a radical structuralist perspective have more often developed the critique of the functionalist approach (Burrell & Morgan, 1979, p. 366). European organizational theorists, however, have developed several theories, including contemporary Mediterranean Marxism, Russian social theory, conflict theory (which can be seen as a subset of critical theory), and radical organization theory, that fit within the assumptions of the radical structuralist approach.

Martin and O'Connor (1989) could not identify direct practice theories that guide practice with individuals, families, or groups that fit into the Radical Structuralist Paradigm. However, they place the social action model of community change in this paradigm. We include perspectives embraced by activists such as the Islamic Jihad, Ghandi, Martin Luther King, Saul Alinsky, the Black Panthers, and Latin American liberation theologians. Box 2.3 provides an overview of the assumptions held by radical structuralists.

Box 2.3

ASSUMPTIONS OF THE RADICAL STRUCTURALIST PARADIGM

From the Objectivist Perspective

1. Reality is above and beyond individual knowledge.
2. Knowledge about social reality is hard and concrete.
3. People are products of their environments; they are shaped.
4. Natural science methods can be applied to the study and understanding of social reality.

From the Regulation Change Perspective

5. Society is characterized by deep-seated structural conflict, modes of domination, and even contradiction.
6. Knowledge for change and action should be the goal.
7. Conflict, rather than consensus, is important.

Source: Adapted from Burrell and Morgan (1979), Chapter 1.

Interpretive Paradigm   In this paradigm, subjectivism meets regulation. The Interpretive Paradigm is informed by a concern to understand the world as it is. It assumes that to understand the fundamental nature of the social world it must be at the level of subjective experience. It seeks explanation of the reality of individual consciousness and subjectivity, within the frame of reference that people are participants as opposed to observers of action. The interpretive approach tends to be nominalist, antipositivist, voluntarist, and idiographic. The social world is seen as an emergent process that is created by the individuals concerned. Social reality is little more than a network of assumptions and intersubjectively shared meanings based on multiple perspectives. The problems of conflict, domination, contradiction, potentiality, and change play little part in this frame of reference, because regulation predominates. Instead, there is much more orientation toward obtaining an understanding of the subjectively created social world as it is in terms of an ongoing process. The Interpretive Paradigm is involved with issues relating to the nature of the status quo, social order, consensus, social integration and cohesion, solidarity, and actuality. It assumes a relativist position in that the world, though ordered, is an emergent social enterprise that is continually being created. It assumes that meaning is created and that intersubjectively shared meaning influences decision making and behavior (Weber, 1947b).

Given their interest in socially constructed and socially sustained meaning and their assumption that meaning can be understood only in the immediate social context, Burrell and Morgan (1979) place Dilthey, Husserl, Schutz, Gadamer, Garfinkle, Berkeley, Heidegger, and Merleau-Ponty in the Interpretive Paradigm. It is clear that, like the functionalists, these thinkers were influenced by the German idealists, but they were more interested in understanding through **Verstehen** (complete understanding) than through positivism. Because of this focus on holistic understanding, some works of Kant, Weber, and Mead exhibit this paradigmatic perspective, while others (the majority of their work) fit within the functionalist perspective.

Though there seems to be a natural philosophical affinity between the assumptions of the Interpretive Paradigm and the social work perspective, particularly in regard to the context dependence of individual experience, only a few social work practice theories are identified by Martin and O'Connor (1989) as belonging within this paradigm: client-centered therapy, problem-solving casework, and Gestalt therapy. More recently developed interventions guided by social constructionism, social constructivism, and symbolic interactionism also are a part of an interpretive perspective. So, too, are some therapies under the rubric of narrative therapy.

Until recently, there were few theories of organization that could be placed within the interpretive perspective. However, the surge of organizational

---

Box 2.4

ASSUMPTIONS OF THE INTERPRETIVE PARADIGM

From the Subjectivist Perspective

1. Social reality exists primarily in the human mind.
2. Knowledge about social reality is soft, subjective, and natural.
3. People can be proactive in creating their own realities.
4. Given that individuals create, change, and interpret the world, qualitative approaches to understanding are useful.

From the Regulation Perspective

5. Society is characterized by social order and equilibrium.
6. Knowledge for knowledge's sake is acceptable.
7. Consensus, rather than conflict, is important.

Source: Adapted from Burrell and Morgan (1979), Chapter 1.

---

culture and sensemaking perspectives in the past two decades has emerged from assumptions held in the Interpretive Paradigm. Studies of the subjective experience of individuals within organizational contexts are guided by phenomenology, hermeneutics, phenomenological sociology, constructivism, ethnomethodology, and phenomenological symbolic interactionism. Box 2.4 provides a summary of assumptions undergirding the Interpretive Paradigm.

Note that the Interpretive and the Functionalist paradigms both hold assumptions about there being order (regulation) in the world. Persons coming from these different perspectives would, however, disagree about how order comes to be. Whereas the functionalist would see order as superimposed by the environment, the interpretivist would see order as socially constructed. Both would seek consensus, but what constitutes consensus would be defined differently; however, each would see the importance of understanding organizations, even if action or change did not occur as a result of that new understanding.

Radical Humanist Paradigm   In this perspective, subjectivism connects with radical change. In this paradigm, the central emphasis is on human consciousness, believing that consciousness is dominated by the ideological superstructures with which humans interact, which drive a cognitive wedge between humans and true consciousness. Without true consciousness, fulfillment is inhibited or prevented. Emphasizing radical change, modes of domination, emancipation, deprivation, and potentiality from a subjectivist standpoint, this perspective rejects the concepts of structural conflict and contradiction in favor of a view of the social world that is nominalist, antipositivist, voluntarist, and idiographic. The major concern from this perspective is the release from the constraints that the status quo places on human development. Society is assumed to be antihuman; therefore, human beings must develop ways to transcend the spiritual bonds and fetters that tie them to existing social patterns in order to realize full potential. The goal is radical change to release constraints that hamper human development.

The philosophers who can be placed in this paradigm have also been influenced by German idealism. They share a common concern for individual freedom of the human spirit. Burrell and Morgan (1979) place Kant, Hegel, Husserl, Lukács, Gramsci, the Frankfurt School, young Marx (before the influence of Engels), Habermas, Horkheimer, Marcuse, Adorno, Sartre, Illich, Castaneda, and Laing in the Radical Humanist Paradigm, based on their emancipatory aims.

There are no well-developed human service practice theories in the Radical Humanist Paradigm. However, with the emerging interest in spirituality and holistic treatment modalities, fully developed approaches may be on the horizon. Some of the emergent practices, such as transpersonal work, transcendental meditation, and spiritual counseling would fit here. Given the general assumptions of the perspective, it is doubtful whether any fully formed theory (using the expectations of the functionalist perspective to define what constitutes theory) will ever develop due to the unabashed connection to an individualized subjectivist view of social reality.

From an organizational theory perspective, the major theory that fits within the paradigm is what could be called *anti-organization theory* (Farmer, 1998), in that it suggests that any organization theory is naïve since no organizations exist outside of individual consciousness. Therefore, any theory developed about organizations is misconceived and politically distasteful. There are, however, a few other theories that hold some of the major assumptions of the paradigm: anarchistic individualism, French existentialism, and one branch of critical theory. **Solipsism**, or the assertion that there exists no independent reality outside of the mind, would also fit within this perspective. Box 2.5 summarizes the assumptions of the Radical Humanist Paradigm.

Note that the Radical Humanist and the Interpretive paradigms have a subjectivist perspective in common. Persons in both these paradigms would agree that reality is a social construction, subject to change. However, the radical humanist would view the interpretivist as too focused on consensus to take on the important changes that need to be made. It is also important to note that the Radical Humanist and the Functionalist paradigms have nothing in common. In fact, their assumptions are contradictions of one another.

One further issue is important: These perspectives are mutually exclusive, alternative views. As such, they represent four different ways of seeing,

---

Box 2.5

ASSUMPTIONS OF THE RADICAL HUMANIST PARADIGM

From the Subjectivist Perspective

1. Social reality exists primarily in the human mind.
2. Knowledge about social reality is soft, subjective, and natural.
3. People can be proactive in creating their own realities.
4. Given that individuals create, change, and interpret the world, qualitative approaches to understanding are useful.

From the Regulation Perspective

5. Society is characterized by deep-seated structural conflict, modes of domination, and even contradiction.
6. Knowledge for change and action should be the goal.
7. Conflict, rather than consensus, is important

Source: Adapted from Burrell and Morgan (1979), Chapter 1.

---

knowing, and practicing. Certainly, one can operate in different paradigms at different times, but no organization or person can operate in more than one at any given time without confronting contradictions in understanding and practice. In fact, when one encounters paradox in organization practice, it is likely that different, incompatible perspectives are trying to coexist. For example, consider the cognitive dissonance you would feel as a new worker entering what has been called a *collaborative organization*. The agency director and your supervisor have both told you that everything is done collaboratively, yet you notice that "team meetings" include only upper administration. Decisions and directives flow to you *hierarchically*. You are never asked for input. In this example, the decision process is hierarchical, coming from a functionalist perspective, while the upper administrators seem to articulate a collaborative mandate from an interpretive perspective. Lower-level workers in this organization are destined to live in the frustration and **paradox** created in this organization, which is attempting to work from two very different sets of assumptions that actually contradict one another. Our research (O'Connor, Netting, & Fabelo, in press) indicates that working within this type of contradiction is rather normal, in that various levels of an organization may embrace entirely different paradigmatic assumptions. This leads us to believe that operating within complex human service organizations is intrinsically paradoxical.

As we explore in depth our integrative perspective, one will see that most authors who approach organizations from alternative paradigmatic perspectives have often critiqued functionalists without really developing their own perspectives. It is our hope that our approach, which utilizes a series of integrated frameworks, will provide the foundation for working within and respecting fundamentally different perspectives. Multiple frameworks expand the horizon of modes of theorizing, modes of behaving, and modes of approaching the business of organizing. Different concepts and different analytic tools are logically derived in each framework that should aid in managing what is at times very confusing.

More importantly, multiple frameworks validate the existence of respectable, different perspectives. Understanding the extent of the differences between worldviews will provide vehicles for bridging the real alternative realities for true communication and understanding. *Multiparadigmatic thinking* allows paradoxical practice in recognition of the degree to which you and your colleagues in organizations may be participating in mutually exclusive, although viably different, ways of seeing the world. We think facility in multiple paradigms is one clear way to move toward multicultural practice.

Multicultural practice leaves functionalist orthodoxy behind and expands one's possibilities to see organizations not just as mechanical or organistic, but also as socially constructed entities full of creativity and possibilities. The analytic schemes discussed in this chapter can become tools for negotiating those possibilities. They are also tools for negotiating life in organizations. All the frameworks, essentially built on the assumptions of four paradigms, give the multiparadigmatic thinker the ability to attend to key assumptions, thereby sorting out precise issues that might differentiate approaches to practice and problem solving within organizations. We have found (O'Connor, Netting, & Fabelo, in press) that approaching an organization from the four paradigms becomes a tool for analysis to determine where an organization is presently, where it has been, and where it might be possible to go. In the next section, it should become clear how paradigms are related to organizational cultures that tend to determine what becomes expected and accepted performance among organization members.

A COMPETING VALUES FRAMEWORK

When organizational members come together to design programs and services to carry out their agency's mission, they act on their beliefs about what is valuable and important to do. These actions are based on agreed-upon worldviews and assumptions that determine what is valued. When conflict arises in the process, it can be due to different working styles or even to people having a bad day or many other related factors. However, when conflict escalates and people feel strongly that their views cannot be compromised, they may simply be holding different values, or more fundamentally, they may be working out of different paradigms in which different assumptions prevail. They may be operating from differing organizational cultures. Communication between individuals is not easy when they are coming from such different perspectives. Literally, their views of the world and how it works (or should work) are in conflict. This makes changing an organization's culture very difficult. In fact, according to Glisson (2007, p. 738), "The expectations, norms, and perceptions that form the organization's social context can inhibit, truncate, reinvent, or adapt core technologies in ways that render the technologies ineffective."

Conflicts in organizations are inevitable, and we believe it is healthy to acknowledge them because they have consequences. To squelch conflicts of assumptions would be to ignore the strengths that come from persons embracing different views. It would also mean sidestepping issues and not fully communicating with one's colleagues. In fact, recognizing differences among organizational stakeholders is so important that we hope to convince you to engage in multiparadigmatic practice within organizations. **Multiparadigmatic practice** means being able to identify assumptions-in-use within an organization and then using one's critical thinking and practice skills to move in and out of different ways of thinking. Leaders enacting multiparadigmatic practice have respect for organizations and individuals who embrace different worldviews than their own and even make the conscious choice to work from a different set of assumptions when that is the best fit for the problem at hand. This is not easy. Individuals typically feel more comfortable in certain paradigms than in others. We believe, however, that it is necessary for the human service leaders of the future to be able to think and act multiparadigmatically in order to fully actualize their organization practice.

In their extensive work in business contexts, Kim Cameron and Robert Quinn have developed an understanding of organizations and change within them based on their cultures. Their **competing values framework** (Cameron & Quinn, 2006) is a result of their empirical research and consulting experience. Their contribution includes instruments for diagnosing organizational culture and management competency and provides a theoretical framework for understanding organizational culture that is built on intersecting continua very similar to those created by Burrell and Morgan. In this case, the four perspectives on culture are the result of the intersection of one continuum with an external focus and differentiation at one end and an internal focus and integration at the other end. To see the congruence with Burrell and Morgan, one should recall the regulation–radical change continuum. The intersecting continuum has **flexibility and discretion** on one end and **stability and control** on the other. Remember that Burrell and Morgan place subjectivity on one end and objectivity on the other. Figure 2.2 details the dimensions of the values framework.

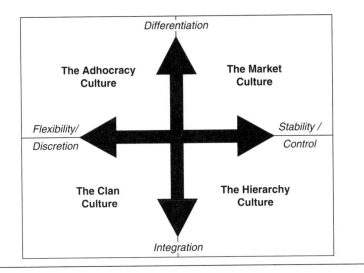

Figure 2.2 Cameron and Quinn's Competing Values Framework. *Source:* Adapted from Cameron and Quinn (2006). *Diagnosing and changing organizational culture* (rev. ed.). San Francisco, CA: Jossey Bass.

Cameron and Quinn's intersecting continua create a competing values framework containing value orientations that characterize organizations. From their perspective, these value orientations are competing and at times contradictory to one another. Their framework details the organizational values and the organizational cultures that derive from them. Even though this approach was developed with a business perspective, it is clear to us that these competing values also operate in the human service arena. We think their framework helps make sense of many of the dimensions of organizational life, including an organization's preferred structure, standards of quality, and leadership and management styles.

The following look at the different cultural profiles will probably remind you of the differences between business organizations and human service organizations, but the flavor of the different cultures should also help to distinguish different norms for organization practice. Later in the text, we will return to this particular framework as an aid in diagnosing and changing an organization's culture when we look more closely at management and practice skills in different organizational types.

THE HIERARCHY CULTURE

According to Cameron and Quinn (2006), the **hierarchy culture** is a very formalized and structured place to work. Everything that people do is governed by procedures and protocols. Efficiency-minded leaders pride themselves on being good coordinators and organizers who are skilled at maintaining a smooth-running organization. The glue that holds the organization together is comprised of formal rules and policies. Of long-term concern is stability and performance with efficient, smooth operations. Dependable delivery, seamless scheduling, and efficient costs are viewed as signs of success. Managers create a work environment in which employees feel secure and things are predicable. The hierarchy culture produces an organization focused on internal maintenance with expectations for stability and control. Management in this culture involves monitoring and coordinating (p. 64).

THE MARKET CULTURE

The **market culture** is found in a results-oriented organization, where the major concern is getting the job done. People are competitive and goal oriented. Leaders are hard-driven producers and competitors. They are tough and demanding because they are sure of their vision. Success is the glue that holds the organization together. Most of the time, this means winning against the competition, and sometimes by any means necessary. Common concerns include maintaining one's reputation and being successful. The long-term focus is on being competitive and achieving measurable goals based on clear targets. Success is defined in terms of size of market share and level of penetration. Market leadership and the ability to compete are important values. The organizational style is hard-driving competitiveness where the ends justify the means. The market culture produces an organization that focuses on external positioning with some recognition of a need for stability and control. Management expectations here involve being competitive and productive (Cameron & Quinn, 2006, p. 94).

THE CLAN CULTURE

The **clan culture** is an engaging and friendly setting to work where people share much of their personal selves. The organizational patterns and communications are like an extended family. Leaders are considered to be members of the group, but are also mentors or even parent figures. Tradition and loyalty hold the organization together. Commitment to the organization and its members is high. Emphasis is placed on the long-term benefit of human resources development and great importance is attached to cohesion and morale. Success is defined in terms of sensitivity to customers and concern for people inside and outside the organization. The organization views teamwork, participation, and consensus as essential elements. This organization values flexibility and concern and sensitivity for people. The manager in this culture is expected to be a facilitator and mentor (Cameron & Quinn, 2006, p. 94).

THE ADHOCRACY CULTURE

The **adhocracy culture** creates a dynamic, entrepreneurial, and creative work setting. People take risks, even sticking their necks out. Leaders are seen as innovators and risk takers and expect that of others. A commitment to experimentation and innovative methods is the glue that holds the organization together. Great emphasis is placed on being on the leading edge, even if sometimes it looks like the fringe. The organization's long-term emphasis is on growth and obtaining new resources. Obtaining new products or services is a sign of success. Being a product or service innovator is important. The organization expects and encourages individual initiative and freedom. This is an organization with great flexibility and individuality. Management is innovative and visionary (Cameron & Quinn, 2006, p. 94).

Figure 2.3 shows how congruent the philosophical paradigmatic perspective of Burrell and Morgan is with the empirically tested competing values framework of Cameron and Quinn. Paradigmatic perspectives based on deep-seated assumptions about how the world works and how one comes to know it can be usefully extended to include what is valued once it is known. Not only will standards of excellence by way of performance change from quadrant to quadrant, but this also suggests that expected management skills and leadership roles will be different in each quadrant.

Multiple researchers have used Cameron and Quinn's tools with thousands of organizations, and findings repeatedly reinforce the fact that organizations do not sit neatly within one culture. Cameron and Quinn themselves used their four-part cultural matrix to plot out the scores of

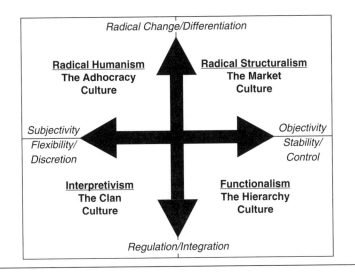

Figure 2.3 Paradigms and Competing Values Combined.

over 1,000 corporations and in the process identified five trends. We list the five trends here, along with comments regarding how they might relate to human service organizations:

1. Top managers were more oriented to clan cultures than lower-level managers. Thus, whereas top managers viewed their organizations as more serendipitous, others were not as convinced. This finding indicates that persons in leadership positions may be more predisposed to family or connectional metaphors, but when it comes to daily oversight, supervisors and program coordinators may find it easier to work in cultures with more established, defined rules and regulations to guide their actions.

2. Adhocracy cultures are typically less evident across the board, and are therefore less dominant than the three other cultural types. In Chapter 9, we will introduce I Help, an entrepreneurial example that had an adhocracy culture.

3. Over time, companies tend to move toward hierarchical and market culture types. Once this happens, it seems they have difficulty moving toward clan or adhocracy cultures. Thus, there could be a tendency for the Washington County Office on Aging, with which we will begin Chapter 3 (a Traditional Organization), and the Consumer-Directed Advocacy Agency in Chapter 5 (a Social Change Organization) to move from their objectivist perspectives into a more subjectivist type of culture, but it might be difficult. It is as if the gravitational pull is toward objectivism as agencies age in place.

4. Although some writers have taken the competing values framework and tried to apply the concept of management to some and leadership to others of the identified cultures, Cameron and Quinn are very clear that both management and leadership are relevant in all four cultures. "All four culture types (and the management competencies that accompany them) are valuable and necessary. None is better or worse than the others (2006, p. 80)." Thus, their conclusion fits well with the Myers-Briggs personality inventory, to be discussed next.

5. Cameron and Quinn's findings underscore our contention that it is highly likely that paradox is to be expected, even in highly functioning organizations. They assert the importance of flexibility in assessing cultural profiles, pointing out that it is typical to find hard-driving productivity coexisting with informality and fun in the same organization (2006, p. 81).

The idea of a perspective that generates preferred structures, goals, and relationships in organizations is only part of what is necessary to create an integrated understanding of organization practice. Next, one must look closely at the people acting within these different organizational standpoints. We do this by first looking individually and then from the point of view of those who manage those individuals in organizations.

THE MYERS-BRIGGS FRAMEWORK

Based on our earlier discussion of Myers-Briggs in Chapter 1, you may have begun thinking about the similarities between personality types and the multiple perspectives involving worldviews and cultural preferences. In this section, we will illustrate how certain aspects of the personality types can be placed on the same intersecting continua that brought paradigms and cultures together. The valid and reliable Myers-Briggs instrument seems to identify how the mind is used—how the individual feels most comfortable, natural, and, thus, confident. It shows how people have different interests, ways of behaving, and ways of viewing strengths and needs for growth.

The Myers-Briggs identifies separate and unique types, the four paradigms define fundamentally different perspectives for the analysis of social phenomena, and the competing values framework defines four very different organizational cultures. Those familiar with the Myers-Briggs framework know that there are 16 personality types identified, according to four dimensions. The dimensions are based on the following questions:

1. Where do you prefer to focus your attention, get your energy?
2. How do you prefer to take in information?
3. How do you make decisions?
4. How do you deal with the outer world? (Myers, 1998, pp. 9–10)

The first question is answered along the extroversion–introversion continuum. The second question is answered along the sensing–intuition continuum. The responses to these two questions pertain to preferences of the individual that will determine how they become personally energized and how they take in information. For example, an extrovert may need the stimulation of working closely with others, whereas the introvert may like to interact with others and then move to her own computer and work alone for a while. Both introverts and extroverts, however, can work in various organizational cultures. Similarly, persons take in information differently. The sensing person enjoys observing what is going on around him (focusing outward) to gather information, whereas the intuitive person may be seen as creative and imaginative, seeing patterns and trusting inspiration (focusing inward). Having a diverse staff who both observe (sense) and make connections (intuit) would be valuable in any of Quinn and Cameron's organizational cultures. Their different ways of processing can be complementary in their respective settings, just as qualitative and quantitative data are important and complementary in the various settings.

Whereas the first two questions relate to how individuals draw energy and process information (focused on how the individual works internally), the next two questions focus on how persons relate to their context or surroundings. The third and fourth questions posed by Myers-Briggs relate to decision-making and social behaviors (actions) taken. Thus, the thinking–feeling continuum that responds to "How do you make decisions?" has implications for individual behavior within a group or organizational context. For example, in human service agencies they are constantly making decisions that influence their colleagues and their clients. Professionals in planning and policy settings make decisions that have broad impact on what occurs at the service delivery level. Myers-Briggs recognizes that this constant decision-making activity is done in different ways by different people. For example, the "thinking" person attempts to decide on an objective basis, whereas the "feeling" person likes to decide in a relative or subjective manner, including the uniqueness of each situation.

Similarly, how a person responds along the judging–perceiving continuum and answers the question, "How do you deal with the outer world?" has important implications for how that person behaves in an organizational context. The "judging" person appreciates order and sticking to plan, trying to avoid the stresses of sudden or rapid change. The "perceiving" person, conversely, thrives on spontaneity and feels energized when pressures mount. Table 2.3 provides an overview of characteristics of

Table 2.3
Myers-Briggs' Characteristics Along Two Behavioral Dimensions

Feeling ←——————→	Thinking
Is empathetic with others	Is analytical
Is guided by personal values	Uses cause-and-effect reasoning
Assesses impacts of decisions on people	Solves problems with logic
Strives for harmony and positive interactions	Strives for an objective standard of truth
Is compassionate	Is reasonable (rational)
Views fairness as treating everyone equally	Can be "tough-minded"
Judging ←——————→	**Perceiving**
Likes schedules	Is spontaneous
Has an organize life	Is flexible
Is systematic	Likes things to be casual
Is methodical	Is okay with things being open ended
Makes short- and long-range plans	Is adaptable; changes course
Likes to have things decided	Likes things loose and open to change
Tries to avoid last-minute stresses	Feels energized by last-minute pressures

Source: Myers (1998), p. 10.

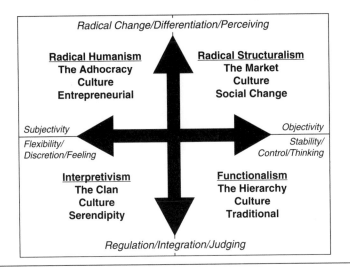

Figure 2.4 Two Myers-Briggs Behavioral Dimensions Placed Within Multiple Frameworks.

thinking–feeling and judging–perceiving as two continua from the Myers-Briggs framework (Myers, 1998, p. 10).

Figure 2.4 shows how the thinking–feeling and the judging–perceiving dimensions of the Myers-Briggs types might also be located in our multiple perspectives framework based on similar assumptions about two questions: (1) How do you make decisions?; and (2) How do you deal with the outer world? Figure 2.4 translates these two dimensions of the Myers-Briggs into a multiparadigmatic framework.

THINKING–JUDGING (TJ)

Persons described as *thinking–judging* (TJ), with their realism, organizing abilities, and command of the facts based on logical pragmatism, can be seen to be functionalists. Their tendency for logic and analysis in their decision-making behaviors as well as their desire to work in a systematic, orderly manner in their interactions with the outer world places them squarely within a functionalist perspective. These personality types could be said to hold a traditional, functionalist, or hierarchical perspective created by the intersection of objectivity/stability/control and regulation/integration when added to thinking and judging. Persons holding this perspective would likely be comfortable being monitored and informed by those in charge and would welcome the structure and coordination provided by dependable and reliable leadership.

The personality types holding a traditional perspective tend to have the following expectations about decision making and organizational culture:

Thinking

- Likes to look at the logical consequences of a choice or action
- Seeks objectivity by mentally removing herself from the situation and examining the pros and cons
- Is energized by critiquing and analyzing using a problem-solving process
- Looks for a standard or principle that will apply universally in similar situations

Judging

- Likes to live in a planned, orderly, predictable manner
- Wants to come to closure on decisions and move on
- Likes to have things settled and structured
- Is energized by sticking to a plan and getting things done

THINKING–PERCEIVING (TP)

Persons described as *thinking–perceiving* (TP), with their need to be analytical and rational in their approach to decision making, will bring those characteristics to situations in the real world that are subject to change. Their perceiving predisposition may give them a sense of adventure in that change is perfectly acceptable as long as one approaches it in an objective, facts-based manner. These personal characteristics are compatible with radical structuralism. With their need to analyze and bring to logical order all aspects of their world, TPs as radical structuralists will seek highly organized change that brings their organization (community or society) into alignment with a new order, invigorated by the pressures that are associated with engaging in collective change. These personality types hold a social change, radical structuralist, market perspective created by the intersection of objectivity/stability/control and radical change/differentiation combined with thinking and perceiving. Persons holding a social change perspective would likely be comfortable with aggressive, decisive leadership that is mission driven, task oriented, and work focused and all about changing.

The personality types holding a social change perspective tend to have the following expectations about decision making and organizational culture:

Thinking

- Likes to look at the logical consequences of a choice or action
- Seeks objectivity by mentally removing herself from the situation and examining the pros and cons

- Is energized by critiquing and analyzing using a problem-solving process
- Looks for a standard or principle that will apply universally in similar situations

Perceiving

- Likes to live in a flexible, spontaneous way
- Views detailed plans and final decisions as confining
- Prefers to stay open to new information and last-minute options
- Is energized by adapting to the demands of the moment

FEELING–JUDGING (FJ)

Those described as *feeling–judging* (FJ), with their deep-felt empathy and compassion for others, fit within the Interpretive Paradigm. FJs are excited about continuous involvement in activities and relationships. Their feeling nature in terms of decision-making processes makes them highly aware of how their decisions impact others, which makes them highly connectional. They show their caring in warm and pragmatic gestures of helping and are often seen as "tender-hearted," which places them within the assumptions of the interpretive perspective. These personality types can be said to hold a serendipitous, interpretive, clannish perspective that is created by the intersection of subjectivity/flexibility/discretion and regulation/integration when combined with judging and feeling. A person having this perspective would likely be most comfortable with leadership that is people and process oriented while being caring and empathic. Mutual respect and trust would be desirable.

The personality types holding a serendipitous perspective tend to have the following expectations about decision making and organizational culture:

Feeling

- Likes to consider what is important to self and others
- Identifies with others in making decisions that honor people
- Is energized by appreciating, supporting, and praising others
- Seeks harmony and treats people as unique individuals

Judging

- Likes to live in a planned, orderly, predictable manner
- Wants to come to closure on decisions and move on
- Likes to have things settled and structured
- Is energized by sticking to a plan and getting things done

FEELING–PERCEIVING (FP)

Personality types with *feeling–perceiving* (FP) characteristics could be said to fit in the Radical Humanist Paradigm in that they are highly respectful of individual differences (subjective) and are very comfortable with change. They embody a concern for human potential and uniqueness as well as being open to possibility. FPs can be said to hold an entrepreneurial, radical, adhocracy perspective that is created by the intersection of subjectivity/flexibility/discretion and radical change/differentiation when combined with feeling and perceiving. Those holding this perspective would appreciate clever, creative leadership that generates hope and potentiality. Continuous improvement (particularly personal improvement) toward possibilities through innovation and adaptation would be welcomed.

The personality types holding an entrepreneurial perspective tend to have the following expectations about decision making and organizational culture:

Feeling

- Likes to consider what is important to self and others
- Identifies with others in making decisions that honor people
- Is energized by appreciating, supporting, and praising others
- Seeks harmony and treats people as unique individuals

Perceiving

- Likes to live in a flexible, spontaneous way
- Views detailed plans and final decisions as confining
- Prefers to stay open to new information and last-minute options
- Is energized by adapting to the demands of the moment

A few examples may help to show how different personality characteristics will have implications for practice in organizations. For instance, leaders and employees holding these different perspectives would develop different expectations for employee performance. Employees with different decision-making styles would need to be aware that some persons are seeking universal "one best ways" or "best practices" in designing and delivering services, while others are more concerned with respecting individual differences in program design and service delivery. Similarly, some people will be more concerned with keeping peace, compromising, and respecting the status quo, when others would be energized by the prospects of confrontation and change.

Readers will likely have examples from their work experience about what can happen when different personality types clash. For example, one colleague may be a "just-the-facts" type of person, who is advocating for nothing being done unless it is based on empirical evidence. This colleague holds a very traditional perspective about organization practice. You, on the other hand, rail against traditionalism, thinking creativity and intuition might produce a better way to serve clients. Even though you both have clients' needs at heart, the way in which you would go about providing services would be very different.

Say you enter an agency where its members seem very much at ease with one another, very friendly, and very close. They like one another and share very intimate information all the time. They might all be FJs holding serendipitous perspectives about work life. They thrive on harmony and respect for the individual. However, to their traditional supervisor, their decision-making processes seem to be based on what "feels right" with little attention to quantitatively measurable evidence. The supervisor is astounded that they are so successful and well respected. She needs empirical evidence to decide organizational direction and doesn't wish to have organizational members become intimates like family members. She is probably a TJ who appreciates a more traditional, functionalist perspective. This supervisor would probably be more comfortable in a hierarchy culture. Her inclination will be to criticize the others' way of doing business. However, the rest of the organization appears to be functioning from a more subjectivist, interpretive perspective as part of a clan culture. Those FJs will tend to criticize the supervisor for being too rigid and unfeeling. From either direction, dissonance is inevitable.

More and more, the Myers-Briggs test is being used to help people make better career choices and manage close relationships. It is used in counseling, parenting, business, teamwork, leadership and spirituality development, and education. It seems there is a growing acceptance that uniqueness brings strength, different styles are useful, and differing perceptions are assets. These attitudes are entering the organizational field with the recognition that personality type is related to career satisfaction and organizational competence (Tieger & Barron-Tieger, 1992), team members' types affect team building (Hirsh, 1992), and ways of describing and analyzing organizational situations set the stage for organizational change (Lawrence, 1993). The management challenges related to diversity lead us to yet another framework for understanding organization practice.

A STRATEGIC MANAGEMENT FRAMEWORK

By now, it should be clear that successful management in such complex and potentially paradoxical environments must be strategic. Mintzberg, Ahlstrand, and Lampel (1998) have identified a variety of schools of thought about management that appear to be congruent with the various frameworks that we have already introduced. Just as we did with the

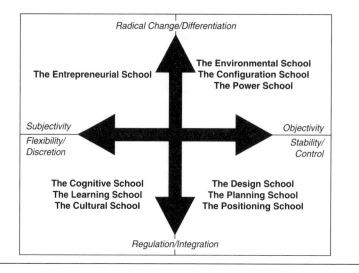

Figure 2.5 Schools of Management Thought Placed Within Multiple Frameworks. *Source:* Mintzberg, Ahlstrand, and Lampe (1998).

Myer-Briggs approach, we have taken the liberty to distribute the various schools representing distinct points of views on management practice according to the paradigmatic and values perspectives that we have been using. Some of these schools are prescriptive, others are descriptive, but all provide ideas about ways to achieve excellence, given differing assumptions about what constitutes excellence. Figure 2.5 shows the distribution of these schools according to differing perspectives about organizations and the behavior within them. As the discussion unfolds, it should become clear that the chosen management strategies have much to do with the existence of differing organizational goals.

FUNCTIONALISM/THE HIERARCHY CULTURE

According to Mintzberg et al., (1998), the three schools in this perspective are *prescriptive* in nature, being concerned with how strategies should be formulated rather than what the strategies are or how they should be enacted.

The Design School Initially developed by Selznick (1957) and Chandler (1962) and further developed by Andrews (1987), this managerial approach focuses on the process of conceiving the appropriate management strategy. The Design School involves appraising external and internal situations, threats and opportunities in the environment, and organizational strengths and weaknesses (often called the *SWOT analysis*—assessment of *strengths and weaknesses of the organization* in relation to the *opportunities and threats in the environment*). By reviewing key success factors and distinctive competencies and linking them to managerial values, strategies are created. Alternatives are considered and the best choice is selected that creates a unique, tailor-made strategy for each organization. The goal is the creation of the right strategy for the conditions at hand. Mintzberg, Ahlstrand, and Lampel indicate the premises of the Design School as:

- Strategies are deliberately formed in an intentional process.
- The formal leader of the organization serves as the primary strategist, with other persons being subordinate in strategizing.
- Strategy formation needs to be simple.
- Best strategies come from tailoring what will happen to the specific situation.
- Once selected, strategies are implemented in a planned and prescribed way.
- Clearly stated and easy-to-follow strategies help everyone know what to do.
- Only after a fully developed, explicit strategy is fully formulated can it be finally implemented (Mintzberg et al., 1998, pp. 29–32).

As one reviews these premises, one can see that this approach to strategy in an organization is based on functionalist assumptions. From the Myers-Briggs discussion, it should be clear that the Design School of management would be a comfortable fit for persons who have a predisposition to thinking–judging, in which decision making is logical and the outer world is viewed as being organized and systematic.

The Planning School   According to Mintzberg, Ahlstrand, and Lampe, the Planning School developed based on the influence of H. Igor Ansoff (1965), who, along with Steiner (1969), developed a linear approach to the creation of a formal process of strategic planning and management. The Planning School set forth steps and to-do lists and used techniques such as developing objectives, establishing a budget, and writing a plan. This school maintains a specific focus on goals. The Planning School accepted most of the premises of the Design School but considered the process of strategy selection and implementation much more formal and mechanistic. Thus, the premises of the Planning School can be summarized as:

- Formal conscious planning can result in specific strategies with specific details identified.
- The executive director is ultimately responsible for that overall process, but implementation rests with staff planners/practitioners.
- Explicit strategies appear from this process ready to be implemented through detailed attention to objectives, budgets, programs, and plans (Mintzberg et al., 1998, p. 58).

In a way, the Planning School tightened up an already-rational model in the Design School, remaining even more functionalist in the assumptions that guided the practice of decision making, strategy formation, and implementation. Although both schools of thought were embraced and used, in 1980, the Positioning School, still based on functionalist assumptions, extended strategic thinking by focusing on the power of positioning one's organization within the economic marketplace.

The Positioning School Strategic formation as an analytic process is the vision of this school, based on the assumption that there exist only a few key strategies or positions in the marketplace that are desirable in a given industry. Various "waves" of this school have existed over time (see Clausewitz, 1968; Henderson, 1979; Porter, 1980). Regardless of the wave, a primary idea behind the positioning school is that generic strategies allow defense against competitors. The generic strategies involve product differentiation and focused market scope through competitive industry analysis. The CEO in concert with planners/analysts select rather than design a strategy that is systematic and empirically supported, resulting in the ideal strategy for an organization under a given set of conditions.

The premises of the Positioning School are:

- Strategies are generic, identifiable positions in the external environment.
- Economics and competition drive the organization's context.
- Planning must be performed in a systematic way, with the primary goal being to select the right generic strategy for the situation at hand.
- Expert analysts play a major role in the strategy selection process, handing the results of their calculations to managers who officially control the choices.
- Fully developed strategies come from this process ready to be implemented; market structure drives positional strategies that drive organizational structure (Mintzberg et al., 1998, p. 85).

The three schools of management just described (design, planning, and positioning) are solidly rooted in functionalist assumptions of the world. Note that a strategy must always be fully developed before it is implemented, and implementation must happen in a systematic manner. The prescriptive nature of these schools may be comforting to persons who want to work in a predictable organization, know what to expect and what is expected of them, and avoid being subject to rapid, unexpected change. Human service professionals who rely on best practices to guide what they do are using the Positioning School's approach. They systematically assess and analyze the situation, then seek the best approach available, fitting strategy with situation and then implementing that strategy in a predetermined manner according to practice directives. An example of this is seen in health-care organizations when professionals use prescribed critical pathways, first diagnosing the problem and then finding the pathway that fits with that diagnosis and finally linking the two.

RADICAL STRUCTURALISM/THE MARKET CULTURE

According to Mintzberg, Ahlstrand, and Lampel (1998), the schools that fit within the assumptions of radical structuralism are less prescriptive and more focused on describing how strategies get selected and enacted. The schools discussed in this section are also much more attuned to the *transformative potential* of strategic management.

The Power School Recognizing that organizational strategy formation is a process of negotiation, the Power School is built on the idea of use of influence. This influence can be political and can include the exploitation of power in other than purely economic ways. This school recognizes that power relations surround organizations both inside and outside, so the divisions is the school represent both micro and macro concerns. MacMillan (1978), Sarrazin (1978), Zald and Berger (1978) and Bolman and Deal (1997) give a flavor of the macro-to-micro continuum in the school.

The premises of the Power School are:

- Power and politics shape strategy formation from inter- and intra-organizational and environmental behavior.
- Strategies that may result from such a process take the form of positions and ploys.
- Micro power sees strategy development as an interplay of persuasion, bargaining, and sometimes direct confrontation, in the form of political games, among parochial interests and shifting coalitions, with none dominant for any significant period of time.
- Macro power sees the organization as self-promoting and controlling of other organizations, through the use of strategic maneuvering as well as collective strategies in various kinds of interorganizational relationships (Mintzberg et al., 1998, p. 260).

The Environmental School This school positions the environment as one of the central forces in the management process along with leadership and the organization itself. The important contribution here is the recognition of the environment as relevant and interactive in the strategic management process. Mintzberg (1979) and Hannan and Freeman (1977) are often cited as framers of what has become known as the *contingency view of management*, which suggests that what is the best way depends on the size of the organization, its technology, the stability of the context, and what is happening external to the organization.

The premises of the Environmental School are:

- General forces in the environment influence the organization's strategy-making process.
- If the organization doesn't respond to these forces, it may not survive.
- Leadership must be savvy in assessing the environment and ensuring proper adaptation by the organization.
- Organizations cluster together in ecological-type niches until conditions change or become too tense. Aggressive responses are needed for survival (Mintzberg et al., 1998, p.288).

The Configuration School   This school sees strategy formation as a process of transformation. The belief here is that if an organization adopts a certain state, then strategy making becomes a process of moving (or leaping) from one state to another, thus transforming itself as a result of new configurations. Borrowing from the revolutionary ideas of Brinton (1938) and Toynbee (1957), Firsirotu (1985) applied the ideas of political or cultural revolutions to organizational turnarounds.

The premises of the Configuration School are:

- Typically, organizations have stable configurations of characteristics that they adopt for a time. This temporary structure is matched to a context that causes it to engage in particular behaviors and strategies.
- Major leaps and transformations to other configurations occur amid periods of stability.
- These successive configurations, interspersed by periods of transformation, may demonstrate patterned sequences or organizational life cycles.
- Strategic management is committed to maintaining stability (or at least adaptable strategic change) most of the time, tempered by managing times of disruption without destroying the organization.
- Timing becomes very important in strategy making, as well as a savvy understanding of the politics in which the organization is engaged.
- Strategies must match the time and situation (Mintzberg et al., 1998, pp. 305–306).

The assumptions of these three schools of thought (power and politics, environment, and configuration) are closely aligned with radical structuralism. Note how important the environment is, as compared to more functionalist assumptions that tend to be more insular. Human service organizations that seek advocacy causes as their mission fit comfortably in the often-volatile power-and-politics approach to strategizing, organizing their structural configurations to align with those causes. Personality types who see targeted ways to make transformative change will enjoy the "thinking" methods of decision making that strives for universal rights, and the change orientation aligned with "perceiving" to achieve social change. Human service professionals who are looking for fast-moving, controversial positions will prefer the strategies in these schools.

INTERPRETIVISM/THE CLAN CULTURE

The schools that fit within this perspective are more attentive to the *communal connections* among organization members than hierarchical approaches. According to Mintzberg, Ahlstrand, and Lampel (1998), values and beliefs play an important part in strategic decision making for the following three schools of thought.

The Cognitive School Drawing from the field of cognitive psychology, this school sees strategy formation as a mental process. The school began by looking at the requisites for thinking about what the strategist needs to know, and later shifting the focus to the strategic reasoning process as either an objective or a subjective one (see Bogner & Thomas, 1993; Reger & Huff, 1993; Simon, 1957) on the part of the strategist. Information processing, cognitive mapping, heuristics, and biases have all been the focus of research in the Cognitive School. This is a continually evolving school, with premises such as:

- Strategy formation is a cognitive process.
- Strategies emerge as concepts, maps, schemas, or frames that shape how people deal with information from the larger environment.
- These inputs (according to the "objective" wing of the school) flow through distorting filters before they are decoded by cognitive maps, or (according to the "subjective" wing) are merely interpretations of how the world is perceived.
- Strategies are hard to capture, are considerably less than optimal when actually attained, and difficult to change when no longer needed (Mintzberg et al., 1998, pp. 171–172).

The Learning School This school sees strategy formation as an emerging process based on learning over time. Strategies emerge as people individually and collectively come to know situations and their organization's capabilities to deal with them. This then is not "management of change but management by change" (Lapierre, 1980, p. 9). The learning school has a foundation based in descriptive research on how strategies actually form in organizations (see Braybrooke & Lindblom, 1963; Kiechel, 1984; Mintzberg & McHugh, 1985; Nelson & Winter, 1982).

Basic premises of the Learning School are:

- Deliberate control is not possible, because the environment is unpredictable, making strategy formation and implementation a learning process that runs together.
- Everyone in the system is a learner and potential strategist.
- Strategizing is an emergent learning process in which sense making (thinking retrospectively to make sense of action) occurs.
- Leaders do not preconceive strategies, but manage the learning process as strategies emerge.
- Strategies first appear as past patterns and only later as future plans. In the end, strategies become perspectives to guide overall behavior (Mintzberg et al., 1998, p. 208–209).

The Cultural School Influenced by anthropology, culture in organizations was discovered about 20 years ago, and organizational culture has been viewed as a form of collective cognition. While individual activities are certainly recognized, their significance in an organization is collective. Pettigrew (1985), Johnson (1992), and Edwards (1977) have all contributed to understanding the cultural aspect of the strategy process imbedded in the culture of the organization and its context.

The premises of the Cultural School are:

- Beliefs and understandings guide strategy formation in a shared, interactive process.
- These beliefs and understandings are acquired as individuals are acculturated or socialized to the organization's culture in both subtle (and not-so-subtle) ways.
- Employees are so well socialized that the assumptions that undergird their culture become second nature. If asked, they would not remember what the actual assumption is because it has become so much a part of how they think and act.
- Strategies are perspectives more than they are positions, rooted in collective expectations and reflecting patterns that protect deeply embedded organizational resources.
- Existing strategy is perpetuated, based on culture and ideology. Instead, any change in direction tends to promote major shifts in position within the organization's overall strategic perspective (Mintzberg et al., 1998, pp. 267–268).

The assumptions of the Cognitive, Learning, and Culture schools fit within the Interpretive Paradigm and sound very much like the clan culture described by Cameron and Quinn. The feeling–judging personality type would be particularly comfortable with these schools of thought because strategies would be jointly developed with colleagues in an atmosphere respectful of their individuality. As strategies emerged, an organized system would be constructed almost by serendipity because those within would build it through a sense of togetherness. Once constructed, the deeply held beliefs that hold it together would become a secure place from which to go about one's work until things changed and new, jointly agreed-upon norms and strategies were embraced.

RADICAL HUMANISM/THE ADHOCRACY CULTURE

The perspective represented here is one of *innovation and complexity*, with rules existing only when necessary to support expertise. Mintzberg, Ahlstrand, and Lampel (1998) identify only one school that fits the freewheeling nature and the assumptions of radical humanism.

The Entrepreneurial School This school views strategy formation as a visionary process of a leader who uses intuition, judgment, wisdom, experience, and insight. This school of thought is more intent on the individual leader's leadership than the organizational or contextual environment. Much attention has been given to the entrepreneurial personality (Kets de Vries, 1985; Pinchot, 1985; Westley & Mintzberg, 1989).

The premises of the Entrepreneurial School can be summarized as:

- Leaders have a perspective, a long-term direction, or a vision for the future. Thus, strategy is tied to the leader's vision.
- Strategy formation is a semiconscious process, rooted in the leader's experience and intuition, regardless of whether he or she actually conceives the strategy or adopts it from others and then internalizes it.
- Close oversight and control occurs in reformulating strategy as the leader individually promotes the vision.
- The leader's strategic vision is malleable and strategies are emergent as details unfold.
- The organization has to be flexible so that the visionary leader has a good deal of latitude for making change.
- There is a sense of forming a niche, because entrepreneurial strategy tends to find the most competitive place in which to focus energies (Mintzberg et al., 1998, p. 243).

The Entrepreneurial School focuses on the leader, a visionary who seeks to transform without being fettered by rigid structures such as those rejected by radical humanism and an adhocracy culture. The feeling–perceiving (FP) type in the Myers-Briggs is a natural in the entrepreneurial school, given the preference for making decisions guided by personal values and views of human uniqueness with spontaneity and change as energizers. In human services, founders who have alterative visions of empowerment for groups who have traditionally been underserved are entrepreneurs. They often give a great deal of thought to where they will incubate their ideas so that they are kept alive in a vital manner. It is during that process of translating their dreams into reality, before they join with others, that they may be most closely aligned with the premises of the Entrepreneurial School (Netting, O'Connor, & Singletary, 2007). It is there that they are somewhat outside the traditional forces of the larger environment, because others are not clamoring to do what they are dreaming to do—these entrepreneurs are literally dreaming what *could be*, rather than trying to join in what *is*.

This quick survey of Mintzberg and his colleagues' categorization of schools of management thought is provided in order to demonstrate differing assumptions about how strategies are developed and used. We have placed these schools of thought into the culture and paradigms frameworks previously discussed. By referring to the ways in which different personality types make decisions and deal with the context in which they practice, we are developing the links between paradigms, cultures, individuals, and practice strategies.

AN INTEGRATED FRAMEWORK BUILT ON ORGANIZATIONAL GOALS AND PERSONAL PREFERENCES

Many organizational thinkers have identified varieties of typologies and configurations to capture the reality of organizational life. Most of these are based on work within the business environment, and are not always useful for human service organizations. We propose an integrated framework that has specific resonance in human service organizations, bringing together the frameworks just discussed as an aid to understand more clearly how chaos, misunderstanding, and paradox can reign within complex organizational environments. When a paradigmatic perspective framework is combined with a cultural framework and placed in congruence with personal and managerial preferences, identification of a clear and direct correspondence with a particular type of organizational goal is possible. When all these aspects of organizational life are in alignment, "fit" occurs. In the next section, we briefly describe this "perfect" congruence to clarify the fundamental differences among organizations when worldview, preferences, and organizational goals are connected. When the goal is structure and control, a Traditional Organization fits. When the goal is consciousness-raising for change, the fit occurs with a Social Change Organization. When the organization aims for connection and collaboration, fit occurs in a Serendipitous Organization. Finally, if the organizational goal is individual empowerment, then an Entrepreneurial

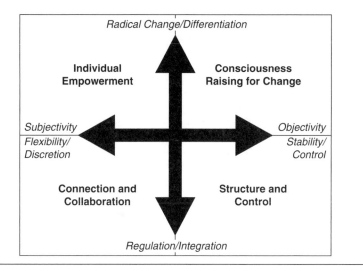

Figure 2.6 Organizational Goals Within Multiple Frameworks.

Organization will be a fit. Figure 2.6 shows the organizational goals that actually represent the full integration of the series of frameworks in this chapter.

TRADITIONAL ORGANIZATION

In Part I, Chapters 3 and 4, you will see the historical and theoretical origins of the Traditional Organization. This is the organization that seeks to operate as a well-calibrated machine, based on a belief that the best work is provided when the organization is ordered and predictable. The organizational goal in a Traditional Organization is structure and control. These goals are based on functionalist assumptions about how the world works. The idea is to manage people and information so that performance and results are predictable and generalizable. These expectations about organizational structure, communication, performance, and decision-making create or are created by a hierarchy culture where leaders are in charge and workers do what they are told. People within the organization fit and work best when a traditional perspective in personal preferences and management style is enacted. Box 2.6 gives a synopsis of what constitutes the Traditional Organization with traditional organizational goals of structure and control.

SOCIAL CHANGE ORGANIZATION

In Part II, Chapters 5 and 6, we will introduce the Social Change Organization. While appreciating the order and predictability of the Traditional Organization, the Social Change Organization is absolutely against the

---

Box 2.6

TRADITIONAL ORGANIZATIONS

- History and tradition are respected as important parts of their programs, seeking external *objective sources of recognized expertise to design and develop programs.*
- *Stability and control* are promoted so that programs run smoothly as workers conform to established protocols.
- Programs are *integrated* by establishing interrelated duties and tasks to be carried out, assuming these duties and tasks establish best practices.
- Well-defined organizational and programmatic structures are created, and are typically *hierarchical*, so lines of authority are clear.

---

status quo and the existing social order. These organizations exist for the purpose of effecting change, so the internal and external goal of such organizations is consciousness-raising for transformative change. These are organizations not satisfied with incrementalism, preferring instead sweeping fundamental change. This positioning comes from a radical structuralist perspective that assumes that change occurs best when the status quo has been disturbed by those who have come to understand reality in its more oppressive dimensions. The culture that is created within these organizations is one of aggressive competition. This is a market culture, where goals will be achieved by any means necessary. Employees fit best within this type organization when conflict and controversy are stimulants. Those with social change perspectives in personal preference and management and who possess courage and expect courage from leadership will fit best in this organization. Box 2.7 summarizes the Social Change Organization with its goals of consciousness-raising for change.

Box 2.7

SOCIAL CHANGE ORGANIZATIONS

- The historical significance of social movements, social reform, and advocacy motivates programs to seek external *objective sources of recognized expertise to mobilize/organize change.*
- *Differentiation and external focus* are promoted so that programs have the capacity to respond to larger community/societal needs for change.
- *Stability and control* of programs is promoted through interrelated duties and/ or tasks to be arrived at by focusing on best practice standards in activist activities.
- Conflict and competition is expected, building organizational and programmatic structures to recognize competing interest groups in a *market culture.*

SERENDIPITOUS ORGANIZATION

As one of the alternative organizational approaches, the Serendipitous Organization does not embrace the factory or machine approach to service delivery. This type organization will be examined in Part III, Chapters 7 and 8. In this organization there is a great deal of attention to the people side of the enterprise, not just to understand human needs and wants in order to create conditions for greater productivity, but in order to establish quality networks of relationships for improved practice. The organization goals of connection and collaboration suggest an interpretivist worldview, where meaning, understanding, and good performance come from connections within the particulars of a context. What is acceptable is that which is acceptable among organization participants who operate with the connectivity of a clan culture. In many ways, rather than a hierarchical structure, the Serendipitous Organization works more intimately with a network of relationships being actively pursued and engaged by those holding a serendipitous perspective as both a personal preference and a preferred management style. Box 2.8 provides an overview of what we have termed the Serendipitous Organization, with its goals of connection and collaboration.

ENTREPRENEURIAL ORGANIZATION

The Entrepreneurial Organization, to be treated in Part IV, Chapters 9 and 10, is probably the most inventive and most difficult to capture or describe of all the organizations precisely because of the organizational goal, which is one of individual empowerment. This is the organization that tends to be at the cutting edge (some say fringe) of new developments with people who may tend to think and act nontraditionally. Rigid rules and roles

---

Box 2.8

SERENDIPITOUS ORGANIZATIONS

- The capacity of human beings to bring their *subjective* differences together is respected in seeking to continually redesign and develop programs and the organization.
- *Integration* is supported so the organization runs smoothly through agreed-upon structure, created by team members and subject to change by consensus as needs shift.
- *Flexibility and discretion* to gain consensus, listening to multiple voices, constructing new realities, and allowing programs to emerge permits individuals to find meaning in their roles.
- Coordination rather than management creates *clan culture* where each has a voice. Hearing all perspectives is a norm in the organization's culture.

Box 2.9

ENTREPRENEURIAL ORGANIZATIONS

- The *subjective* nature of persons who provide valuable insights, perform significant deeds, and think outside the box is recognized and respected. It is recognized that contributions may not be corralled into a group effort
- *Flexibility and discretion* are promoted. It is understood that workers will not only be mavericks in their programs but may question or resist most aspects of what they are trying to do.
- Individual contribution is expected with a recognition that individuals are so *differentiated* that they work best on their own without the confines of a program.
- Conflict is expected when *radical change* is being pursued individually. Causes are supported in nontraditional ways.

---

are rejected in favor of a more liberated view of the work environment. Individual liberation is both the goal and the process within which work is organized, so that an adhocracy culture is enacted where whatever is necessary to get the work done is what occurs, as long as individual creativity is not impinged on. Freewheeling, entrepreneurial styles and perspectives in personal preferences and preferred management are a perfect fit for this approach to organizing. Box 2.9 captures the Entrepreneurial Organization with its goals of individual empowerment.

This brief overview of how organizations and the behavior within them differ was intended to give you a sense of what is to follow in the rest of the text. Each part that follows details the frameworks that can be used to guide each type of organization in a chapter that focuses on understanding that organization's primary identity, immediately followed by a chapter on understanding practice within that type of organization to aid in understanding the sources of the fundamental differences that may be found between and even within organizations.

CONCLUSION

The continuing search to understand differences reveals that, no matter how much a manager or leader would like to have people conform to a shared set of assumptions and create an organizational culture that reflects shared values, there will always be people who do not share assumptions or values. The reasons for these differences are myriad. The depth of differences and the ability of anyone to change those differences vary. Categorizing differences in order to understand them offers some possibilities in organization practice. Managing the complexity of all this becomes the challenge. We think that an integration of the frameworks introduced in this chapter has great potential. An important question, then, is, how does one learn to think in this complex way so that one can maximize strengths amid this diversity of strongly held worldviews?

Efforts to critically analyze organizations and the practice within them, with an eye to cultural competence and social justice, have been greatly enhanced by the work of Burrell and Morgan (1979). Their thinking helps to incorporate scholarship on organizations with more recent and seemingly contradictory efforts of modern and postmodern thinkers. In their classic work, *Sociological Paradigms and Organisational Analysis*, Burrell and Morgan provide a framework for making sense of the many, competing, and often contradictory theories of organization and organizational behavior. Their way of framing the multiple approaches to researching and understanding organizations is central to our thinking about human service practice within an organizational context. We see their framework as a useful way to organize and manage one's simultaneous attention to social work values, complex situations, and multiple perspectives. Cameron and Quinn's competing values framework clarifies how deeply imbedded culture is in all aspects of organizational life. Their work is not only compatible with that of Burrell and Morgan, but it also helps to clarify the consistency and depth of the paradoxes that are possible in complex organizations.

We think these two frameworks are also compatible with the Myers-Briggs' efforts to promote understanding, respect, and acceptance of differences between people of different nations, races, cultures, and persuasions (Briggs Myers & Myers, 1995). These multiple perspectives have the potential to help people in organizations "to recognize and enjoy their gifts" (Briggs Myers & Myers, 1995, p. xv). This leads us to Mintzberg and his associates and their ideas of strategic management. The diversity of approaches to developing strategies and managing within an organization add another clarifying agent to the intricate world of human service organizations. Our goal in later sections of the book is to show just how much each of these frameworks contributes to one's competent understanding of the world and practice within organizations.

For direct practice or clinical students among our readers, serious effort will be given throughout the text to identifying the practice skills that a well-trained clinician can bring to leadership in organization practice. Much of what you have learned in direct practice, such as conducting multidimensional assessment, problem identification, planning change, and managing barriers to change, will come in handy when translated into an organizational context, but we offer a word of caution. As Resnick and Patti (1980) made clear, organizations are not just collections of personalities; they are much more complex phenomena. We explore just how complex in the chapters that follow.

DISCUSSION QUESTIONS

1. Identify at least three ways human service organizations differ from other types of organizations. What might be the costs and benefits of those differences?
2. In your own words, detail the important assumptions that distinguish the four paradigms from one another. Could you identify a type of music that would fit in each paradigm? What about a color? Could you identify an action hero that might fit in each paradigm?
3. In this chapter, we link four Burrell and Morgan's paradigms with Cameron and Quinn's four cultures. How do paradigms differ from cultures? How might these linkages assist you in understanding a setting with which you are familiar?
4. Based on the discussion of the Myers-Briggs personality types, where do you think you are on the thinking–feeling and judging–perceiving continua? What might your response mean for you and your comfort zone when looking at different paradigms and cultures?
5. Look at all the management schools discussed in this chapter. Identify the school with which you most identify and explain why. Now assess how that preference might connect to your personality position on the two dimensions of the Myers-Briggs discussed in question 4.
6. Look at the four types of organizations discussed at the end of this chapter. Given your thinking and preferences, where would you be most comfortable right now? In your journal, take note of where your challenges might be because of your current preferences.

PART I

STRUCTURE AND CONTROL

P ART I FOCUSES on understanding practice within Traditional Organizations with goals of structure and control. The first chapter (Chapter 3) investigates theories that can be used to understand Traditional Organizations intent on maintaining and sustaining order. In Chapter 4, the focus switches to understanding practice in traditional human service organizations. Starting with the *functionalist* paradigmatic perspective, followed by a thorough look at the *hierarchy culture*, we will investigate the identities, values, preferences, standards, and strategies congruent with organizations holding structure and control goals.

In Chapter 3, approaches to understanding Traditional Organizations are introduced along with details of the underlying assumptions that form the Traditional Organization's identity: that there are universal truths and that maintaining order and stability is most important in a turbulent environment. Classical, neoclassical, and "modern" structural organizational theories provide a historical perspective on functionalist assumptions that have been embraced by traditional human service organizations. Early human relations theories emanating from now-famous studies are reviewed in this chapter, because their original intent was to control workers and keep them focused on organizational goals rather than respond to their needs in any way. Two types of systems theory (mechanistic and organismic) are included with their focus on inputs, throughputs, outputs, and outcomes. Not all systems theories hold functionalist assumptions. Because of that, other types within the systems theory school will be reviewed in later chapters.

The content of Chapter 3 will likely seem familiar to the reader, as the majority of human service agencies have survived by at least attempting to articulate conformity to assumptions in which maintaining the status quo is a high priority. Since Traditional Organizations are designed to resist change, there are costs as well as benefits. Both will be examined.

In Chapter 4, the focus switches to understanding practice in traditional human service organizations. Using the lens of strategic management and the roles of managers and leaders within the hierarchical culture, important dimensions of practice will be explored. Here we will examine programming, management, research, accountability, relationships, prescriptive planning, and paradox, along with the type of advocacy most often used where structure and control are goals. It will become clear that practice in organizations having traditional perspectives fits well with the current push toward outcome and performance-based measurement, which assumes that if one does certain things on the front end (inputs), and then knows what technologies to use with clients (throughputs), one can select predetermined measurements for the quality of what happens (outcomes). Further, there is congruence with the belief that the only worthwhile outcomes are those that are measurable. This chapter demonstrates why planned change approaches in which incremental change is appropriate also work well with hierarchical cultures, as do research methods dedicated to theory building and testing. Discussion of the paradoxical nature of measurement within organizations where individual change is the output is also included in keeping with our discussion in earlier chapters on critical thinking, self-awareness, and multiculturalism. End-of-chapter discussion questions and activities are aimed at enhancing readers' critical thinking about understanding and practicing in traditional, bureaucratic human service organizations with established and legitimized identities and reputations.

To introduce our focus on traditional human service organizations with goals of structure and control, we begin with a case example. In the next two chapters, you will see the structure and behavior standards within this type of organization, so that as the text unfolds you will come to understand how this perspective differs from what will follow in the rest of the text.

The Washington County Office on Aging

The Washington County Office on Aging came into being in the late 1970s as small allotments of Title III funds from the Older Americans Act trickled down to the grassroots level. Jayne remembers it well, because she was just graduating from her master's program, hoping to find a job. Having worked for the Central Capital Area Agency on Aging (AAA) as a field intern, she had watched as each of eight counties conducted a search to hire a qualified professional to head up their county offices. It was her good fortune to graduate just in time to capture the directorship of the office in Washington County.

The AAA was housed in a regional health and human services planning and development district office, and the director had developed a very organized way to approach the distribution of federal aging dollars. Even though funds were limited, there was just enough to hire a director for an office on aging in each county as long as the county judge and county commission (later called the *county executive* and *board of supervisors*) gave their approval and offered matching funds to sweeten the deal. All but one county jumped at the opportunity, and the one outlier was a mostly rural county with a county judge who was up on charges of drug possession. However, even with those localized problems, that county had replaced the judge and gradually followed the pattern already established by the other seven counties.

Jayne remembers vividly the beginnings of the county office. Her first day at work found her stumbling over the cinderblock steps that had been stacked in front of the old nurses' building behind the county hospital. The nurses' building was to become the county's first senior citizens' center and the office on aging would serve the dual purpose of center oversight and management as well as establishing the home and community-based service programs to be offered through the countywide office. It was very comforting for Jayne as a newly minted graduate to have directions from the Area Agency on Aging that had been standardized in a Director on Aging job description, an organizational chart showing the relationship of the director to the county and the county to the AAA, guidelines for establishing an advisory council of senior citizens, and requests for proposals (RFPs) to apply for state funding for the senior citizens' center. She remembers thinking that her work was cut out for her, but she didn't have to worry about how to begin, because the directives were clearly stated. First, she wanted to meet with Judge Bill Reynolds, her new supervisor, and ask him about county priorities. Next, she would identify older citizens who would be a part of the advisory council. Finally, she would tackle responding to the RFPs. If those funds could be secured, it would mean that the office would have a mix of federal, state, and county funds in the budget.

Jayne's early recollections about the Office on Aging were fond memories of her first position out of school. She stayed in that position for five years, then moved out of town for another position in the aging network. But she was proud to leave things in good order. In fact, her organizational skills were appreciated by the older persons with whom she worked in Washington County, and she had provided leadership in obtaining additional federal dollars as well as secured an operational budget for the senior citizens' center prior to her departure. The renovation of the senior center had taken place with county funds and the county judge had convinced the commissioners to make the office on aging a continuing line item in the budget. Jayne had designed a brochure that explained how the office on aging worked, outlined the services provided, and advertised the senior center's activities. This brochure had been adopted (with local modifications) in the other seven counties, so that a senior citizen who moved between counties would know exactly what to expect in an adjacent county. One of the things Jayne enjoyed most was talking with senior citizens groups and explaining just how the "aging network" was organized.

Over the years, the offices on aging witnessed turnover in staff in all but one of the offices in the eight counties. With each transition, the AAA staff would provide each new employee with copies of brochures and other public relations information, organizational charts, copies of funded grant proposals to use as examples, pertinent regulations tied to the Older Americans Act, state regulations on senior center operations, and a packet of forms used in all the counties. In recent years, the forms were being sent electronically and completed online. With each office completing the same forms, comparable data were available in the AAA's information system and a report card could be given to each county office. In this way, the director could see how their operation shaped up in comparison with their peers in other counties. This had led to a bit of competition between the offices over the years.

The Central Capital Council on Aging, a regional group, had developed into a force to be reckoned with over the years. Each of the eight county councils on aging elected two delegates to go to the monthly meetings of this regional body. The directors of the offices on aging, the directors of the senior citizens center, and their delegates arrived at these meetings every month and listened to the AAA director and his staff detail any changes in rules, regulations, or protocols. Delegates would take back what they learned to the local councils, keeping everyone informed of the latest political, economic, social, and technological developments. Every year, at the annual meeting, each delegation would report on progress made that year and make any amendments to their county plan. The AAA would then incorporate any changes into its area plan and share the results with the eight counties.

Jayne visited the Washington County Office on Aging periodically when she was in the area. What she liked about her visits was that she could count on some degree of familiarity with what was going on and, therefore, catch up fairly easily. The senior citizens center had grown a great deal over the years and the activities were more diverse than the earlier days, with more groups scheduled to meet at the center. The quilting frames that had dominated the large meeting room had been replaced by an exercise room format, and the activity chart was no longer in paper copy. It was posted on an electronic bulletin board that dominated the view as one came into the lobby. During her last visit, a public forum was being held to gather needs assessment data for the upcoming three-year plan, and issues of transportation, home health care, and nutrition were being discussed. The AAA staff kept emphasizing the importance of effectiveness-based programming and the need for clear, measurable outcome objectives to be stated. She knew that the Washington County Council on Aging members would be preparing their input to take to the regional meeting and that soon a plan would be distributed (complete with process and outcome objectives, as well as action steps), ready for another year.

CHAPTER 3

Traditional Organizations

I N CHAPTER 2, we introduced the Functionalist Paradigm and Traditional Organizations, and in this chapter we deepen that original discussion by exploring what constitute appropriate structures of organizations holding this perspective on appropriate goals for organizing. We start by investigating the themes found in functionalist thinking and the assumptions that constitute the Functionalist Paradigm, resulting in the structure and control goals of what we are calling the Traditional Organization. Following this paradigmatic discussion, the major theories that fit within this perspective are identified. To add to our investigation of Traditional Organizations, we will draw on the Washington County Office on Aging as an example. We close this chapter with a critical analysis, so that the reader is left with the ability to judge what is gained and what is given up when approaching organizations from a functionalist worldview. We then transition to Chapter 4, which focuses on the culture and the behavioral theories that guide the standards of practice within organizations with structure and control goals. Of the four types of organizations, we begin with the most familiar and traditional views of organizations, because they are generally assumed to be the gold standard of organizing, although many other competent approaches have developed as worldviews and organizational theories have become more complex.

We want to caution the reader that we are referring to the Traditional Organization as a *prototype*, because today there may no longer be "pure" Traditional Organizations. Even agencies that are definitely functionalist in nature may have units, programs, and/or staff members that operate under different assumptions. For example, Jayne did observe when she returned to visit the Washington County Office on Aging that one of their newest programs had been designed by volunteers and was not quite the same as the other programs. The volunteer-caregiver program was much more loosely structured and was heavily volunteer run and operated. Volunteers were meeting on a regular basis, often without paid staff involved in the decision-making process. The director had privately expressed some concern about not feeling "on top of" what they were

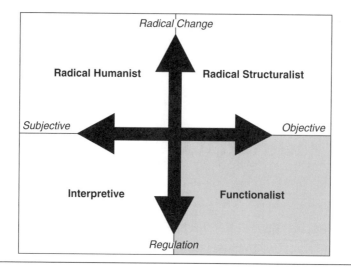

Figure 3.1 Burrell and Morgan's Paradigmatic Framework *Source:* Adapted from Burrell and Morgan (1979). *Sociological paradigms and organizational analysis.* Aldershot, England: Ashgate. Figure 3.1, p. 22. Used by permission.

doing. Jayne was curious to see how this program would fit within what traditionally had been a hierarchical structure controlled by paid staff members. When something such as what Jayne noticed happens, organizational members and units will encounter paradoxes as differing assumptions clash. As you read further into the book, it is our hope that you will understand why functionalist assumptions may collide with assumptions from other paradigms. But, first, let's focus on the themes and assumptions of the Traditional Organization.

Recall from Chapter 2 that Traditional Organizations count on stability and control to assure that programs run smoothly. There is attention to and appreciation of history and tradition, along with objective sources, to design, develop, and evaluate organizational activities. Activities are undertaken with a division of labor achieved through well-defined organizational and programmatic structures that are usually hierarchical with clear lines of authority with promise for efficient and effective practices. Figure 3.1 shows where the Traditional Organization fits within the paradigms introduced in Chapter 2.

FUNCTIONIALIST THEMES

Most traditional approaches to understanding organizations are based on assumptions held within the boundaries of the Functionalist Paradigm. Additionally, most of the theories that were developed during the early stages of organizational research are positivist and, therefore, functionalist in nature. These theories are based on the presumption that research and analysis of organizational data are exclusively rational and research methods should be traditionally scientific. Therefore, organizational study should be oriented to carefully defined designs, including variables, sample, data collection, and data analysis. Further, there is an assumption that good organizational study is impersonal with the goal of prediction and control of persons and things within the organizational setting. Functionalist theories "seek to search for regularities and attempt to test for the existence of such regularities in order to predict and control organizational behavior" (Vibert, 2004, p. 12). Research is capable of producing generalized principles to guide the replicability of events and procedures in the organizational context. Once there is sufficient evidence, then it is possible to know enough about the organization to control both the process and the product of the organization. With sufficient information, order can be structured and activities within the organization can be regulated in a predictable manner.

The Washington County Office on Aging is an excellent exemplar of these functionalist themes. Each of the eight county offices had the same basic goals and was designed to resemble the others. As the years progressed, these offices collected the same data and those data became the information system for the region. No one ever questioned whether the data collected were the most relevant to the individual county's needs, because the standard was uniformity across offices.

Functionalism holds a traditional view of knowledge building about organizations that has its genesis in the natural sciences, where controlled experiments are the preferred method of knowing and understanding. This expectation and the assumptions on which it is built present challenges for research and practice in ever-changing, complex organizations where all the variables may not be known and order is not part of the organizing experience. To more fully understand these challenges, it is helpful to look more closely at the basic terms and assumptions that define the paradigm.

ASSUMPTIONS OF THE FUNCTIONALIST PARADIGM

The Functionalist Paradigm is objectivist in its perspective. Recall that in Chapter 2 we presented four terms that define *objectivism*. Box 3.1 provides a brief review of those terms.

The functionalist perspective assumes there is reality apart from the individual and his or her perceptions, and that there are universal truths. The functionalist ontology is *realist*, assuming that what is known is independent of the human mind and that understanding anything is abstracted from an independent reality that exists "out there." Given this view, the accepted functionalist **epistemology**, or what can be known and how scientists can be expected to know it, is *positivist*. This means that theoretical propositions must be tested or built according to the rules of

---

Box 3.1

OBJECTIVISM: DEFINING TERMS

Realism (external)
Positivism (hard, real, tangible)
Determinism (people are products of their environments)
Nomothetic (use methods of natural science to test hypotheses in accord with scientific rigor)

Source: Adapted from Burrell and Morgan (1979). *Sociological paradigms and organizational analysis.* Aldershot, England: Ashgate. Figure 1.1, p. 3. Used by permission.

---

formal logic and based on methods derived from the natural sciences to create scientific (trusted) knowledge. Positivism seeks hard, real, and tangible knowledge. Knowledge can be acquired in this way because it is assumed that reality is deterministic, comprised of antecedents and consequences, making everything totally determined by a sequence of causes that can be identified or uncovered. This identification or discovery is the role of scientific research, including research about organizations.

Since functionalism takes an objectivist position regarding human nature, humankind is viewed as rational, able to use reason to support a position. It is also thought that human experience is just as deterministic as reality, based on identifiable causes and consequences, which require only identification or discovery to be understood and managed. Human nature, like reality in general, is based on law-like generalizations that describe everything about the human experience exactly the same way for all time. There is "truth," which means that the functionalism takes a nomothetic position that describes reality and human nature based on what is generally the case. This is a rule-governed reality.

Recall that functionalism sits within the intersection of objectivism and regulation. Regulation, combined with a belief in universal truths, assumes that generalization is possible and desirable. This is why, according to Burrell and Morgan (1979), the functionalist perspective holds interest in maintaining the status quo and achieving social order. In this perspective, it is believed that consensus, social integration, solidarity, needs satisfaction, and actuality are possible. Box 3.2 summarizes the concerns of this regulation perspective.

Now we turn to how functionalism guides organizational theory. But before we do, look at Box 3.3, which was originally introduced in Chapter 2.

This box provides a quick summary of the basic assumptions of the Functionalist Paradigm. Keep these assumptions in mind, and return to this box as often as you need to see how many of the theories used by human service practitioners and others in organizations fit within this paradigm. You may find that you recognize some, possibly all, of these assumptions, because the organizations you have experienced may have

---

Box 3.2

CONCERNS OF THE REGULATION PERSPECTIVE

1. Status quo
2. Social order
3. Consensus
4. Social integration and cohesion
5. Solidarity
6. Need satisfaction
7. Actuality

Source: Adapted from Burrell and Morgan (1979). *Sociological paradigms and organizational analysis.* Aldershot, England: Ashgate. Table 2.2, p. 18. Used by permission.

Box 3.3

ASSUMPTIONS OF THE FUNCTIONALIST PARADIGM

From the Objectivist Perspective

Reality is above and beyond individual knowledge.
Knowledge about social reality is hard and concrete.
People are products of their environments; they are shaped.
Natural science methods can be applied to the study and understanding of social reality.

From the Regulation Perspective

Society is characterized by social order and equilibrium.
Knowledge for knowledge's sake is acceptable.
Consensus, rather than conflict, is important.

Source: Adapted from Burrell and Morgan (1979), Chapter 1.

---

been shaped by this perspective. You may also recognize these assumptions in the Washington County Office on Aging case. The use of federal dollars to fund an office on aging in each county seemed logical and assuring parallel structure was never questioned. Tying the office to the county executive made for conformity in that each office would have the same reporting system, and it would leverage the county to allocate funds to support the office. Even though implementation occurred at the local level, there was respect for an external locus of control based on universal principles for how each unit should go about its business.

TRADITIONAL ORGANIZATION THEORIES SUPPORTING STRUCTURE AND CONTROL GOALS

Since the majority of theories about organizations have emerged from the functionalist perspective (Vibert, 2004), functionalism is sometimes seen as the *only* scientific approach to understanding organizations and the behavior within them. In subsequent chapters, as you move further into the discussion of alternative perspectives about organizations, you will recognize that there are many other rigorous ways of understanding organizations. But we start with the theories that can be located within the Functionalist Paradigm because they will probably be the most familiar. They have the longest history of guiding organizational research and have received the most critical analysis. As the chapter develops, you will also discover that these theories present some of the most interesting challenges to organizational leaders in operationalizing a multicultural frame of reference.

In Chapter 1, we focused on the search for order in understanding organizations. Shafritz, Ott, and Lang identified a number of major perspectives on organization theory. Most of the earlier perspectives developed based on functionalist assumptions. In this chapter, we focus on five of the major groupings identified by Shafritz, Ott, and Lang (2005):

1. Classical organization theory
2. Neoclassical organization theory
3. Human resource theory/organizational behavior perspective
4. "Modern" structural organization theory
5. Theories of organizations and environments

Each theoretical perspective is briefly discussed, along with some of the major contributors so as to fully develop the functionalist view of organizations and what is pivotal to understanding Traditional Organizations.

CLASSICAL ORGANIZATION THEORY

Organizational theory really began during the Industrial Revolution in Great Britain and the United States. Theories were developed to manage complex economic organizations. These early theories have been grouped into what has been termed *classical* theories since they were the first, with their influence beginning in the late 1700s and continuing until the 1930s and even beyond. In Chapter 1, we introduced the primary contributions of each collection of theories. In Table 3.1, we identify the fundamental assumptions of the classical theories and tie them to the functionalist perspective.

Table 3.1

Classical Organization Theories and the Functionalist Perspective

Assumptions of Classical Organization Theories	Assumptions of the Functionalist Perspective
Organizations exist to accomplish production-related and economic goals.	Society is characterized by social order and equilibrium. (Regulation)
	Knowledge for knowledge's sake is acceptable. (Regulation)
There is one best way to organize for production, and that way can be found through systematic, scientific inquiry.	Knowledge about social reality is hard and concrete. (Objectivist)
	Natural science methods can be applied to the study and understanding of Social reality. (Objectivist)
Production is maximized through specialization and division of labor.	Consensus, rather than conflict, is important. (Objectivist)
People and organizations act in accordance with rational economic principles.	People are products of their environments; they are shaped. (Objectivist)
	Reality is above and beyond individual Knowledge. (Objectivist)

Source: Shafriz & Ott (2001), p. 28.

It is within the context of classical theory that workers were understood not as individuals but as parts of a factory system, much like machine parts. The goal of classical theory was to guide understanding so that employers could take advantage of people, money, and machines for productivity. The goal was to locate the "best way" to organize for production.

Adam Smith (1776) is credited with creating the first method to structure organizations and the people within them so that people would be more machine-like in their work. He proposed that the best way of operating a factory was to centralize equipment and labor, have a division of labor, manage through specialization, and give attention to the economics of the competitive marketplace.

After this strong attention to structure, theorists focused on managing that structure and the people within it through the development of the science of administration. Henri Fayol (1916) was the first theorist to create a comprehensive theory of management, but because he was French and outside of the British/American mainstream, his real influence was not felt until his work was translated into English in the late 1940s. Fayol identified the important elements necessary to organize and manage an organization. His six principles—technical, commercial, financial, security, accounting, and managerial—still have currency today. His areas of interest continue to present modern challenges: division of work, authority and responsibility, discipline, unity of command, unity of direction, subordination of individual interest to the general interest, payment of personnel, centralization, chain of command, order, equity, stability of personnel, tenure, initiative, and *esprit de corps*.

Probably the most famous and influential classical theorist was Frederick Taylor (1916), who, with his principles of scientific management, proposed that organizations could be more productive if designed scientifically. He believed this design could be achieved through *time-and-motion studies* that would uncover the fastest, most efficient, least fatiguing way of doing the business of the organization. He assumed this would allow management to impose this best way on workers, thus creating the best way of social organizing. From his early work came many derivations by his followers, who looked for ways of planning and systematically controlling the work environment through scientific principles. One of his most notable followers was H. L. Gantt (1861–1919), who developed the Gantt chart for planning output so that ammunition could be tracked during World War I. **Gantt charts** are bar graphs illustrating who is expected to do what task at what time. The charts were used for purposes other than ammunition tracking following the war. Prior to computerization, Gantt charts were important guides to monitor progress in early social service agencies. In fact, in our case example at the beginning of this part of the text, Jayne remembers using a Gantt chart to monitor the progress made by the senior citizens' program in getting things accomplished.

Other noteworthy contributors to classical theory were Max Weber and Luther Gulick. Weber (1922) characterized the core features of bureaucratic organization and the pattern of behavior that followed. Basically, his description of the ideal type of bureaucracy had the following dimensions:

- Positions in the organization are grouped into a clearly defined hierarchy.
- Job candidates are selected on the basis of their technical qualifications.
- Each position has a defined sphere of competence.
- Positions reflect a high degree of specialization based on expert training.
- Positions demand the full working capacity of their holders.
- Positions are career-oriented. There is a system of promotion according to seniority or achievement. Promotion is dependent on the judgment of superiors.
- Rules of procedure are outlined for rational coordination of activities.
- A central system of records is maintained to summarize the activities of the organization.
- Impersonality governs relationships between organizational members.

- Distinctions are drawn between private and public lives and positions of organizational members (Weber, 1947a and Rogers, 1975, as cited in Netting, Kettner, & McMurtry, 2008, p. 217).

Gulick, influenced by Fayol, identified the major functions of management within a hierarchical, bureaucratic organization. Gulick's contribution includes his mnemonic, POSDCORB, for the seven functions of management: planning, organizing, staffing, directing, coordinating, reporting, and budgeting. Weber and Gulick's contributions, like Taylor's, are still present in the thinking of today's functionalist theorists.

Mechanistic approaches, generated from classical theories, continue to shape how organizations are defined and structured. It is little surprise, then, that Morgan (1997) framed these theories as machine metaphors in which routines, efficiency, reliability, and predictability were expected organizational characteristics. Yet, another metaphor is relevant here, as well. One might ask why Taylor was so adamant about there being "one best way." Morgan explains that Taylor's metaphor of *organization* was the *psychic prison in which there was no order.* Taylor "was a man totally preoccupied with control . . . an obsessive, compulsive character, driven by a relentless need to tie down and master almost every aspect of his life" (1997, p. 221). Taylor's metaphor for organizations, and the accompanying assumptions, led him to create ways to structure organizations as machines so that they would be controlled by managers. We hope that this illustration reveals to the reader how important it is to recognize the assumptions held by theorists and how those assumptions are translated into their work.

From a current standpoint, all this work may look narrow and simplistic. A historical lens helps to identify the degree to which it was really groundbreaking thinking that was steeped in the assumptions of what is now called the Functionalist Paradigm. Classical theorists were seeking the best way to structure and manage organizations so that they would be consensus-based, rational collectivities that performed in the most efficient manner possible. But the challenge was so great that these early classical contributions led to the second major perspective identified by Shafritz, Ott, & Lang (2005)—neoclassical organization theory.

NEOCLASSICAL ORGANIZATION THEORY

Most theoreticians who fit within the neoclassical tradition are placed there because they were critics and revisionists of classical theory. Their work occurred after World War II. While most thinkers of the time continued the interest in organizing for productivity, their criticism of earlier theoretical work was based on some or all of the following: rejection of the minimization of the humanness of organizational members, necessity of coordination of needs among bureaucratic units, the existence of internal–external organizational relations, and the need to understand organizational decision-making (Shafritz, Ott, & Lang, 2005). As statistical technology evolved, criticism also included the lack of empirical grounding for most of the classical thought. The neoclassicists created less a new approach than a *modification* of what had come before. Their developments were based on methods drawn from the behavioral sciences. *Neoclassical theory* presents a transition in the theoretical movement from the oversimplistic, mechanistic perspectives of the classical theorists to more contemporary thinking about complex organizations.

Two of the earliest critics of the classical approach were Chester Barnard and Herbert Simon. Barnard (1938) spoke of the necessity of cooperation among people within organizational settings for goal achievement. Further, he thought it was the executive's responsibility to establish the context for this cooperation by establishing a purpose and moral code of the organization and by instituting a system of formal and informal communication. These efforts were to ensure participants' willingness to cooperate, because within these structures should be found inducements and other means of persuasion to achieve cooperation.

Herbert Simon (1946) rejected the theories of Fayol, Gulick, and others, calling their perspective "proverbs of administration" rather than principles of administration. He strongly reacted to those approaches dominated by excessive formalism and rationalism, which he believed limited both organizations and individuals from making choices. He proposed that being able to define and accurately measure the objectives of administrative organization would move administrative practices from art to science. This could happen with sufficient scientific rigor to control for alternative explanations or effects of the studies. Simon (1947) focused on the importance of organizational decision making, introducing the concepts of "bounded rationality" and "satisficing decisions" to characterize the complexity of decision-making within the context of formal organizations. **Bounded rationality** meant that individuals, no matter how much information they collect, always make decisions within limits. Simon recognized that decision makers would never know everything there was to know about any situation, and when a decision had to be made, they had to recognize the boundaries of their knowledge base. This is called **satisficing** decision making. Decisions are made within these boundaries because human beings do not have the intellectual capability to totally maximize possibilities; therefore, a perfect decision is not possible, only a satisfactory one. Though this moved organizational studies closer to the experience of organizational members, what was missing in Simon's theorizing was "politics, culture, morality, and history . . . [which were] treated as random, extraneous variables beyond the influence, much less control, of rational cognitive processes and organizational procedures. [They became] analytically marginalized, left outside the conceptual parameters of Simon's preferred model" (Reed, 1996, p. 36).

Neoclassicists can be credited with beginning the theoretical movement from interest in purely engineering elements in the organization to contextual elements of the organization's environment. With this change of interest came the involvement of another discipline in the study of organizations and organizational behaviors. Sociologists helped to establish that organizations are not isolated from the environments in which they are located. Talcott Parsons (1956) introduced the general theory of social systems as a way to analyze formal organizations. At the same time, other sociologists were interested in understanding the perspectives and behavior of those within organizations. Phillip Selznick (1948) found that persons within the organization were not purely rational, and without recognition of this, managers were unable to cope with the nonrational. His well-cited case study on the Tennessee Valley Authority revealed that many people within that organization did not necessarily share the organization's goals. Without shared goals among workers, managers had to resort to what Selznick called **cooptation** as a means of controlling alternative perspectives and assuring conformity to the organization and its mission. Other sociologists, such as Melville Dalton (1950) and W. H. Whyte (1956), also contributed to the neoclassical perspective. Dalton recognized the structural friction between line staff and organizational units, while Whyte looked at the consequences of stress and status on human relations within the organization.

In sum, all of these students of organizations and organizational behavior collectively served as a transitional or evolutionary step between formal classical theory and its mechanistic dominance, in recognizing the challenges of a more complex understanding of what is necessary to achieve more satisfactory management of behavior in modern organizations. Even the critics of rational approaches were often searching for the one best way, looking for new sources of power and authority, rather than stepping into a different set of assumptions representing an alternative worldview. Some critics began clamoring to understand how the sense of community among members could be recognized as an important element in organizational theory (Reed, 1996, p. 36). To examine the human side of organizations, we now turn to the third perspective identified by Shafritz, Ott, and Lang (2005)—human relations/organizational behavioral theory.

HUMAN RELATIONS/ORGANIZATIONAL BEHAVIORAL THEORY

All the early theories of organizations were really attempts at dealing with organizational behavior by structuring organizations in ways that would control and standardize human behavior. After all, from a functionalist perspective, if one really believes that there is one best way to do business, then controlling human beings so that they do their work in that best way becomes the goal. Most early theories were used to guide the actions of those who peopled organizations. It was not until the development of the various aspects of human relations or organizational behavioral theory that this focus was finely tuned. It was at this stage that classical organizational theory was actually displaced, making room for the more creative approaches to understanding organizations that followed. At this juncture, theorists realized that organizations were much more than variables to manipulate in order to change behavior of organizational members. Instead, organizations were understood as contexts within which behavior occurs. The people and the organization represent mutual, interactive influences through which people are shaped by the organization and the organization is shaped by the people within its boundaries.

Since the late 1920s, much organization theory developed in reaction to the classical theories of scientific management and bureaucracy. The Human Relations School in the United States recognized workers' needs beyond the economic, and the often-cited work of Elton Mayo and his research team beginning in 1927 at the Hawthorne plant of the Western Electric Company is seen as a breakthrough event. Mayo's team was attempting to fit workers into classical views of organizational productivity by manipulating various factors (e.g., lights, pay incentives, flow of materials). When workers were more productive, even when important factors were withheld, the research team reframed their study in social-psychological terms, recognizing for the first time the importance of paying attention to workers within organizational life.

Understanding organizations, in what later became known as *human relations* or *organizational behavior theory*, meant paying attention to social and cultural needs, not just economic needs of workers. Shifting focus to social rather than physical determinants of output, the goal of human relations theory was to understand the real nature of workers' needs, their informal group life and its relationships to the organization, so that enlightened management could develop the steps necessary to meet workers' needs. Needs could be met when work and organizational structure were related to the social needs of employees. Given previous perspectives on organizations, human relations theory no longer viewed organizations as an entity to be manipulated so that behavior could be changed, but the organization was seen as a context in which human beings interacted. It was beginning to be recognized that context shaped behavior just as behavior could influence context (Shafritz, Ott, & Lang, 2005).

The early studies of people in organizations gave rise to a new discipline, *industrial* or *applied psychology*, in which psychological findings from laboratory experiments were applied to organizational matters. The technology came from the emerging behaviorists and behavioral sciences that developed during and after World War II in response to the need to find appropriate recruits and train them to meet military standards. Behaviorism provided the means to influence employees, their attitudes, and psychological conditions in order to impact productivity. Hugo Münsterberg (1922) helped to move organizational studies beyond behaviorism to the recognition that employees were humans, not machines, who needed to be treated as individuals in order to enhance employee productivity.

Earlier, we mentioned Elton Mayo (1933) and his famous study of the Hawthorne electric plant where results were achieved simply because the research was undertaken. Mayo's study represented a major breakthrough in understanding organizationally based social psychology, group relations, group norms, and issues of control and personal recognition. Researchers began to focus on humans as individuals, respecting their need for accurate information in order to make informed decisions based on free will within the organizational setting (Argyris, 1970).

More than 50 years of organizational behavioral research have focused on people's perspectives on jobs, organizational communication, work groups, one's own work, roles within the organization, and leadership. Few women can be identified as organizational researchers, but Mary Parker Follett's (1926) early work on communication and leadership style was the forerunner for much of the work on motivation. She focused on the manner in which orders were given, seeing orders as mutually agreed on between leaders and followers in light of unique situations that could not always be anticipated.

Perhaps the most influential thinker regarding motivation is Abraham Maslow, who, along with Mayo, set the stage for the clarifying ideas found in Theory X and Theory Y developed by Douglas McGregor. Maslow (1943), as a behaviorist, posited that all humans have needs and these are at the base of their motivational structure. Needs were viewed as hierarchical, and once a need was met it no longer served as a motivator, so that when lower order needs were met, higher order needs became motivating forces. Herzberg (1966) looked at motivation from a different perspective, investigating intrinsic and extrinsic motivators. He found that extrinsic elements such as working conditions and pay kept down dissatisfaction but did not serve as motivators, while workers were intrinsically motivated by the use of their creativity and intelligence. Building on need recognition, McGregor (1957) outlined two different assumption sets held by managers that became self-fulfilling prophecies. **Theory X** captured the perspective of the scientific managers who assumed that it was human nature to hate work and avoid it whenever possible, so that coercion, control, discipline, and direction were essential if employees were to be expected to work toward organizational goals. Further, in order to feel secure, employees preferred to be directed, allowing them to avoid taking responsibility for their actions or inactions. **Theory Y** reflected a more evolved perspective, holding that human beings did not necessarily hate work, if it was satisfying. It was human nature to take control and personal responsibility when there was personal congruence with organizational goals, so that commitment to organizational objectives was possible.

This attention to motivation, group and intergroup behavior, leadership, power and influence, and the effect of organizational context on individuals was the precursor to some of the later work built from alternative paradigmatic perspectives. In later chapters, it will be clear that the interpretive and radical humanist perspectives, and their attention to meaning in context, owe much to the human relations theorists for what has evolved that is subjective. For now, it is important to recognize that early human relations theorists were decidedly functionalist in their perspective. They recognized the human element in a generalized individualistic way, but for the reason of finding the best way to control and regulate people for productive purposes. As human relations and organizational behavioral theory developed, however, it converged with systems theories that focused more on interdependence and balance. This led to "a belief that rationalism provided an extremely limited and often misleading vision of the 'realities' of organizational life" (Reed, 1996, p. 37). Another major growth spurt in organization theory began developing—the modern structural school.

"Modern" Structural Organization Theory

"Modern" structural organization theory is distinguished from classical approaches by time. The classicists developed their perspectives prior to World War II, and the modern structuralists wrote after the war. Classical organizational theorists were interested in the design structure of organizations and its relationship to production processes, so from that standpoint some of the classical theorists were also structural organizational theorists. The "modern" structural theorists were interested, like Fayol, Taylor, Gulick, Weber, and others who came before them, in organizational efficiency based on rationality and the role of rationality in increasing productivity. Influenced by neoclassical, human relations, and systems theorists, modern structuralists saw understanding organizations as requiring a more encompassing, balanced approach.

The modern structuralist assumed that conflict and strain within the organization were inevitable and not always undesirable. The goal was to understand the organizational/personal needs and issues, discipline and autonomy, formal and informal relations, management and worker perspectives, ranks' and divisions' perspectives, and the organizational environment both inside and outside of the organization in order to understand the relationship between material and social rewards related to productivity. Although this perspective did incorporate elements of the approaches that came before it, at its base was an acceptance of conflict and alienation from a Marxian tradition. It was assumed that large, complex organizations had elements of shared interests and other interests that were incompatible. The organization served as a platform for power struggle rather than as a surrogate family. From this perspective, understanding organization required the understanding of the social functions of conflict in order to allow differences to emerge so that testing and adjustments in the organization could be made to ensure greater productivity (Shafritz, Ott & Lang, 2005).

As modern structuralist theory evolved, studies of organizations and behavior of those within them focused on understanding authority and its use, organizational structure, communication, control, leadership, and organizational interaction in its social environment. At this stage in development, researchers on organizations were concerned with both formal and informal elements of structure (Blau & Scott, 1962) and whether to structure an organization according to its products or its functions (Walker & Lorsch, 1968). Modern structuralists assumed that "most problems in an organization result from structural flaws and can be solved by changing the structure" (Shafritz & Ott, 2001, p. 198).

Building on the structuralist approach, the 1970s and 1980s saw the development of organizational research that attempted to understand and predict organizational behavior or create best decisions. The research focus was on describing important variables and the linkages between these variables that influence their effectiveness in organizations. Most of the attempts at understanding were based on quantitative studies at a high level of abstraction (Etzioni, 1975) rather than detailed observations about single organizations. From this research a conceptual framework evolved (Heydebrand, 1973) that identified the important dimensions of organizational life. One dimension involved studies of the nature and complexity of the organizational environment and organizational autonomy. Issues such as the complexity of the organization, the organizational age, and the organization's autonomy were studied.

A second dimension included organizational goals and task structure. Growing out of an interest in the interaction between the environment and autonomy and their influence on organizational structure, this dimension looked at the number and diversity of major organizational objectives, geographical dispersion, variability of tasks, organizational size, organizational change, and dimensions of effectiveness. All of this was seen to be related to another dimension, *internal structure*. Here the interest was in the division of labor: specialization, standardization, formalization, centralization, configuration, and flexibility (Heydebrand, 1973, p. 458). The technical complexity and skill structure of the organization was also at issue, as was the social environment. The social environment was operationalized to include such elements as involvement, rewards, and rationality.

The social environment and its relationship to managerial autonomy were also at issue. This led to yet another dimension of the conceptual framework, *organizational coordination and control*. In this dimension was included the concept of *professionalization*, including nonbureaucratic and bureaucratic approaches, forms of administration, decision-making, and interorganizational networks. Together these dimensions represented the determinants of internal structure. Organizations could be understood and the characteristics of organizations could be identified through this network of internal and external control clusters. In sum, the mathematical approach to understanding organization was the most technologically sophisticated. The hope was that understanding organizational size in relation to complexity and administration could statistically affect efficiency, satisfaction, flexibility, and productivity (Etzioni, 1975).

Bolman & Deal (1991) identified the basic assumptions of the structural theoretical perspective:

- Organizations are rational efforts to accomplish established goals facilitated through rational organizational behavior based on clear rules and authority for control and coordination.
- There is a "best" structure for every organization based on internal and external conditions.
- Specialization and division of labor facilitates the achievement of production quality and quantity.
- Most organizational problems are caused by structural flaws and can be eliminated with a change in structure.

These assumptions fall squarely within the Functionalist Paradigm, which focuses on finding the best way (the right rules, authority structure, etc.) to solve problems by adapting structure (an objectivist approach). Structural theorists take an interest in what goes on horizontally and vertically in organizations. Vertical (hierarchical levels) and horizontal (between units or departments) differentiation and coordination are the focus of their thinking and organizational research.

It is fairly easy to see how the Washington County Office on Aging was based on modern structural theoretical perspectives. A best structure was developed for replication in each of the eight counties. Jayne became the director and knew where to start because the AAA had planned what needed to happen first. Horizontally, all eight county offices performed in parallel fashion, so Jayne could talk with her colleagues in other counties and automatically know how they were operating, according to what protocols.

Interest in specialization, departmentalization, span of control, and coordination and control of specialized units all reflect historical antecedents in organization and organizational behavioral research. Newer influences can be seen in the interest in the difference between stable and more dynamic conditions within the organization as well as organizational climate, management systems, and the formal and informal elements of organizational life. Researchers were beginning to realize that normal organizational conditions may not be stable, so the study of organizations' relationship to structure took on new dimensions.

Burns and Stalker (1961) represent how structuralist thinking developed, allowing for the "one best way" or design of an organization to be dependent on certain conditions rather than assuming that organizations are all alike. Their pivotal work at the Tavistock Institute in London resulted in a widely cited book, *The Management of Innovation*, in which they identified two types of organizations: mechanistic and organic. The **mechanistic organization** was highly traditional in terms of hierarchy, formal rules and regulations, communication, and decision making. This type of organization was particularly useful in producing inanimate products such as those found in factories. The **organic organization**, on the other hand, was one that functioned in a highly changeable environment requiring staff that could make decisions quickly to adapt to this change, such as in a marketing or service organization. People working in mechanistic organizations were viewed as more secure, whereas those in organic organizations faced more uncertainty. The acknowledgment that different environments called for different structures was groundbreaking. It meant that organizations' structures would need to differ, depending on where an organization fell along the mechanistic–organic continuum.

Following the lead of Burns and Stalker, a number of theorists posed questions about structural differences in organizations. Blau and Scott (1962) asserted that the true structure of an organization could be understood only with a concomitant understanding of the informal values and norms of the organization. Walker and Lorsch (1968) wondered whether organizations should be structured according to product or function. Thompson (1967) attempted to capture the essence of complex organizational management of uncertainty by identifying various ways in which units could be coupled (related), further demonstrating the administrative challenges presented by the degree of interdependence among organizational members. Mintzberg, in *The Structuring of Organizations* (1979), masterfully captured, categorized, and synthesized all the theoretical developments to date. His important contribution was to integrate both organization and management theory into a structural representation of the five basic parts of organizations: (1) the operating core, (2) middle line, and (3) strategic apex supported by the (4) technostructure and (5) support staff.

The tumultuous nature of the 1960s had its impact on organizations and the research about them. Many theorists from the 1960s (through the 1980s), whose thinking remained part of the Functionalist Paradigm, either noted or called for changes in Traditional Organizational hierarchies. These changes were needed to respond to changes in society, to respond appropriately to rapidly changing environments. Writers such as Bennis (1966), Toffler (1970), Bennis & Slater (1968), and Thayer (1981) in various ways and for various reasons called for alternative, if not flatter, structures to meet modern challenges. Peter Drucker (1954), best known for his work on developing decision structures such as *management by objectives* (MBO), in his later work (1988) called for flatter, more information-based organizations. Remaining true to the structuralist traditions, however, one can also find thinkers such as Elliott Jaques (1990), who, in *In Praise of Hierarchy*, saw bureaucracies as enduring because he believed they are the best way to assure efficiency while also assuring equity and representativeness in complex structures.

At this stage in theoretical development, as different organizational theories evolved, separating theorists into perspectives or schools of thought became more difficult. Theorists from various perspectives began to incorporate ideas and concepts from others who were writing about organizations, thus blurring the distinctive niches into which their theories might have been categorized. By the time systems theorists were emerging, the "modern" structuralists and human relations theorists were influencing system theory work and vice versa. Where a theorist fit in any classification scheme really depended on which elements were being emphasized at the time of the classification. We think the cross-fertilization of various organizational theories brings excitement and stimulation to the field and reemphasizes the complexity of organizational thought; however, trying to keep theories conceptually clean for analysis and categorization became quite challenging the more mutual theoretical influences became the norm. Keeping this complexity in mind, we now turn to theories about organizations and their environments.

THEORIES OF ORGANIZATIONS AND ENVIRONMENTS

Since Ludwig von Bertalanffy (1951) elaborated general systems theory, organizational researchers have attended to the context in which the organization operates. Based on general systems theory, and with the aid of emerging quantitative tools, organizational researchers sought to understand the complex relations among organizational and environmental variables. Organizational decision processes and information and control systems were a major focus of analysis. Owing much to Simon's (1957) concepts of bounded rationality and satisficing decisions, cause and effect for optimal solutions were topics of continuing interest. Wiener (1948), in his classic, *Cybernetics*, saw organizations as adaptive, self-regulating systems.

In the late 1960s, systems theory came fully to the forefront of organizational thinking with the publication of two pivotal works written by Katz and Kahn (1966) and Thompson (1967). Katz & Kahn (1966) saw organizations as open systems and sought to describe and understand the interdependence and interactions between the organization and the environment. Thompson (1967) extended the system notion by envisioning organizations as rational systems with a contingency perspective. Thompson (1967) distinguished between the organization's task and general environments. **Task environments** included all those individuals, groups, and organizations with which an organization had interaction. **General environments** were defined as broader institutions of society reflected in things such as political structures or societal attitudes. He sought to understand and predict effectiveness of organizational action under what he called *norms of rationality*.

While structuralists had continued to focus on machine metaphors, early systems thinkers were firmly rooted in organism metaphors. Organizations were seen as species in which dynamic interactions transpired, in which there were inputs, throughputs, outputs, outcomes, feedback loops, and a whole range of terms describing interaction between organizations and their environments. Systems theorists recognized the importance of the changing environment. Different schools of thought within systems theory held differing assumptions about organizations. Social scientists have used five analogies to depict social systems: mechanical, organismic, morphogenic, factional, and catastrophic (Burrell & Morgan, 1979). Depending on the analogy used, systems theory can be used to describe both traditional and alternative agencies. Table 3.2 summarizes these analogies.

Martin & O'Connor (1989) explain each of the analogies in Table 3.2. Unlike mechanical and organismic analogies, morphogenic, factional, and catastrophic analogies focus on the dynamic and changing nature of social systems rather than attempting to deny those dynamics. Conflict is seen as a normal part of being an organization within a complex environment. These latter three types of systems theory are based on assumptions from the Radical Structuralist Paradigm, since they are not adverse to radical change. In Chapter 7, we will elaborate on the three systems analogies that are not based on functionalist assumptions. For now, we want the reader to be aware that there are very different ways of approaching systems theory. Table 3.3 summarizes the two analogies that are based on functionalist assumptions. We will return to the other analogies later when we investigate other paradigmatic perspectives.

The mechanical analogy views social systems as if they were physical machines, derived from physics (Martin & O'Connor, 1989). This is a closed-system approach that focuses on internal integration. This is how the early structuralists viewed an organization. One can almost hear the early theorists searching for the one best way to make people in organizations work as interchangeable parts and to locate the right structure that will maintain system equilibrium. This approach to systems is

Table 3.2

Analogies Used by Social Scientists to Depict Social Systems

Analogy	Description and Principal Tendency
Mechanical	Assumes perfect coordination and integration of parts
	Assumes that departures from equilibrium result in correct action to return to equilibrium
	Assumes social systems are like machines
	Emphasizes order and stability over conflict and change
Organismic	Assumes high coordination and integration of parts
	Assumes that departures from homeostasis result in corrective actions to return to homeostasis
	Assumes society is like a living organism with different organs that cooperate closely to contribute to the survival of the whole
	Assumes social systems are cohesive because of consensus of citizens, families, communities, etc.
	Emphasizes order and stability over conflict and change
Morphogenic	Assumes that social systems change constantly through interaction and exchange with their environment(s)
	Assumes that social systems are highly open
	Assumes social systems may be orderly and predictable but may also be disorderly and unpredictable
	Assumes that order may rest on coercion and domination as well as cooperation and consensus
	Places about equal emphasis on conflict and change as on order and stability
Factional	Assumes that social systems are divided into contentious factions that conflict over goals, priorities, resources and strategies
	Assumes that the turbulent division of the system into factions is the principal tendency of the system
	Emphasizes conflict and change over order and stability
Catastrophic	Assumes that social systems are severely segmented and warring
	Assumes that little order or predictability exists
	Assumes that conflict may destroy some component parts
	Assumes complete reorganization of the system is required if the system is to become less chaotic or conflictual
	Emphasizes conflict and change over order and stability

Source: From Patricia Yancey Martin and Gerald G. O'Connor. *The social environment: Open systems applications.* Copyright © 1989 Allyn & Bacon. Reprinted by permission. Adapted from Burrell and Morgan, *Sociological paradigms and organizational analysis.* Aldershot, England: Ashgate, 1979. Figure 4.1, p. 67. Used by permission.

Table 3.3

Functionalist Analogies Used by Social Scientists to Depict Social Systems

Analogy	Description and Principal Tendency
Mechanical	Assumes perfect coordination and integration of parts
	Assumes that departures from equilibrium result in correct action to return to equilibrium
	Assumes social systems are like machines
	Emphasizes order and stability over conflict and change
Organismic	Assumes high coordination and integration of parts
	Assumes that departures from homeostasis result in corrective actions to return to homeostasis
	Assumes society is like a living organism with different organs that cooperate closely to contribute to the survival of the whole
	Assumes social systems are cohesive because of consensus of citizens, families, communities, etc.
	Emphasizes order and stability over conflict and change

Source: Patricia Yancey Martin and Gerald G. O'Connor. *The social environment: Open systems applications.* Copyright © 1989 Allyn & Bacon. Reprinted by permission. Adapted from Burrell and Morgan, *Sociological paradigms and organizational analysis.* Aldershot, England: Ashgate, 1979. Figure 4.1, p. 67. Used by permission.

definitely in the Functionalist Paradigm and has been highly criticized for ignoring complexity and the interdependence of organizations and their environments.

The Washington County Office on Aging was established very much in this mechanistic tradition—rules, protocols, structure, and a host of other characteristics were expected as standard across sites. One of the most obvious enactments of the theory was in the division of labor, so that if any one staff member left, it was assumed that another person could be hired to pick up where the previous person left off. Jayne remembers the search process when she was getting ready to leave the directorship. Several of the council on aging members had said, "We'll never replace you!" and her reply had been swift: "Everything's in place, so that anyone can come into the office and do what I've been doing." She didn't like to think of herself as a replaceable part, but she also prided herself on paving the way for a smooth and seamless transition based on her assumption that organizations should behave in a consistent, predictable manner.

The organismic analogy comes from biology and was a reaction to the machine analogy, much like the human relations and "modern" structuralists reacted to the classical and neoclassical theorists. In this analogy, society is viewed as a biological organism with interrelated parts that are functionally unified. Emerging in the 1940s and 1950s as a reaction to the more mechanistic views of systems, the organismic analogy developed with advances in biology. Talcott Parsons is credited with having advanced this development in his structural-functionalist approach to systems, which dominated theoretical circles between the 1950s and 1960s. "Structural functionalism and its progeny, systems theory, provided an 'internalist' focus on organizational design with an 'externalist' concern with environmental uncertainty" (Reed, 1996, p. 37). According to Parsons, social systems had to perform four functions in order to survive: adaptation, goal attainment, integration, and pattern maintenance. In performing these functions, the goal was to seek **homeostasis**, a state of balance in which every part is working together and integrating with the whole. Focusing attention on the status quo and attempting only incremental change, the organismic type of systems theory leads to a search for order and consensus. Martin and O'Connor (Martin & O'Connor, 1989, p. 54) think that it is unfortunate that open-systems theory "has been used often with an organismic analogy and, as a result, is believed to have limitations that it does not have." This is why one will run into people who talk about how conservative or change aversive systems theory is. They are referring to the organismic type of systems theory that focuses on maintaining the status quo at all costs. Traditional Organizations have often been accused of behaving in this way, of not taking risks, and of focusing on organizational maintenance over client service.

Both mechanical and organismic systems theory are functionalist in perspective. There is an assumption of a reality external to the individual and that knowledge about that reality can be studied with social science methods that allow for generalizability. These approaches to systems theory, combined with structural-functionalism, actually were seen to have the potential to depoliticize the decision-making process within organizations. A generation of managers and system designers educated in these brands of systems theory learned to resist conflict, seek consensus, and aspire to overall control within an increasingly differentiated and complex society" (Reed, 1996, p. 38).

As we write this part of the chapter, we are smiling because this is where we began our careers. We were taught open systems of the organismic type, when it was believed that order (regulation) was possible if only one could find the right combination of variables and then design the organization accordingly. There was hope that with systems theory one's eyes would open to the orderly pattern of the universe, and that social scientists could predict exactly what would happen because they would know how to design the organizations that would work because they would fit within this ordered structure. Soon, however, the limitations of the organismic approach to systems would be clear, and the search would continue for theories to deal with the increasing complexity of organizational life.

Thus far, we have examined five major perspectives on organization theory—classical, neoclassical, human relations and organizational behavior,

Radical Humanist	Radical Structuralist
Interpretive	Systems Theories (Mechanistic & Organismic Analogies) Human Relations Theories **Functionalist** "Modern" Structural Theories Neoclassical Theories Classical Theories

Figure 3.2   Organizational Theories Within the Functionalist Paradigm.

"modern" structural, and organizations and their environments. As these perspectives have evolved and interacted, it has become increasingly difficult to place entire schools of thought into one paradigm. For example, systems theories, depending on the analogies used to elucidate theoretical assumptions, are based on different paradigmatic assumptions. All dimensions of systems theory are not captured in the functionalist worldview.

Figure 3.2 provides a visual location of the theories discussed in this chapter and their placement within the Functionalist Paradigm. The theory's placement is a commentary on its location on the Burrell and Morgan (1979) objectivist–subjectivist and regulation–change continua.

Vibert (2004) also examines those organizational perspectives that fit within each of the paradigms. He places the following within the Functionalist Paradigm, based on their assumptions:

- Bureaucracy perspective
- Contingency perspective
- Strategic choice perspective
- Resource dependence perspective
- Population ecology perspective
- Institutional perspective
- Chaos perspective

Vibert's categorization is different from Shafritz, Ott, and Lang's, but the fit within functionalism is evident. Bureaucracy is a classical structural theory, whereas contingency, resource dependence, and population ecology theories are cousins of systems theory. Strategic choice is inherently rational in its orientation and fits with decision-making theory. An institutional perspective seeks to examine how organizations are the same, pushing toward conformity. And even though a chaos perspective may sound highly unstructured, it is a mathematical approach to reasoning that fits within the Functionalist Paradigm.

As we examine each paradigm in subsequent chapters, we will add theories to our table that fall within the other paradigms. The Functionalist Paradigm has been the dominant paradigm from the time modern organizations developed. Thus, theories that fall within other paradigms will be viewed as "alternative," at least by those persons who hold functionalist views. For now, we hope that you have a beginning understanding of what it means when we say that functionalism is considered the traditional perspective from which the vast majority of organizational theories have emerged. We hope that you have been able to develop a greater understanding of this paradigmatic perspective because of the organizational theories that fit within it. This should also give meaning to the structure and control goals of Traditional Organizations. With this knowledge, you will be much better able to make considered assessments of the usefulness of the theories for your own practice within human service settings.

COSTS AND BENEFITS

THE FUNCTIONALIST PARADIGM AND ITS THEORIES

Even persons who value bureaucratic structures recognize that the level of order and control necessary to maintain the hierarchical standard comes with a price. Overall, the Functionalist Paradigm is open to criticism on several grounds that are relevant to understanding organizations. This perspective rests heavily on the ability to operationalize what is of interest for study. This means that what is to be studied must be defined and be made measurable. This is particularly difficult when many aspects of organizational life cannot be known at this level, but rather on the tacit or intuitive level. The communication style of the manager may not be totally definable by current standards of measurability, but his or her employees "know" when the manager "means business" even if there is no tool to assess this. Articulating what the employees know is next to impossible, but they all can act on that knowledge by attending to business when necessary. Replicating this information for a newcomer is not possible.

The focus of functionalist research is on cause and effect due to the functionalist goal of achieving truth through generalizability. In functionalism there is no acceptance of the need to understand meaning and its implications. The intent is to reduce uncertainty and difference, working toward consensus. In addition, the attention to determinism and reductionism seems misplaced in an organizational world that has become so complex. This means that making predictions in an individual organization is all but impossible. Finally, in the fast-moving context of the beginning of the 21st century, the functionalist perspective is not able to deal with the emergent issues of the day. It becomes more and more clear that functionalism rests on a set of assumptions that are increasingly difficult to maintain. Especially when one looks at current post-positivist efforts, there are violations of basic paradigmatic assumptions everywhere in order for research to be relevant to the current context of organizational life. Experimental designs are all but nonexistent in organizations; objectivity is not maintained due to lack of randomness in sampling. These are just two small examples of how functionalist assumptions must be violated in today's fast-paced organizations.

TRADITIONAL ORGANIZATIONS WITH STRUCTURE AND CONTROL GOALS

Even with these limits and challenges, the theories developed within the assumptions of this paradigm have strengths. For example, bureaucracy maximizes efficiency. Bureaucratic approaches particularly facilitate the management of greater numbers of tasks in large, complex organizations, allowing for increased productivity. Following the bureaucratic tenets of having only those with the skills do the required job assures quality. This structure continues to be quite acceptable for manufacturing environments, but the vast, impersonal setting of a bureaucracy allows little attention to unique needs of either employees or those being served. Top-down dictates of a hierarchical approach mean participants and clients have few rights.

Merton (1952) identified the bureaucratic personality that is derived from this context. The risk of this personality is that the individual becomes more interested in rote rules and procedures than in doing the job as intended. This is a direct result of the technological way in which employees are understood, as if they are cogs in a wheel. Differentiation and attention to subtleties cannot be addressed either by the theories used to guide practice or by the personality types well suited to the perspective. This results in the potential for exploitation of workers, because the bias is toward productivity. This biasing effect may be even more complex. Kelly (1991) asserts that the lack of ability to account for subtleties in goals, decision making, technology, and individual needs creates a male bias in communication and decision-making preferences that has particularly negative effects on women and minorities.

Built on functionalist assumptions, scientific management pays great attention to precision, measurement, and specialization to the detriment of process and meaning. It may be very useful to categorize efforts and to formalize programs, but this does little to understand the human side of service efforts. How do employees feel about the demands of their job description? How do clients relate to the efforts and services rendered? Remember that Taylor's time-and-motion studies were based on men shoveling pig iron, not workers processing human beings. The potential disconnect should be obvious.

The human relations influence served both to under- and overestimate the importance of social factors in the organization. This theoretical perspective provided a humanizing counterbalance to the formalization of the earlier efforts. Needs and interests of the individual became part of the organizational equation, but with no intention of empowering workers. The attention focused on workers was for the purpose of gaining greater productivity. These efforts did not escape the potential consequence of serving to dehumanize, oppress, and exploit workers, because all power and decision making remained at the top of the hierarchy. Attention to personal and social relationships, including networking, continued to disadvantage women and minorities due to their lack of access to powerful networks. Though the human relations school failed to prove that a happier worker was more productive, and though it is now recognized that the relationship between worker needs and productivity is much more complex, this major perspective did contribute to our understanding of organizations by showing the importance of teamwork, cooperation, leadership, and positive attention of management.

Systems theory cemented the recognition of the environment as a critical variable in organizations. This recognition is particularly important for human service organizations. Systems attention to organizational survival also opened doors to new understanding of some of the forces behind organizational behavior. Given the variety of analogies on which systems theories are based, the broad flexibility among these approaches may cause confusion to the student of organization. To assure usefulness of a systems perspective for organization practice, the intentions and standpoint of the particular approach must be clear. Only with this clarity can the student or worker know what standards to apply when considering the usefulness of the theory for their environment.

CONCLUSION

Traditional Organizations have a wealth of theories to guide their actions with a long history of dominance in organization practice. It is important to recognize the strengths of the theories and how deeply their cultural assumptions are embedded in their structures.

Classical organization theories showed the benefits of production-related and economic goals and how organizing for productivity through systematic inquiry maximizes production. Neoclassical theories added to the understanding of the complexity of maintaining necessary discipline while organizing for the best productivity. Human relations theories introduced the human needs side of organizing by recognizing necessary elements of viable work contexts in which organizational behavior occurs. Motivation entered the equation for productive purposes. "Modern" structural organization theory reignited the interest in organizational efficiency based on rationality, but with a much greater attention to human need. We have examined some aspects of the limits and challenges of these theories and the paradigm within which they are lodged. Functionalist approaches are not sufficient to aid in understanding work within the complicated organizations of today and tomorrow. Something more is needed. But in order for you to understand the degree to which additional perspectives are necessary and useful, more information about different approaches to organizational thinking will be highlighted in subsequent chapters.

Next, we turn to mechanisms for understanding the practical aspects of life within Traditional Organizations. Having examined the rich and lengthy theoretical background that forms a structural backdrop for these organizations, we now investigate the behavior and practices congruent with a Traditional Organization. We look at the *hierarchical culture* congruent with a Functionalist Paradigm by translating the themes and theories from this chapter into various aspects of the work of Traditional Organizations. Such aspects as values, preferences, and strategies will help to define standards of practice in human service organizations holding functionalist perspectives where structure and control are goals.

DISCUSSION QUESTIONS

1. Compare and contrast the assumptions of the Functionalist Paradigm with the goals of the Traditional Organization. How are they similar or different? What are the costs and benefits of the similarities? Of the differences?

2. Imagine you are on the search committee for an executive director of a very traditional human service agency. The search committee is engaged in dialogue about the costs and benefits of being a part of a Traditional Organization so that members can provide "words to the wise" for potential candidates for the position. What might the "words to the wise" be? What might you advise the committee to consider in recruiting candidates? How might the committee go about

assessing applicants' potential fit with the organization's goals and expectations?

3. Review the theory discussion and compare the similarities and differences between the classical and neoclassical theoretical approaches. Do the same with human relations and theories X and Y. Which theories are more congruent with your preferences about structure and behavior in an organization, and why?

4. In the beginning of this part of the text, a case example was introduced—the Washington County Office on Aging. Go back to that case and consider the follow questions:
   a. What characteristics of this organization make it a Traditional Organization? Are there characteristics that are less traditional than others?
   b. What assumptions did Jayne appear to bring to her new position and how were they helpful (or not) in carrying out her responsibilities?
   c. With growth and change over the years, how did this organization maintain its tradition?

5. Imagine that you are starting a small organization and that you want to be sure that the structure of your organization is congruent with its environment. What issues would you need to address if you were to choose a Traditional Organizational structure to be sure that it matched a particular environment? Describe the environment for which a Traditional Organization is most suited.

6. You are a supervisor or manager in a human service agency. What would cause you to prefer working in a Traditional Organization with traditional goals? Would there be any challenges for you personally as a leader? If so, what would they be, and how would you deal with them?

CHAPTER 4

Practice in Traditional Organizations

T HE MAJORITY OF organizations in which human service practitioners work have been heavily influenced by functionalist approaches and therefore have goals of structure and control. Yet, it is important to point out that many Traditional Organizations are now using language that implies assumptions that are not functionalist at all. For example, the word *empowerment*, drawn from the more radical and critical perspectives in the 1990s, implies that employees will have more freedom to self-actualize on the job. Unfortunately, this language is present when employees in many organizations live in constant fear of being downsized. It is hardly fertile ground for feeling empowered in one's work. Another example is the widespread use of the more subjectively focused term, *client centered*, where many of the outcomes measured in human service programs are predetermined by professionals with minimal client input and without attention to intervening variables beyond the control of the client or the worker. In some organizations, the only thing that makes the measure and the service client centered is that they are directed toward clients with the arrogance of professionals who think they know what is best for clients.

It is no wonder, then, that people are confused when they hear language that pertains to a less deterministic perspective spoken in organizations that are steeped in determinism. The language signals changes in perspectives that are rarely born out in the organizational structure or standards of organization practice. Practicing in a Traditional Organization is often fraught with contradictions because the language used may not always reflect the underlying values of these organizations. Instead they are a reflection of changes in societal attitudes and assumptions that have not quite permeated traditional assumptions in order to fundamentally change the expectations and the practices in Traditional Organizations.

For the foreseeable future, we see Traditional Organizations as zones of paradox for human service practitioners. We give the reader permission to heave a sigh of relief in knowing that they can expect to encounter paradox in organization practice, rather than beating themselves up because they can't seem to figure out why words and actions contradict one another. Hopefully, as a result of working with the material in this book, you will be better prepared to understand traditional expectations and perhaps change those and the practice that follows from those expectations.

We are confident that anyone reading this book will have encountered Traditional Organizations, because they are a dominant form within the human service planning and delivery system in American society. Even if you have not worked in a human service agency, you will have interacted with people in Traditional Organizations. In this chapter, we focus on what is necessary to practice in Traditional Organizations. In similar chapters for each of the remaining perspectives on organizations, we will use four questions to guide readers so that they will be able to compare and contrast organizations based on different sets of assumptions. These questions are: (1) What are the cultural values and characteristics of organizations derived from the assumptions of this paradigm? (2) What roles and relationships are congruent with the culture of this type organization? (3) What are the standards for practice within this type organization? and (4) What are the implications for practice within this type of organization?

CULTURAL VALUES AND CHARACTERISTICS OF TRADITIONAL ORGANIZATIONS

In Chapter 2, we referred to Cameron and Quinn's (2006) Competing Values Framework, in which four different organizational cultures are identified. The Traditional Organization as described here is most congruent with a hierarchy culture, which is very formalized and structured as a place of work. Everything that people do is governed by procedures and protocols. Efficiency-minded leaders pride themselves on being good coordinators and organizers who are skilled at maintaining a smooth-running organization. The glue that holds the organization together is comprised of formal rules and policies. Of long-term concern is stability and performance with efficient, smooth operations. Dependable delivery, seamless scheduling, and efficient costs are viewed as signs of success. Managers create a work environment in which employees feel secure and things are predicable. The hierarchy culture produces an organization focused on internal maintenance with expectations for stability and control. Management in this culture involves monitoring and coordinating (p. 64).

Box 4.1 is a repeat of a box originally introduced in Chapter 2. It provides a reminder of the basic cultural elements that inform a Traditional Organization.

Box 4.1

TRADITIONAL ORGANIZATIONS

- History and tradition are respected as important parts of their programs, seeking external *objective sources of recognized expertise to design and develop programs.*
- *Stability and control* are promoted so that programs run smoothly as workers conform to established protocols
- Programs are *integrated* by establishing interrelated duties and tasks to be carried out assuming these duties and tasks establish best practices.
- Well-defined organizational and programmatic structures are created, and are typically *hierarchical*, so lines of authority are clear.

VALUES IN TRADITIONAL ORGANIZATIONS

In the Traditional Organization, there is no great need to search for meaning or to spend much time questioning values. The goal of Traditional Organizations is to maintain a sense of structure and control, thus not only would it be wasteful (highly inefficient) to spend a lot of time on meaning, but it would involve process more than outcome. Simply put, efficiency and effectiveness are the values. Nothing else matters. Products and outcomes are highly esteemed, and if end products are considered effective and efficient, then there is proof that the process worked. Being organized and maintaining consistency within the organization is important. This is what is valued.

Remember that the Traditional Organization takes an *absolutist* position. Truth comes from an external source and is not determined by the individual. The Traditional Organization operationalizes dominant opinions, doctrines, and practices. This generally means their funding sources mirror those same dominant perspectives. What is valued in the agency is what is sanctioned in the society and by the funders. For example, when society saw woman's place as in the home, there was no real effort to prepare and hire women professionals; when societal values shifted to allow women into the working world, then organizations began hiring women who would fit within the structures and behavioral norms that were already in place. Funders were required by law or as a societal reflection to attend to women in the workplace, as well. However, responsiveness to environmental shifts comes with a serious effort to maintain what exists. When women entered the workplace, there were expectations that mirrored the expectations for men, with no real attention to women's important role as mothers in society. What had existed in the workplace prior to women entering it in large numbers was maintained.

In Traditional Organizations, interventions need to be logically derived from what was learned in the processes of assessment, diagnosis, and planning. Interventions may take the form of **planned change**, defined as a process of deliberately identifying a problem, analyzing its causes, and carefully determining a strategy to alter the situation according to pre-determined outcomes. Planned change interventions, then, are not done haphazardly, spontaneously, or without a great deal of planful, mostly linear thought.

Since consensus is a core functionalist value, tactics used in planned change interventions are typically conservative and incremental—designed to be acceptable to the majority, especially those in positions of power over the organization. The status quo is also protected during change. For example, some of the early textbooks on change focused on making certain that collaborative or campaign tactics were used before even considering contest tactics (Brager & Holloway, 1978; Resnick & Patti, 1980). Resnick and Patti (1980) focused on the importance of working for change from *inside* the organization, not even addressing the concerns of the outside agitator. Their approaches fit well with Traditional Organizations because they hold highly compatible basic assumptions of stability and control.

Mission/Philosophy of Traditional Organizations

Building on the belief that the status quo and social order are good things for organizations, the Traditional Organization views the social world of the organization as composed of concrete empirical artifacts and relationships that can be identified, studied/measured, and managed through controlled approaches derived from the natural sciences. These methods were first identified by Taylor (1916), who conducted *time-and-motion studies* to develop rules and laws to increase productivity or organizational output. Scientific methods continue to be the acceptable way to measure compliance with or divergence from the ideal or desired state in the organization. This measurement control is directed toward the implementation of logical plans for reaching organization goals.

Mission or philosophical statements are not always easy to decipher, because they typically contain lofty words and are written to inspire the reader. Therefore, missions of Traditional Organizations may contain words that do not fully fit with basic underlying assumptions. For example, many human service organizations will have the verb *advocate* in their mission statements. Certainly the Traditional Organization will advocate for individual clients to a degree—perhaps getting them signed up for food stamps or bringing their needs to the attention of an appropriate agency—but this type of client or **case advocacy** is not intended to create major structural change in oppressive systems (Schneider & Lester, 2001).

Instead, it is a more conservative approach that seeks to bring clients into the existing service delivery system by changing their status. It is therefore important to carefully read statements of mission and philosophy in light of what the words mean for establishing the standard for acceptable practice within the organizational context.

Preferred Structure in Traditional Organizations

With goals and processes, the Traditional Organization is also absolutist. There is one "best" way of defining the problem and implementing the solution to that problem. The way to achieve problem solution and change is with logical order and maximum control of all elements of the organization. The difficult part is to find that best solution so that a formal structure can be designed to support it. In most cases, the solution is organized hierarchically with clear roles and responsibilities delineated.

To serve this aim the Traditional Organization has several structural elements: formality, bureaucracy, and hierarchy. The formal nature of the Traditional Organization is a vestige of the beginnings of social organizing during industrialization and the study of postindustrial organizations. Frederick Taylor (1916) framed the belief that there is one best way of accomplishing any task, including social organizing. Once the one best solution is discovered, then rules and laws are put into place to create the formal structure geared to increase output.

Adam Smith (1776) was the first proponent of divided, coordinated work. The functionalist perspective fits the tradition that began with *The Wealth of Nations*. Functionalism welcomes a division of labor and work assignments between management and labor with clear expectations regarding performance, good treatment, respect, and discipline if the rules are broken. The expectation is that management does the planning, organizing, staffing, directing, coordinating, reporting, and budgeting (Gulick, 1937), and labor does as it is told. This division is pragmatic and acceptable, because it is believed the approach enhances the skills, and, thus, the effectiveness, of each. It saves time and expands creativity in developing best practice methods and technology. All this serves to increase productive quantity, as the narrow focusing of activities increases abilities, which in turn increases quality of performance. It is assumed with this focusing that it is much more likely that workers or managers will discover easier, more effective and efficient methods of achieving objectives. When this occurs, better pay, and, thus, more satisfied employees will result.

Types of Programs and Services in Traditional Organizations

In Chapter 1, we introduced different types of programs and services. Recall that *direct service programs* directly serve clients. *Staff development and training programs* focus on staff, and *support programs* undergird direct service and staff-focused programs. Traditional Organizations may contain all three types of programs. Regardless of the program type, programs in Traditional Organizations will be more concerned about *outcomes* or results than they will be about the quality of the process. What will be important about process is that it efficiently leads to results.

Program and service goals and objectives require using gradual change to alter people's status so that they can function best within the larger society. For example, a program designed for persons with disabilities will attempt to make clients as proficient as possible, using whatever assistive technology available, for as much independence as possible, as quickly as possible. Another program targeting welfare mothers may teach interviewing skills so that the mothers can get jobs. Retention of the job will not be of initial interest—until job retention is later identified as a problem. Yet another program may assist older persons to remain in their own homes in order to save the costs associated with out-of-home care. All of these programs are change oriented, but these are not radical or structural changes. Clients are changed so that their increased abilities or changed situation will allow them to access existing societal resources without actually changing the resource availability picture until that becomes a societal priority.

Traditional Organizations generally have programs and services that have well-defined, measurable objectives. Management and funding sources will expect this. Program budgeting rather than simple line-item budgeting may be in place. This allows investigation of each program separately in terms of its revenue sources and its expenditures and shows what costs are being shared across programs. It also provides for cost-per-unit-of-service efficiency measures. Programs may be viewed as cost centers, with program directors or coordinators responsible for their oversight. This combination of identifiable program objectives and a budget that is directly related adds to the stability of the organizational structure, enhances management's ability to discipline the structure, and ensures division of labor and evaluation of productivity for efficiency as well as effectiveness.

Summary Characteristics of Traditional Organizations

Traditional Organizations can be distinguished from organizations in the other three paradigmatic perspectives that are considered alternative. One might ask, "alternative to what?" Essentially, the Functionalist Paradigm has dominated organizational thought for so long that alternative agencies are literally *alternative to Traditional Organizations*. Public, private nonprofit, and private for-profit agencies can be either traditional or alternative in their approaches. We summarize the characteristics of Traditional

Table 4.1
Characteristics of Traditional Organizations

Characteristics	Traditional Organizations
Values	To operationalize dominant opinions, doctrines, and practices, focusing on efficiency and effectiveness
Mission and Philosophy	To use the best knowledge available to enhance and achieve the highest social order
Organizational Structure	To establish clear relationships between organizational members and among units within the organization, and to be part of service delivery structures that are established by agency staff and protocols that have been used over the years
Programs and Services	To use incremental or gradual change to alter people's status so that they can function best within society

Organizations in Table 4.1. These characteristics apply to any category of agency operating with traditional, functionalist assumptions. In many ways, these have become the standard against which all organization structure and operation is judged.

The characteristics in Table 4.1 reveal a great deal about Traditional Organizations. These organizations wish to preserve and protect their position and, therefore, will be more conservative or preservative in their decisions and actions. They are typically well-established agencies with much to lose if radical change occurs. Since they have clients who are viewed as worthy of receiving services (or members of the larger society believe should be served) and predictable funding sources, Traditional Organizations generally seek to maintain some sense of predictability through maintenance of the status quo. When an organization has resources, it has much more to lose by way of money, status, and power than an alternative agency that may not have gained credibility with powerful environmental forces. Traditional Organizations tend to have been around for a while, because they have protected the reputation and positioning that has garnered them an identifiable space in the human service landscape.

Traditional Organizations can be of any size, but the large public human service agency that serves thousands of clients is an excellent example of the complexity that can be managed following traditional assumptions. The bureaucratic structure and hierarchical culture are necessary to manage the numbers of people, the amount of paperwork expected to document decisions and actions, and the other demands of a complex political economy. Traditional Organizations may be well-established, turn-of-the-20th century nonprofit agencies that have long been affiliated with religious groups. They may have begun as alternative agencies when certain population groups needed services, but have developed and grown in response to community needs. These agencies may still be quite innovative, spinning out new programs as times change, but their size and structural complexity are indicators of their functionalist nature. They may call themselves advocates, but they are fully aware of how far they can go without alienating the community or a funding source. Thus, they are advocates within boundaries. Traditional Organizations may also be for-profit agencies that have entered the social welfare domain in more recent years, cognizant of the importance of productivity and efficiency and in competition for the service dollar—terms well established in business. Traditional Organizations cut across sectors and are a large portion of the human service landscape as it is currently developed.

Within Traditional Organizations there are basic assumptions about locus of control and change. From an objectivist perspective, locus of control is external—there is a greater source of truth and knowledge beyond the individual. If people are products of their environments (a functionalist assumption), then Traditional Organizations help people adjust to those environments so that their quality of life will be improved. For example, when one goes to a health-care clinic, one hopes to have an accurate diagnosis so that successful treatment will follow. In a human service agency that provides counseling, consumers hope to be able to cope better with life's stresses as a result of service. In these situations, persons are helped to adjust to their circumstances. The idea is they have their needs met without major structural upset. Services have been delivered in a socially acceptable manner, a solid *best practices* model. Finding the *best* practices and the *best* fit and working toward the *best* possible outcomes is what the Traditional Organization is all about. A long tradition of looking for *best* ways to enhance organizational effectiveness and efficiency dominates in the Traditional Organization.

Given its regulation perspective, the Traditional Organization is not designed to seek radical change. These organizations are essentially very conservative. Persons within Traditional Organizations can be change agents, but they focus on changes that are controllable and manageable so that harmony can be maintained or restored quickly. The most profound changes within this context are acceptable only if they are incremental in nature. If an agency sees that a funding source has changed its service interest, there will be an effort to reconceptualize its service to fit the funding source's new vision. These changes rarely change what service providers do with clients; the change is in the language that describes the services. Changes in Traditional Organizations are not intended to alter basic internal or external structures, but to help people lead quality lives within those existing structures. The environment in which the organization operates is viewed by functionalists as a set of forces to be controlled as much as possible, so that social order both inside and outside of the organization can be maintained or reestablished.

ROLES AND RELATIONSHIPS WITH AND WITHIN TRADITIONAL ORGANIZATIONS

Given the functionalist objectives and regulation perspectives that guide Traditional Organizations, Table 4.2 provides a summary of some of the ways in which roles and relationships develop in Traditional Organizations. This same framework will appear in subsequent chapters as we examine the differing goals of various types of organizations.

ORGANIZATION-ENVIRONMENT RELATIONSHIPS

We begin with how Traditional Organizations view their relationships with the larger environment. We will then examine the Traditional Organization's internal roles and relationships, particularly elaborating on funding and clients.

Task Environment Relationships   The task environment comprises all those groups, organizations, and individuals with which an organization relates (Thompson, 1967). It is important to know how the Traditional Organization views those assorted relationships beyond their immediate control.

In the previous chapter, Table 3.2 introduced analogies used by social scientists to depict social systems. We pointed out that mechanical and

Table 4.2
Roles and Relationships With and Within Traditional Organizations

Type of Relationship	Purpose
Task Environment Relationships	To recognize that the environment is uncertain and turbulent, and to do whatever possible to control environmental forces
Relationships With Funders	To obtain funding that flows from long-established and multiple sources
Relationships With Client Populations Referral Sources	To fund, plan, or deliver socially acceptable programs to socially acceptable clients in need
Internal Organizational Roles and Relationships:	
◦ Managing	To designate administrators and supervisors within a defined structure and to work toward consensus (agreement) so that tasks can be logically addressed; value hierarchical communication and decision-making
◦ Communicating	To develop established protocols, such as organizational charts and information systems, so that expectations about communication are clear
◦ Recognizing Staff Expectations	To hire people who will work in the most efficient and effective manner

organismic systems analogies fall squarely within the Functionalist Paradigm. According to organismic systems theory, the organization's goal is to seek homeostasis, a state of balance in which every part is working together and integrating with the whole. Organismic systems theory guides the Traditional Organization as it seeks to focus attention on the status quo and attempts only incremental change in its search for order and consensus. If there is trouble in the environment by way of dissatisfied clients, unmet service demands, or funding sources that are somehow not happy with agency services, the organization listens to the complaint and does what is necessary to assuage the criticism without making major modifications to the agency structure or programming. The Traditional Organization is aware of environmental influences, but attempts to control their impacts.

The environment, in the language of systems theory, is looked upon by the Traditional Organization as a sea of uncertainty and turbulence. Guiding one's organization through this sea requires active leadership. The task is to maintain as much order within the organization as possible, even as the waves splash and the ideological or political tide ebbs and flows. The leader must maintain stability at the helm of the agency, responding in ways that do not create monumental change. The Traditional Organization interprets the environment as an ever-present challenge to be controlled as much as possible. Adjusting to the environment is a survival requirement, but maintaining a semblance of order is the goal. Thus, only gradual change is required, for to rock the boat would send the agency into greater uncertainty and would upset the status quo.

Martin does an excellent job of identifying the "major economic, political, social and technological forces in the external environment [that] can play an important role in shaping" administration in social welfare organizations. Beginning with the collapse of communism, he identifies the global economy, national political power, the devolution of social welfare policy, the "graying" of America, the rediscovery of community, the accountability movement, and advances in information technology as powerful environment forces (Martin, 2000, p. 55). For the contemporary Traditional Organization, these forces cannot be ignored and are viewed as both threats and opportunities, depending on how much they may force a change in the position of a particular agency in the human service arena.

Relationships with Funders　Traditional Organizations seek to obtain funding that flows from long-established, multiple sources. Stability and predictability are desired. This is expected, given their perspective on the environment. If the environment is viewed as uncertain and if the goal is to keep the agency stable, then one would want to seek funding from sources that are likely to remain viable. In addition, leaders in Traditional Organizations have learned what it takes to survive. For example, leaders know that receiving funds from multiple types and sources (diversification) will assist in providing a cushion should one source no longer be available. Traditional Organizations of any size will tend not to put all their financial eggs in one basket if they can help it, unlike alternative agencies, which might feel fortunate to even locate a funding source for their cause.

Traditional Organizations and their funding sources develop close relationships, and funders actually influence the agency's direction or its programming. Policies and regulations that accompany the receiving of funds will become part of the environmental forces that must be constantly considered. For example, in home health organizations, staff members are very cognizant of the potential to be accused of fraud under Medicare. Fear of not following regulations to the letter could actually hamper how much practitioners think they can do for patients. Massive closures of home health agencies because of fraud in the previous decade attest to the realities in which these fears are grounded (Lechich, 2000).

Relationships With Client Populations and Referral Sources   Just as funding is a critical environmental influence, so are clients. And clients often come to agencies from referral sources, other organizations that have enough confidence in making a referral that a client will be well served (or the Traditional Organization may be the only agency providing the needed service). In any case, maintaining a positive public image is critical both to obtaining clients and to ongoing relationships with referral sources.

The Traditional Organization typically serves clients who are viewed as "deserving" or that a funding source has found acceptable to serve. This is a practical matter—if clients are socially acceptable, then chances are that public or private charitable dollars will be available to fund services for them. For example, serving children who have terminal cancer will quickly generate funds for a local children's hospice as people overidentify with the vulnerability of these children and the testimonies of their parents. Socially acceptable clients usually do not require personal or social radical change or transformation in order for service success to occur. They do not have to first convince the public that they are "worth" serving even before they receive service. Socially acceptable clients will tend to "go along with the program" more often than persons who are outside the mainstream or feel alienated from society. When they are voluntary recipients of service, socially acceptable clients are likely to be those persons whose values are compatible with those of the organization and its funders.

However, socially acceptable clients may also be persons who have involuntarily been commanded to be served. For example, prisons are Traditional Organizations. Clients in prison are anything but socially acceptable. However, the larger society supports the building of new prisons and even the taking of lives because prisons perform a socially acceptable function—keeping violent criminals off the streets. Involuntary clients fit within Traditional Organizations because its mode of operation is to maintain the status quo—to fit people within the existing structures of society—not to push for transformation in the social structures serving them. Similarly, Traditional Organizations serve clients that society wants to control, such as mothers on Temporary Assistance for Needy Families, who are given limited monies with the stipulation that they must go to work. In this instance, the Traditional Organization attempts to co-opt or force mothers to conform to standards established as socially acceptable: Work to achieve economic independence in order to support a family, rather than being dependent on the public dole.

INTERNAL ORGANIZATIONAL ROLES AND RELATIONSHIPS

The Traditional Organization is definitely aware of its environment, but it is also exceedingly concerned about the ways in which it internally operates as an organization. The internal workings of the Traditional Organization are influenced by a broad repertoire of theories identified in the previous chapter. These theories guide both the expected structure and behavior within that structure.

Managing   The Traditional Organization of today is bureaucratic, following a Weberian (1946) tradition. There are stated, official areas of responsibility for all persons within the organization. A hierarchy culture is established in that rules and regulations establish levels or gradations of power and authority about organizational processes. The hierarchy is organized either *"top down"* or *"top up"* (Gulick, 1937). The organization that has been ordered through a system of subdividing the enterprise under the control and responsibility of a chief executive is top down. A Traditional Organization uses top-down management where information and directives flow downward through various levels of management. The system may be created in a top-up way by combining individual work units into aggregates that are then subordinated to the chief executive, but top-up approaches are more congruent with other approaches to management geared to more collegial ways of decision-making. For top-up management hierarchies to maintain congruence with the assumptions of the Traditional Organization, information flows upward, but directives still flow downward. Regardless of the form of the hierarchy, there are formal means of written communication used to conduct the business of the organization. Written or understood rules also govern behavior within the organization. Management within the bureaucracy is specialized and trained, so that job performance expectations for management differ from expectations for those providing other services within the organization.

Mintzberg et al. (1998) have helped to clarify the schools of management that are congruent with the hierarchical culture of the Traditional Organization. In keeping with the desire to find the "best" way, all the schools are

prescriptive, describing how strategies should be formulated to arrive at that best way. The Design School focuses on the process of conceiving the appropriate management strategy, providing a formula for *who* should attend to *what* related to strategy selection, including how the explicit strategies should be articulated. The Planning School also is formulaic, with a formal process of strategic planning, including steps, checklists, and techniques for implementation. The Positioning School provides for the identification of the explicit strategies for competitively positioning an organization within its environment. All schools have a commonality of systematically assessing and analyzing a situation, and then seeking the best approach available, fitting the strategy with the situation and implementing the strategy according to a fully developed plan.

Whatever the management formula for management decision making in the Traditional Organization, leaders and managers develop job descriptions and organizational charts that provide information on what employees do and how they relate to one another. Clear lines of authority are a goal for such organizations, so that valuable time is not lost in trying to figure out who is supposed to do what task. In large organizations, the benefits of bureaucratic structure are evident in the way large numbers of employees are coordinated. Time is spent in making roles and relationships clear, with little attention to debating how people feel about these roles and relationships. Traditional Organizations that hire large numbers of professionals tend to have undercurrents of tension, because professionally educated people do not always conform to expected roles and relationships, no matter how hard managers work to make this happen. In fact, if employees are critical thinkers, they will likely question roles, relationships, rules, and procedures according to their personality preferences and professional frames of reference.

Leaders who want to succeed in a Traditional Organization will find that there are certain characteristics that are rewarded by organizations holding a functionalist perspective. Box 4.2 provides a list of characteristics of functionalist leaders.

Communicating Formal communication in the Traditional Organization is facilitated by having defined, predictable structures. Written rules and procedures are designed to communicate work-related expectations. Job descriptions and organizational charts convey role and relational expectations, whereas flowcharts provide visual images of how work is to be performed, decisions made, and communication accepted. Handouts, memos, websites, and various other methods are used to formally and officially disseminate information to employees.

Communication among employees is facilitated by computerized information systems in most contemporary Traditional Organizations. Voice mail, e-mail, cellular phones, palm pilots, and other technological devices

---

Box 4.2

CHARACTERISTICS OF TRADITIONAL LEADERS

- Is comfortable with clearly defined rules, procedures, and directions
- Seeks consensus among colleagues
- Sees conflict as something to be reduced
- Truly appreciates collegiality and mutual respect for organizational goals
- Is comfortable with maintaining the status quo
- Likes concrete, measurable artifacts
- Works toward identifying best practices, best ways of doing the work
- Likes having maximum control at work
- Is viewed by others as rational under stress
- Tolerates process but sees outcomes as most important
- Is able to separate personal from professional life, believing in the importance of clear boundaries
- Follows the rules
- Makes incremental change as needed

---

are embraced in a hierarchical culture as tools to get the work done in as efficient a manner as possible. Managers spend much of their time looking at ways to promote a more efficient, disciplined operation so that outcomes can be achieved in a more timely, less costly manner. In human service organizations, this means finding ways to enhance and streamline methods of communication among employees, between agencies, and with clients. The result is that clients are expected to take most of the responsibility for their goal achievement, as the amount of face time between staff and clients is limited in order to be more efficient. In modern Traditional Organizations, accountability regarding service outcomes seems to have shifted from the professional to the service recipient as fewer and fewer professionals are expected to serve more clients in service of agency efficiency goals.

The formal structure of Traditional Organizations includes the deliberate selection of employees and attention to their career development, followed by expectations for increased productivity and subsequent increased pay. Today's Traditional Organization operates with formal rules and procedures that govern hiring, firing, training, and motivating workers. These rules are provided formally. Traditional Organizations typically have formalized pay scales that are also rule governed but may or may not be easily accessible to the interested employee or client, because pay still represents a mechanism for controlling behavior within the organization. Freely communicating the rules for how behavior is financially rewarded makes organizational financial rewards more predictable and less vulnerable to management power and politics.

Recognizing Staff Expectations   Handbooks that elaborate policies and procedures are available to employees so that everyone is aware of the rules that govern their working lives within Traditional Organizations. Whenever a new issue arises, the predisposition in the Traditional Organization is to clarify things in writing. The quest for clarity about roles, relationships, and responsibilities is reflected in the vast number of written policies and procedures. However, any serious look at the language of these policies and procedures will suggest that language precision for *documentation*, rather than meaning, is generally the case.

The formal structure of Traditional Organizations includes the deliberate selection of employees based on needed knowledge, skills, and/or attitudes, with subsequent attention to their career development in service of the needs of the organization, followed by expectations for increased productivity and subsequent increased pay. Everyone knows the rules and is expected to follow them or suffer the various disciplinary consequences that are available in a hierarchy.

We believe that there are functionalist personality types, persons who are more likely to fit in Traditional Organizations than others. In Chapter 2, we introduced the possibility that the Myers-Briggs personality types can be related to the various paradigmatic perspectives. Persons described as *thinking–judging* (TJ), with their realism, organizing abilities, and command of the facts based on logical pragmatism, can be seen to be functionalist in their worldview. Their tendency for logic and analysis in their decision-making behaviors as well as their desire to work in a systematic, orderly manner in their interactions with the outer world places them squarely within a functionalist perspective. These personality types could be said to hold a traditional, functionalist, or hierarchical perspective. Persons holding this perspective would likely be comfortable being monitored and informed by those in charge and would welcome the structure and coordination provided by dependable and reliable leadership. This Myers-Briggs type needs to know how objects, events, and people work in order to create logic and provide the analysis of the outer world. Congruence and comfort are present with those preferring this approach when a sense of what is real is achieved and one's life and work experiences make sense.

Given the preferences of these personality types, there are certain aspects of Traditional Organizational structure and behavior that are decidedly congruent with their approaches to work. The presence of a clear division of labor, direct communication regarding giving and taking orders, along with incentives directly tied to work performance are important to the behavior and satisfaction of these personalities within Traditional Organizations. They expect their managers to be in charge and to take charge when necessary.

A match between personality type and organizational expectations in the Traditional Organization occurs when agreed-on special skills, knowledge, or behavior are focused on clearly stated organizational production goals. The match deepens when there is a belief in the efficacy of specializations regarding training and separate, independent work assignments as a way to be more productive. Match is complete when rules and rewards are clearly articulated and evenhandedly applied.

STANDARDS OF PRACTICE WITHIN TRADITIONAL ORGANIZATIONS

LANGUAGING IN TRADITIONAL ORGANIZATION

In recent years, the terms *assessment* and *diagnosis* have been used to approach data gathering about larger systems (organizations and communities) as much as they have been used in direct practice situations. An overview of the terms *assessment* and *diagnosis* as used in one field (social work) may help to clarify some of the challenges in the transfer of these concepts from small to larger systems, and will facilitate our examination of practice within Traditional Organizations and the others that follow.

The uniqueness of a social work approach to assessment of clients and their problems has been seen as its distinguishing professional characteristic (Kirk, Sirporin, & Kutchins, 1989, p. 295). Social work assessment has been described as multifaceted, client-in-situation centered, focused on problems in living, and nonpathological (Miller, 2001). Yet the terms *assessment* and *diagnosis* are often used interchangeably, causing some confusion over what the assessment process is.

The diagnosis–assessment differentiation debate may be at the base of the struggle of social work to develop into a full-fledged profession (Rodwell, 1987). Based on early criticism by Abraham Flexner (1915), that social work was not a profession because it was not scientific in its practices, much of the early efforts to characterize social work focused on creating a scientific approach to professional practice by absorbing the medical model of solving patients' problems through study, diagnosis, and treatment. A classic example of the profession's adaptation to the medical view of scientific rigor can be seen in Mary Richmond's work (1917), which she called *social diagnosis*. She attempted to demonstrate medical model rigor by using the language of a dominant profession, while simultaneously distinguishing social work diagnosis from medical diagnosis.

Diagnosis comes from Greek and means "to distinguish, discern, to learn to know, perceive" (*Oxford Dictionary*, p. 596). There are, however, discipline-specific definitions of this term. In medicine, *diagnosis* can mean "determination of the nature of a diseased condition; identification of a disease by careful investigation of its symptoms and history." From biology, the meaning is "distinctive characterization and precise terms" (*Oxford Dictionary*, p. 596). In the *NASW Dictionary* (Barker, 1999), *diagnosis* is defined as a "process of identifying a problem (social and mental, as well as medical) and underlying causes and formulating a solution" (p. 127). Barker underscores the strong medical implications of this definition and suggests that there is a preference among practitioners for the term *assessment*.

Miller (2001) clearly distinguishes between assessment and diagnosis by stating that *assessment* and *diagnosis* are not interchangeable, even though they have been used interchangeably in her profession of social work (see, for example, Goldstein, 1995; Hepworth, Rooney, Rooney, Strom-Gottfried & Larsen, 2006; Kirk, Siporin, & Kutchins, 1989; Rauch, 1993; Turner, 1994; Woods & Hollis, 2000). She sees assessment as an ongoing, continuous process, in that different tools may be used at different points, given the various roles professionals play. The initial assessment process provides the information for making a diagnosis (i.e., using the DSM-IV in clinical practice), which is folded into the ongoing reassessment process. Diagnosis from this perspective is a labeling process for the problems identified as a result of initial assessment and is reformulated as reassessment informs practice.

In the organization literature, similar struggles about the distinction between assessment and diagnosis exist, but unlike a definable controversy that impacts direct practice in social work, the struggle in organization practice appears to be simply a question of language usage. Even though some writers on organization recognize that the terms are often used interchangeably (see Lawler, Nadler, & Cammann, 1980; Seashore, Lawler, Mirvis, & Cammann, 1983), others distinguish between the concepts of assessment and diagnosis. Harrison and Shirom (1999) view assessments as more focused on specific programs or services, whereas diagnosis is designed to be a more systematic look at the entire organization. They point out that one can assess without diagnosing; in other words, one might know there is a problem but have no understanding of its underlying causes. Harrison (1994) suggests that during diagnosis the current state of an organization is compared to a preferred state. The diagnostic study is a search for ways to narrow the gap between the current and the desired state of affairs. However, this label is not static, because continuing reassessment refines and shapes diagnoses.

In this book, we borrow from both micro and macro practice to use the terms *assessment* and *diagnosis* as follows: **Assessment** is a process in which a person or group gathers information about a service, program, or organization. How wide the net is cast will depend on the purpose of the assessment. Some assessments may gather information on a single agency program, whereas others may examine an entire organization. The type of data collected and the method of collection will also depend on the reason one is undertaking an assessment. For functionalism, regardless of the theoretical perspective guiding the assessment methodology, diagnosis cannot be done well without first some elements of assessment occurring. From this perspective, diagnosis is taking assessment data and analyzing them into information that can be used as the basis of identifying problems, resolving issues, or enhancing organizational effectiveness. Assessment involves accurate data gathering or construction. **Diagnosis** occurs when data are understood and translated into information, so that problems and needs are labeled and analyzed.

Following assessment and diagnosis is planning. **Planning** is defined as preparing to resolve problems and address organizational needs. Regardless of the difficulties in distinguishing between diagnosis and assessment, there are commonalities in many of the skills used to perform the tasks of either professional action in large or smaller systems. The performance of these tasks is usually called *planned change* in Traditional Organizations. Professional judgment, information acquisition and processing, and critical thinking are essential skills for effectiveness in all phases of the assessment, diagnosis, planning, and planned change process.

Having examined the use of language for practice and the accompanying debates, we now turn to the specifics in a Traditional Organization. As you will see, assessment, diagnosis, planning, and intervention are viewed as stages used to approach the work in most Traditional Organizations. No matter the type of organization in which one practices, there will always be times when something needs to change. When change agents attempt to change something within the Traditional Organization, they typically will be expected to follow a non-emotional, rational process. Radical change or strategies that increase conflict are not well tolerated in Traditional Organizations. This suggests that assessment, diagnosis, and planning for deliberate, planned change will occur through the use of rational, linear decision making with passionate approaches being viewed as inappropriate.

Assessing Situations

In the Traditional Organization, assessment is viewed as a rational, beginning attempt to gather data about organizations, programs, clients, and any situation or problem that needs to change. Initial assessments are first-time, typically quantitative snapshots of a situation, to be followed by periodic reassessments in which the results of changes are identified. Assessment, then, is an ongoing process, important to the functionalist perspective because of the assumption that reality is above and beyond individual intuitive knowledge. Hard-and-concrete facts are collected because it is important to have as much objective information as possible before diagnosing the organizational or programmatic problem. Information systems that contain statistics on agency performance are important resources in the assessment process.

Given functionalism's predisposition to standardized measures, tools designed to assess organizations are welcomed. For example, a strategic planning guide that begins with the mission statement, moves to the external environment, identifies best practices, analyzes clients and stakeholders, assesses internal operations, and develops components of a plan (Austin & Solomon, 2000, p. 346), or a planned change model that begins with assessing all the components of the organization (Netting, Kettner, & McMurtry, 2008), or a management audit that examines all facets of the organization (Lewis, Lewis, Packard, & Souflee, 2001, pp. 331–337) are acceptable tools in Traditional Organizations. These tools offer the traditional leader a place to begin looking at what is happening in the organization or program so that a change process can begin.

Program data collected by staff offer another information source for managers and workers alike who want to assess an organization's progress or analyze a client's situation. Here again, the staff would use instruments that gather concrete facts and figures, highly valuing standardized tools, tested for reliability and validity, because they are considered to be as objective as possible. Numbers, not words, are preferred. Programs that fit well within Traditional Organizations will tend to keep field notes and qualitative data collection to a minimum, because these types of data are time consuming to collect and hard to code for translation into computer systems. They are more subjective than objective. Progress notes in traditional programs are written in behaviorally measurable terms so that an objective reviewer unfamiliar with the situation can quickly discern exactly what happened. If judgments are recorded in the assessment or progress note process, they are to be clearly flagged as personal or professional interpretations so as not to be confused with objective data. Methods selected to gather traditional assessment information should be well established and acceptable to members of the scientific community. For example, systematic quantitative data collection that can be computer analyzed is highly desirable.

Assessment, then, is a process of gathering data that can be translated by professionals into information and used in determining as objective a diagnosis as possible. It is also very important to use the same tools in order to ask the same questions in subsequent reassessments. In the assessment and reassessment process, it is also important to control relevant stakeholders to guard against bias and other "chatter" in the data. Although conflict is inevitable whenever anyone is assessing a problem situation, the Traditional Organization will prefer communication strategies that muffle conflict. For example, organizational change agents will attempt to co-opt unwilling stakeholders to be a part of the assessment process, perhaps shaping their responses toward "appropriateness" so that conflict can be kept to a minimum. Assurances will be made that there is no desire to make radical changes, only to assess the situation so that interventions compatible with the organization can be planned. In reality, who determines what is compatible once data are analyzed rests with those in positions of formal organizational power.

DIAGNOSING PROBLEMS

Logically, if accurate and reliable data are gathered, then professional judgment can be used to diagnose or label the problem or situation. Although it is recognized that assessment and diagnosis are ongoing, and will change as things change, there are practical reasons for labeling problems quickly without deep investigation or interpretation. For example, if an organization wants to maintain reimbursement from established funding sources, managers must be certain that all forms are filled out in their entirety before site reviewers from funding and regulatory bodies arrive to monitor files. If an assessment reveals that this is not being done, then the diagnosis may be that the program is out of compliance and must come into compliance in order to avoid funding consequences. Note that in other types of organizations, with different perspectives and organizational goals, the diagnosis might be that the restrictive policies of a funder might need to be changed into something more feasible for the organization to implement. This reframing or reconstruction of a problem is less likely to occur in Traditional Organizations due to commitments to following the rules and not questioning authority or in any way "biting the hand that feeds them."

Earlier we elaborated about how *diagnosis* has traditionally been a medical term, appropriated by other helping professionals as a method of gaining legitimacy. The term continues to be used today in more clinical circles, only recently being applied to organizations. Another term that historically has implied the labeling or diagnostic process in organizational settings is *problem definition and analysis*. If assessment is a data gathering process, then problem definition and analysis is the process of determining from those data what problem or problems need to be addressed. In the definitional/diagnostic process, analysis occurs because the organization leader/manager in the Traditional Organization is trying to examine the potential causes of the problem so that a plan for intervention can be designed.

In macro arenas (organizations and communities), planned change models have dominated the literature. For example, in a popular framework for understanding the problem and the target population, the first task is to identify the organizational condition. This is followed by reviewing the literature on the condition, problem, or opportunity; collecting supporting data; identifying relevant historical incidents; identifying barriers to problem resolution; and, then, determining whether the condition is a problem (Netting, Kettner, & McMurtry, 2008). This approach to diagnosis is very systematic and scientific, based on finding the concrete facts that will help in naming the problem and deciding why it exists.

Although assessment can be seen as a broadening exercise, attempting to gather as much knowledge as possible across domains (i.e., financial, physical, mental, social, economic, environmental, pragmatic), diagnosis in the Traditional Organization is a focusing or narrowing opportunity. Being able to label a problem or problems and then focus specifically on the accompanying issues makes planning more manageable. It is *reductionistic.* It reduces what is being considered to its simplest form. In the Traditional Organization, manageability is very important. For example, a diagnosis may require that the organizational process under study be placed on a flowchart so that there is a clear visual representation of what steps are expected. Each step is simplified and connected linearly to the next in a cause/consequence format. Creating flowcharts is an appreciated functionalist tool, grounded in the Taylorist classical tradition because it takes all the chatter from the environment and the data and reduces what is to be done to its simplest, most precise form—not just for assessment and diagnosis, but also for planning.

PLANNING INTERVENTIONS

In Traditional Organizations, the link between assessment, diagnosis, and planning is critically important. Once a diagnosis has been made, then planning must follow logically from what is known about intervening with organizations having the particular diagnosis. If the diagnosis changes, plans must be revised in order to reflect other interventions that fit with the new diagnosis. Similarly, in the process of reassessment, new data about an organization's situation must be considered in light of current diagnoses. A change in diagnosis will warrant a change in the plan. The inherent logic and linearity of the process is based in organismic systems theory.

Planning in Traditional Organizations has a long history in the Design, Planning, and Positioning schools described by Mintzberg, Ahlstrand, and Lampel (1998). You may recall from Chapter 2 how these approaches to planning are congruent with the assumptions of the functionalist perspective. From the Design School, strategies are viewed as deliberate and intentional, kept as simple as possible, and tailored to a situation. The Planning School views the strategies selected as composed of explicit steps, and the Positioning School reminds the planner to consider the environment in which one is planning. All three schools see the planning process as tied to the organizational structure, with the managers or leaders having control over final approval before the implementation process begins.

Most changes occur for organizational maintenance rather than fundamental change. The desire for broader scale, radical change may be entertained by some organizational members who are not satisfied with the conservatism of the Traditional Organization, but their voices are expressions of preference from a different paradigmatic perspective. What is most often heard in Traditional Organization hallways are statements like, "If it's not broken, then why fix it?" or "We've tried that before and it didn't work" or "If we're going to make a change, let's be sure we know all the implications of what we are planning." One of the criticisms of this perspective on organizing is that those holding this view are slow to change, making rapid responses to changing environments almost impossible to achieve.

An excellent program planning model for use in Traditional Organizations has been developed by Kettner, Moroney, and Martin (2008). Called an effectiveness-based approach, this model begins with problem analysis and needs assessment, and then moves to planning, designing, and tracking interventions. Grounded in systems theory, the model is widely used in schools of social work throughout the country to prepare students to design outcome-based programs. Kettner, Moroney, and Martin (2008) explain why their model comes from a functionalist perspective by using three examples. The first example focuses on the political economy as a factor contributing to unemployment. They explain that if the program planner attempted to address capitalism as the cause of unemployment, "proposed solutions would be likely to involve a radical transformation of the existing system or at least its modification. Although the analysis can be theoretically and technically correct, it is unlikely that a planner or administrator at the local level will be in a position to change the system, whether it is a form of capitalism or socialism" (p. 102). They conclude that it is important to recognize these larger systems problems, but also to accept that they are not within the purview or control of the local human service agency. Therefore, a planner may design a program to provide incentives for unemployed persons within the local community to find jobs, but she would be naive to think she and her collaborators will tackle capitalism as an oppressive system.

In their statements, Kettner, Moroney, and Martin (2008) explain the distinctive difference between the Traditional Organization and the Social Change Organization (elaborated on in Chapters 5 and 6). The Traditional Organization is focused on incremental, controllable change so that social order and homeostasis can be established or restored. In the Traditional Organization, having knowledge that there are preconditions that set up problems to be addressed does not mean that one has to tackle those preconditions. Not only are they outside the purview of the organization, but they are rife with conflict. The Traditional Organization plans programs that are built on consensus, that are designed to address problems that can be controlled, and that move toward establishing or reestablishing a sense of order. Gradual change is seen as the preferred change here. In the next several chapters, we will investigate approaches that see change quite differently.

PRODUCING PRODUCTS AND OUTCOMES

Products in Traditional Organizations called *organizational outputs* and *human service outcomes* are the quality-of-life changes for participants that have occurred as a result. Products and outcomes are highly valued in Traditional Organizations. The current push for outcome measurement is very compatible with the perspectives held by Traditional Organizations.

In designing programs in Traditional Organizations, one always starts by defining the problem, for it is the rational, problem-solving process that drives traditional programs. "The rational approach views the organization as an efficient machine to attain specific goals" (Hasenfeld, 2000, p. 91). Well-designed traditional programs are ones in which the problem is carefully defined and the causes of the problem are analyzed. A complete search of the literature and relevant studies will reveal what is known about these causes and will then logically lead to decisions about effective interventions. If interventions do not work, it is likely that the problem has been ill defined or that the causes were not well established. Rarely is the linear model of thinking and decision making questioned. There is a generally held assumption that problem definition leads to the identification of problem causation, and intervention is based on the definition and cause. The Traditional Organization seeks to link problems to interventions to outcomes. Given a specific problem, the intervention is directed at what is understood to be the problem's cause in order to eliminate (or at least ameliorate) the problem.

This brings us to the implications for practice in Traditional Organizations. In the section that follows, we will examine the relevance of understanding the cultural values and characteristics, the roles and relationships, and the standards of practice in human service organizations based on functionalist assumptions.

IMPLICATIONS FOR PRACTICE IN TRADITIONAL ORGANIZATIONS

There are aspects of the functionalist perspective that are congruent with the values of the social work profession and others that present challenges, particularly to its social justice mission. One of the greatest challenges is that this perspective forces a position of *ethical absolutism*. This means there must be one best way of defining what constitute the acceptable core values of professional organization practice. Further, ethical absolutism means starting with the organization within its own context and perspective.

Moving into unique and different ways is impossible or at least professionally unacceptable, because there is only one true best way of proceeding with all organizations.

Iglehart and Becerra (1995) criticize functionalist approaches to practice, because students learn to attempt less conflictual tactics first before moving to more aggressive methods when trying to address larger systems change. They also criticize these approaches for taking the middle course, avoiding controversy, and supporting determinism (p. 137). Iglehart and Becerra are critical of those practice approaches that avoid addressing larger societal issues. Basically, they are critical of Traditional Organizations because aggressive, radical change is purposefully avoided in favor of incremental modifications of the status quo.

There are, however, some aspects of the Traditional Organization that are congruent with the social work and other helping professions. From bureaucracy, the preference for specialization based on professional training and practice expertise, career orientation, and upward mobility, and valuing abilities on the job more than who one knows, all fit well with the concept of professionalism. But the bureaucratic approach is also impersonal and inattentive to the individual in context. Further, the possibility of attention to procedure over effectiveness on the job means that human service workers in a bureaucratic environment might not meet the real needs of those they intend to serve. Instead, because of what is rewarded in a hierarchical structure, practitioners may move to unthinking compliance with rules rather than critical analysis of the organization's policies and procedures vis-à-vis their clients.

The "scientific" approach supported by theories congruent with Traditional Organizations makes sense in social work service delivery and programming as a means of documenting effects and improving practice. The present focus on accountability and outcome measurement for reimbursement from managed-care entities or for financial support by other funding sources may be answered by the rigorous designs of interventions and valid and reliable measures called for by functionalist assumptions. But the fact that most program evaluations produce no significant findings suggests that quantitative measures may not be the only way of knowing what really results from a social work intervention.

However, the influence of management by objectives (MBO) and the focus on strategic planning that dominated organizational thinking in the late twentieth century makes annual plans an expected part of human service organizations. Functionalist support of outcome measures is good and useful, but the narrow definition of what can be assumed to represent quality results may tend to overlook the process of the intervention. Focus on outputs and outcomes has helped Traditional Organizations become more proactive, but this proactivity continues to assume rationality and an ability to control what goes on in an organization. Since there may be other dimensions overlooked in a functionalist perspective, lack of goal achievement may not indicate lack of success or incompetence on the part of practitioners. It may only mean that the wrong aspects of the organization are being investigated or that the assumption of rationality among organizational members does not hold.

Off targeting of what should have attention in organizational studies is a potential problem in Traditional Organizations. This is especially true for organizations favoring a social-work-values perspective. The social justice target of the profession may suffer in this type organization. For example, in the hierarchical structure of Traditional Organizations, women and minorities may be disadvantaged in the expected movement from lower to upper levels of the organization. Given the biases within the structure, many capable people who look, speak, and act differently from the traditional administrators of organizations may experience what is known as the **glass ceiling**, where the upper reaches of the organization are visible but not attainable. This may be due to some of the negative influences of early human relations theory, where power and decisions were always intended to remain at the top with no empowerment in the ranks, just control for productivity. This leaves the potential for oppression, exploitation, and dehumanization of those in the lower portions of the organization. Even though there is attention to personal and social relations in a traditional approach, women and minorities continue to be disadvantaged in Traditional Organizations due to lack of access. This leads to their exclusion from the important networks that serve to open opportunities for promotion and advancement.

Table 4.3 provides an overview of the practice characteristics in Traditional Organizations.

CONCLUSION

The Traditional Organization is committed to the discovery of the one best way of conducting assessment and diagnosis to achieve the one best way for change. This sets up the expectation that discovery of a generalizable truth is possible and so, too, is control of planning and intervention. When the unexpected happens somewhere in the process, the assumption may be that there is a lack of competence at the bottom of this absence of control. In actuality, it might be that an inappropriate theory or paradigm is being used to guide the decision-making process around assessment, diagnosis, and planning.

What the organizational leader does gain from functionalist assumptions is the promise of valid and reliable instruments to "norm" organizational structure and behavior. The leader gains outcome measurement tools to aid in response to the productivity pressures of outside funders, but this comes with the risk of lack of effectiveness in the outcomes when

Table 4.3

Practice Characteristics in Traditional Organizations

Practice Element	Characteristics
Assessment	Systematic data gathering is a first step in addressing any situation.
	Standardized, quantitative forms, guides, or tools are helpful in the assessment process.
	Assessments provide hard, concrete, objective data that can be used by professionals to diagnosis the situation or problem.
	Data collection methods should be consistent.
Diagnosis or Problem Definition and Analysis	Diagnosis flows from objective assessment data.
	With reassessments, diagnoses may change.
	Diagnosis requires consideration of objective data known about identified problems.
Planning	Planning follows logically from diagnosis or problem definition.
	Planning is incremental in its orientation.
	A change in diagnosis will warrant a change in the plan of action.
	In planning, preconditions are recognized, but the goal is to design realistic interventions.
Incremental Change	Interventions may be at the individual, group, organization, or organizational unit level.
	There is a best or better intervention identified.
	Change-from-within tactics (collaboration and campaign), rather than contest (conflict), are preferred.
	The goal is to intervene in the situation so that homeostasis is reestablished.

the significance standard in statistics is used as the only measure of effectiveness. Structural change is not the expectation from this perspective. Cost effectiveness is.

When adopting this perspective for assessment, diagnosis, planning, and gradual change, the practitioner loses a view of what is unique to the organization and its members in the organizational environment. Some of the subtle influences regarding processes are not captured in the data collection for decision making. This happens because there is little room for consideration of the more qualitative, affective, intuitive aspects of organizational life due to the rigor expectations that are assumed to be necessary for "knowing."

For the human service leader, there is another serious challenge. This perspective and the theories within it offer no help in assessment, diagnosis, planning, and incremental change in attending to the special opportunities and challenges provided by that which is different from the norm. There is little if any attention to cultural differences. Further, there is no room for the chaotic and the unexpected, which seem to permeate today's organizational life. The presence of chaos or unpredictability is attributed to incompetence in the administration, the program design, the organizational structure, or the personnel, when chaos might instead be the norm for contemporary organizations both here and in other parts of the world.

We now turn to a second type organization—the Social Change Organization. You will soon see that this organization has some assumptions in common with functionalism. Just as important for organization practitioners, however, are the differences in how change is viewed.

DISCUSSION QUESTIONS

1. Why is planned change so valued in Traditional Organization practice? What paradigmatic and cultural assumptions support it? What benefits are gained by engaging in planned change? What might be potential problems?

2. What type(s) of advocacy are typically performed in Traditional Organization practice? What type of tactics might be most congruent with advocacy or change efforts in Traditional Organizations?

3. Given the preferred structure and management style in Traditional Organizations, what are the challenges and opportunities for your own practice? How would working in a Traditional Organization fit with your comfort zone?

4. Review the characteristics of Traditional Organizations in Table 4.1. Where are the potential strengths and challenges for you as a practitioner in this type organization? Are there other characteristics that you would add to this table? If so, what would they be and why would you add them?

5. Characterize the roles and relationships that are expected in a Traditional Organization. How do these fit with the practice standards and expectations related to managing and being managed in this type organization? Reflect on what the meaning of all this might be for you as a developing practitioner. (This reflection could become part of a regular journaling exercise.)

6. As a practitioner in a Traditional Organization, what would you expect the challenges and opportunities might be in relationship to the environment in which this type organization operates? What

would you assume the standards and expectations to be vis-à-vis the environment?

7. In reviewing the expectations regarding assessment, diagnosis, planning, and interventions in a Traditional Organization, what do you foresee as the strengths and challenges when the organization is engaged in a multicultural environment? What might be social justice issues and opportunities?

8. From the standpoint of a professional practitioner in a Traditional Organization, what are the costs and benefits of the preferred manner for evaluation of practice and performance within the organization?

9. Going back to the Washington County Office on Aging case example in the beginning of Part I, use the content in this chapter to conduct an organizational analysis looking at both organization structure and practice expectations. What insights are gained from your analysis?

PART II

CONSCIOUSNESS RAISING FOR CHANGE

I N PART II, we seek to understand practice within Social Change Organizations with identity and goals of collective change through *consciousness raising*. Ways in which power and politics are operationalized within Social Change Organizations are examined, along with the risks that may be involved when the stakes are high and when incremental change is not the object. Implications of the promotion of radical transformation of oppressive (often traditional) systems are considered for both service providers and service recipients. The collective transformational challenges presented by organizing goals seeking to be congruent with a radical structuralist perspective will be the focus of Chapter 5. Chapter 6 is designed to help the reader understand standards of behavior and practice in Social Change Organizations with goals of consciousness raising for change. Transformative change that constitutes fit within this perspective is investigated. Part II reveals the paradoxical nature of practicing in an organization that is so tied to collective initiatives that its goal is to empower entire groups and whole communities at all costs without focusing on the complexities of diversity. Starting with the *radical structuralist* paradigmatic perspective and moving to the *market culture*, attention in this part of the text will be given to the values, preferences, and decision-making strategies that are congruent with organizations having consciousness raising for change goals.

In Chapter 5, theories derived from assumptions that collective change or transformation is ultimately important are discussed. Comparisons are made with incremental change entities in order to highlight how Social Change Organizations are tied to power and politics theories, critical theory, radical branches of feminist theory, system theories (morphogenic, factional, and catastrophic types), and population ecology and transorganizational theories. It is important to note that power and politics and critical theories are also influenced by the Radical Humanist Paradigm and will be touched on again later in the chapters that investigate organizations and their practices from that perspective.

Additional discussion of the differences in theoretical emphasis between organizational perspectives is designed to illustrate just how far apart traditional and radical change organizations are in their thinking and theorizing. The recognition of diverse types of systems theory that treat conflict entirely differently than the status quo forms a provocative back-drop against which to explore the nature and consequences of organiza-tions determined to transform community and societal structures. The chapter closes with a consideration of the Social Change Organization as a viable organizational model for radical change. Also explored will be the costs and benefits of radical structuralist assumptions within this organi-zational perspective.

Continuing use of the lens of strategic management and the roles of managers and leaders within this more radical approach and the issues of organizing within organizational structures seeking collective change are considered in Chapter 6. The idea of well-conceived structures for organizing is introduced as a potential means of organizing multitudes of individuals to work toward an agreed-upon universal cause. Conflict in these type organizations is also examined for transformation potential. Organizational practice seeking consciousness raising for change often means involvement with large-scale advocacy organizations or entire social movements. Special considerations will be highlighted when organizational members seek to alter the status quo, replacing a tradi-tional version of universal truth with their own alternative version of truth.

We offer this perspective as a second consideration of multiple perspec-tives on organizing and practicing with the hope that the critical thinking skills, the growing self-awareness, and the increased understanding of the need for ethnic competence in practice might allow the reader to engage in an even-handed examination of the potential of practice in such a radical, alternative perspective. As an aid in moving away from the typical view of human service agencies to an expanded view, end-of-chapter discussion questions focus on the challenges of transforming groups within controlled organizational boundaries that challenge the status quo at the societal or structural levels.

To begin our examination of organizations that are dedicated to con-sciousness raising and social change, we offer the following case example. In the next two chapters, you will see in detail the paradoxical nature of organizational structure and behavior when goals are more communal than individual and when the call for change is foremost in the minds of members.

The Consumer-Directed Advocacy Agency

It had been a hard fight to get legislation in place for a consumer-directed initiative. David Lyons had organized the effort through the Consumer-Directed Advocacy Agency, established a few years earlier. He and a large cohort of consumer advocates had recruited volunteers from around the state, training recruits in the methods of community organizing and legislative advocacy. They had a cause related to empowering consumers and they believed in it to the fullest extent. The commitment, dedication, and compassion of this tireless network of advocates were something to behold.

David was part of the disabilities community and proud of it. Having lost his leg in an industrial accident, now almost a decade ago, he had suddenly found himself as a member of a community about which he knew very little. His physical therapist had been incredibly helpful and had introduced him to a number of other men and women who were trying to find a way to live in a world that was not always sensitive to disabilities. Recently he was meeting young, vital veterans who were coming home from the war with devastating wounds. The push for assistive technologies could not keep up with all the needs.

But what David had discovered in his own journey to regain his health and a sense of dignity was that the service delivery system was incredibly paternalistic in how it rationed services and connected him with personal attendants who could help him perform instrumental activities of daily living. Lying on his back in various rehab facilities, he had accessed the Internet to locate consumer groups who were pushing for change. He found that the consumer-directed movement was struggling against the status quo of a system in which professional providers served as the link between personal attendants and persons with disabilities. Many of the providers he encountered were used to serving frail elders who needed someone to live in with them. To him it was obvious that these providers were highly protective of these dependent consumers. They carried these strategies to new clients needing service, not even considering the fact that many persons needing personal attendants now were actually in good health other than for the disabilities they had. Providers were taught to be benevolent, to serve as experts, and to oversee the connections between consumers and attendants.

David had wondered over and over again—*What happened to personal choice? Why can't I hire my own attendant? Why do I need a middle person or provider to make the link? Why is the system so damned set on controlling this situation in the name of protection and safety?*

As soon as he had recovered to the point that he could return to his apartment, he was mobilizing other people with disabilities to take on the provider system. He recognized that some older persons and some people with disabilities might need a more protective, less market-oriented approach. However, he knew that he and many others desperately wanted a sense of empowerment so that they could take hold and be as independent as possible in a world that did not always see them as having the abilities to work and support themselves. Having access to the resources one needed, in this case personal attendants, could make all the difference.

When David and 12 of his friends started the Consumer-Directed Advocacy Agency, they had no idea how much interest they would attract. Not only were people with disabilities drawn to their cause, but personal care attendants were triumphant because this provided the possibility that they could directly contract with consumers without being subordinated to provider agencies. Fees between consumers and attendants could be negotiated between two parties, without a third party taking a cut for "coordination." To his mind, they succeeded in transforming the structure of the service network, probably because all the stakeholders wanted the change. It was a win-win for everyone.

Things changed when David began to disseminate his empowerment model agency to other consumer initiatives in neighboring states. Their first few years were spent almost entirely assisting with the writing of legislation based on model statutes, in lobbying for sponsorship, and then testifying in front of any committee that would hear their plea. They worked within the system. Probably because of that, donations from disabilities groups, combined with a series of fundraising events, provided enough money to keep the agency going until a foundation grant underwrote operating costs for a five-year stretch.

After a while, there were rips in the fabric of the coalition. Their structure was tight and organized, with committees dedicated to each piece of legislation, and a committee composed of grassroots advocates who set up guidelines for consumers and attendants in the negotiation process as well as public relations materials on what it meant to be truly consumer-directed. Sometimes, they were assailed by local providers who saw the agency as being too aggressive and as advocating for autonomy over beneficence. When this happened, the coalition splintered about ways to respond, though all agreed they were advocating for social justice in the form of disability rights. Some members wished to exhibit radical resistance, rather than trying to reason things into consensus. This really started happening when formerly able-bodied vets became vocal organizers. They would not put up with the "put downs," and they organized several sit-ins on the steps of recalcitrant legislative bodies in several states.

That got them some good press related to responses to veterans; but concern started being expressed by multiple consumer protection advocates who were not convinced that the agency should have any say in the political process. Externally, the agency was often tagged as a renegade or maverick organization, trying to change the system too soon, too fast, while internally there was talk of "war." Most of the members were coming to the conclusion that changes needed to be made by any means necessary—and some of the members were quite familiar with a variety of means that David would never consider.

It was quite chaotic for a time, with threats going back and forth. David felt he was under siege for wanting to take a more moderate approach, all along knowing that incrementalism would not replace the service structure in his own lifetime. Finally, according to the other advocates in the organization, including the Board of Directors, David "got with the program" and agreed to be involved in much more aggressive action as long as it was peaceful and did not lead to violence. Some organization members were not happy with this directive, but agreed to follow his rules since even passive action was better than trying to reason with those in power. The general assessment was that the only way to transform the system was to match power with power to force change. A series of training sessions were undertaken for all the members and whomever else they could get to join them. People were well prepared to suffer the consequences of the pacifist actions envisioned, even if that meant being arrested. They even created a bankroll to support legal defense and maintenance needs of those arrested and their families who might be placed at risk. They were ready to mount their alternative assault. The plan was to embarrass the legislature in all the states where reason had not served to change the system. The intervention occurred with military precision in each state. Hundreds of people with disabilities, a "rainbow coalition" of people in need, sat together quietly on the steps of each state capitol. They stayed there for a week, refusing to leave until the service delivery formula was changed. They locked themselves together, so that when the police came to move them away it was impossible to disentangle all the wheel chairs, motorized vehicles, and assistive devices. Of course, the media was there from the beginning, because some media insiders were longtime friends of some of the disabled vets. In every state, it was the same—front-page pictures and headlines about how we ought to be ashamed.

David and his colleagues had banded together as a collective and pushed forward with the desire to raise consciousness within each state about the rightness of having people with disabilities be in control of their lives. Some of their members were arrested, and that provided a great opportunity for more consciousness raising and outrage, among both members and the public in general. Their tight structure and righteous indignation bonded them together so they could power down the various legislative bodies. Bills were introduced everywhere they had staged sit-ins. The Consumer-Directed Advocacy Agency had become a formidable force for the free market economy and consumer's rights. The questions then became: What would be the target of their next radical action? Was such a tightly structured organization with David in charge really necessary?

CHAPTER 5

Social Change Organizations

I N CHAPTER 2, we introduced the Radical Structuralist Paradigm and Social Change Organizations. In this chapter, we expand on our original description by focusing on what goes into the structure of organizations holding consciousness raising for change goals for organizing. We begin by examining themes found in radical structuralist thinking and the assumptions that flow from the Radical Structuralist Paradigm, resulting in the radical change goals of what we are calling Social Change Organizations. Following this paradigmatic grounding, the major organizational theories that can be said to fit within this perspective are identified. To add to our investigation in Part II, we will draw on the Consumer-Directed Advocacy Agency as an example of a Social Change Organization. We close Chapter 5 with a critical analysis, so that the reader is left with the ability to judge what is gained and what is given up when approaching organizations from a radical structuralist worldview. We then transition to Chapter 6, which focuses on social change culture and rather radical behavioral theories that guide the standards for practice in organizations with social change and consciousness-raising goals.

As with the other organizations with differing paradigmatic perspectives and goals, the Social Change Organization is a prototype. We recognize that in day-to-day experience, it is not always so easy to classify organizations. As with organizations based on assumptions from other paradigms that may have staff members and contain units that operate under different assumptions, the same may be true of Social Change Organizations. Some of this was beginning to be evident in our case example. When this happens, staff may experience paradoxes and discomfort as differing assumptions clash around what is "right" and what should be done. Having read this chapter, it is our hope that the reader will understand why radical structural assumptions about organizational goals may collide with status-quo-oriented goals. We hope to set the stage so that later it will also be clear that both Social Change Organizations with radical change goals and Entrepreneurial Organizations with individual empowerment goals seek radical change, but differ in what they think is necessary and possible.

For example, David Lyons suffered a tremendous blow to his ability to ambulate and to do what he had done in the past after he lost his leg. He was certainly bent on becoming empowered as an individual, but he also realized the potential of collective action in getting change accomplished. By founding the Consumer-Directed Advocacy Agency, he was able to mobilize others to work as a network for systemic change. By raising consciousness in the disability and aging communities, this network of advocates was able to effect broader scale change. But some of the organization members continued to work separately for their own empowerment by initiating change on their own. It was, however, through collective effort that structural social change was forced into the system, thus representing a radical structuralist perspective.

Recall from Chapter 2 that in this type of organization the goals of consciousness raising for social change are congruent with the radical structuralist worldview. Commitment to a cause and collective action come from a context in which **cause advocacy** is to be pursued and conflict is inevitable (even embraced). The Social Change Organization works in a tightly structured, rules-governed, focused manner designed deliberately and powerfully to push toward targets of change. The paradoxical idea is that through the use of structure, transformed structures to better serve needs can result. Figure 5.1 is a reminder of where the Social Change Organization fits within the paradigms introduced in Chapter 2.

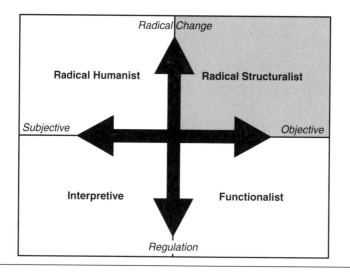

Figure 5.1 Burrell and Morgan's Paradigmatic Framework. *Source:* Adapted from Burrell and Morgan (1979). *Sociological paradigms and organizational analysis.* Aldershot, England: Ashgate. Figure 3.1, p. 22. Used by permission.

RADICAL STRUCTURALIST THEMES

Some of the more conflict-oriented theories to understanding organizational dynamics are based on assumptions that create the boundaries of the Radical Structuralist Paradigm. From this perspective, the study of organizations holds assumptions regarding the possibility and desirability of rationality and realism. This approach is very ideologically driven, oriented to traditional science assumptions that control and shape organizational study. Here organizational variables are carefully defined and operationalized with an expectation of rigor derived from natural science on how one selects samples and collects and analyzes data. Further, there is the expectation that research will be objective, and oriented to prediction and control, so that results can be generalized. This may sound familiar, because both radical structuralists and functionalists are objectivist in their approach. The major departure from functionalism involves the purpose of organizational study. In addition to the obvious expectations about controlled procedures for knowing and understanding organizations, there is an expectation that the consequence of knowledge building is change, including radical or revolutionary change, which also must be measurable.

The radical structuralist perspective is principally positivistic, requiring that propositions be tested or built according to rules of formal logic and based on methods derived from the natural sciences; however, there is a values sensitivity that also frames organizational studies. From this perspective, the choice of a value system tends to empower or enfranchise certain persons while disenfranchising and disempowering others. When one takes a position and that position is accepted, the person is empowered, while those holding another position are left without a strong position. They are disenfranchised or disempowered. The role of inquiry into organizations, then, is to determine the gainers and the losers related to the problem selected for study. This makes any inquiry from this perspective a political act. It is a political act because the purpose of study is to understand the consequences of situations, thus creating transformative knowledge. Knowledge is transformative when participants' awareness has been raised to a level of **true consciousness.** It is with this consciousness that participants (assumed to be oppressed people) will act to transform the situation under investigation in the direction of more empowerment, even if forcing the transformation is necessary. It is assumed that this transformation can be predicted and controlled because decisions are based on true consciousness aimed at liberation. In this way, radical structuralism differs from functionalism regarding the perception about how change occurs. Functionalism sees acceptable change happening incrementally. Radical structuralism holds that substantive, permanent alternative structures are achieved only through transformation of the type that usually occurs as a result of revolutionary actions. These actions need not be violent, but they will be groundbreaking and structure shattering.

For example, in the Consumer-Directed Advocacy Agency, David Lyons led a committed group of disabilities advocates who believed that their role was to alter the system, not interject disabled persons into the existing system. These advocates were incensed at the provider network that sought to tell them how to get the care they needed. They felt that this network posed a barrier, rather than serving as a vehicle for helping people. Their coalition was cause oriented and powerfully unstoppable. Righteous indignation and implied threats caused a change in the status quo. They were able to shatter the currently accepted service structure.

The methods to achieve true consciousness in the organization are not necessarily as **interventionist,** or controlling, as those used in the Functionalist Paradigm to define and control the organization. Research methods consist of dialogue where participants (sometimes including the researcher) come to a common point of view. Sometimes this is a point of view about the interpretation of traditional organizational research findings; sometimes it is a point of view regarding their common organizational experiences; sometimes it is related to outside forces. It is assumed that through a dialectical process in which conflicting views are aired, agreement can occur around the features of the organization under investigation; judgments can be made together about what can and should be altered, thus setting the stage for concerted, sometimes aggressive, efforts at transformation. This dialectical process happened both internally and externally in our case example. There and in any radical organization, beyond the expected elements of natural science rigor that must be exhibited for the research to be considered scientifically sound, there is an additional rigor expectation: Did a transformation result from the process? In the case of David's organization it did—for now.

Given a radical structuralist perspective, critical thinking and analytic questioning of arguments and methods within the organization are acceptable sources of knowledge. Theoretical reasoning can come into question, as can the procedures for selecting, collecting, and evaluating traditional empirical data. Everything within the organizational context can be open to scrutiny from this perspective, based on the attention to social regulation and unequal distribution of power. This was precisely what caused David to change his approach.

Even though human nature from the radical structuralist perspective is a deterministic product of the environment, there remains human possibility. The recognition that circumstance and the environment shape human nature is mitigated through consciousness raising. There is an assumed power/knowledge connection such that human nature reaches the realm of ultimate possibilities through understanding how boundaries and structures are formed and how they serve to limit. The research participants, in a kind of participatory action research process, become cognizant of the elements within and outside the organization that serve to disempower and disenfranchise. Understanding develops about how individuals participate in the creation of oppression and oppressive structures, both consciously and unconsciously. This understanding only comes through struggle in the face of forces that pervade common sense and become part of the ordinary way of seeing the world (Angus, 1992).

The theme here is that people need to become conscious of a situation that seems to be normal and acceptable but that is actually oppressive, just as in the case example providers needed to see how oppressive their actions were with the newly disabled. There, as well as in most situations, it is difficult to see past common practices to real, if not intended, effects. Struggles will ensue as intended and unintended consequences are highlighted. Working for conditions in which critical reflection is fostered as part of the organizing process usually also requires a struggle. It is assumed that there are forces at work to maintain the dominant order as a universal and unalterable existence. For radical structuralism, it is only through the dialectical struggle that the advantaged will be forced to engage in the full range of options for consideration so that all, including the marginalized and disadvantaged, can reach their potential. In the Consumer-Directed Advocacy case, the provider network was holding to traditional ways of delivering services that were supported and maintained statutorily. The consumers created public crises and forced structural transformation.

ASSUMPTIONS OF THE RADICAL STRUCTURALIST PARADIGM

A radical structuralist perspective holds a commitment to radical change, emancipation, and potentiality. This is assumed to be achievable through an analysis of structural conflict, modes of domination, contradiction, and deprivation. This perspective shares with functionalism realism, positivism, and determinism, which produces nomothetic (rule-governed) understanding of the social world.

In both Chapters 2 and 3, we reviewed four terms that define objectivism. We repeat this (see Box. 5.1) once again so that the reader will have a handy reference for review in understanding radical structuralism.

A radical structuralist perspective assumes that truth is determined by the larger environment, but because the paradigm sits at the intersection of objectivism and radical change, it assumes that having knowledge derived from rigorous study is insufficient unless that knowledge is *used to make change happen*. Radical structuralism rejects being satisfied with knowledge for knowledge's sake in favor of knowledge as a means of consciousness raising and transformational change. Different from functionalism and

---

Box 5.1

OBJECTIVISM: DEFINING TERMS

Realism (external)
Positivism (hard, real, tangible)
Determinism (people are products of their environments)
Nomothetic (use methods of natural science to test hypotheses in accord with
    scientific rigor)

Source: Adapted from Burrell and Morgan (1979). *Sociological paradigms and organizational analysis.* Aldershot, England: Ashgate. Figure 1.1, p. 3. Used by permission.

Box 5.2

CONCERNS OF THE RADICAL CHANGE PERSPECTIVE

1. Radical change
2. Structural conflict
3. Modes of domination
4. Contradiction
5. Emancipation
6. Deprivation
7. Potentiality

Source: Adapted from Burrell and Morgan (1979). *Sociological paradigms and organizational analysis.* Aldershot, England: Ashgate. Table 2.2, p. 18. Used by permission.

---

related to radical humanism, organizations with consciousness raising for social change goals embrace conflict to generate radical change through crisis.

In Box 5.2, the concerns of a radical change perspective are summarized.

Radical structuralism offers a different way to approach organizational studies. Instead of looking at structural and behavioral relationships to understand mechanisms of organizing, the radical structuralist begins with a critical stance oriented toward investigating exploitation, modes of domination, repression, unfairness, uneven power relationships, and the communication and thinking patterns that engender and maintain them within structural and behavioral relationships. The radical structuralist perspective engenders activism aimed at overthrow of organizational limits for classes of organizational participants.

This expectation of radical change based on critical analysis represents a challenge to traditional views about organizations and organizational behavior. No more is there authoritative control for disciplined and

---

Box 5.3

FROM THE OBJECTIVIST PERSPECTIVE ASSUMPTIONS OF THE RADICAL
STRUCTURALIST PARADIGM

1. Reality is above and beyond individual knowledge.
2. Knowledge about social reality is hard and concrete.
3. People are products of their environments; they are shaped.
4. Natural science methods can be applied to the study and understanding of
   social reality.

FROM THE RADICAL CHANGE PERSPECTIVE

5. Society is characterized by deep-seated structural conflict, modes of domination, and even contradiction.
6. Knowledge for change and action should be the goal.
7. Conflict, rather than consensus, is important.

Source: Adapted from Burrell and Morgan (1979), Chapter 1.

---

productive behavior. Revolutionary action is the expectation. It also presents a challenge for research in organizations where structure and control
of results is expected at all levels of organizational life. The degree of
difficulty, as well as the opportunities that this perspective represent, may
be made clear by looking at Box 5.3, in which all assumptions of this
paradigm are viewed together.

This box provides a summary of the basic assumptions of the Radical
Structuralist Paradigm. Keep these assumptions in mind, and return to this
box as often as you need to see how many of the theories used by human
service practitioners and others in organizations fit within this paradigm.
As you read about the theories highlighted in this chapter, Box 5.3 provides
a reminder of their underlying assumptions. It is also a way of testing the
degree to which organizations with which you are familiar could be said to
fit within this paradigm. You should recognize these assumptions in the
Consumer-Directed Advocacy Agency case.

SOCIAL CHANGE ORGANIZATION THEORIES SUPPORTING CONSCIOUSNESS-RAISING GOALS

For further grounding in this paradigmatic perspective and the organizational goals derived from this perspective, we will now investigate the
major organization and organizational behavioral theories that can be
placed within this paradigm, given their assumptions about organizational
structure and organizational life. Though there are as yet few organizational theorists identified with this perspective, those who do hold these

views are part of a broader critical tradition. This tradition includes philosophers who have challenged the status quo and supported those who are marginalized so that their voices are no longer suppressed. The work from this position is in response to social conditions of domination and is motivated by a desire to provide mechanisms for a more inclusive dialogue and dialectic. This dialectic is assumed to produce a radically different future for all. From this philosophical and theoretical stance, a presentation of difference, a different perspective, and the resultant disruption of the current dominant discourse opens the way for contested or subjugated knowledge to serve as a medium for the creation of societies and organizations that are free from domination (Alvesson & Deetz, 1996). When new voices are allowed to be heard, new ideas create opportunities for a freer structure for organizations and society. The anti-domination themes, which include advocacy, grassroots activities, and radical reform, will become clear as we look at the radical structuralist theories and then move in Chapter 6 to understanding the culture of organizations, practices, and personality types that are compatible with this perspective.

In Chapter 2, we introduced a number of major perspectives on organization theory identified by Shafritz, Ott, and Lang (2005). Several schools of thought, categorized differently by different writers, emanate from the assumptions of radical structuralism and lend insight into the way in which Social Change Organizations embrace change. These are:

- Systems theory
- Population ecology theory
- Power and politics theories
- Radical feminist theory
- Critical theories
- Postmodern theories

Several ideas seem to pervade the theories of interest here. First, organizations are not considered in isolation, but in relationship to total environmental contexts. Second, these theories are attentive to structure, but not just of organizations. They include interest in the configurations of social relationships even at the class level that create totalities separate from and independent of the individuals' consciousness of them. A third important idea is that of *contradiction* seen at various levels of organizational structure and behavior. Contradictions include the hope that oppressive structures contain the seeds of their own destruction in a radical sense. Contradictions also exist between various organizational goals and individual needs, in class conflicts or the contradictions between technology and humanity. A fourth idea is *crisis*, where change comes through crisis of a political, economic, or emotional nature and serves as a point of transformation from one type of totality, one type of social structure, to another more inclusive one.

We begin our theory discussion with certain types of systems theories. Although systems theory was originally introduced in the Functionalist Paradigm, there are some schools of systems theory that fit well within the Radical Structuralist Paradigm.

SYSTEMS THEORY

When we examined systems theory in Chapter 3, different analogies used by social scientists to depict social systems were highlighted. Whereas mechanical and organismic analogies of systems theory are tied to functionalist assumptions, *morphogenic, factional,* and *catastrophic* analogies are based in the Radical Structuralist Paradigm. Table 5.1 provides a reminder of the assumptions in these three versions of open-systems theory.

Unlike mechanical and organismic analogies, those within the Radical Structuralist Paradigm focus on the dynamic and changing nature of social

Table 5.1
Analogies Used by Social Scientists to Depict Social Systems

Analogy	Description and Principal Tendency
Morphogenic	Assumes that social systems change constantly through interaction and exchange with their environment(s)
	Assumes that social systems are highly open
	Assumes social systems may be orderly and predictable but may also be disorderly and unpredictable
	Assumes that order may rest on coercion and domination as well as cooperation and consensus
	Places about equal emphasis on conflict and change as on order and stability
Factional	Assumes that social systems are divided into contentious factions that conflict over goals, priorities, resources, and strategies
	Assumes that the turbulent division of the system into factions is the principal tendency of the system
	Emphasizes conflict and change over order and stability
Catastrophic	Assumes that social systems are severely segmented and warring
	Assumes that little order or predictability exists
	Assumes that conflict may destroy some component parts
	Assumes that complete reorganization of the system is required if the system is to become less chaotic or conflictual
	Emphasizes conflict and change over order and stability

Source: From Patricia Yancey Martin and Gerald G. O'Connor. *The social environment: Open systems applications.* Copyright © 1989 Allyn & Bacon. Reprinted by permission. Adapted from Burrell and Morgan, *Sociological paradigms and organizational analysis.* Aldershot, England: Ashgate, 1979. Figure 4.1, p. 67. Used by permission.

systems rather than attempting to deny those dynamics. Conflict is seen as a normal part of an organization located within a complex environment.

Morphogenic means *structure change,* as opposed to **morphostasis,** which means *structure maintaining.* A morphogenic approach views systems as capable of change. In actuality, the possibility that an organization will return to a previous state of stability (through morphostasis) is only one of many possible options. The expectation is that as organizations gain more knowledge and experience, they will change their structures, forms, goals, policies, and so forth. In doing so, maintaining a steady-state equilibrium would indicate that the system has not grown and developed. Systems theory based on a morphogenic analogy expects interaction with the environment to influence what occurs within the organization so that the organization adjusts and changes accordingly. There is a sense of fluidity that comes from recognizing differences and learning from those differences. New organizational forms will emerge over time, hopefully leading to more highly ordered, complex systems (Martin & O'Connor, 1989).

While a *morphogenic analogy* works well to explain an organization that has members who are in general agreement about direction and purpose, or at least get along reasonably well, a *factional analogy* views organizations as being somewhat fragmented among various, somewhat contentious groups. This lack of cooperation is characterized by internal conflict, complete with disagreement, domination, competition, and lack of cooperation rather than harmony among members. Given that members change and staff turns over in organizations, a factional analogy may apply at times within systems, depending on the presence of controversy and strife. This analogy is also compatible with the morphogenic analogy, because both assume that organizations are within ever-changing environments in which conflict and disorder are to be expected. The difference is that in the factional system, conflict among groups is also occurring within the organization (Martin & O'Connor, 1989).

The third analogy is *catastrophic* and, like the other two analogies, assumes that social systems are in constant change. In this view of organizations, however, internal competition is harsh. Severe conflict is occurring on an ongoing basis, making all aspects of the system in flux. To survive, reorganization is ongoing. Due to this fluctuation, parts of the system may literally be on the verge of collapse. Again, like the morphogenic and factional analogies, change is a predictable part of the organizational experience (Martin & O'Connor, 1989), but here it is of the cataclysmic variety.

These three analogies of systems theory bring organizations beyond a simple view that they are shifting in an environmental sea, attempting to regain stability and homeostasis. Instead, they recognize that organizations and environments are in a constant state of interaction and that organizations have various degrees of stability within them. There is no expectation that organizations will remain the same. In fact, the potential for change is the constant. Being able to transform may make the difference in whether the organization grows, develops, or survives as a viable entity. Change is a productive way of life in these open systems. Systems theory as represented by these three radical analogies does not assume that staying the same and achieving a steady state is desirable.

Population Ecology Theory

Population ecology theories are often included with systems theories, since they are both very much based in open-systems theory. Rather than focusing on just one or one type of organization, population ecology theorists are interested in sets of organizations that are engaged in similar activities, how they interact with the environment, and how they relate to one another.

Concepts of particular interest to these theorists are population dynamics and density dependence. **Population dynamics** reflects the idea that as new organizations are founded, resources are often more difficult to obtain since these sets of organizations typically depend on similar funding sources. This idea is particularly relevant to human service agencies that often compete with one another for limited dollars. As organizations fail, and if new ones are not founded, then the remaining organizations may be able to obtain needed resources more easily, unless the cause for which they were founded becomes unpopular. Population dynamics postulates that if more new agencies are founded, without others failing, then the density of organizations rises and competition for resources increases. **Density dependence** is the number of organizations in the population. As more organizations are founded, this may signal increasing legitimacy of the service provided by these organizations in the larger environment. However, with increasing density comes an increase in competition and a potential risk for higher rates of failures within this population of agencies due to lack of resources. Technological developments also influence the founding and failing of sets of organizations. Changes in the political and cultural institutions and shifts in demographics also impact organizational stability (Hasenfeld, 2000, p. 98). This may have been at play when war veterans entered the disabilities scene in our case example.

Of interest to population ecologists are macro-level strategies that influence sets of organizations, such as creating institutional linkages with government agencies that increase the legitimacy of the agencies providing human services. These strategies, unfortunately, are less well developed than the understanding of the consequences to organizations that do not have appropriate coping strategies (Hasenfeld, 2000, p. 99). In the future, look for further developments in perspectives that may add to the work of population ecologists and may contribute to understanding how organizations interconnect and relate to one another within population groups.

Weiner (1990) provides an overview of what he calls "the emerging theory of inter-organizational relations [which] has become the very foundation of social welfare and other human service organizations" (p. 12). Growing concern about fragmentation and alienation in service organizations has led to an additional focus on organizational theory development that includes attention to the organization within its social environment and interorganizational relations. Only some branches of this theoretical development can truly be seen to be radical enough to fit within the Radical Structuralist Paradigm. Those influenced by a Marxian tradition would be interested in how the links between government agencies, corporations, and others ensure the continued dominance of certain powerful groups and capitalist interests even within human service organizations (Mizruchi & Galaskiewicz, 1993). The social control element involved in the creation of a complacent working class and a clearly defined deviant population would be of interest. Here the assumption is that integration and coordination of services is a way to continue the functioning of the current welfare system with more efficiency and less resources, thus maintaining the accepted dominant structure (think about the dominant mode of service delivery in our case as an example of this) (Morris & Lescohier, 1978). This theoretical perspective draws attention to the political functions of an integrated human service system, in order to understand how conflict and crisis will be necessary to overcome the capitalistic market economy's effect on the nature of human service organizations.

A more recent approach to transorganizational theory would posit that traditional management concepts are not acceptable in the postmodern world and especially in organizations linked in nontraditional ways. Of interest is the increased self-government of employees in networks created by interorganizational structures. Employees and managers behave differently when they hold allegiance to a network rather than to a particular organization. Kikert (1993) asserts that facilitative incentives and invitations to perform the work replace hierarchical commands in networks. The network is a "kinder and gentler" environment. In addition, with practice guided by this theory the role of government recedes, allowing deregulation, decentralization, and privatization. Marginalized populations have more voice in these antiauthoritarian and antimodernist organizations. This is because the patriarchal structure serving the interests of men (Wilson, 1996) gives way to a collective environment designed in opposition to bureaucratic domination (Hyde, 1992; Iannello, 1992).

The recognition of constant change in open-systems theory, the potential for factional and catastrophic dynamics, acknowledgment of population ecologies, and the increasing emphasis on transorganizational theory all lead to the development of the next set of theories. Theories of power and politics are steeped in assumptions of constant change and are focused on the dynamic nature of interpersonal and organizational relationships.

POWER AND POLITICS THEORIES

Although power and politics theories represent a more recent development in organizational theory, the concept of power has long been a source of interest and concern. Hardy and Clegg (1996) trace the emergence of two voices, "the critical and the rational," in the development of power and politics. The *critical voice* emanates from an older tradition based in the work of Marx and Weber. Marx's work on class structure viewed organizational life as one in which the interests of workers were subjugated to the control of production by a dominant class. Weber was actually the first writer to take Marx's view to a more complex level of thinking, when he focused on power as being tied to *both* ownership and control of production. Ownership was only one facet of power; having the knowledge that allowed one to control production activities was a second form of power. Thus, dominance required both economic power (ownership) and the knowledge to do the work (labor power). Another voice (Hardy & Clegg, 1996) emerged from 1950s studies in management. This *rational voice* asserted that the structures established by organizations represented legitimate power.

For example, Bennis and his colleagues (1958) distinguished between the formal organization, in which authority was based on one's position, and the informal organization, in which power came from a number of factors in addition to one's position in the organization. French and Raven (1959) identified reward power, perceived coercive power, legitimate (authority) power, referent power, and expert power and suggested that different sources of power produce different consequences in the organization. Management studies focused on the manifestation of both formal and informal power caught on during the 1960s. Managers were instructed to use their formalized power (authority) to control informal power viewed as illegitimate and dysfunctional. Baldridge (1971) studied changes in the balance of power and demonstrated how organizational goals show the official version of who is in power. This power structure was also of interest to Thompson (1967) in his study of the transitory nature of power and the interdependence among units of an organization.

This led Pfeffer (1981) and others to see power as a structural issue. Power was viewed as a result of a division of labor and professional specialization. Those who have the expertise to complete critical tasks hold organizational power. Organizational authority through an established organizational hierarchy then becomes only one of many sources of power. Allen and Porter (1983) identified downward power (hierarchical) as only one type, along with lateral and upward power. Other sources of power that reflect the consequence of multiple coalitions within organizations were identified as control of resources (including information and skills), access to power, coalition membership, and credibility. Cohen and March's study of universities (1974) revealed a very modern concept called **organized anarchies** to describe the confused power present in universities based on ambiguity of power, purpose, experience, and what constitutes success. All of these theorists saw power and politics as fundamental concepts for understanding behavior in organizations. They represent the rational voice that framed power from a functionalist perspective, maintaining power to engender desired control.

The critical voice, based on the Marxist/Weberian tradition, held assumptions of the Radical Structuralist Paradigm, understanding power in order to use it for liberation. "The Marxist/Weberian tradition equated power with the structures by which certain interests were dominated; while the management theorists defined power as those actions that fell outside the legitimized structures, and which threatened organizational goals" (Hardy & Clegg, 1996, p. 626). In this chapter, we are interested in the critical voice of power and politics because it is this view that fits with a radical structuralist perspective and organizations holding consciousness raising for change goals.

Of great curiosity to theorists who viewed power and politics as oppressive to various groups was why these groups seemed relatively passive in organizations (Hardy & Clegg, 1996). Some writers suggested that groups were passive because they were satisfied. Others recognized that access to political and organizational structures and their decision-making processes might be so impermeable that interests and grievances might remain unarticulated (Hardy & Clegg, 1996). From this standpoint, groups were not necessarily passive; they just couldn't break through organizational and societal barriers to make their voices heard. The possibility emerged that key decisions might be made by less visible leaders to whom workers did not have access in their organizations. Studies of power began to focus on why issues were suppressed, conflict was not evident, and how people might be manipulated into compliance. It was possible that dominant classes actually controlled reality by defining and thus creating it in their own way (Clegg, Hardy, & Nord, 1996).

Mann (1986) introduced the concept of **organizational outflanking,** a process used by those in dominance to gain consent and subordination of organizational members. Instead of viewing the oppressed as in denial and the elite as outwitting the masses, Mann theorized that outflanking occurs because the oppressed do not have access to or know the rules. Their affiliations are with others who have little power and by being ignorant of organizational rules and procedures their affiliations do not gain them a collective strength. If you do not know the manner in which decisions are made and if you do not associate with decision makers, then you and those with whom you do associate have little impact on decision making. This situation creates a sense of futility when considering resistance as an alternative to the current situation. In fact, the gain one might achieve from advocating for change would require too much energy to make it worthwhile. Organizational members become self-monitoring and self-controlling. They are outflanked. Outflanking could occur when people are unaware of the rules, but it could also occur when they know the rules but do not have the emotional energy to challenge them. Outflanking certainly did not occur in our case example. Interestingly, while the critical power and politics theorists were concerned with the oppressive nature of out-flanking in keeping with radical structuralism, power and politics theorists in the rational/functionalist tradition were seeking ways to set up barriers to control others based on what they were learning about outflanking. David could have followed that tradition, but because he, too, held a radical structural perspective, change occurred within the organization.

When organizational theorists began dealing with power and politics, they were strongly reacting to structural and systems theories based on functionalist assumptions in which organizations were considered to be rational. Rationality meant that organizations would have agreed-upon goals, around which there was consensus. However, once power and politics theorists acknowledged that consensus was rarely present and that there was often conflict and competition among members and units within organizations, work became more radical. To fully appreciate power also required understanding dominance, control, and oppression within the organization. Rationality was replaced by passion.

Power and politics theorists are open to criticism, because they represent less than 30 years of focused attention with less empirical grounding than other theories we have seen to this point. Even so, as they are moving beyond the older definition of **power,** which focuses on the ability to get things done by influencing people (Shafritz, Ott, & Lang, 2005), those holding the radical structuralist perspective no longer assume that the organization's primary purpose is to accomplish organizational goals. There is a rejection of the idea that organizational goals are determined and designed by those in charge and measured only for effectiveness and efficiency, restraining personal issues in favor of organizational needs. Power and politics theories reject the notion that power is vested in formal authority. Instead, there is a complex system of individuals and coalitions with interests, benefits, values, perspectives, and perceptions that act in competition for organizational resources and enter into conflict to acquire influence. There is recognition that behaviors and decisions are not rational, but the result of influence. This influence is necessary for use in competition and conflict to shape decisions. The coalitions and the individuals within them hold organizational power, but the power and the coalitions are always shifting and so are the behaviors and decisions that result.

We have chosen to place the political economy perspective within the power and politics school of thought. Zald (1970) defines this perspective as "the study of the interplay of power, the goals of power-wielders, and productive exchange systems" (p. 233). Focus on an organization's political economy includes looking at how the management of power and of resource acquisition and distribution occurs, and then seeing how these two systems interrelate. The organization is an arena in which various groups, external and internal to the agency, compete to optimize available resources. The political economy perspective has been used in extensive research on human service organizations, their development, maintenance, and destruction (Hasenfeld, 2000, p. 96).

From a radical structuralist perspective, power has been viewed as a tool of domination, and resistance to power is seen as a way to gain emancipation. Much of the work in this area is still highly theoretical, with little by way of specific practice models. Hardy and Clegg (1996) caution us to be wary of any theory that poses as *the* theory of power. There are many ways of viewing power and, therefore, any general theories of power at this stage in their development are more likely to be some group's or individual's attempt to define all situations from one biased standpoint.

Although Shafritz, Ott, and Lang (2005) do not elaborate on feminist and critical theories, we believe that some dimensions of each are appropriate to include here under the power and politics radical structuralist perspective. Both theoretical approaches also emanate from the Marxian tradition. We will briefly highlight important elements of each, and then turn to the postmodern theories that are also highly influenced by the critical voice.

RADICAL FEMINIST THEORY

The recognition of the relevance of gender within the workplace did not occur until the 1970s, when scholars began to reassess previous studies in light of their total neglect of gender. Until then, power and politics theorists were men who studied men in organizations. Hardy and Clegg (1996) contend that the gender bias in organizational studies was yet another way that male dominance permeated the workplace. The sheer force of theory that formed organizational ideology for decades had ignored gender and power and politics.

Certain branches of feminist theory fit more comfortably in a more radical change approach to understanding organizing against dominance than in other approaches. Liberal feminist theory, with its roots in the liberal political tradition, advocated for reforming organizations, instead of transforming organizations as advocated by radical feminist theory. Similar to the two rational and critical voices identified earlier in the power and politics perspective, liberal feminists took a reasoned perspective that sought to gain access to existing organizations and to incorporate women into these agencies as full and equal participants following traditional rules of behavior. This approach did not require a transformation of the social and political system, because all that was called for was an opening for women. This approach was functionalist in its view.

The majority of the organizational literature beginning in the 1960s reflected a liberal feminist approach and focused on women in management. Liberal feminist theory acknowledges conflict and tension within organizations, but with a focus on how women who do reach managerial positions are "rendered structurally powerless" (Kanter, 1987, p. 354). Early work on women's roles in organizations was conducted by Rosabeth Moss Kanter (Millman & Kanter, 1975), whose case studies were the first serious examination of women's numbers, status, and opportunities in the workplace. Kanter (1979) looked at powerlessness in organizations and found that first-line women supervisors, staff professionals, and top executives exhibited a great sense of powerlessness. She also found that dominance, control, and oppression are more likely to result from a lack of sense of power within the organization and that women managers experienced special types of power failures. Therefore, she called a *sense of powerlessness* more of a problem for organizations than power itself. Janet Wolff (1977) examined women's roles in organizations and how they related to more general societal roles for women. Her work was expanded by Gutek and Cohen (1982), who coined the term **sex role spillover,** defined as carrying socially defined gender-based roles into the workplace. None of these theorists sought to move much beyond definition of the problem for women within organizations. There was no call for radical change or for alternative ways of understanding women's perspective in organizations. Therefore, it is important to recognize that just because a theory is feminist in its orientation does not necessarily place it within the Radical Structuralist Paradigm.

Calás and Smircich (1996) have referred to feminist approaches that fit within the Radical Structuralist Paradigm as *radical feminist theory and alternative organizations* (p. 227). Taking subordination of women as a fundamental organizing principle of patriarchal society, radical feminist theorists call for organizational and institutional transformation rather than individual change. A woman should not necessarily change her behavior; instead, the organization should change to make way for a woman's way of communicating and decision making. Since radical feminism is *woman centered*, these theorists envision alternative, often separatist, organizations in which women are not subordinated to men. Rejecting functionalist assumptions grounded in regulation and control, radical feminists spurn male forms of power, seeking to create *womanspace* through alternative organizations designed to meet women's nurturing and collaborating needs.

In the 1970s, case studies of feminist organizations sought to identify how they would be different from traditional hierarchies. For example, Koen's (1984) study of three feminist businesses identified five elements indicative of feminist values: participatory decision making; rotating leadership; flexible, interactive job designs; equitable distribution of income; and political and interpersonal accountability (we will return to these sorts of values when we discuss organizations built on an interpretivist perspective that is not merely feminist in its orientation). Studies such as these are seldom seen in the mainstream management literature since they often seek to change strongly held values in traditional organizational structures (Martin, 1990). Whereas liberal feminist functionalist approaches take a how-to-succeed-in-organizations perspective, radical feminist theorists attempt to view the world of work from a woman's vision, placing women in the center of the analysis in order to create radically different organizations (Calás & Smircich, 1996, p. 229). Other radical feminist theorists, including those developing Marxist and socialist feminist theories, also are grouped within the Radical Structuralist Paradigm. All focus on gender inequality and the demand for major structural transformation in organizations.

CRITICAL THEORIES

Any discussion of power and politics would not be complete without an examination of how critical theorists have influenced the study of organizations. Coming from Marxist thought, in which organizations are viewed as instruments of the dominant class, many critical theorists (see, for example, Beechey & Donald, 1985; Bourdieu, 1977; Dreyfus & Rabinow, 1983; Giddens, 1987; Habermas, 1971, 1984; Mannheim, 1936; Williams, 1977) are concerned with the ways in which social, cultural, and economic conditions produce a type of selectivity in the processes and structures of organizations. There is skepticism regarding anything that is accepted as the norm or the socially accepted convention because they constitute social practices derived from power and domination. Critical organizational research is designed to challenge everything accepted as standard in order to unmask the dominant perspectives and establish the arena of conflict. Conflict is created in order to dislodge the natural state. Order indicates domination and suppressed conflicts. In order to achieve real consideration of the organizational status quo, various perspectives must be allowed voice in addition to the dominant view. When various perspectives are present, conflict is inevitable; but this conflict is believed to be necessary in order to achieve a full picture more amenable to fundamental change.

Insight and praxis are of central concern; knowledge or consciousness inevitably leads to change, but an anti-management stance is not always necessary. According to Alvesson and Deetz (1996), "Contributions include input to reflection on career choices, intellectual resources for counteracting totalitarian tendencies in managerially controlled corporate socialization, and stimulation for incorporating a broader set of criteria and consideration in decision-making—especially in cases where profit and growth do not clearly compete with other ends or where uncertainty exists regarding the profit outcomes of various alternative means and strategies" (p. 199). At least for some theorists, full overthrow of the administrative structure is not necessary in order to amend the consequences of organizational oppression.

Generally speaking, critical theorists have paid more attention to the societal issues of unequal power and subsequent oppression, but institutions that engender lack of equality are also of interest. Use of critical theory to guide organizational and management studies is still relatively new, emerging in the late 1970s and early 1980s. In many cases, critical theory has been linked to postmodern theory (see Alvesson & Deetz, 1996, for a good description of similarities and differences).

As the name implies, critical theory generally takes a critical stance on contemporary society. To find new and different responses to the changes that have led to new social conditions, scholars like Benson (1977), Frost (1980), Deetz and Kersten (1983), Fischer and Sirianni (1984), Alvesson (1993), and Willmott (1993) have looked at the size of organizations, technology, globalization, the nature of work, professionalization, stagnant economies, ecological problems, and generalized turbulence. Human service organizations are of particular interest to critical theorists, because these agencies are viewed as buffers between capitalists and the working classes, providing services that keep deviants from challenging the capitalist system (Hasenfeld, 2000, p. 105). The goal of critical theory is to create societies and workplaces free from oppression and domination. These theorists see an environment where all people have equal opportunity to contribute to meeting societal needs. Progressive development is the ideal.

Of particular interest to organizational scholars here is how technology and rationality are protecting dominant interests. Modernity is a focus of inquiry because it, too, in its resultant science, industrialization, communication, and information technologies presents problems that include the danger of domination. The rise of modernity has created new conflicts. Critical organizational theorists have focused on "the skewing and closure of the historical discourse through reification, universalization of sectional interests, domination of instrumental reasoning, and hegemony" (Alvesson & Deetz, 1996, p. 195). They hope to "recover a rational process through understanding social/historical/political constructionism, a broader conception of rationality, inclusion of more groups in social determination, and overcoming systematically distorted communication" (Alvesson & Deetz, 1996, p. 195).

With the critique of domination, sometimes called *ideological critiques*, the hope is that all stakeholders will come to enlightened understanding that can result in "communicative action" (Alvesson & Deetz, 1996, p. 199) leading to institutional reform. This can occur through research that focuses on organizations' relationship to the larger society, domination and distortion, politics, and identifiable disenfranchised groups. What is hoped is that morally driven discourse will result in action with direction and orchestration provided by the theoretical framework. But when all else fails, the power resulting from knowledge can lead to resistance or revolution, leading to transformation of the social order. Critical theorists are very explicit about the purpose of their research: to make organizations communities of authentic dialogue rather than instruments of domination (Handler, 1990). These theorists have greatly influenced postmodern theory development.

POSTMODERN THEORIES

Postmodern theorists continue the interest in the marginalized and disadvantaged and see the organizational world as anything but natural, rational, or neutral. These theorists look at conflicts as opportunities to reconsider and question the social order. Postmodern theories are the most esoteric of the theories examined thus far, and without the influence of critical theorists they might not have had much relevance or provided much direction for organizational structure or behavior. In addition, as with a few of the other theories discussed in this text, at least one branch of the postmodernists will be found in another paradigm, radical humanism. Those postmodern theories, more attune to the subjective in domination, will be discussed in a later chapter on the radical humanist perspective. Here we focus on those taking a more generalized or class-based view of organizational reality.

Postmodern theories are hard to delimit since many different philosophical approaches have been labeled *postmodern*. Postmodern organizational work began in the later 1980s, with the work of Smircich and Calás (1987) and Cooper and Burrell (1988). Guided by philosophers who focused on concepts such as fragmentation, textuality, and resistance, and growing out of the social mood, the historical period, and the major social and organizational changes that were occurring, postmodern theories represent a different philosophical approach to understanding organizations and behavior within them. A major postmodern theme is that culture is a source of control in organizations because "it objectifies the values, norms, and knowledge of those in power; and . . . perpetuates patterns of dominance" (Hasenfeld, 2000, p. 102). **Deconstruction,** therefore, is a way of demonstrating just how artificial these values, norms, and knowledge are. The exercise of deconstruction also reveals how the concept of rationality is socially constructed. What seems reasonable depends on the historical moment.

Featherstone (1988), Kellner (1988), Parker (1992), and Hassard and Parker (1993) are a few of the scholars who have investigated the power/ knowledge connection, the role of expertise in systems that oppress or dominate. Their investigations also include the role of the media and information technology in the contemporary world of modern organizations. As do critical theorists, postmodern scholars challenge the status quo and support those without voice. This is accomplished through research efforts that take apart language in order to understand its relationship to the theoretical, political, and affective dimensions that have created it. A deep understanding is important to really see current organizations so that they can be rethought. Theorists are interested in identifying what goes into the production and sustaining of domination in organizations. They are interested in identifying and understanding systematically distorted communication that tends to subjugate others (see Knights & Willmott, 1989; Linstead, 1993).

Postmodernists see power as achieved in discursive formation. Power is a social construction. They are interested in studying how social institutions organize around language, reasoning, and specific practices that create power and domination. Research is intended to challenge the guiding organizational assumptions, meanings, and relationships in order to move beyond the current constructions to more acceptable ones. This is accomplished through investigation of texts, deconstruction, and the use of words instead of just numbers as a way to extend the understanding of empirical research. Rather than the revolutionary reform envisioned by the critical theorists, postmodern theorists propose that people step back and explore feelings heretofore unknown. Many postmodernists can be placed in the Radical Structuralist Paradigm, because they would agree that there is a higher social order somewhere in the universe and the goal should be to find it (objectivist). They would also strongly agree that the functionalists have claimed to know what that objectivism or universal truth is, have named it, and have imposed it on others. Consistent with the Radical Structuralist Paradigm, postmodernism seeks transformational change so that a dominant group does not impose their defined reality on others.

To summarize, as theories have become more complex, so have the divisions and alternative views within the various schools of thought. In systems theory, we have seen that there are five analogies, two of which are built on functionalist assumptions and three of which can be placed in the Radical Structuralist Paradigm. Beginning with power and politics, there are multiple divisions and controversies among theorists who disagree over how theoretical knowledge should be used. For example, theorists coming from a rational approach study power and politics as

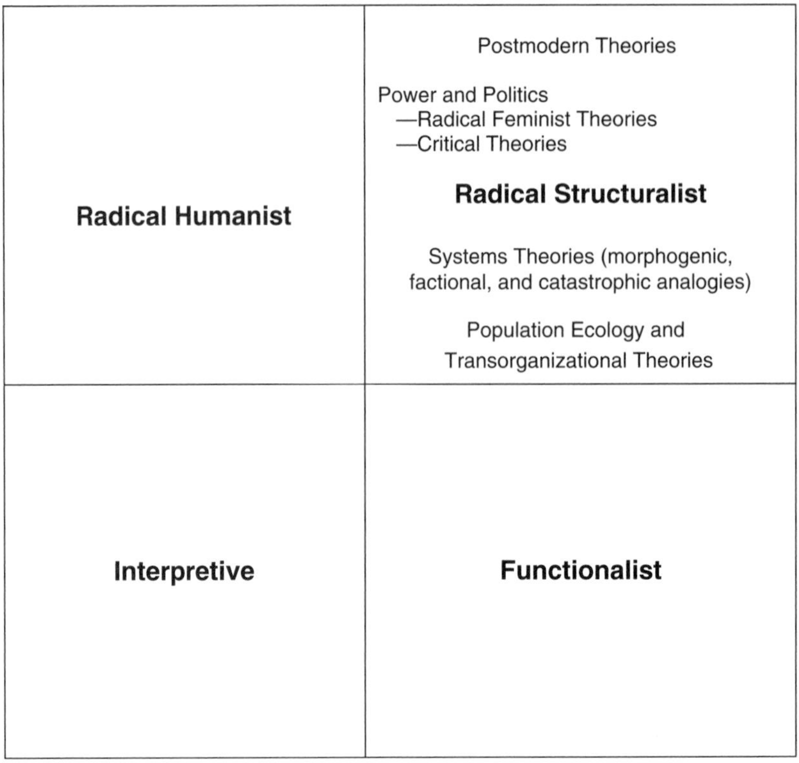

Radical Humanist	Postmodern Theories Power and Politics —Radical Feminist Theories —Critical Theories **Radical Structuralist** Systems Theories (morphogenic, factional, and catastrophic analogies) Population Ecology and Transorganizational Theories
Interpretive	**Functionalist**

Figure 5.2 Organizational Theories Within the Radical Structuralist Paradigm.

something to use in order to control subordinates and remain in the Functionalist Paradigm. However, power and politics theorists coming from a critical Weberian or Marxian perspective seek to understand organizational power so that members will be empowered and so that social change can occur. They are radical structuralists. Similarly, radical feminist theories share the quest for social change. Liberal feminist voices advocate for rationality in the ways of making room for women to remain within the Functionalist Paradigm. Those voices rising from a critical perspective fit with assumptions in the Radical Structuralist Paradigm. Figure 5.2 provides a visual distribution of the theories discussed in this chapter. Their placement within the Radical Structuralist Paradigm reflects their similarities and differences related to assumptions held in other perspectives.

COSTS AND BENEFITS

THE RADICAL STRUCTURALIST PARADIGM AND ITS THEORIES

The critical theories presented here serve a very important function in relation to those from other perspectives. They are seriously and rigorously critical of the status quo. Use of radical structuralist theories to guide understandings of organizational structures, formalized programs, and their impact in communities helps to target the collective social conscience of the organization to avoid rationalization and cooptation in service of job security and satisfaction. Though revolution may not be the preferred outcome of situations assessed and understood through critical theories, feminist theories, and postmodern theories, they do serve to help the manager and staff members consider situations from a very unforgiving lens.

Radical structuralism aspires to sweeping, non-incremental changes to the fundamental structure and belief systems within society. Organizational researchers from this perspective want the same for organizational life and develop theories in service of these goals. However, most Americans prefer individual merit and individual achievement to class action. The American culture is more likely to support efforts aimed at individual changes instead of sweeping class-based changes and incrementalism to more radical forms of change. Preference goes to evolution over revolution in the North American ideology. No matter what the impact of social problem definition, most leaders, workers, and clients in human service systems will prefer order and control over chaos to achieve change. They will prefer incrementalism with all its costs to revolution with all its unknowns. It is from this American cultural perspective of pragmatic individualism that radical structuralism will receive most of its criticism.

Social Change Organizations with Consciousness-Raising Goals

Regardless of the intellectual attractiveness of the theories presented here, especially for those with a well-hewn conscience regarding social justice, the practice that results from these theories may not be acceptable in the current context of organizational life. While the theories will aid in the understanding of the experience within Social Change Organizations, even when taken together, the possibility of this worldview predominating in organizational life is unrealistic. Few organizational leaders will risk the consequences, intended or otherwise, of an outright assault on the social structure in order to achieve change within or outside the organization. This will particularly be the case as an organization ages and gains legitimacy within its environment. This is the risk for the Consumer-Directed Advocacy Agency. The Social Change Organization of the past may become the Traditional Organization of the future as forces toward conservatism from funding sources trump idealism. Brilliant's (2000) analysis of women's fundraising organizations illustrates this point. She concludes that in politically conservative climates it becomes harder for social movement organizations to maintain their cohesion, as ''larger organizational members become institutionalized philanthropies, whereas small funds continue to struggle to obtain minimal resources . . . the network's continuation as a social movement may depend on both new skills (such as marketing) and the renewed continuation of a changing leadership to the old passions of the movement's founding mothers" (p. 567). The delicate balance between maintaining passion for social change and surviving as an organization represents a tension between radical structuralist passion and functionalist rationality that is not easily resolved.

CONCLUSION

In this chapter, we discussed theorists who focus on the same general concepts (e.g., power) but who disagree over basic assumptions introduced earlier. For example, systems theory was introduced in Chapter 3, because two of its analogies were strongly functionalist. In this chapter, we have examined three analogies that fit within a more Radical Structuralist Paradigm. Similarly, theorists interested in power can be in different paradigms, depending on how they choose to view and use their concepts. Rational management theorists, acting from a functionalist perspective, want to understand power so that managers can use their knowledge to keep others in their respective places. Conversely, radical structuralist power and politics theorists who come from a domination and oppression stance will view the study of power in organizations as a means of understanding how to raise the voices of the powerless. Feminist theories run a parallel course in that liberal feminists (functionalists) study organizations in an attempt to make women fit within existing structures, whereas radical feminists (radical structuralists) come from a set of differing assumptions about change and fundamental transformation in order to find authentic space for women in organizations.

Critical theorists have provided a foundation for much of what is known about radical structuralism and have given power and politics, feminist, and postmodern theorists valuable understandings on which to build. However, all critical or postmodern theorists do not necessarily fit within one paradigm. Beginning with this chapter, and throughout the remainder of the book, we will often examine categories of theories that hold views so different that they fall within different paradigms. We hope that this does not confuse the reader, but instead raises interest and extends capacity for critical thinking and analysis, for our approach reflects the complexity of the current organizational world and the theoretical developments aimed at understanding them.

In the next chapter, we examine the Social Change Organization. It is time to see how the theories in this chapter can be used to understand the work and establish standards of practice in organizations that come from a radical structuralist perspective. We will seek to understand their particular view on organization values, preferences, and decision-making strategies in order to see the implications for human service organizations holding this perspective. In Chapter 6, the Social Change Organization that advocates for, plans, and delivers human services with consciousness raising for change goals will be described in detail.

DISCUSSION QUESTIONS

1. Compare and contrast the major assumptions of the Radical Structuralist Paradigm with the goals of the Social Change Organization. How are they similar or different? What are the costs and benefits of the similarities? Of the differences?

2. Imagine you are on the search committee for an executive director of a very progressive human service agency. The search committee is engaged in dialogue about the costs and benefits of being part of a Social Change Organization so that members can provide "words to the wise" for potential candidates for the position. What might the "words to the wise" be? What might you advise the committee to consider in recruiting candidates? How might the committee go about assessing applicants' potential fit with the organization's goals and expectations?

3. Review the theory discussion and compare the similarities and differences between the major theories supportive of this type of organization that is dedicated to consciousness raising. Look at systems theory, population ecology theory, power and politics theories, radical feminist theory, and critical theories. What theories are more congruent with your preferences about structure and behavior in an organization, and why?

4. In the beginning of this part of the text, a case example was introduced: the Consumer-Directed Advocacy Agency. Go back to the case and consider the following questions:
   a. What characteristics of this organization make it a Social Change Organization? What are the characteristics that are less social change oriented than others?
   b. What assumptions did David appear to bring to his new position and how were they helpful (or not) in carrying out his responsibilities?
   c. As this agency developed, what did members do to insure that it remained focused on radical change?

5. Imagine that you are starting a small organization and that you want to be sure that the structure of your organization is congruent with its environment. What issues would you need to address if you were to choose a Social Change Organizational structure to be sure that it

matched a particular environment? Describe the environment for which a Social Change Organization is most suited.

6. You are a supervisor or manager in a human service agency. What would cause you to prefer working in a Social Change Organization with consciousness raising and radical change goals? Would there be any challenges for you personally as a leader? If so, what would they be, and how would you deal with them?

CHAPTER 6

Practice in Social Change Organizations

S OCIAL CHANGE ORGANIZATIONS are more dedicated to making much broader changes and upsetting the status quo than their functionalist counterparts in Traditional Organizations. If there is a basic philosophical difference between these two types of organizations, it is their attitude toward change. While Traditional Organizations plan and provide human services that facilitate incremental change and attempt to keep a lid on conflict, Social Change Organizations face conflict head on, raising consciousness about needs that are not being met, and making conflict manifest in order to shake things up enough to allow for fundamental change.

As do Traditional Organizations, Social Change Organizations recognize that concrete empirical artifacts and relationships can be identified and studied through scientific methods. However, these organizations use the results of these studies differently. Whereas a Traditional Organization uses study findings to work toward gradual interventions, Social Change Organizations seize study findings to mobilize a critical mass of people to advocate for transformative change. They may use the study process itself to create the critical mass for change demands. This transformation, depending on the problem identified, can be focused internally or externally to the organization. For example, in the Consumer Advocacy case, David was faced with internal as well as external transformational challenges.

It is important to recognize that Social Change Organizations may be developed by many different groups that come together for causes as diverse as there are groups to sponsor them. Cause-driven people are committed people, dedicated to making a difference, often in a dramatic way. Thus, cause-driven organizations bring together collectivities of people who have strongly held beliefs; otherwise they would not care enough to form, develop, and continue to participate in the time-consuming activities necessary to operate the Social Change Organization. Passion and commitment are propellants in these organizations. Keep in mind that the causes these types of organizations embrace can vary greatly and represent many different political ideologies, philosophies, and values. The Religious Right, the Southern Poverty Law Center, the NAACP, the KKK, and the Center for Human Rights Education, and even Al Qaida could be said to hold radical structuralist assumptions—all these groups want to essentially change the status quo, and all are very familiar with conflict. All have definite notions about existing external truths that need to be vigorously pursued and replaced with an alternative truth. Obviously, these diverse organizations are not advocating on behalf of the same people and some are even in extreme opposition to one another.

Although there are fewer "pure" Social Change Organizations than Traditional Organizations, the language of radical structuralism is very familiar to human service practitioners. Principles such as social justice and fairness, calls for changes that address the oppression of diverse groups, emphases on empowerment, and advocacy are common in professional jargon. These concepts are often embraced by persons working in Traditional Organizations, resulting in disillusionment and frustration when employees recognize that the assumptions undergirding these organizations and practice within them do not support or allow for the more radical change such social justice rhetoric envisions.

In this chapter, we look at ways to understand practice in Social Change Organizations. We return to the four questions originally introduced in Chapter 4 to guide the reader. These questions are: (1) What are the cultural values and characteristics of organizations derived from the assumptions of this paradigm? (2) What roles and relationships are congruent with the culture of this type of organization? (3) What are the standards for practice within this type of organization? and (4) What are the implications for practice within this type of organization?

CULTURAL VALUES AND CHARACTERISTICS OF SOCIAL CHANGE ORGANIZATIONS

In Chapter 2, we referred to Cameron and Quinn's (2006) Competing Values Framework, in which four different organizational cultures are identified. The Social Change Organization as described here is most congruent with a market culture in which there is an expectation that the organization will be results oriented in getting change accomplished. People are competitive and goal oriented, and leaders are hard drivers, producers, and competitors. They are tough and demanding because they are sure of their vision. David and his friends who started their advocacy effort lived the experience against which they were fighting. This was not the intellectual journey of a committed advocate, but the journey of people whose actual survival depended on their achieving success. The glue that

---

Box 6.1

SOCIAL CHANGE ORGANIZATIONS

- The historical significance of social movements, social reform, and advocacy motivates programs to seek external *objective sources of recognized expertise to mobilize/organize change.*
- *Differentiation and external focus* are promoted so that programs have the capacity to respond to larger community/societal needs for change.
- *Stability and control* of programs is promoted through interrelated duties and/or tasks to be arrived at by focusing on best practice standards in activist activities.
- Conflict and competition is expected, building organizational and programmatic structures to recognize competing interest groups in a *market culture.*

---

holds the organization together is an emphasis on success. Most times this means winning against the competition, sometimes by any means necessary. Reputation and success are common concerns. The long-term focus is on competitive actions and achievements of measurable goals based on clear targets. Success is defined in terms of how broad a focus one can have and levels of market penetration. In human service, this means level of acceptance and support for the change vision. In human services organizations, this translates into having a highly influential vision. The organizational preferred approach is hard-driving competitiveness where the ends justify the means. The market culture produces an organization that focuses on external positioning with some recognition of a need for stability and control. Management expectations here involve being competitive and productive; for human services this means being persuasive and successful regarding the desired changes.

Box 6.1 is a repeat of a box originally introduced in Chapter 2. It provides a reminder of the basic cultural elements that inform a Social Change Organization.

VALUES IN SOCIAL CHANGE ORGANIZATIONS

As with the Traditional Organization, Social Change Organizations have goals and processes that can be termed *absolutist*. They are absolutist in the sense that Social Change Organizations reject false consciousness in favor of true consciousness. **False consciousness** may be a set of values strongly held by dominant interests who are believed to be in error. True consciousness, on the other hand, is determined through critical analysis and dialectical discussion with the stakeholders about the problem(s) under consideration. True consciousness is achieved when there is enough energy to reject the current situation and its accompanying values, create a crisis, and move to structural change at the organizational or societal levels. For example, David rejected the providers' benevolent position as a false notion of personal empowerment. He wanted that position changed and went after that change by organizing in whatever way was needed.

For these reasons, the Social Change Organization does not have so much an identifiable structure as a *definable change mission*. These organizations will tend to have a social justice focus directed at creating access in a social and/or political economy for those who have been deprived of their human rights, but access comes through conflict. Therefore, organizations whose major activities involve advocacy at any level could be considered radical structuralist if fundamental structural change is their goal *and* their intention is to create the possibility for that change through serious, sometimes violent struggle. This conflict does not necessarily need to be violent, nor does it need to be directed from the outside of the social structure intended for change, but structural dislocation in an extreme form must be seen as desirable. Radical reform must be the goal, whether the organization is involved in legal services, welfare reform, mental health, or health-care reform. Evolutionary or incremental change (such as is possible in Traditional or Serendipitous Organizations) would be seen to be too conservative and be rejected in favor of *catastrophic change* (Burrell & Morgan, 1979, p. 359).

Social Change Organizations are built on radical structuralist assumptions. Thus, they are absolutist, because their members believe that there is an external source of truth to be discovered. The functionalist version of truth is the false consciousness of the radical structuralist, because functionalist truth represents the dominant version of what is real, acceptable, and valued. The radical structuralist is willing to accept that there is a greater external truth, but that truth is often a completely different reality than the truth held by those in power. Radical structuralists in their absolutism may find themselves accused of being fanatics because they tirelessly push for change. They are also somewhat fundamentalist in their orientation on what ultimate truth is all about. Everyone else could be wrong, but they are never wrong about the oppressive nature of structural power and what must be done to overcome it.

Not only do radical structuralists search for and identify what they believe to be *real* external truth and universal values, but there can be conflict among Social Change Organizations when they strongly disagree about what true consciousness is. For example, in response to the rise of the Religious Right and their version of truth, a nonprofit organization called Interfaith Alliance developed to counter the views of the Religious Right. Similarly, the Southern Poverty Law Center developed Klanwatch to monitor the activities of the KKK. As Social Change Organizations emerge, there are usually other Social Change Organizations created in reaction to the values they are promoting. These value conflicts are predictable due to the passionately held positions and the vocal nature of these types of organizations.

Social Change Organizations seek logic, given their objectivist assumptions. Therefore, they will use the processes of assessment, analysis, and organizing to intervene in what might be called *radicalized planned change*. Instead of an incremental process, collective transformational change will be sought in which planned change processes are intensely used in a broadscale way to revolutionize internal or external structures.

Collective transformation in the Social Change Organization is based on a social advocacy approach that "deems the application of pressure as the best course of action to take against people or institutions that may have induced the problem or that stand in the way to its solution—which frequently involves promoting equity or social justice. When interests clash in this way, conflict is a given" (Rothman, 2007, p. 12). The social advocacy model uses confrontational strategies and tactics such as demonstrating, picketing, striking, marching, boycotting, engaging in civil disobedience, and even violence. This approach has been used by organizations such as "Children Now or People for the Ethical Treatment of Animals—PETA . . . Pressure as a means of influence is also evident in some advocacy groups that focus on conventional lobbying and legislative reform rather than grassroots organizing. Examples include Mothers Against Drunk Driving, The Women's Campaign Fund, Rock the Vote, AIDS Action Council, the Gray Panthers, and the American Association of Retired Persons (AARP) . . . the militant social action approach has been embraced by the Industrial Areas Foundation—IAF (the Alinsky group) and ACORN (Association of Community Organizations for Reform Now) as well as unions and radical political action movements" (Rothman, 2007, pp. 31–32).

Social Change Organizations have a history grounded in social action at the turn of the 20th century and the causes of the 1960s. Today, their interventions are more refined and their adversarial strategies more sophisticated as public tolerance of disruption has decreased. Whereas collaborative strategies may suffice in functionalist organizations, campaign and contest tactics are the tactics of choice used by Social Change Organizations, including within their own organizations. There is little tolerance for neglecting the organization's cause or any of its constituencies.

MISSION/PHILOSOPHY OF SOCIAL CHANGE ORGANIZATIONS

The Social Change Organization has a mission grounded in advocacy, social action, empowerment, and change. Advocacy may take different forms. For example, **case advocacy** occurs when someone persuades others regarding the interest of an individual, whereas cause, legislative, and administrative types of advocacy cast a much wider macro-net, focusing on social conditions that affect many. Schneider and Lester (2001) define **cause advocacy** as "promoting changes in policies and practices affecting all persons in a certain group or class, for example, the disabled, welfare recipients, elderly immigrants, or battered women" (p. 196). Legislative advocacy occurs when persons seek statutory change that will improve the lot of others; administrative advocacy happens when change from within an organization is proposed. Social Change Organizations may do all types of advocacy, having units that provide direct service advocacy and others that focus on broader scale change. Some organizations will focus solely on cause and legislative advocacy. The point is that advocacy is a word heard frequently in the hallways of these organizations.

Social action, as a philosophical approach to change, is a collective effort in the face of opposition to promote a cause or make a progressive change (Hardcastle, Wenocur, & Powers, 2004). Social action, then, is highly related to advocacy but may go beyond traditional limits, not staying within the boundaries of acceptable (even legal) policies and procedures so common in Traditional Organizations. Compared with advocacy, social action has a broader goal and emerged out of insurgency movements that championed the cause of the oppressed. Hardcastle, Wenocur, and Powers (2004) identify three change modalities relevant to direct service: (1) ensuring individual rights, (2) public interest advocacy, and (3) transformation. Ensuring individual rights includes assuring that persons have what is legally theirs to have. For example, due process rights may involve access to a public hearing. **Public interest advocacy** involves having the opportunity to take part in the civic process, literally having a seat at the table, giving voice to the voiceless. **Transformation** involves structural change and is more concerned with a vision of a greater society than either individual rights or public interest advocacy. Certainly all these change modalities are related, but fundamental transformation is the ultimate, visionary cause-oriented approach.

Social Change Organizations may engage in all three change modalities, depending on their missions. All types of advocacy can be used simultaneously to advance the conditions of invisible population groups. But it is likely that the transformational type of advocacy providing a vision of a better world is the best fit with the driven nature of the Social Change Organization and its mission/philosophy. These organizations hold to an assumption that social structure, including organizational structure, has the potential for oppression and domination; therefore antidomination themes permeate their mission/philosophy.

Preferred Structure in Social Change Organizations

Social Change Organizations are often created in defiance of existing service delivery structures that are not meeting the needs of certain groups.

Given their contempt, they often try not to replicate organization and program structures that are viewed as instruments of oppression in Traditional Organizations. Since most human service agencies are hierarchically structured, "those wishing to create empowering organizations must look beyond the status quo to models that show some promise for providing increased consciousness, confidence, and connection to the world interacting with the organization" (Gutierrez & Lewis, 1999, p. 81). These organizations can be viewed as a work in progress, in which member education is paramount, staff and consumer participation in all aspects of organizational life is encouraged, and leaders recognize the importance of an empowered workforce as much as an empowered constituency. The actual structure of the organization would be characterized by a flattened hierarchy, flexibility, teamwork, and a shared philosophy that supports the ability for everyone to take risks (Gutierrez & Lewis, 1999, p. 83).

However, Social Change Organizations face a dilemma when it comes to structuring their organizations. The concepts of flat structures and shared decision making sound reasonable until leaders try to mobilize the masses for action. There are times when strict protocols, coordinated efforts, and timing of orchestrated procedures are necessary to move change ahead in a timely fashion. In such times, the flexibility and sometimes seemingly chaotic structure of Social Change Organizations may take a turn closer to their more orderly functionalist counterparts, as another aspect of "by any means necessary" comes into play. The Consumer-Directed Advocacy Agency faced these challenges.

Types of Programs and Services in Social Change Organizations

Different types of programs and services were discussed in Chapter 1. Recall that *direct service programs* serve individual clients. *Staff development and training programs* focus on staff, and *support programs* facilitate direct service and staff programs. The Social Change Organization may contain all three types of programs. For example, a case advocacy approach that defines its direct service programs may be combined with an emphasis on staff development and education. An agency directed toward accessing appropriate community-based services for the persistently mentally ill does so by training staff and volunteers in innovative ways to create services while also educating the public at large about the special needs of this population. However, the organization's signature program may be what human service professionals would call a support program—cause advocacy that seeks more radical change. This same agency is known, not for its educational pamphlets that they distribute to family members and service providers to educate them, but rather for the executive director's quotable quotes that appear in the area newspapers whenever structural inequities and unacceptable services for those challenged with mental illness are uncovered. A Traditional Organization serving persons with mental illness would see advocacy programs as supportive of its direct service work; a Social Change Organization sees its direct service work as supportive of its primary mission—to empower consumers with mental disorders.

The implementation of empowerment-type programs requires the Social Change Organization to consciously think about how clients or consumers will be involved in every aspect of organizational functioning. Programs will be designed to be more strengths-enhancing and responsive than in more traditional systems. In addition, dialectical processes that open communication for potentially conflicting views will be particularly important to all levels of the organization. The Consumer-Directed Advocacy Agency case example demonstrates these issues in many ways. David and his friends were both consumers and members of the advocacy organization. They intentionally developed their structure and processes to achieve the utmost in structural changes, but this did not occur without major controversies within and outside the organization.

SUMMARY CHARACTERISTICS OF SOCIAL CHANGE ORGANIZATIONS

Just as readers will have encountered Traditional Organizations in their daily lives, we are certain that readers are familiar with Social Change Organizations. Even if you have not worked in such an organization, you will likely have received mailings from or heard about the work of Social Change Organizations. Since these organizations are not "shrinking violets," the fact that you have heard their names or seen their ads or heard about their activities means that they are doing their job of lifting the voice of the silenced. However, witnessing what Social Change Organizations do is not the same as working in these organizations. We summarize the characteristics of Social Change Organizations in Table 6.1. These characteristics apply to any category of agency operating with social change/radical structuralist assumptions.

The characteristics in Table 6.1 reveal a great deal about Social Change Organizations. They are formed to meet needs that are often not recognized by the larger society, and their clients are persons whose needs are not being met by Traditional Organizations. Their advocacy orientation makes them vulnerable in seeking funding, for funders will have to feel comfortable with, and be willing to support, the cause-oriented approach taken by the organization. The funders must be as willing to take risks as is the organization itself. Their use of volunteers and the type of internal leadership required set them apart from their functionalist counterparts. Although they may work closely in coalitions and alliances with more traditional agencies, their methods will definitely stand out as more

Table 6.1
Characteristics of Social Change Organizations

Characteristics	Social Change Organizations
Values	To provide avenues for nondominant opinions, doctrines, and practices
Mission and Philosophy	To use the best knowledge available to enhance and achieve the highest social change for the common good
Organizational Structure	To allow structure to emerge so that the organization's cause is best facilitated, and to use less bureaucratic, flatter structures whenever possible
Programs and Services	To develop advocacy-based programs and services designed to change oppressive structures and empower people

radical. There may even be times when traditional agencies use their social change colleagues to make changes that they feel they cannot make. The more conservative Traditional Organizations tend to be allied with more conservative groups or more hampered by rules and regulations regarding the degree to which advocacy can be undertaken. People within Traditional Organizations who have the same vision of necessary change will choose to have the Social Change Organization stand in the forefront of articulating problems and seeking needed changes rather than risk losing established funding sources. We have seen Traditional Organizations go so far as to provide the needed data or other information to radical staff in Social Change Organizations in order to facilitate their activities, while still maintaining their own less radical position in the community.

Social Change Organizations will likely be smaller in size than Traditional Organizations, because their radical approaches and resource limitations may limit their ability to grow. However, there are Social Change Organizations at the national level that actually grow to have millions of dollars in funding because they have established credibility about the needs for which they advocate. For example, large associations that are cause-oriented groups advocating for their constituencies may have been originally grounded in radical structuralist assumptions. The American Association of Retired Persons (AARP), for example, advocates for the needs of older citizens and could be seen as attempting to lay the groundwork for elder empowerment. Its network of chapters throughout the country attest to the incredible cadre of members who belong to this association and its lobbyists are active in advocating for or against proposed bills before the Congress. Compare AARP to those Social Change Organizations at the grassroots level that are struggling to survive in local communities and one can readily see how incredibly diverse these organizations can be. Also, given the way in which AARP has developed, one could argue that its original radical structuralist orientation has been muted by a distinctive functionalist perspective as it has moved into the mainstream of power in more recent years.

Working in a Social Change Organization requires management of basic underlying assumptions about locus of control and change. From an objectivist perspective, locus of control is external—there is a greater source of truth and knowledge beyond the individual. These collective or universal truths become the rallying cry of radical structuralists. The Social Change Organization uses these external truths as guides in raising awareness and consciousness. In a way, radical structuralists are proselytizers—they are attempting to convert others to their way of thinking, to seeing the truths that they hold dear. For example, the National Citizens Coalition on Nursing Home Reform (NCCNHR) was established as a nonprofit membership organization in 1975 to spread the message that quality care in America's long-term care facilities must be a top national priority. This group emerged out of concerns over the conditions in America's nursing homes and the need to protect vulnerable older residents who are invisible to the larger society. NCCNHR's advocacy role, combined with the work of many committed volunteers throughout the country, has influenced changes in federal legislation. Its newsletter, *Quality Care Advocate*, serves as a vehicle to raise consciousness about conditions in long-term care facilities and changes that need to occur. If you are unfamiliar with NCCNHR, we suspect you have heard of groups like Prevent Child Abuse America, Greenpeace, Mothers Against Drunk Driving (MADD), or Common Cause. These advocacy organizations are firmly in the radical structuralist tradition.

Given its radical change perspective, the Social Change Organization seeks transformative change that not only affects the organization itself but has an impact on the community and even the larger society. That's what David and his colleagues wanted in their consumer advocacy efforts. In this example, one can readily see that when one works within a Social Change Organization, one has no choice but to become part of a transformational process. O'Donnell and Karanja (2000) define **transformation** as the process by which people come to understand their own internal spirit and strength in order to develop alternative visions of their community. **Transformative community practice** seeks to change: (1) how individual people see themselves, developing deeper understanding of who they are and what they can accomplish; (2) how they see themselves in relationship to others in the community, building a collective identity and senses of common purpose and efficacy; and (3) how people outside the community view the community and its people (pp. 75–76).

Note that radical structuralists are collectivists, building a common identity among people. Radical structuralists seek transformative change for the collective, not the individual alone.

ROLES AND RELATIONSHIPS WITH AND WITHIN SOCIAL CHANGE ORGANIZATIONS

Given radical structuralist objectives and radical change perspectives that guide Social Change Organizations, Table 6.2 provides a summary of some of the ways in which roles and relationships develop in Social Change Organizations. This same framework appears in each of the practice chapters in this book as we examine the differing goals of different types of organizations.

ORGANIZATION–ENVIRONMENT RELATIONSHIPS

We begin with how Social Change Organizations view their relationships with the larger environment. We will then examine the Social Change Organization's internal roles and relationships, particularly elaborating on funding and clients.

Task Environment Relationships   The task environment comprises all those groups, organizations, and individuals with which an organization relates (Thompson, 1967). It is important to know how the Social Change

Table 6.2
Roles and Relationships With and Within Social Change Organizations

Type of Relationship	Purpose
Task Environment Relationships	To recognize environmental uncertainty as an opportunity to interact with and mobilize diverse forces to benefit the organization's cause
Relationships with Funders	To obtain any funding that will support the organization's cause
Relationships with Client Populations and Referral Sources	To advocate with, rather than for, consumers and to encourage the development of programs that have full community participation
Internal Organizational Roles and Relationships:	
• Managing	To establish a participatory, inclusive approach to management and leadership in which dialogue and debate are freely exchanged
• Communicating	To develop open communication in which the voices of clients, volunteers, and staff are equally heard, and to engage in face-to-face exchanges in which conflict is accepted as part of the dialectical process
• Recognizing Staff Expectations	To hire persons who will embrace the cause and who have advocacy skills

Organization views those assorted relationships beyond their immediate control.

In the previous chapter, Table 5.1 reintroduced three systems analogies (morphogenic, factional, and catastrophic) used by social scientists to depict social systems and that fall within the Radical Structuralist Paradigm. Morphogenic systems are in constant interaction with their environments and are highly open. Change and conflict receive equal emphasis. In factional systems, conflict divides contentious factions as disagreements over goals, priorities, resources, and strategies prevail. The catastrophic analogy focuses on severe fragmentation among groups in which conflict has the potential to threaten the organization's survival or create major shifts. In each, the environment is highly defining for the organization.

Social Change Organizations see the environment as a set of forces with which the organization is in constant interaction. Rather than fearing conflict and trying to squelch disagreement, the Social Change Organization recognizes this instability as presenting opportunities to change existing structures, even to change its own internal structure if needed. This organization listens to its neighbors; it encourages criticism and disagreement about its service, and has organizational members who are very visible outside the structure of the organization itself. Guiding this type of organization through the environment requires leaders who are not afraid of conflict and who see the organization as developing over time. David was this sort of leader; he was not threatened by how this development might actually move the organization to a new and different place. In fact, the concept of maintaining organizational homeostasis would be seen as somewhat of a copout, in which organizational change goals are displaced by keeping things the same. The status quo is of no interest to this organization, except in how to change it.

The Social Change Organization views *change as normal*, even useful. This is a great departure from traditional views of agency–environment relationships in which the *normal* organization seeks stability and equilibrium amid environmental uncertainty. The social movement type of organization would not be adverse to radical internal change, sometimes called **organizational transformation,** which implies a "profound reformulation of not only the organization's mission, structure, and management, but also fundamental changes in the basic social, political, and cultural aspects of the organization" (Leifer, 1989, p. 900). Normalizing change, even embracing it as a continuous menu of new options, is exhilarating to the radical structuralist.

Relationships With Funding   Social Change Organizations often have trouble developing and maintaining a stable funding base because they embrace nontraditional, even unpopular causes. Unless there are funding sources in the larger environment that agree with their mission, they may literally operate on a shoestring budget, with continuing questions about their long-term survival. This may be out of their own fear of cooptation or due to potential funders' fear of agency processes and outcomes. Social Change Organizations see little benefit in working to achieve value consensus or consonance with funders, believing instead that their position speaks for itself and should be supported for what it is.

O'Donnell and Karanja (2000) studied Centers for New Horizons, an organization dedicated to work in extremely low-income urban African-American communities to empower parents of childhood education programs and to advocate for local residents. Fighting to maintain their radical structuralist orientation, their continual "fear is that we have become a 'vendor' rather than a community partner in providing child and family welfare services" (p. 71). Since its original founding in 1971, Centers has secured public dollars to hire, educate, and promote community residents. However, they point out, "so-called minority agencies like ours in extremely low income communities also lack access to unrestricted funds, such as major donor and endowment funds. One organizing training institute, the Southern Empowerment Project, has taken on fund-raising and funding cooperatives as a core organizing strategy; the Project is encouraged that this effort will strengthen the institutional infrastructure for grassroots groups throughout the South" (p. 80).

The concerns expressed above have been reflected in studies of alternative agencies for years (for example, see Brilliant, 2000). Wilkerson (1988) summarized the findings from a series of case studies of alternative agencies, focusing on the tenuous nature of external funding. Funding sources, Wilkerson contends, follow "front-burner social issues and crises. Governmental, foundation, and corporate-giving programs all have a bent toward a somewhat whimsical nature: When a more attractive or urgent social need attracts their attention or when social themes change—due to politics, economics, or new social threats—the money route can move in a mercurial flow, contributing to the typically short life-span of the alternative human service agency" (p. 124).

Wilkerson's observation raises an important point about working in an alternative agency. If the Social Change Organization is successful in raising the public consciousness, then the novelty of its cause may attract temporary funding interests. However, the fickle nature of funding streams means that working in a Social Change Organization could mean that one's job (with funding) disappears as suddenly as it appeared if soft monies are not continued or if another cause catches the eye of funders. The volatility of funding, then, is an ongoing issue for agencies that assume a radical structuralist orientation. Working in them may feel very much like a rollercoaster ride, invigorating yet somewhat risky and uncertain.

Relationships With Client Populations and Referral Sources   Just as funding is a critical input from the environment, so are clients. Traditional referral agencies may see a new Social Change Organization as a resource to which they can send clients who have nowhere else to go. This may sound appropriate at first glance, but this referral process may be seen as a dumping mechanism by the receiving organization. In most cases, the referral will not include a mechanism to pay for services since, for the most part, these clients' needs will not have reached the public agenda, much less been institutionalized as a societal obligation worthy of funding.

Just as Traditional Organizations typically serve clients who are "socially acceptable," because of the clients or the way in which they are served, Social Change Organizations may be seen at worst as troublemakers or at best as a refreshing approach to an unresolved community or societal problem. Whatever the popularity of the cause, Social Change Organizations engage clients in a very different way than their functionalist neighbors. First, Social Change Organizations may be developed by the very persons they are intended to serve, as with our case example. In neophyte organizations, the entire staff may be volunteers, many of whom are drawn to the cause because of their own needs. Second, use of the term *client* might be offensive, and words like *member* or *participant* may be used to describe persons who benefit from what the organization does. Third, use of power among members, participants, and staff is different than in Traditional Organizations, in which there may be a clearer demarcation between persons who work in the organization and those who volunteer or receive services. A dialectical approach in communication and problem solving may be used in which various community stakeholders participate on equal footing with persons who are employed by the agency. Inclusion of community members and participants in the decision-making process assures that conflict will be inevitable. This inclusionary process is not efficient, and may be messy, meaning the process might not be viewed as sufficiently efficient by those persons with more traditional views of organization practice, but might be very satisfactory to those inside.

In summary, Social Change Organizations view funding and clients differently than do their functionalist colleagues. Funding is far less certain, often short-lived, and a continual struggle. Even if funding is obtained, the organization may have to guard against being co-opted into more traditional ways of working. Survival is not assured and environmental forces are constantly being scanned for resources. Clients may not be called *clients* at all, because clients imply that professionals do something *for*, when in the Social Change Organization doing *with* is the goal. This view of the environment sets a context for examining the organization's internal structure.

INTERNAL ORGANIZATIONAL ROLES AND RELATIONSHIPS

The Social Change Organization is highly aware of its environment, and consequently it seeks a structure that will be able to respond to the many forces with which it is constantly interacting. The internal workings of the Social Change Organization are influenced by theories that are loosely grouped under *systems, power and politics*, and *postmodern* perspectives. These theories are reflected in the organization's internal operations.

Managing   Given such a radicalized stance toward change, many Social Change Organizations might be easier to identify by personalities, groups, or movements that could be considered radical structuralists. Mitch Schneider and Saul Alinsky could be called radical structuralists. The Black Panthers and the radical wing of the Right to Life Movement are also radical structuralists. None share the same methods of organizing or manner of establishing organizational structures. None have similar management or leadership styles. What they do have in common is the desire for change based on consciousness raising of those affected by the identified problem. In order to create the atmosphere conducive to change they are willing to create crisis, which at times could be violent in nature.

The concept of charismatic leadership is very relevant to Social Change Organizations. Often these organizations have emerged because someone rose to the occasion and others joined the cause. Given the charismatic nature of management in Social Change Organizations, Wilkerson contends that the leader is considered "first among equals" and others follow her or his lead because they admire and believe in this person's ability. "Thus, the dilemma in the non-exercise of implicit role requirements for an executive is dissolved by the power of the leader's real or imputed charm" (1988, p. 125).

It would be naive to assume that a charismatic leader can carry the organizational banner indefinitely. Should the Social Change Organization survive, eventually leadership will change because people move on to other areas, retire, or die. It can be expected that in terms of leadership succession, an organization that has depended on the charisma of a founder/leader will have major adjustments to make when a new person assumes the leadership role. These organizations may suffer from "founder's syndrome" (Netting, O'Connor, & Singletary, 2007). It is not unusual for these transitions to be fraught with intense power and political dynamics as people adjust. For example, in situations in which there are self-appointed heirs, "the dynamics finally become self-centered; and the group fervor that characteristically carries the flow of democracy, enthusiasm, and compliance ultimately breaks. How many minor cracks can be sustained and whether they can be repaired . . . short of moving to the bureaucratic model, is an intriguing area for more experimentation and investigation" (Wilkerson, 1988, p. 126). Sometimes it seems that during these times of leadership vacuum, the organization will shift to a more conservative posture vis-à-vis goals and services as a way to seek the comfort and stability that had formerly been supplied by the charismatic leadership.

Mintzberg, Ahlstrand, and Lampel (1998) have helped to clarify the schools of management that are most congruent with the market culture of the Social Change Organization. The Power School recognizes that organizational strategy formation is a process of negotiation and the use of influence. This influence can be political and can include the exploitation of power in other than purely economic ways. Managers in this school of thought see strategy making as interplay, through persuasion, bargaining, and sometimes direct confrontation, in the form of political games, among parochial interests and shifting coalitions, with none dominant for any significant period of time. The Environmental School positions the organization's environment as central to the managerial decision-making process. Managers who focus heavily on the environment will use contingency approaches, determining the best approach depending on the organization's size, technology, and stability. In the Configuration School, managers literally leap from one state, structure, or condition to another, thus transforming the way in which the organization operates. Periods of stability are interrupted by transformational processes that result in quantum leaps to another way of operating, requiring great adaptability among employees. Managers in Social Change Organizations are much more attentive and responsive to environmental forces than their traditional colleagues. The Social Change Organization that seeks advocacy causes as their mission will have managers who fit comfortably in the often-volatile power and politics approach to strategizing, organizing their structural configurations to align with those causes.

Management in these types of organizations actually may be a misnomer. Terms such as *organizer* or *leader*, rather than *manager*, are more reflective of the activities. Depending on the size of the organization, there may be no management positions, certainly not in the traditional sense. However, those leaders who want to succeed in Social Change Organizations will find that there are certain characteristics that are rewarded because of their usefulness to the organization. Box 6.2 provides a list of characteristics of radical structuralist leaders.

Communicating Open, frank communication is valued in Social Change Organizations. In the empowered and empowering organization, Gutierrez and Lewis (1999) identify organizational processes for workers with good communication underlying every process. First, they focus on *consciousness*, in which workers are educated about organizational factors, organizational processes are demystified, and there is dialogue about

---

Box 6.2

CHARACTERISTICS OF SOCIAL CHANGE LEADERS

- Questions existing rules, procedures, and directions
- Actively engages in conflict
- Can incite conflict when necessary
- Is comfortable with dialectical interaction
- Is thick skinned, able to deal with insults
- Is cause or mission driven
- Makes no distinction between personal and work life (sees what one does as a higher calling)
- Makes radical change as needed
- Believes passionately in what one does
- Can be aggressively assertive when necessary
- Is invigorated and challenged by taking on "the system"
- Can support cause with factual information
- Believes there are higher truths to be pursued

---

organizational mission. Second, they examine *confidence* in which skills are built to increase leadership capability, areas of power and control are identified, and professional growth and development is encouraged. Finally, they address *connection*, in which teams are developed to make program decisions, bottom-up and top-down approaches are coordinated, and there is ongoing evaluation of the change process. These processes to empower workers can form an intentional and ongoing communication network that describes the standard in Social Change Organizations. Instead of workers, members, volunteers, participants, or consumers feeling left out and wishing for communication from designated leaders, the Social Change Organization's cultural norm is that there should be no surprises, conflicts should be openly addressed, and everyone should have a voice in decision-making processes.

As Chapter 5 illustrated, there are a number of theories that pertain to radical structuralism, and these theories challenge the status quo. Practicing in a Social Change Organization is not for persons who are uncomfortable with conflict or want to avoid it altogether. One's practice in this type organization will be fraught with conflict and will fully engage the practitioner in a constellation of roles that requires constant communication. There will be a healthy irreverence for credentials and titles and an enthusiasm for partnering with consumers. The culture will feel vibrant and alive, with a heavy dose of righteous indignation and moral outrage.

Recognizing Staff Expectations   Since Social Change Organizations arise out of the consciousness of community people who see injustice, personnel policies, procedures, and practices are more likely to be seen as part of the problem, rather than an aid to problem solution. Therefore, a recently established Social Change Organization may have minimal policies in place and will take pride in not being as formalized as Traditional Organizations. In fact, such technical details may be seen as tools of impending bureaucratic oppression. This makes sense in the early life of an organization, where the few employees might have little need for policies and procedures. The vision or mission establishes the structure that embraces the "by any means necessary" approach.

When Social Change Organizations formally incorporate in order to receive funds, then the need for some policies will arise. Primary energy will not be devoted to these administrative or technical details. Even when policies and manuals are developed, everything contained therein will be under constant scrutiny for oppressive or limiting consequences. Rules will always be suspect, because if they serve to help one segment of the organizations they may impinge on the liberty and potentiality of another segment.

Just as there are functionalist personality types, we think there are persons who are more likely to excel in Social Change Organizations. In Chapter 2, we introduced the possibility that the Myers-Briggs personality types can be related to the various paradigms based on their descriptions and defining characteristics. Persons described as *thinking–perceiving* (TP), with their need to be analytical and rational in their approach to decision making, will bring those characteristics to situations in the real world that are subject to change. Their perceiving predisposition may give them a sense of adventure in that change is perfectly acceptable as long as one approaches change in an objective, facts-based manner. They are theory driven. These personal characteristics are compatible with radical structuralism. With their need to analyze and bring to logical order all aspects of their world, TPs as radical structuralists will seek highly organized change that brings their organization (community or society) into alignment with a new order, invigorated by the pressures that are associated with engaging in collective change. These personality types hold a social change/radical structuralist/market perspective created by the intersection of objectivity/stability/control and radical change/differentiation combined with thinking and perceiving. Persons holding a social change perspective would likely be comfortable with aggressive, decisive leadership that is mission driven, task oriented, and work focused. They are all about changing.

Given the preferences of these personality types, there are certain aspects of a Social Change Organization's structure and behavior that are decidedly congruent with their approaches to work. The mission-driven nature of most human service organizations will draw them to join the work, but their natural approaches to problem solving may present difficulties should they land in traditional, more conservative organizations. These personality types represent the very contradictions that are so much the focus of the Social Change Organization. They are drawn toward order, but they are also drawn toward action.

Perhaps, because of these contradictions, even within the most radically forward-looking organization, these personalities may present challenges to persons who are trying to provide leadership. Since staff members having these personality traits tend to be critically analytical, everything will be analyzed before being accepted. Sometimes the critical analysis will be received as criticism. Other times, based on commitment to a change vision, the analysis will not be balanced in a way to consider costs and benefits, positives and negatives of the phenomena under analysis. This may mean that these personalities can represent very negative organizational energy without receiving support from others for their questioning and critiquing of ideas.

These personality types comfortably question authority so that the highly hierarchical, bureaucratized organization would not provide a comfortable fit. Rather, the Social Change Organization that is open to criticism and sees dialogue and dialectic as ways to improve performance and direction would be a more appropriate fit. There is room here for passion and charisma. Confrontation will be a desired strategy, requiring those in leadership positions to respond with equal strength, or the necessary organizational rules and procedures will be ignored in favor of more radical action. For some of the personality types, confrontation may move into aggression. This aggression could also include violence to prove a point or to set the stage for their desired change.

STANDARDS OF PRACTICE WITHIN SOCIAL CHANGE ORGANIZATIONS

LANGUAGE IN SOCIAL CHANGE ORGANIZATIONS

When we discussed the Traditional Organization, we focused on a debate over the use of terms such as *assessment* and *diagnosis*. This debate is irrelevant to the Social Change Organization. Whereas *assessment* is an acceptable term, *diagnosis* implies a medical, expert, or dominant orientation and will rarely be heard in the hallways of these agencies even if they provide direct services. Similarly, although *planning* might be used, the term *organizing* is more relevant to the Social Change Organization because it implies mobilization. *Social planning* has traditionally been used to mean that experts are in charge, bringing special skills to the design of programs and interventions. Radical structuralists do not use *planning* in this way, for it is important to demystify the planning process away from an expert–client dichotomy. Instead, planning is viewed as an all-inclusive dialectical process with participant engagement or participatory action as a cornerstone of the process. In Social Change Organizations, the term *intervention* may be used, but remember that whatever the intervention is, the goal will be to empower people to transform the organization, community, and society. Note that we are using *collective transformational change* to reflect the more radical language of intervention one finds in Social Change Organizations.

Having examined the language of practice, we now turn to the specifics of practice in Social Change Organizations. As you will see, assessment, problem analysis, organizing, and collective transformational change are viewed as stages in organizational change in most Social Change Organizations.

ASSESSING SITUATIONS

Assessment is critically important in Social Change Organizations, because, as in Traditional Organizations, gathering as much objective knowledge as possible about the situation at hand is important. Initial assessment of an organizational situation or problem that needs to change is usually approached with less finesse and diplomacy than it would be approached by functionalists. It is, however, approached with the same kind of objectivist logic. Given the culture of the Social Change Organization, there is little need to tread softly or to worry about hurting colleagues' feelings. The focus of what is being assessed will depend on the organization's goals and concerns. What is important to remember is that assessment is an ongoing process, and that in this process hard and concrete facts are collected. Radical structuralists are very concerned that vast and rigorous information is gathered so that their analysis of the problem can be enhanced. Given their objectivist perspective, those in Social Change Organizations are predisposed to standardized measures or established tools that are designed to assess organizations.

Needs assessments that convey the problems of vulnerable population groups are ideal sources of information if the organization is seen as not properly addressing identified needs. Program data collected by committed volunteers and staff members is another source of information. When needs assessment data on the local level are not available to address an organizational change or perhaps set a new direction for the organization, the expectation is to search for quantitative data that indicate gaps in service and document just how oppressed a group is. When primary data sources are not available, organizational leaders can extrapolate from existing studies, use resource inventories to identify gaps in services, and collect and analyze service statistics from community agencies. They may collect primary data by conducting their own survey, and even hold or participate in public forums in order to assess needs of at-risk groups (Kettner, Moroney, & Martin, 2008). Each needs assessment method has its strengths and limitations. For the Social Change Organization, needs assessment methods must be critically reviewed to determine inherent biases toward certain population groups. For example, conducting one's own needs assessment survey is costly, but may be the only way to fully explore the perceived needs of an at-risk population. **Perceived needs** are those that have not come to the attention of service providers, are therefore invisible in the power domain, and are ignored in the planning of services. Social Change Organizations want to bring these needs to the attention of decision makers, and if their own organization is not meeting those needs they do not hesitate to prompt leaders, board members, or others about what the organization needs to be doing. Just as in our case example, there is no tolerance for an organization not following through on its own advocacy mandate.

Those Social Change Organizations that do provide direct services as part of their mission will collect assessment data for their programs using standardized forms. They are interested in gaining knowledge through the collection of facts and figures. But assessment forms used in traditional agencies may not meet their needs since these tools may be insensitive to the very population groups the organization is championing. Development of tools that are normed to various population groups will be an issue, as will the biases in most existing instruments. When assessment data are collected, the focus will be on the patterns and trends that reveal the need for structural change. The Social Change Organization will collect those data primarily to use the knowledge gained in the interests of drastic change. They may use the information to make the case that their own organization, programs, and services need to change in order to be sensitive to client needs.

In the assessment process, all the relevant stakeholders are included. In internal change demands in Social Change Organizations, it will be typical for volunteers and client-participants to be a part of the assessment process and recognized as change agents. Change agents will face conflict head on if there are disagreements about how to begin the assessment process or what data to collect. Given the volatility of the Social Change Organization, assessments may unapologetically lead to identifying numerous fundamental changes that need to occur within the organization rather than one specific program or service that is needed or must be changed.

ANALYZING PROBLEMS

With assessment data collected, the members of a Social Change Organization view problem analysis as a broadening experience. Rather than trying to prematurely label and narrow, problem analysis becomes a time to engage others in the process, attempting to gain as much new information as possible. Consciousness raising is important in order to avoid false consciousness about what constitutes the problem. Labeling the problem is a group process, in which a successful collective commitment to change the organization is as much a goal as the labeling. Thus, the practitioner who doesn't enjoy dialectical group process will be miserable in the Social Change Organization, because the inclusionary nature of practice will continue as one engages in problem identifying, organizing, and transforming.

In cause-oriented organizations there is a need for multiple constituents to own the problem and to be adamant that some action be taken. The importance of working closely together in naming the problem creates a bonding experience, and the commitment to the problem definition must be total so that the necessary zeal can be garnered so there is energy to overcome obstacles and effect fundamental change. Working out differences and dealing with conflict about what are the most urgent needs, problems, or issues in the organization takes time. Every voice must be heard and every participant must be more sophisticated in his or her understanding of the situation, or the problem analysis is not complete.

ORGANIZING INTERVENTIONS

Mobilization toward a common goal in a Social Change Organization emerges from the consciousness raising that occurs in assessment and problem identification. Organizing or mobilizing constituents is nothing new to social work. There is a long tradition of community organizing, and entire casebooks have been written about partnerships among community agencies and multiple constituencies (Nyden, Figert, Shibley, & Burrows, 1997). In the Social Change Organization, it is assumed that the analyzed problem leads to consciousness of the need for change in the organization or one of its units because that is the nature of organizations and social problems. Social Change Organizations exist in order to tackle social problems by organizing staff members, participants, volunteers, or others involved so that change can occur.

Fenby's (1991) action model is in keeping with the transformative, empowerment expectations of the Social Change Organization. The empowerment perspective is also a longtime part of the social work tradition (see Levy, 1994; Mondros & Wilson, 1994). Fenby builds her model from a critical approach that moves from the technical aspects of management to mechanisms used to understand the process of action. She identifies the need for deep understanding of underlying values and perceptions on the part of those calling for action in order to appropriately and ethically advocate for desired institutional change. Seeing connections, viewing people holistically, and changing established organizational patterns are elements of the action model understood as "radical action within the patriarchy" (p. 32). In addition, the literature on feminist organizations (for example, Bordt, 1997; Ferree & Martin, 1995; Handy, Kassam, Feeney, & Ranade, 2006; Hyde, 2000; Kravetz, 2004; Metzendorf, 2005) and women and power (Odendahl & O'Neil, 1994) goes beyond empowerment to provide explicit examples of the link between power and politics theory and feminist theory in an alternative view of organization practice.

The action model asserts that altered power relationships and reallocation of economic and social resources through structural change in social institutions is the goal of social change. This approach continues the tradition of social reform in social work with a primary focus on community organization and development, but it is relevant to organizational development as well. It is also most akin to the radical social work perspective as seen in the work of Galper (1976), Piven and Cloward (1971), and Bailey and Brake (1975). Asserting that economic, political, and social class stratification is created by and creates structures and institutions that allow some segments of society to suffer while others prosper, the effort is for the organizer, partnering with the oppressed or disadvantaged, to overcome the oppression (Alinsky, 1969; Rothman, 2007). Thus, in Social Change Organizations it is not unusual to have staff join with clients to advocate for change in the very organization they helped design to address those changes.

Recognizing injustice, inequity, and exploitation, the idea is to organize the disenfranchised to exert power such that change, by way of concessions from the dominant groups, is extracted. In organizations, dominant groups may take multiple forms—boards of directors, factions, formal or self-designated leaders, and even colleagues who have become comfortable in their power positions and have lost sight of the cause. Since resources are scarce and those with resources will not give them up willingly, conflict is inevitable. But it is only through this show of power by way of mass organizing and use of the political process that those with power are forced to share that power. There must be active advocacy, agitation, brokerage, and negotiation to overthrow current institutional arrangements.

When the interests of the powerful and the powerless are irreconcilable, harmonious solutions are impossible. Rather, struggle and conflict are inevitable in order to arrive at a new social order. Sometimes this struggle leads to the overthrow of current administration; other times the struggle spawns a totally new organization more appropriately targeted to the desired change. The struggle does not abate until reordering has been accomplished. Interestingly, there is an assumption by some that this new social order will inevitably oppress some segment of society, leading to other waves of dissent, struggle, conflict, and change. It is a cyclical process embedded in consciousness raising and responsive to the intended and unintended consequences of even the most desired change. Therefore, organizing for organizational renewal and change is an ongoing element in Social Change Organizations.

PRODUCING PRODUCTS AND OUTCOMES

Products in Social Change Organizations may take the form of well-researched educational materials used to inform various constituencies about issues and causes. Although direct service programs will have client-centered outcomes that focus on empowerment goals, ultimate outcomes will likely be seen at policy, community, and organizational levels, indicating that revolutionary structural changes have occurred in existing systems. Social Change Organizations value those products and outcomes that work toward broader transformational change.

This brings us to the implications for practice in Social Change Organizations. In the section that follows, we will examine the relevance of understanding the cultural values and characteristics, the roles and relationships, and the standards of practice in human service organizations based on radical structuralist assumptions.

IMPLICATIONS FOR PRACTICE IN SOCIAL CHANGE ORGANIZATIONS

The nature of this worldview and the theories that are derived from it make the radical structuralist perspective a very dangerous and yet a very attractive one. It is dangerous because it may be so attractive to those it draws that they may overlook the possibility that many others will be repelled by it. This visceral reaction may mean that reasoned analysis of costs and other potentially negative consequences will not be assessed in an even-handed manner in advance. The passion of the perspective may overtake the reason necessary for success and organizations dedicated to a specific "cause" may be seen as having tunnel vision. At the same time, regardless of whatever reasonableness an approach guided from this perspective may represent to some persons, the mere fact that it is designed from such a radical and potentially violent worldview will make others fearful of even considering the perspective. This fear may make them overreact to the ideas put forward in the perspective, making reasoned dialogue and analysis impossible.

One of the greatest challenges faced by members of Social Change Organizations is the radical structuralist position of *ethical absolutism*. Once critical consciousness is achieved, there is assumed to be a best way of defining what constitutes the core values of the organization. Granted, this best way will be a progressive one, but an absolute one nonetheless. Radical structuralists are fundamentalist in their orientation. In fact, they may be rabid fundamentalists for their cause, failing to see other alternatives. For the Consumer-Directed Advocacy Agency used as an example earlier, there is no way to define what constitutes consumer direction but their way; there is no way to work with disabled persons but their way; there is only one way to advocate for needed change—head on and aggressively.

Individualized attention to the person within a particular situation will also present a challenge to the absolutist vision. Each individual is not a unique person, but a member of a certain class of individuals representing either the powerful or the powerless. Understanding and managing complexity regarding individual experiences and motivations becomes a great challenge and mostly beyond the scope of this perspective.

There are some aspects of this perspective that will be difficult in an essentially human service system. For example, radical structuralists eschew organizational structures that tend to impinge on or prevent radical responses to mediate known needs. The manager or worker coming from this perspective may be seen in a Traditional Organization as the loose cannon unable to determine which battle to pick because all battles within the oppressive structure merit waging. They may be loose cannons because they will not wait for the right time or place for change, preferring to act because no one else will; and they do so with righteous criticism of all those preferring a more measured or reasoned response.

This suggests that focus for change action may be difficult. Organizing for change may also be difficult because setting priorities may be impossible. As with the functionalists, assuming rationality and the ability to control what goes on, the Social Change Organization may overlook important dimensions of individual reality in favor of class issues. Overlooking important dimensions of reality because of the focus on quantitatively valid and reliable measures may mean that radical responses become overkill. In addition, other types of off-targeting are also possible. An effort to overcome oppression, exploitation, and dehumanization of one class of individuals may result in yet another class of individuals becoming disadvantaged. Opening opportunities for women and minorities in an organization does not guarantee that a new way of doing business will evolve. Without other important changes, the shift will represent merely a different combination of who has power and who does not. Table 6.3 provides an overview of the practice characteristics in Social Change Organizations.

CONCLUSION

The Social Change Organization is committed to the alternative best way of approaching change. This sets up the expectation that discovery of a generalizable truth is possible and so, too, is control of organizing for

Table 6.3

Practice Characteristics in Social Change Organizations

Practice Element	Characteristics
Assessment	Systematic data collection is a first step in gathering information about identified issues.
	Standardized, quantitative forms are preferred, although instrument sensitivity to at-risk groups is a concern.
	Assessments provide hard, concrete, objective data to be used by interested parties to analyze the situation or problem.
	Data collection methods should be consistent.
Problem Analysis	Problem analysis flows from objective assessment data.
	With reassessments, analyses may change.
	Analysis requires consideration of objective data known about identified problems.
	Data gathering among all constituencies means engaging in a dialectical process to listen to all voices and to achieve consciousness about what constitutes the problem.
Organizing	Mobilizing people for change is critically important.
	Organizing is very action oriented, inclusive, and fraught with conflict.
Collective Transformational Change	Interventions may be at any level of the organization, but change is framed in the context of the organization's cause.
	Campaign and contest (conflict) tactics are used without reservation if necessary.
	The goal of organizational change is to keep the focus on the advocacy mission, making the organization more viable in its societal transformation.

change. The intent of the social change is revolution by superimposing a better way to meet identified societal needs.

What the organizational leader gains from the assumptions of this perspective on organizing is guidance on the creation of new valid and reliable instruments to assess organizational structure and behavior, tools that may be more sensitive to the collective needs of the groups for whom they advocate. The leader also gains guidance for the creation of outcome-measurement tools that measure change as a result of the consciousness raising that results from the distribution of the results of needs assessment activities. Both sets of data aid in responding to the productivity pressures of outside funders. However, the nature of the change process presents the risk of lack of effectiveness measures in the outcomes when the significance standard in statistics is used as the only measure of effectiveness. Structural change is the expectation from this perspective. That type of change may be so long in coming that funders' interests will have come and gone. What could be worse is that the need for measurement works against the process or development needs that might assure long-term success (Netting, O'Connor, & Fauri, 2007).

When adopting this organizational perspective for assessment, analysis, organizing, and collective transformational change, the practitioner loses a view of what is unique to the organization and its members in the organizational environment. Some of the subtle influences regarding processes are not captured in the data collection for decision making. This is true because there is little room for consideration of the more qualitative, affective, intuitive aspects of organizational life due to the rigor expectations that are assumed to be necessary for a critical consciousness.

For the leader in a Social Change Organization there is another serious challenge. This perspective and the theories within it offer little help in attending to the special opportunities and challenges provided by that which is different from the norm. Certainly, the practitioner within a Social Change Organization seeks to change existing norms, but the assumption that there should be definitive norms remains. In other words, a set of traditional norms may be replaced by a set of nontraditional, but equally rigid, norms and expectations.

We next turn to a third type of organization—the Serendipitous Organization. You will soon see that this organization holds assumptions about change and the use of knowledge in common with the functionalists. However, The Serendipitous Organization has a distinctively different perspective on absolutism that distinguishes it from both Social Change and Traditional Organizations.

DISCUSSION QUESTIONS

1. Why is planned change so valued in Social Change Organization practice? What paradigmatic and cultural assumptions support it? What benefits are gained by engaging in planned change? What might be potential problems when transformational change is the goal?
2. What type(s) of advocacy are typically performed in Social Change Organization practice? What types of tactics might be most congruent with the type of change most appreciated in a Social Change Organization?
3. Given the preferred structure and management style in Social Change Organizations, what are the challenges and opportunities for your own practice? How would working in a Social Change Organization fit with your comfort zone?
4. Review the characteristics of Social Change Organizations in Table 6.1. Where are the potential strengths and challenges for you as a practitioner in this type organization? Are there other characteristics

that you would add to this table? If so, what would they be and why would you add them?

5. Characterize the roles and relationships that are expected in a Social Change Organization. How do these fit with the practice standards and expectations related to managing and being managed in this type of organization? Reflect on what might be the meaning of all this for you as a developing practitioner. (This reflection could become part of a regular journaling exercise.)

6. As a practitioner in a Social Change Organization, what would you expect the challenges and opportunities to be in relationship to the environment in which this type of organization operates? What would you assume the standards and expectations to be vis-à-vis the environment? What might be the consequences of conservative environmental expectations for the development and successes of a Social Change Organization?

7. In reviewing the expectations regarding assessment, problem analysis, organizing, and collective transformational change in a Social Change Organization, what do you foresee as the strengths and challenges when the organization is engaged in a multicultural environment? What might be social justice issues and opportunities?

8. From the standpoint of a professional practitioner in a Social Change Organization, what are the costs and benefits of the preferred manner of evaluation of practice and performance within the organization? What are the challenges in program and service evaluation when advocacy and other more radical inputs might not produce immediate outcomes?

9. Going back to the Consumer-Directed Advocacy case in the beginning of Part II, use the content in this chapter to conduct an organizational analysis related to both structure and practice expectations. What insights are gained from your analysis?

CONNECTION AND COLLABORATION

I N PART III, we seek to understand practice within Serendipitous Organizations that are intent on context-based meaning making achieved through connection and collaboration. In Chapter 7, we look at the important aspects that go into the structure of these types of organizations with particular focus on the organizational theories that are congruent with this perspective on organizing. Chapter 8 looks at the behavior and practices that are congruent with these organizations. Starting with the *interpretive* paradigmatic perspective and moving to the *clan culture*, attention will be given to the values, preferences, and decision-making strategies that are congruent with organizations that have connection and collaboration goals.

In Chapter 7, two schools of organizational theory are highlighted: organizational culture and sense-making theory. Consideration is given to the consequences of interpretive theory for organizational structure and products, including how individuals within these organizations are expected to conform to norms that are often unstated and difficult for outsiders to understand. Implications are provided for understanding organizations as social constructions, including the subjective dimension of how people find meaning within them. Also included is a consideration of the implications of a comparison of these organizations to their traditional counterparts along the dimension of maintaining the status quo. While Traditional Organizations control for order, collaborative organizations revel in diversity.

The degree to which practice in meaning-making organizations is different from work in traditional and radical change organizations is explored through a close look at the values held in such organizations, especially related to the assumptions about how the organization and its employees should be. Consequences of the interpersonal, collaborative norm within meaning-making organizations are underscored with a goal of helping the practitioner understand the standpoint of persons who do not find the search for meaning in such a collaborative environment to be productive.

Through the lens of strategic management and the roles of managers and leaders within this approach in Chapter 8, we will highlight why individuals practicing from different perspectives may view change in meaning-making organizations as soft, subjective, and difficult to achieve. The paradox of process orientation in human services is addressed with attention to the differences in process orientation depending on organizational goals. The challenges of seeking consensus within a multiplicity of meanings will be explored, including the advocacy mechanisms considered congruent with this type of organization's goals.

As with the rest of the text, critical thinking, self-awareness, and multiculturalism will be of interest as programming, management, research, accountability, collaboration, emergent planning and paradox, along with advocacy are considered, especially in the end-of-chapter discussion questions. There the reader will focus on understanding and practicing in organizations that enhance meaning making and engage participants in the appreciation of differences while also seeking consensus. Issues of personal preference of organizational and decision-making style will be included.

To begin the investigation of organizations with the goal of connection and collaboration, take a look at the case example that follows. In the next two chapters, you will begin to see in detail how the structure and behavior within this type of organization differs markedly from what you have dealt with before in this text. Enjoy the adventure!

The Orange State Child Abuse Prevention Agency

One Saturday morning, more than 25 years ago, two young mothers were sitting at their kitchen table talking about the horrible stories they had heard regarding a couple of children who had been maltreated by their parents. At first, they were shocked about how any parent could harm his or her defenseless child; but as they talked more, they began to realize that during times of stress they also had come close to the kind of anger and reactivity that had resulted in harm to those children. When they first recognized this, they were alarmed at themselves. As they talked they became clear about why they did not maltreat their children; they had options; they had support. Out of this realization came the seed of an idea about making a difference for mothers and their children who lacked options and support. Together they decided that there ought to be a program that could help stressed-out parents care for and protect their children. That hour of conversation in the kitchen was the beginning of what was to become an influential statewide child abuse prevention organization committed to the development of options and support for struggling families.

The two founders of the organization had a great deal of experience running households of growing families with very busy husbands. They both were college educated, but they did not have human service experience. They had important community connections, knew how to balance a checkbook, and could sell their ideas. Within a couple of weeks, there were seven other women working with them on the idea of establishing a child abuse prevention organization that would offer support, education, and understanding to families at risk of losing their children to the child protection system. Each woman came with her own skill set and network of friends. Each woman identified with the vision of a supportive environment where families could find the resources necessary to keep everyone safe. From their own bank accounts, along with donations from families and friends, enough money was collected over several months to rent a small space, get some furniture, and hook up the utilities and a couple of phone lines. The Orange State Child Abuse Prevention Agency had become a reality!

During those first months, the nine women would meet a couple of times a week to establish the vision of what they were going to do. First, they decided what the answering machine would say about the agency and what the caller could expect when leaving a message. Then, one of the women with a marketing background helped them think through how they could declare who they were to both the service community and those clients who might need their service. The lawyer among them helped to prepare the papers to create their legal status, and the rest of the women began thinking about the kinds of programs they could deliver.

Someone heard about a grant that would be available from the state. All of them looked over the RFP (request for proposals) and decided that they could write a proposal focusing on *child abuse prevention education*. One person agreed to write the narrative about the need because she had access to state and local data. Another had a great idea about a public education campaign, and a third, using her accounting background, wrote the budget. They all decided that one of the women with the original idea, Pat, needed to be identified as the executive in charge of the agency because Myra, the other woman at the kitchen table that day, had already been designated as the chairwoman of the board of directors, as required to establish the agency's nonprofit status. Everyone was among the identified board members, but a couple of the women decided that they would rather volunteer in other ways, so by the time the funding became available, the prevention agency had identifiable staff, a board of directors, and a few volunteers, including some men, who became involved as a result of hearing about the whole idea.

With the three-year grant, it became clear that the small office would not support all the activities to which the group had committed. Pat and Myra located a lovely, bright office in an old office building downtown. They thought this would be good because it was on a bus line and close to many of the social service agencies that might be eventually sending referrals. (They continued to think in terms of direct, supportive services, even though the funding they had received was for large-scale education and prevention efforts.) Everyone pooled their resources and some of them even cleaned out their basements and attics to decorate this office. They wanted it to be warm and charming, inviting and safe for all who came in. They had comfy seats, toys for the children, and educational materials in several languages and at several reading levels. They used this as a test of the prevention material they were developing. Whoever came to the office was offered material and asked what they thought about it. The feedback would then shape the next versions of material.

They instituted teatime every day, where whoever was in the office at the time was invited to stop for a while, sit, relax, and enjoy the company and the conversation. It was at those times that they would ask whoever was there, from the building custodian to the representative of the state funding agency, what they thought about the ways to target child abuse prevention and what they thought about the marketing strategies that they had developed. It was also at those times that Pat began to hear about other needs that could be met only through direct services. At teatime and during the ongoing planning meetings, more and more discussion focused on developing family support services and how to staff them. Was a volunteer-led effort needed, or was it necessary to begin hiring professionals? What was clear to all was that if professionals were hired they would need to be those special types who really wanted to work collectively with many people possessing very different gifts and challenges. Some of the original nine thought that professionals, especially social workers and psychologists, would be more work than help. They wanted to remain a volunteer-led organization providing paraprofessional help in a very warm but professional way.

Now, 25 years later, most of those originally involved have moved on, but the professional-versus-volunteer question is still alive. The agency, depending on the funding source and cycle, has three to six programs and, on average, 20 employees representing a mix of full- and part-time workers with a variety of educational backgrounds. Everyone pitches in wherever they are needed, so programs come and go almost seamlessly. There is, however, a good deal of nervousness about job stability as one grant winds down and another has yet to hit. The board has expanded and diversified, but remains a close-knit group committed to the prevention ideal. Affiliate groups have developed all over the state. The biggest challenge now is with affiliates that think the home office needs to be more businesslike.

CHAPTER 7

Serendipitous Organizations

I N CHAPTER 2, we introduced the Interpretive Paradigm and Serendipitous Organizations; in this chapter, we expand on our original description by focusing on what goes into the structure of organizations holding this perspective on appropriate goals for organizing. We begin by examining themes found in interpretive thinking and the assumptions that flow from the Interpretive Paradigm, resulting in the *connection and collaboration* goals of what we are calling Serendipitous Organizations. Following this thorough paradigmatic grounding, the major organizational theories that can be said to fit within this perspective are identified. We close the chapter with a critical analysis, so that the reader is left with a perspective on what is gained and what is given up when approaching organizations from an interpretive worldview. We then transition to Chapter 8, which focuses on the culture and behavioral theories that guide the standards for practice in organizations with connection and collaboration goals.

As with the other organizations with differing paradigmatic perspectives and goals, the Serendipitous Organization is a prototype. We recognize that in day-to-day experience, it is not always so easy to classify organizations. As with organizations based in assumptions from other paradigms that may have staff members and contain units that operate under different assumptions, the same may be true of Serendipitous Organizations. When this happens, staff may experience paradoxes as differing assumptions clash. Having read this chapter, it is our hope that the reader will understand why interpretive assumptions about organizational goals may collide with radical change goals. It will also be clear that both Serendipitous Organizations with connection and collaboration goals and Traditional Organizations with order and control goals seek order and stability, but differ in what they think is necessary and possible.

Recall from Chapter 2 that in this organization there is a great deal of attention to the people side of the enterprise. The organization goals of connection and collaboration are congruent with the interpretivist worldview, where meaning, understanding, and good performance come from

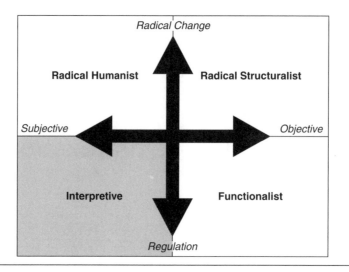

Figure 7.1 Burrell and Morgan's Paradigmatic Framework. *Source:* Adapted from Burrell and Morgan (1979). *Sociological paradigms and organizational analysis.* Aldershot, England: Ashgate. Figure 3.1, p. 22. Used by permission.

connections within the particulars of a context. Rather than having a hierarchical structure, the Serendipitous Organization works more intimately with a network of relationships being actively pursued and engaged. Figure 7.1 is a reminder of where the Serendipitous Organization fits within the paradigms introduced in Chapter 2.

INTERPRETIVE THEMES

Some of the more modern sociologically or interpretively oriented approaches to understanding organizations are based on assumptions that create the boundaries of the Interpretive Paradigm. From this perspective, the study of organizations is a mix of rational, nonrational, and intuitive thinking for both data collection and analysis. This approach is very personal, oriented to process within the organization and interested in *understanding*, rather than controlling organizations or organizational behavior. The assumption is that this very understanding is sufficient for successful organizing. Inquiry from this perspective accepts many ways of knowing. One can come to know and comprehend the organization from experience, from the use of the senses, from intuition and in conversation, among other ways. In addition, those taking this standpoint hold an interest in the meaningfulness of research findings to both the scholarly and the user communities. Therefore, relevance is a measure of the quality of organizational research. The results need to make sense to those within the organization, as well as to the scholars. The focus is on what is unique, although frequently occurring within a certain context. Because the particular context influences what meaning is constructed, it is assumed that the organizational context is central to understanding meaning of any phenomena under investigation in an organization.

For interpretivism, good research represents a re-humanization of the study process, in which organizational researchers are human beings dealing with human problems in human ways. Knowledge building is based on the recognition of the gifts of the human instrument, namely creativity, flexibility, and reflexivity. Language and its interpretation are at the base of the research process because through language comes shared meaning. Therefore, qualitative methods, including observation, participant observation, and various forms of interviewing, are recognized as the most helpful ways to make sense of complex situations. There is an appreciation of both induction and deduction as ways of analysis along with recognition of tacit, intuitive knowledge as a rigorous way of coming to an understanding of the views held by those people involved in the situation. From this perspective, truth emerges not as one objective view, but as the composite picture of how all those involved think. Observation is shaped by what is observed. Respondents are shaped by their interacting perceptions, expectations about the organizational research, and how the data will be used. What questions are asked and by whom largely determine what the results will be.

In the traditional view of knowledge building, the structural elements of the research design establish objectivity to guard against investigator bias. In interpretivism, objectivity is not expected; therefore, one gets adaptability, insight, and intuitive knowledge. There is no statement about human behavior in organizations being time and context free. There is no certitude, just tentatively held working hypotheses about what is occurring here and now. The most that can be expected as a result of an interpretive process is a statement about characteristics and presumed relationships in this time and this place. What is known is understood to be limited to the organizational context under investigation.

For example, in the Orange State case, what the board, the volunteers, or the founders needed to know was dependent on what was happening at a particular time. What they could do with the information was dependent on the resources at hand, which were always emerging as they all became more sophisticated about the needs they wanted to address and how they needed to go about addressing them. How the organization looked one year did not resemble how it looked the next, but connection and collaboration remained keys to the organizing process.

Generalizable theories are of little use in a socially constructed and socially sustained environment. Instead, tentatively held hypotheses or grounded theories, those that are derived from the inquiry itself, are acceptable for the purposes of knowledge building. What is known is held tentatively, because it is always changing. Knowledge building occurs within the context of the phenomena under investigation and is aimed at capturing not only the content but also the process of meaning making about the phenomena. The context and its values bound the rules that guide rigorous knowledge building, thus preserving the frames of reference of the participants. Those involved in the research in the context of their organizational practice help to determine what should be researched by whom and what constitute acceptable results. Both those providing and those receiving service in the Orange State prevention organization participated in this determination. There is no expectation that results should have meaning to anyone beyond those who participate. No generalizability is called for or expected. Findings may be useful in another time or context, but the responsibility for this determination rests with the consumer of the results, those who hear or read about the research product, not the researchers or research participants. This is why the board of directors in the Orange State Child Abuse Prevention Agency was not dismayed by the concerns of affiliates. They understood what was working for them in their context and expected the affiliates to work out their own solutions.

ASSUMPTIONS OF THE INTEPRETIVE PARADIGM

Unlike both the functionalist and radical structuralist perspectives, the interpretivist perspective sees reality as a product of human consciousness. Reality is what a human thinks it is. *Interpretivism* embraces a belief in a subjective, rather than an objective, reality. *Subjectivity* assumes that the social world exists as an emergent process that is created by the individuals concerned. Reality, then, is not independent of the human mind, but inextricably linked to individual experience. This makes reality little more than a network of assumptions and intersubjectively shared meanings that are always in flux due to the shaping of multiple individual perspectives. How reality is constructed depends on who is involved in the construction. Rather than the realism of more traditional perspectives, here there is a relativist assumption, that the world, though ordered, is emergent and always being created intersubjectively. Nothing holds as true across time and context.

In Chapter 2 (Table 2.1), we reviewed four terms that define subjectivism. We repeat them here so that the reader will have a reference for review (see Box 7.1).

A subjectivist perspective assumes that social reality exists primarily in the human consciousness (a product of one's mind). A subjectivist would say that knowledge about reality is soft, subjective, and natural (antipositivism). Human nature is based in voluntarism; people can be proactive in creating their own realities. Free human beings participate actively in the creation and construction of social reality. Further, reality to be transmitted and understood must be experienced. One cannot understand without

---

Box 7.1

SUBJECTIVISM: DEFINING TERMS

Nominalism (in the mind)
Antipositivism (soft, subjective, must be experienced)
Voluntarism (people create their environments)
Ideographic (analyze subjective accounts that one generates by "getting inside"
    situations of everyday life)

Source: Adapted from Burrell and Morgan (1979). *Sociological paradigms and organizational analysis*. Aldershot, England: Ashgate. Figure 1.1, p. 3. Used by permission.

---

experience. Finally, a subjectivist perspective is idiographic, meaning that concern should not be focused on universal principles or in an absolutist view. Instead, subjectivists emphasize what is unique and relative to the individual and the ways in which individuals create, change, and interpret the world. This is an insider's view, not the objective view of an outsider.

Since interpretivism sees the world subjectively, there is no universalism in which there is "one best way." An interpretivist perspective is not congruent with a functionalist or radical structuralist perspective about the nature of reality. Interpretivism does not look for universal truths, derived from some external force. Instead, the search is for multiple truths that arise from within people. Therefore, the Serendipitous Organization in its congruence with the interpretive perspective would provide an alternative to traditional ways of thinking about organizing. Traditional thinking based on a functionalist perspective seeks order through locating the best way to do the work of the organization. The Serendipitous Organization seeks order, but that order is socially constructed by those involved and will change over time. What is considered a best way today may no longer be a best way tomorrow. In our child protection case, what worked during one funding cycle generally was not what was necessary to accomplish during another funding cycle. Dynamic change was expected, but not chaos.

Interpretivism seeks order, rather than conflict. This position is related to functionalism. These two paradigms may disagree on how truth is derived, but both interpretivism and functionalism are interested in maintaining order. Like functionalism, interpretivism holds a regulation perspective in which consensus, social integration, solidarity, needs satisfaction, and actuality are possible and desirable. Box 7.2 summarizes the concerns of this regulation perspective.

Interpretivism believes in the status quo. However, the status quo will have been constructed through a consensual process very different from a functionalist consensual process. In functionalism, consensus is gained when there is agreement on universal principles or assent to the average (those with the most votes win), whereas interpretivism requires the

---

Box 7.2

CONCERNS OF THE REGULATION PERSPECTIVE

1. Status quo
2. Social order
3. Consensus
4. Social integration and cohesion
5. Solidarity
6. Need satisfaction
7. Actuality

Source: Adapted from Burrell and Morgan (1979). *Sociological paradigms and organizational analysis.* Aldershot, England: Ashgate. Table 2.2, p. 18. Used by permission.

---

refocusing of consensual decisions depending on the current need. The source of truth in interpretivist thought is found in interaction and is, therefore, subject to change as new ideas emerge and new perspectives are included. Consensus is a process, not a product. It is ongoing, so that the process builds solidarity. When individuals are in constant conversation and communication, they become more conversant about the issues under discussion, but they also become more familiar with those in the conversation. These connections of ideas and people establish the possibility for solidarity, an important element of interpretive stability achieved through connection and collaboration, as was the experience in the child abuse prevention agency.

The assumptions of the Interpretive Paradigm are summarized in Box 7.3. This box may serve as a reference for you to determine the degree

---

Box 7.3

ASSUMPTIONS OF THE INTERPRETIVE PARADIGM

From the Subjectivist Perspective

1. Social reality exists primarily in the human mind.
2. Knowledge about social reality is soft, subjective, and natural.
3. People can be proactive in creating their own realities.
4. Given that individuals create, change, and interpret the world, qualitative approaches to understanding are useful.

From the Regulation Perspective

5. Society is characterized by social order and equilibrium.
6. Knowledge for knowledge's sake is acceptable.
7. Consensus, rather than conflict, is important.

Source: Adapted from Burrell and Morgan (1979), Chapter 1.

to which organizations with which you are familiar fit within this paradigmatic perspective.

In sum, human nature for the Interpretive Paradigm involves ultimate possibilities. Human consciousness creates reality through consensus, social integration, and cohesion. Human nature is social. It is within social interaction and solidarity that self-actualization and meaning are created. Truth is what the individual thinks it is, based on personal, subjective experience. Coming to truth is an ongoing process because truth is socially created and recreated. Truth is personally derived or socially constructed. Truth in the organization is a social construct, as well. Serendipitous Organizations are intimate organizations with the same sort of feeling as the Orange State case. To understand how this intimacy is achieved, let's look at the major organizational theories in this paradigm.

SERENDIPITOUS ORGANIZATION THEORIES SUPPORTING CONNECTION AND COLLABORATION GOALS

A number of organizational theories were introduced in previous chapters. These theories tended to seek universal approaches to an ideal organizational structure and practice and to guide managers toward the best way to encounter the environment and achieve traditional or social change goals. It is important to note that functionalism and radical structuralism are not necessarily naive about subjectivism. Indeed, these other two paradigms acknowledge that there are differences in the ways people think and in the ways organizations function. However, knowing that there are differences is one thing; embracing them is an entirely different matter. For example, systems theorists recognize the complexity and diversity of organizational environments. With objectivist assumptions, this plurality is something to be controlled. In interpretivism with a subjectivist focus, this multiplicity of difference is stimulating and interesting, assisting in understanding the complexity of the organization in its context.

Perhaps some theories previously introduced could be adapted to fit an interpretivist perspective without violating the basic propositions of the theories. However, in the 1970s and beyond, the limits of existing theories led to the development of most of the theories that are placed within the parameters of the Interpretive Paradigm. Since they are relatively new, they are not as well tested or as well developed as some of the more traditional theories that have already been discussed. It should be clear why testing for generalizability is not of interest in this perspective; meaning and meaning making in context is. This lack of traditional testing and the mandate for relevance of what is developed leaves these theories open to criticism, even within interpretivism.

Given the objectivist nature of both Functionalist and Radical Structuralist paradigms, interpretive theories are often viewed with disdain since they have not proven to be generalizable through rigorous "scientific" testing, even though most represent insights about organizations that make intuitive sense. Ironically, from an interpretive perspective, if theories attempted to reach this generalizability standard, then this achievement would be contrary to the assumptions of uniqueness and the impossibility of generalization found in the Interpretive Paradigm. To avoid criticism from traditionalists, an interpretivist theoretician would have to violate the assumptions of the paradigm that was developed to overcome their own criticisms of traditional ways of understanding organizations—quite a paradox, indeed.

In previous chapters, we used Shafritz, Ott, and Lang (2005) as a resource to identify major perspectives in organizational theory. In this chapter, we focus primarily on theories within one of their groupings: *organizational culture theory.*

Other theoretical perspectives have influenced the development of interpretive theories, but we consider theories of organizational culture to have originated from interpretive assumptions, so they represent the purest examples of this paradigmatic perspective. For us, organizational culture theories are pivotal in understanding the Serendipitous Organization.

ORGANIZATIONAL CULTURE THEORY

Organizational culture theorists discovered a very different construction of organizational reality by rejecting the methods of traditional organizational research. The units of analysis and the methods and approaches undertaken to understand organizations and their cultures were very different from those used in the functionalist quantitative tradition. Borrowing from sociology and anthropology, organizational researchers adapted qualitative research designs and methods to get at the *meaning dimension* of organizational life. They recognized that inquiry into organizational structure, management information systems, planning processes, market decisions, goals and objectives development, and other areas of focus in the Functionalist Paradigm will give clues to what the organization is about, but the traditional quantitative methods miss important subtle, unconscious, forgotten elements. Based on their research results, they assert (see, for example, Van Maanen, 1979, 1983; Van Maanen, Dabbs, & Faulkner, 1982) that to understand the organization's behavior it is necessary to understand the organization's culture. For these researchers, organizational culture is more easily identified and understood using ethnographic and phenomenological methods rather than standard quantitative methods.

Interest in organizational culture dominated organizational thinking during the 1980s and 1990s. Martin and Frost (1996) metaphorically referred to the struggle among researchers interested in organizational culture as a game of King of the Mountain, in which different theoretical perspectives about cultures vied for control. Later Martin referred to this vying for control as "culture wars" (Martin, 2002, p. 29). They categorize three groups of cultural research: (1) revolutionary vanguards; (2) value engineering and the integration perspective; and (3) the differentiation perspective. We focus on each category below.

Revolutionary Vanguards   Although the language of culture in organization began to appear in the 1950s, originally it was mostly used as a way to describe the necessity of socializing individuals into the organization so that they would conform to the culture and thus assure better productivity. Books such as *The Changing Culture of a Factory* (Jaques, 1951) and *The Organization Man* (Whyte, 1956) focused on how the individual conformed to corporate life. Not until the 1960s and 1970s did several books begin to pay increased attention to the natural socialization that occurs within organizations and professions. Widely read were books like *Boys in White* by Becker, Greer, Hughes, and Stauss (1961), which focused on the socialization of students into the medical profession, and Kaufman's *The Forest Ranger* (1960), which studied conformity among remotely stationed rangers in the U.S. Forest Service.

Early organizational culture theorists viewed functionalist approaches to organizations as too reliant on rational ways of understanding human behavior. What was known about organizations was typically based on quantitative analyses, and managers were expected to control numbers rather than to understand people. The emergence of this interpretive approach to understanding organizational culture was filled with hope and expectation as theorists actually advocated for thinking beyond the structural boxes, so common in functionalist thinking, to the humanity of the persons working in the structures. Organizational culture theory gave managers permission and encouragement to examine the human, affective factors often seen as irrelevant in Traditional Organizations.

The understanding of the mental processes of how organizational participants come to understand organizations is based on a groundbreaking work by Berger & Luckman (1967), who described the cognitive and affective dimensions of what they termed a *socially constructed reality*. Their work, the basis of the social constructivism and constructionism so popular in direct practice today, was based on their study of the process of organizing. For them, it did not matter whether things were real in and of themselves; it is the perceptions of these things that have impact and are real. Thus, perceptions of the organizational symbols that result from organizational culture became an integral part of organizational culture theory and became *symbolic management*.

Bolman and Deal's (2003) basic tenets of symbolic management help in setting the stage:

1. What is most important is not what happens but what it means.
2. Activity and meaning are loosely coupled; events have multiple meanings because people interpret experience differently.
3. In the face of widespread uncertainty and ambiguity, people create symbols to resolve confusion, increase predictability, give final direction, and anchor hope and faith.
4. Many events and processes are more important for what is expressed than what is produced. They form a cultural tapestry of secular myths, heroes and heroines, rituals, ceremonies, and stories that help people find purpose and passion in their personal and work lives.
5. Culture is the glue that holds an organization together and unites people around shared values and beliefs (pp. 242–243).

The culture theories that are congruent with Japanese management and the perceived failures of traditional approaches to organizations began to appear in the 1970s. They represented, and continue to represent, alternative perspectives to traditional organizational theories based on very different assumptions about organizational realities and relationships. These early theorists were interested in understanding how organizational cultures form and change and how culture affects leadership and relationships in establishing organizational directions. As a result, organizations began to be understood in more symbolic ways.

With this vanguard, the struggle among cultural theorists for supremacy was just beginning (Martin, 2002; Martin & Frost, 1996, p. 604). There was almost a playfulness among theorists as they focused on new ways of understanding dimensions of organizations that had long been neglected. Martin and Frost (1996) categorize these earlier theorists as *revolutionary vanguards* because they opened the way for others to begin thinking about socialization to organizational culture. This focus on socialization and the impact of existing cultures on workers did not yet include questions about how cultures are formed and change, or how leaders affect culture. In fact, as late as 1987, traditional writers such as Shafritz and Ott (1987) introduced organizational culture in an earlier edition of their book on classic theory as being *countercultural*, indicating that this approach to understanding organizations had not yet been accepted as part of mainstream organizational thought.

Value Engineers and Integrationists   Martin and Frost (1996) categorize the next wave of organizational culturalists as *value engineers* and *integrationists*. In the early 1980s, more and more popular literature appeared on the topic of organizational culture, and writers declared that a culture could be established by leaders who were in touch with their values or the values one wished to create within the organization. This approach was termed **value engineering,** because these theorists assumed that a leader could actually instill her or his values within the organization and practice.

In attempting to go beyond what earlier theorists had discovered about socialization to an organization's culture, Louis (1980) began to explore what happens when newcomers enter unfamiliar settings. Identifying a number of ways in which newcomers are surprised when they enter cultures, Louis expanded the understanding of the complexity of the transitional process from being an outsider to being inside. This move toward more complex thinking about organizational culture occurred simultaneously with a number of developments in the popular management literature.

When Peters and Waterman published *In Search of Excellence* in 1982, the concept of corporate culture burst into the management literature like a welcomed boost to morale. They promoted a unified corporate culture as the key to organizational success. *Corporate culture* became a buzzword in the popular management literature. Consultants on the development of corporate culture proliferated. Full of practical information on how to develop a unified culture, Peters and Waterman were the first in a barrage of books on how to create and change culture.

In some ways, this energy was built on the popular influence of Ouchi's *Theory Z* (1981), where excellence was seen in organizations that promoted a sense of family. Focus on simplicity and consensus permeated the field. Bored by traditional organizational research, some academicians were enthralled with the possibilities of this approach. The idea of creating a unified culture, without focusing on potential conflicts, was well received and studies that looked for this consistent, consensual organizationwide cultural experience were labeled as *integration* research (Martin & Frost, 1996, p. 602).

An integrationist perspective fit well with interpretive assumptions. There was a search for consensus, and if conflict did occur it was seen as a natural transition that occurs when change is about to take place. If an organization was going through a cultural transformation, then some discomfort and uneasiness would naturally need to occur, but the point was to get to a place where everyone could collaborate within a culture that all parties could embrace. Harmony among members of the organization was the goal. The concept of shared values, vision, and culture revealed an underlying message that organizational members could forge a joint subjective consensus.

Whereas Peters and Waterman's book hit the popular press and influenced both academic and managerial audiences alike, Edgar Schein's (1985) book, *Organizational Culture and Leadership*, offered a more theoretical or academic approach that spelled out the cultural concept in detail. Schein (1992) provides a list of concepts used by various writers to allude to culture:

1. "Observed behavioral regularities when people interact," including their language, customs, traditions, and rituals
2. "Group norms" that evolve as standards and values for working together
3. "Espoused values" that people announce as the beliefs that guide what they do
4. "Formal philosophy," the board policies and ideologies that direct the work
5. "Rules of the game," often known as *the ropes*
6. "Climate," the physical layout and how it *feels*
7. "Embedded skills," the ability to pass on competencies to the next generation
8. "Habits of thinking, mental models, and/or linguistic paradigms," as things taught to new members as they are socialized to the organization
9. "Shared meanings," group understandings that develop as they work together
10. "Root metaphors or integrating symbols," the ideas, feelings, images, and even physical layout that represent the group's artifacts (Schein, 1992, pp. 9–10)

Schein's point is that all of these concepts reflect aspects of an organization's culture, but that none of them are culture unto themselves. He adds that culture implies two additional elements: *"structural stability* in the group," and *"patterning or integration* of the elements into a larger . . . gestalt that ties together the various elements and that lies at a deeper level" (p. 10). The point of view needs to hold together and permeate the structure, perspectives, and behaviors of organizational participants.

Schein (1992) defines **organizational culture** as "a pattern of shared basic assumptions that the group learned as it solved its problems of external adaptation and internal integration, that has worked well enough to be considered valid and, therefore, to be taught to new members as the correct way to perceive, think, and feel in relation to those problems" (p. 12). Note that Schein begins with "shared basic assumptions." Yet, one often enters organizations in which those basic assumptions are so ingrained that they are often not even recognized on a conscious level. Have you ever entered an organization and known that you had stepped into another culture in which you did not know *the rules?* Perhaps you had a sense that you had said or done something *wrong*, but you didn't have a clue about what it was. Chances are that you tripped over a basic unstated assumption that everyone else held as the correct way of behaving in that culture. Note that Schein indicates that these assumptions are *considered valid*, whereas Louis (1980) would call these *surprises*. Did you ever try to change an organization and wonder why you met resistance, when the change seemed so logical to you? Perhaps what you considered valid was not what others considered valid. Perhaps the stated norms or rules were not *really* the norms guiding behavior in that organization.

Looking again at the Orange State case, for years the organization operated within norms of connection and collaboration without thought being given to how that shaped the organizational structure and practices. It was only when the organization grew to include programs and individuals coming from different perspectives that organizational participants began to question what was there.

Solving problems of external adaptation and internal integration refers to the ways in which organizational members go about working on their relationship with the larger external environment and dealing with issues internal to the organization. Schein (1992) contends that *adapting externally* includes gaining a consensus on the following elements:

1. *Mission and strategy:* coming up with a shared understanding of the organization's mission, major task, and manifest and latent functions
2. *Goals:* using the core mission to develop a consensus around goals
3. *Means:* figuring out ways to attain the goals (e.g., organizational structure, staffing, incentive systems, power and authority relationships)
4. *Measurement:* establishing criteria to measure how the work is going, including an information system to track effectiveness
5. *Correction:* identifying remedial or repair strategies to use when goals are not met (Schein, 1992, p. 52)

According to Schein, if these five areas are minimally necessary for an organization to structure itself to survive in its environment, then there is great potential for misunderstanding when persons from different backgrounds enter the organization. What if you came from a voluntary organization with a very loose structure in which power and authority relationships were considered unimportant, where people worked as colleagues, and teams worked toward goal achievement with minimal supervision? What would happen when you entered a large public bureaucracy in which authority and power were differently defined and in which teamwork was not encouraged? No matter how much one liked one's colleagues, this would be an adjustment to a different culture. Would you become acculturated, meaning you would embrace this new culture? Or might you accommodate, missing the familiar culture from which you had come? Might you even want to change the culture you had entered?

Schein also elucidates the factors required for *internal integration* of an organization's culture. These include the development of a common language and conceptual categories; group boundaries; power and status dimensions; norms concerning relationships; rewards and punishments;

and even ways to explain uncontrollable events (Schein, 1992, p. 66). Schein explains that cultural assumptions provide a filter for how one views the world and that if one is stripped of that filter, anxiety and overload will be experienced. Cultural solutions offer routine answers to what normally would be complex problems. The major reason organizational members resist cultural change is because it challenges deeply held assumptions that stabilize one's world—it questions the status quo. This is why members of a dysfunctional culture might choose to retain current assumptions rather than risk having their cultural roots challenged. Schein also lists three levels of organizational culture as reflected in Box 7.4.

Identification with artifacts, values, and assumptions allows the group to develop, and group development results in culture. These are also clues about ways an outsider can get to know an organization's culture.

Box 7.4

LEVELS OF ORGANIZATIONAL CULTURE

Level 1: Artifacts

- Most visible level of the culture
- The organization's constructed physical and social environment
- Use of physical space
- Output of group
- Written and spoken language
- Metaphors used
- Artistic productions
- Members' behavior

Level 2: Values

- Cognitively transformed into a belief, when holding that value works.
- Ultimately, some values will be transformed into assumptions.
- *Espoused values* are what people say they believe, but they don't always act in accordance with them. This would be a separation of culture from behavior.

Level 3: Basic Underlying Assumptions

- So taken for granted that one finds little variation in a unit
- Theories-in-use
- Often hard to assess whether we are dealing with organizational culture or
  - professional culture
  - Disciplinary culture
  - Regional variations
  - Ethnicity
  - Gender

Source: Adapted from Schein (1992), Chapter 2.

In the theoretical literature, it was Schein's work that revealed the necessity of identifying the assumptions that leaders bring to an organization. He contended that it is those assumptions that will help to identify how acceptable change occurs within an organization. Kilmann et al. (1985) and other writers also recognized that values, beliefs, assumptions, perceptions, norms, and artifacts in organizations are the forces behind organizational activities and change. In fact, organizational culture is the social dynamic that moves people; culture is the behind-the-scenes, yet motivating theme that adds guidance and meaning for actions within an organization. These internal actions are dependent on the patterns of assumptions held by those in the organization. Those assumptions are linked to what worked in the past. They are not necessarily a conscious part of the current organizational ethos, but remain forceful even when the organizational context changes. The culture tends to remain an underlying force—unquestioned, universally accepted, and not open to critical analysis. The culture remains the unquestioned reasons for what is done; it controls behavior. Unlike what has been asserted in other theories, it is not personal preferences, nor formal rules, authority, or norms of rational behavior, that control organizational behavior. Instead, it is cultural norms, values, beliefs, and assumptions that maintain the status quo in the Serendipitous Organization. Context is everything.

It is very important to recognize that traditional leaders with a functionalist perspective who wanted to know how to manipulate and persuade employees also embraced the more popularized version of the corporate culture discussion. The discussion was attractive because it facilitated employees embracing a common point of view so that productivity could increase. The functionalists' language may have been interpretive, but the use of culture was anything but a subjectivist appreciation of difference. Instead, managers looked for ways to change existing cultures and to engineer (or reengineer) values for the organization's benefit. For example, managers couched their desires for change in terms such as *empowerment* of employees and *teamwork*, when they were unwilling to relinquish control over decision making. Persons with no intention of relinquishing control can appeal to a sense of group identity and espouse norms of inclusiveness. Such a use of organizational culture to place one's own values over the values of others is anything but collaborative in its intent. One could say that such a manager is a functionalist in interpretive clothing.

An example of the functionalist perspective usurping an interpretive concept can be found in Shafritz, Ott, and Lang (2005), who devote a chapter in their book, *Classics of Organizational Theory*, to what they call *reform through changes in organizational culture*. The perspectives under reform are viewed as concessions to readers and reviewers who frequently requested articles representing the current management trends. These reform pieces share a common theme—the centrality of organizational culture. Included in Shafritz, Ott, and Lang's reform section is the work of William Ouchi on the Z Organization, Peters and Waterman's Excellence Movement, Senge's work on the learning organization, Acker's work on gendering organizations, Al Gore's report on reinventing government, and Taylor Cox's work on managing diversity. We refer the reader to Shafritz, Ott, and Lang or to the literature on how to change organizational culture that can be seen on the bookshelves of any management library. However, beware of the underlying assumptions in most of these works. The language is interpretivist, but the goals are often functionalist. For the most part, these movements have been focused on applying the concept of organizational culture with the purpose of providing prescriptive techniques for managers and leaders whose better understanding of organizational culture could then be used to control and change the organization. Connection and collaboration are not the goals; structure and control are. This is not Interpretive Paradigm or serendipitous organizational thinking.

Differentiators   Within interpretivist thought, as excitement about organizational culture and the proliferation of integration research grew, another group of scholars were working independently on similar concepts. They agreed that traditional organizational theory and research was uncreative and dull. Some of these scholars were qualitative researchers who were relieved finally to see interest develop in more than quantitative methods. Others were persons who had been on the fringe of organizational research, convinced that something new had to happen in understanding organizations, and were hoping to capture new ways of thinking that would go beyond traditional ways of knowing.

Like integration studies, differentiation studies focused on topics such as values, symbolism, meaning, and emotion—topics neglected in traditional organizational research. However, differentiators did not limit their focus to the informal, interactional, and esthetic aspects of culture. They advocated for a more holistic view in which formal practice and structural aspects of organizations were considered as well.

Reacting to the value engineers and integrationists, some differentiators faced the challenges of conflict head on, believing that a good organizational study could not ignore the complexities of deep-rooted conflict, inconsistencies, and differences in interpretation among cultural members. Given their predisposition to focus on conflict and inconsistencies, differentiationists drew heavily from Marxist/critical theory and took a more critical than interpretive perspective. Having less concern about consensus than their interpretive colleagues, organizational culture theorists and researchers who came from a *differentiation* perspective eventually became more aligned with the assumptions of the Radical Humanist Paradigm. Therefore, when we summarize the placement of organizational theories within the Interpretive Paradigm later in this chapter, we will place organizational culture differentiators very close to the line between the two paradigms.

Sense-Making Theory

Closely related and highly compatible with organizational culture theory is *sensemaking theory*. The idea of sense making in organizations developed when Roethlisberger and Dickson (1939) suggested that an organization's structure and environment could be understood based on the meaning that employees attach to objects or events. More modern thoughts about sense making are concerned with language and symbols and understanding.

Historically, sensemaking theory emerged from the legacy of Festinger's (1957) *cognitive dissonance theory*. This theory holds that explanations of events are often based on a retrospective, rather circular, thinking, instead of a reporting of a linear process based on linear logic. For example, when a person chooses among mutually exclusive alternatives, he or she will have to live with his or her choice. Since most such choices have negative as well as positive consequences, the person may experience anxiety or feel agitated. This is dissonance. To reduce dissonance, the person will quickly focus on the negative features of the alternatives they did not take, while simultaneously playing up the positive traits of the selected option. Retrospectively, the person alters the meaning of his decision or what he did and changes the meaning of the other possible options, thus constructing a plausible story that makes "sense" and helps to reduce the dissonance and explain the "rightness" of the choice.

Some feminist scholars on organization can be placed in the Interpretive Paradigm for their contributions to sensemaking theories. The feminist theorists in the interpretivist perspective are those who focus on how gender impacts culture and leadership. Calás and Smircich (1996) categorized feminist theories and their contribution to organizational studies as liberal, radical, psychoanalytic, Marxist, socialist, poststructuralist, and third world/(post) colonial (p. 220). We see the liberal and socialist traditions as fitting with interpretive assumptions, although Calás and Smircich would argue that the liberal feminist tradition is functionalist in orientation. We think that because liberal feminists tend to use quantitative methods, they might be considered functionalists; but because they base their work on interpretive assumptions regarding meaning making for women in organizations, they are very much within the Interpretive Paradigm. (We do this also because we believe that research methods are not paradigmatic; both qualitative and quantitative methods may be used in any of the paradigms.)

Many of these feminist organizational scholars (see, for example, Davies, 1975; Hearn & Parkin, 1987; Kelly, 1991) assert that male control of organizations has been accomplished by the use of a male lens to under-stand organizations. It is the feminist perspective, with questions in the woman's voice, that shows that organizations are not gender neutral. Further, research and theories used to understand organizational structure and behavior are also not gender neutral.

Gherardi (1995) brings culture and gender together for sense making by arguing that "organizational cultures differ according to their gender regimes and, consequently, according to the social patternings that they give to gender citizenship. . . . How gender is 'done' in an organization is a crucial cultural phenomenon; and how it can be 'done' differently is a challenge to all those who work for organizations . . ." (pp. 3–4). She further asserts, "in a gender regime which systematically devalues everything connected with the female, the organization can never be-come democratic, whatever affirmative action it may introduce, and whatever equal opportunity legislation may be promulgated" (p. 9). It is from the socialist feminists that the intersections of gender, race, class, and sexuality have been highlighted (see Acker, 1990, 1994; Collins, 1990; Lugones & Spelman, 1983) to expand sense making about organizations.

Without necessarily adopting a gender lens, the mental processes used to make sense of organizational environments are central to sensemaking theory. For example, conscious thought in understanding and coping with organizations is the focus of the work of Louis (1980) and features change, contrast, and surprise for newcomers to organizations. Her research on retrospective accounts to explain organizational surprises indicates that "newcomers often attach meanings to action, events, and surprises in the new setting using interpretation schemes developed through their experiences in other settings." Based on these, "inappropriate and dys-functional interpretations may be produced" (p. 450). From this research came a call for practices that facilitate sense making, including research techniques that produce relevant and useful information for the context in which the research is undertaken.

Gareth Morgan (1986) provided more clarity about the symbolic aspects of making sense of organizations in his *Images of Organizations*. In 1997, Morgan published a second edition, further attempting to define and understand organizations. Morgan demystified what was often seen as "a kind of magical power to understand and transform the situations [successful managers and problem solvers] encounter" (p. 3). His premise was "that all theories of organization and management are based on implicit images or metaphors that lead us to see, understand, and manage organizations in distinctive yet practical ways" (p. 4). Defining metaphors as "attempt[s] to understand one element of experi-ence in terms of another" (p. 4), he proceeded to elaborate on the meta-phorical images most frequently used when people try to define and understand organizations. Here is an updated list of Morgan's (2007) metaphors:

- Organizations as Machines
- Organizations at Organisms
- Organizations as Brains
- Organizations as Cultures
- Organizations as Political Systems
- Organizations as Psychic Prisons
- Organizations as Flux and Transformation
- Organizations as Instruments of Domination

Morgan details each metaphor, identifies theories that reflect each metaphor, and examines the strengths and limitations of each. Morgan's metaphors highlight certain interpretations of the organization. For example, if one encounters organizations as prisons, then he or she will act within the organization as if it were a prison. Morgan goes beyond connecting the metaphor to understanding and behavior by saying that the metaphor can also be used as an instrument of change. Metaphorically imagining an organization as different from what it is can be the first step to changing the character and culture of the organization. Since the ways in which individuals read organizations are distinctive, but also only partial pictures, the metaphor can be used as a device for expanding conversations within the organization. Understanding each other's use of metaphor is to understand each other's way of thinking and seeing the organizational world. This is a step to understanding the complex, ambiguous, and paradoxical world of the organization. For Morgan, metaphorical thinking presents new ways of approaching and solving organizational problems.

As another mechanism for sense making and problem solving, Starbuck and Milliken (1988) focus on how individuals place stimuli into some kind of framework. Sackman (1993) was interested in the mechanisms organizational members use to attribute meaning to events in order to understand the "standards and rules for perceiving, interpreting, believing and acting that are typically used in cultural settings" (p. 33). These scholars of sense making in organizations are interested in how individuals organize information structurally, and how they comprehend information, compensate for surprise, construct meaning, and interact with others in the organization in pursuit of mutual understanding.

Weick (1995), who recognizes the instability of organizational contexts and the real challenges in providing "relevant and reliable" information, sees sense making as less about discovery and more about invention. Because in interpretivism, there is no reality "out there," but only that which can be constructed in the mind, to engage in sense making is to construct, filter, frame, and create that which can act as fact (Turner, 1987). Weick embraces the ambiguity and uncertainty of organizational life. He sees sense making as the way to take advantage of the situation and has identified its seven properties:

1. *Identity.* As individuals name, describe, and analyze organizations, they rethink their understandings based on their changing experiences and their effects on sense of self. Therefore, "making sense" of an organization is tied to a person's identity, and understandings about that organization change as the person grows and develops.
2. *Retrospection.* Understanding organizations is based on "lived" experience because people make sense of what happens after they have experienced reality. "Students of sensemaking find forecasting, contingency planning, strategic planning and other magical probes into the future wasteful and misleading if they are decoupled from reflective action and history" (p. 30).
3. *Enactment.* Organizations are understood in the context of the actions that are possible within them. Action in organizations such as enacting policies, writing rules, setting timelines, organizing space, establishing categories, and changing the environment in numerous ways give meaning to the organization and life within it.
4. *Social.* The actions that occur in organizations are interactive—people working with people. Shared experiences and processes do not always mean agreement or shared understanding, but there is shared history. How a person is socialized, and the groups to whom one looks for feedback, will influence what a person does and thinks about in organizational life.
5. *Ongoing.* Weick contends "that sensemaking never starts [because] people are always in the middle of things, which become things" (p. 43). Connecting events, seeing how things fit with the past, and even puzzling over interruptions to routines are ongoing. People's interests and experiences continue to change, and therefore understanding the organization itself is ongoing.
6. *Extracted cues.* Extracted cues are pieces of information from which people draw implications about organizations. What people make of an extracted cue depends first on themselves and their lived experience and then on context, in terms of both what cue is extracted and how it is interpreted.
7. *Plausibility.* Sense making does not require that people in organizations know the "truth." In fact, they piece together extracted cues, so that they know enough to do current projects acceptably. This means that "sufficiency and plausibility take precedence over accuracy" (p. 62).

Weick sees both organizations and sense making as "cut from the same cloth," because to organize is to "impose order, counteract deviations, simplify, and connect, and the same holds true when people try to make sense" (p. 82). In summarizing his approach to sense making in organizations, he sees it as necessary to understand ideologies, paradigms, theories of action, traditions, and stories, because their content pervades organizations and colors interpretations. All of these are in play all of the time. For him, moments of meaning occur when any two of the paradigms, theories, and so forth become connected in a meaningful way. Those meanings vary as a function of the content and the connection. Thus, there is no such thing as a fixed meaning for the content resources of sense making; but simply because the meanings of content shift is no reason to ignore content and focus only on the process of connecting. Sense making, after all, is about the world. What is being asserted about that world is found in the labels and categories implied by frames. Words express and interpret. Words include and exclude. These words matter (p. 132).

The concepts of organizational culture and sense making are grounded in the Interpretive Paradigm and give meaning to the connection and collaboration goals of Serendipitous Organizations. These theories are designed to recognize subjectivity and to focus on interactions within the organization. Figure 7.2 provides a summary of where these theories can be placed within the Interpretive Paradigm.

Radical Humanist	**Radical Structuralist**
Organization Culture Diffusionists **Interpretive** Organization Culture Integrationists Organization Culture Revolutionary Vanguard Sensemaking Theory	**Functionalist**

Figure 7.2   Organizational Theories in the Interpretive Paradigm.

COSTS AND BENEFITS

THE INTERPRETIVE PARADIGM AND ITS THEORIES

The antipositivistic, antideterministic stance of the Interpretive Paradigm is troublesome to many who think that humans are not as free and undetermined as interpretivism asserts they are (see Reed, 1993; Thompson, 1993). In addition, the move from realism to relativism that is a logical consequence of this paradigm's assumptions is unacceptable to those who believe in immutable truth. However, most of the criticism about organizational research derived from this perspective is due to its subjectivist, insider perspective. It is not generalizable, and therefore not useful to the traditional scientific community. Preference for language-based research that relies on qualitative methods and is attentive to various perspectives makes it impossible to escape the criticism of the traditionalist researcher whose scientific standards include randomization, objectivity, and other controls for generalizability. To date, the alternative approaches to research rigor proposed in a variety of methodologies developed from this perspective (see Lincoln & Guba, 1985; Rodwell, 1998) have yet to receive acceptance in the more powerful traditional scientific community, though respect and acceptance is growing with scholars from other paradigmatic perspectives.

As with any criticism of qualitative methods, qualitative interpretive research in organizations is not efficient. Though research based on the language and the thinking of the participants provides a certain richness and attention to subtleties and is responsive to the complexity of modern organizational environments, it is not produced without great costs. Interpretive organizational research takes much more time in the process of data collection and data analysis. Overall, the research is more expensive. The answers that are provided via the research product are not as "clean" and precise as those produced in traditional research, even if they do provide more visceral meaning to the consumers of the research results. However, research participants benefit more noticeably in interpretive research because of the change in power of the inquirer. Research "subjects" become inquiry "participants" who help to shape the process and evaluate the quality of the product. Since there is recognition that the participants own their data and have their own perspective on the phenomena under investigation, the power differential between the research and the researched is changed. Participants have a say in the process, and by virtue of this involvement, unintended consequences, both positive and negative, accrue to all involved. The research is never easy and the researcher is never really in charge once the research has begun. This suggests that much less control of the research process is possible so that those organizations that cannot risk negative findings will not have the capacity to accept inquiry processes that can emerge in surprising ways.

SERENDIPITOUS ORGANIZATIONS WITH CONNECTION AND COLLABORATION GOALS

As far as we can tell, Theory Z (Ouchi, 1981), a pure guide for structuring a Serendipitous Organization, has not been fully implemented within an organization in the United States, even though our Orange State case seems to have created a version of a Serendipitous Organization. Perhaps the communal, all-encompassing nature of the approach is not technologically appropriate in a culture that has such respect for individuality. Perhaps the time necessary to introduce such a dramatic departure from a traditional hierarchical bureaucracy has rarely been afforded organizations choosing to experiment with the approach. However, many of the elements of a Theory Z approach have found their way into the organizational excellence literature popularized by Peters and Waterman (1982). The same is true for most of the organizational culture and sensemaking theoretical work with the focus on recognizing and working with diversity.

Each of these approaches offers interesting insights into the processes involved in developing policies, practices, and organizational structures that can benefit both the organization and the individuals within them. These theories do not provide an easy fix for organizations wanting quality and efficiency while also addressing the human side of the enterprise, including connection and collaboration. None can provide the one best approach, no matter how much managers and employees wish that were possible. In fact, many of these theories will provide more questions than answers. Further, the answers that are produced will be unsettling, because they will underscore how much more is needed to achieve both political and economic wisdom within organizations, to say nothing of the diversity of response necessary for cultural competence.

Serendipitous Organizations with goals of connection and collaboration generally will not be efficient organizations due to their high attention to process. However, because of the importance of consensus among the various stakeholding populations inside and outside of the organization, the chances of effectiveness are increased. This is true, if effectiveness is measured by the quality of the decision-making process and satisfaction among all participants with both the process and the results of the structure and practices within the organization.

CONCLUSION

The theories that are based on the Interpretive Paradigm are in their youth developmentally, but are congruent with organizations whose goals are connection and collaboration. The theories have opened up new ways of viewing organizations that were not considered appropriate, much less central to organizational thinking, by early theorists. Depending on the use of theoretical concepts, or on the school of thought within a theoretical category, theories in one paradigm have influenced theory development in others. In the Interpretive Paradigm, the focus has shifted to the way in which meaning and culture develop and impact diverse organizational players.

With this shift has come the recognition that there exists no one best way of doing organizational practice. Instead, the best that is possible is what makes sense and works for the here and now. No quest for certainty persists in this paradigm. It is replaced with an acceptance of complexity, ambiguity, and uncertainty within a process that values connections on many levels. Along with the tenuousness and due to the attention to the humanity of organizations comes a depth of understanding and local knowledge that provides its own security and solace within organizational life. The search for perfection has been replaced with pragmatics. It is enough to know what works now.

We next turn to the behavior and practices congruent with a Serendipitous Organization by way of a deeper understanding of the clan culture, also congruent with an Interpretive Paradigm. It is time to see how the themes and theories in this chapter can be translated into the work of Serendipitous Organizations in order to practice within an interpretive perspective. The next chapter showcases values, preferences, and decision-making strategies as ways to understand the practice of human service organizations that come from an interpretive perspective. The idea is to detail standards for practice within organizations where connection and collaboration are the goals.

DISCUSSION QUESTIONS

1. Compare and contrast the major assumptions of the Interpretive Paradigm with the goals of the Serendipitous Organization. How are they similar or different? What are the costs and benefits of the similarities? Of the differences?

2. Imagine you are on a search committee for a team leader of a serendipitous human service agency. The search committee is engaged in a dialogue about the costs and benefits of being part of a Serendipitous Organization so that members can provide "words to the wise" for potential candidates for the position. What might the "words to the wise" be? What might you advise the committee to consider in recruiting candidates? How might the committee go about assessing applicants' potential fit with the organization's goals and expectations?

3. Review the theory discussion and compare the similarities and differences between the various aspects of organizational culture theory and sensemaking theory. How might these theories impede or enhance connection, collaboration, and consensus in an organization?

Which of these theories is most congruent with your preferences about structure and behavior in an organization, and why?

4. In the beginning of this part, a case example was introduced—the Orange State Child Abuse Prevention Agency. Go back to the case and consider the following questions:

   a. What characteristics of this organization make it a Serendipitous Organization? Are there characteristics that are less change oriented than others?

   b. What assumptions did the women founders appear to bring to the table and how were they helpful (or not) in carrying out their responsibilities?

   c. As the agency developed, what did members do to insure that it remained focused on interpretivist assumptions?

5. Imagine you are starting a small organization and that you want to be sure that the structure of that organization is congruent with its environment. What issues would you need to address if you were to choose a serendipitous organizational structure to be sure that it matched a particular environment? Describe the environment for which a Serendipitous Organization is most suited.

6. You are a supervisor or manager in a human service agency. What would make you prefer working in a Serendipitous Organization with connection and collaboration goals? Would there be challenges for you personally as a leader? If so, what would they be, and how would you deal with them?

CHAPTER 8

Practice in Serendipitous Organizations

SERENDIPITOUS ORGANIZATIONS MAINTAIN a status quo that has been established through ongoing collaboration and consensus-building processes. As with the Traditional Organization, incremental change and minimal conflict is acceptable in Serendipitous Organizations. Both types seek a status quo, but they go about determining the nature of that status quo in different ways. While organizations with a functionalist perspective hold there is a best way that forms *the* status quo guided by universal truths, those from an interpretivist perspective accept a more fluid status quo. Given this fluidity, the status quo is simply what is agreed on today. This will shift and change as new ideas and thoughts emerge and as a new consensus is established; thus, the Serendipitous Organization status quo *evolves* as an ongoing process.

Serendipitous Organizations may be developed by different groups that come together because there is a need to *understand* a situation or set of circumstances neglected by other organizations. The intent is to increase awareness, to promote collaboration, and to enhance understanding. The concept of a *think tank* is interpretive in that these organizations emerge so that scholars and practitioners can engage in dialogue and begin to understand complex situations. The think tank is particularly interpretive when multiple perspectives are garnered to create a consensus. Think tanks may be affiliated with or used to promote different political agendas (a more functionalist or radical structuralist notion); but for those who come together to seek more understanding, the process of thinking things through is highly interpretive and such an organization would be considered a Serendipitous Organization if structure and performance in the organization were also interpretive.

Similarly, some professional associations formed to increase knowledge about specific groups of people may also be Serendipitous Organizations. For example, the Gerontological Society of America (GSA) is an association of persons interested in studying and understanding aging, whereas the

Child Welfare League of America (CWLA) is dedicated to increasing providers' awareness and competence about services to children. Organizations created by study commissions or designed to educate clients and staff about complicated problems and issues can be interpretivist in their orientation. To be true Serendipitous Organizations, they must also have connection and collaboration as their organizational goals enacted through their structure and practices.

While think tanks and associations are dedicated to promoting awareness and understanding and typically stop short of delivering direct services, there are Serendipitous Organizations that do plan and deliver human services. These organizations are those that promote client awareness and understanding, seeing knowledge as a way to empower clients. Instead of seeking broad social change (cause advocacy), these organizations seek to provide case advocacy in that they encourage clients to fully participate and work with staff toward the goal of deep understanding to achieve personal or group change. An example of this type organization would be a freestanding hospice that uses a team of professionals and paraprofessionals to work with families and patients. Such an organization, dedicated to preparing families and patients for a good dying process, would provide staff to assist clients as they seek meaning in their final months, weeks, and days. This meaning making is an interpretivist experience when there is recognition that each patient's journey will be highly individualized and where the expectation of staff is to be flexible in encouraging the patient's process to emerge rather than imposing their own views of how it should happen. This fluid, evolving experience engages staff, families, and patients in a customized process constructed by all those involved. Awareness and understanding are encouraged and supported, with the focus on meaning being tied to the process, since death is the ultimate outcome. In this example, organizational connection and collaboration goals are enacted by the services provided generally in a nonlinear, emerging process determined by preferences and needs.

Freestanding hospice organizations are interpretive in their approach, as are hospice programs that are housed in larger health-care networks. In the latter case, when interpretive programs are placed within traditional organizations with structure and control goals, staff will encounter contradictions bordering on paradox. While the larger system may be stressing outcome measurement and efficiency, hospice staff will be highly focused on processes that may be perceived as anything but efficient. Service will probably be structured in ways that support notions of connection and collaboration. Both sets of organization goals are being held at the same time—a perfect recipe for paradox. In this case, a hospice team dedicated to making joint visits is using interpretive techniques—gathering persons with different perspectives together to make their best joint decision about patient care. Seen as highly inefficient and labor intensive in tying up so many professionals simultaneously, a functionalist perspective would suggest that joint visits are too costly and should be limited. When connection and collaboration are goals, a mandate to make fewer joint visits contradicts the importance of multiple viewpoints. Connection and collaboration opportunities would be reduced, as would the meaningfulness and civility of the process. The paradox would occur with staff members who recognize the need to create the network of relationships within the process in order to be successful, while their organizational directives create expectations that ignore meaning and overlook process. We suspect that many readers have experienced these sorts of contradictions. But we are not as certain that readers have experienced the congruence with a Serendipitous Organization as was seen in the Orange State Child Abuse Prevention Agency case at the beginning of Part III. Hopefully, by the end of this part, you will be able to envision practice within this alternative context.

In this chapter, we focus on what is needed to understand practice in Serendipitous Organizations. We return to the four questions originally introduced in Chapter 4 to guide the reader: (1) What are the cultural values and characteristics of organizations derived from the assumptions of this paradigm? (2) What roles are congruent with the culture of this type of organization? (3) What are the standards of practice within this type of organization? (4) What are the implications for practice in this type of organization?

CULTURAL VALUES AND CHARACTERISTICS OF SERENDIPITOUS ORGANIZATIONS

Earlier we referred to the Competing Values Framework (Cameron & Quinn, 2006) to identify a variety of organizational cultures. The collaborative, consensus-based fluidity of the Serendipitous Organization harmonizes with the friendliness and connections of the clan culture in the workplace. Connections support what people do. Leaders are more mentors than supervisors. Civility, tradition, and loyalty are hallmarks of the members of the organizational "family." A focus on human resource development is embedded in cohesion and positive morale, making it difficult to say whether the long-term mutual commitment in this type of organization is a cause or a consequence of the organizing process. Whatever the reason, teamwork, participation, and consensus are norms and serve as a measure of the quality of the process. In this culture, success is defined by sensitivity to customers or clients and overall concern for the people connected to the organization.

Box 8.1, originally introduced in Chapter 2 as Box 2.8, provides a reminder of the cultural elements that inform the structure and practices in Serendipitous Organizations.

Box 8.1

SERENDIPITOUS ORGANIZATIONS

- The capacity of human beings to bring their *subjective* differences together is respected in seeking to continually redesign and develop programs and the organization.
- *Integration* is supported so the organization runs smoothly through agreed-upon structure, created by team members and subject to change by consensus as needs shift.
- *Flexibility and discretion* to gain consensus, listening to multiple voices, constructing new realities, and allowing programs to emerge permits individuals to find meaning in their roles.
- Coordination rather than management creates *clan culture* where each has a voice. Hearing all perspectives is a norm in the organization's culture.

VALUES IN SERENDIPITOUS ORGANIZATIONS

The Serendipitous Organization is grounded in *subjectivism*, which takes a *relativist* stance on values. The organization is very open to **situational ethics,** in which choices made in one situation may actually change in light of new information or a shift in this or future scenarios. Taking a relativist perspective, Serendipitous Organizations hold that principles change; values change with time, there are multiple truths, and there are multiple ways of knowing and doing. Therefore, Serendipitous Organizations are particularly sensitive to the dignity and worth of the individual and the importance of human relationships.

Because these organizations respect difference, they value each individual and the individual's opinions, thoughts, and contributions. Also, because these organizations seek to establish a status quo, they are particularly attentive to human relationships and the importance of connectedness. How people feel about the work context and the process of receiving help will be important. Central to work will be a genuine respect for the perspectives of individuals because they are expert in their own experience. Managing the consequences of such fundamental and closely held differences is important in Serendipitous Organizations.

Serendipitous Organizations are open to different ways of understanding that emerge in context. They are formed to meet needs that are often not recognized by the larger society. Their clients are persons whose needs are not being met by other organizations. Their case advocacy, which is highly attendant to process, makes the organization vulnerable in seeking funding, for funders will have to recognize and respect the importance of meaning making at a time when outcome measurement dominates.

Here, outcome is less important than process. This is because the Serendipitous Organization will seek to engage clients in collaboration with staff to better understand their problems prior to determining any action. The voice of the client is understood from an **emic** or insider's perspective, rather than an **etic** or expert outsider's perspective. This makes the work appear to be somewhat wishy-washy and tedious, because practitioners in this culture examine every aspect of a problem and seek multiple perspectives to enhance understanding prior to acting.

Change will take time, at least at the start. The focus is on the individual, so most efforts lead to individual rather than class or collective change. But because change will be based on deep insight and understandings about social problems, larger scale incremental change may be possible in the long run. Because of the complexity and the detail involved in processing information and problem solving, Serendipitous Organizations will tend to value smaller size in order to assure that all stakeholders have a voice in the construction of the agency and the services provided. The way in which Serendipitous Organizations include and use volunteers extends the clan culture of inclusion with little attention to hierarchy and expertise and much attention to the intentions and inclinations of the volunteer in a mutual process of program shaping. Leadership is also collaborative, allowing for close working relationships inside the organization and with all types of agencies and organizations in the environment. In consensus building, the Serendipitous Organization listens to multiple perspectives inside and outside of the organization on every issue.

Mission/Philosophy of Serendipitous Organizations

The Serendipitous Organization seeks knowledge to enhance awareness and understanding for meaningful information and programming, regardless of the chosen topic. Since it is not satisfied with simplistic answers, dominant methods, or one way of knowing, this organization's philosophy is very open and accepting of diversity. In fact, if there is any organization that is particularly sensitive to dealing with multiculturalism and diversity, it is the Serendipitous Organization. All opinions and perspectives are valued and listening to every voice is important. Organizational structures are established to ensure this.

The interpretive philosophy of the clan culture is that people need complete understandings of issues, problems, and concerns from the point of view of all those with a stake in order to make informed, effective choices. Every choice is recognized as a value-laden contextual decision. A good choice at one time will not necessarily remain the best choice when things change. Being flexible and collaborating with others allows new choices, understandings, and meanings to emerge. This means that the agency's mission today may not be the same in two or five years because situations in the service context change, requiring the organization to change in order to assure its relevance in problem solving.

PREFERRED STRUCTURE IN SERENDIPITOUS ORGANIZATIONS

The Serendipitous Organization's structure and process is influenced by theories that are mostly grouped under *organizational culture* and *sense making* perspectives. These theories are reflected in the organization's internal operations. Organizational structure is not of utmost importance in the Serendipitous Organization. Instead, the process of organizing the work and the perspectives of those who are involved in this organizing are of interest. Much more attention is placed on understanding the individuals who come together in the organization, because through this comes an understanding of the organization itself. It does not matter so much who is in charge or who is deemed accountable. What matters is that all participants have a space to offer their opinions, and responsibility to exercise their expertise, for the good of the whole effort. What is needed structurally at one time may shift with the times. This was clear in the Orange County case example. How the organization was structured over time depended on the players, the needs, and the circumstances.

Most Serendipitous Organizations, as in our case example, will be more informal than bureaucratic and hierarchical in their structure. There is attention to order, but that order is more likely based on the personalities and the preferences of the participants and their perceptions of need than on any vision of "ideal" structure. Attention is consistently focused on how organizational participants feel about the social world of the organization. Organizational attention, then, will not be based on concrete empirical artifacts alone. Workload and salary structure, though important, are not the only elements considered in job satisfaction and performance. In fact, the intuitive and the ephemeral will be included in decision making about how to structure work or proceed toward the connection and collaboration goals of the organization. Does the structure of the process feel right to all involved? If not, why not? If not, how should the process or the structure change?

TYPES OF PROGRAMS AND SERVICES IN SERENDIPITOUS ORGANIZATIONS

In Chapter 1, we introduced different types of programs and services. Recall that *direct service programs* directly serve clients. *Staff development and training programs* focus on staff, and *support programs* undergird direct service and staff programs. Serendipitous Organizations may contain all three types of programs, but these will look very different from the same types of programs offered in organizations enacting other perspectives because their purposes and goals are different.

When direct service programs are provided in a Serendipitous Organization, they will focus on empowering clients through personal awareness and understanding, so clients can gain consciousness about meaning in life in order to respond to problems and challenges. Interpretive programs in a clan culture are particularly sensitive to assisting individuals in finding meaning in unsolvable situations in which they must learn to adjust and in redefining or reframing problems so that understanding can occur and useful resources identified. Therapies used in programs congruent with this perspective are intended to enhance insight, such as are seen in services provided in victim assistance programs or women's shelters.

Perhaps the signature type of program for a Serendipitous Organization is its staff development and training sessions, because Serendipitous Organizations are intent on developing staff and educating others to understand complex issues and to seek meaning through their professional and personal development. In this organization, special emphasis is placed on drawing from the strengths of diversity both inside and outside of the organization and at all levels and with all perspectives.

Serendipitous Organizations offer support programs, particularly in the area of research and development. The broader, macro outcome of these programs is to disseminate new ways of thinking that are of interest to varied audiences. Note that these organizations are satisfied to distribute this information without using it themselves to make large-scale change, believing that with knowledge comes desired incremental improvement. Because of a commitment to diversity and alternative perspectives, there would be no objection to having radical structuralist colleagues seize on their interpretive findings to use for their own, more radical change purposes.

SUMMARY CHARACTERISTICS OF SERENDIPITOUS ORGANIZATIONS

The basic underlying assumptions about locus of control and change in a Serendipitous Organization differ from what has been seen so far. Given its *regulation* perspective, the Serendipitous Organization is not designed to seek radical change. As with functionalists, people in Serendipitous Organizations can be change agents, but they focus on changes that are controllable and manageable so that harmony can be restored or maintained. One could say that their clan culture is steeped in a standard of civility.

This position places the Serendipitous Organization within what has been called the *alternative organizational perspective*. It is alternative because of its profound differences from the Traditional Organizations discussed in Chapter 4; but it should also be clear that all the organizational perspectives based on assumptions other than those found in the functionalist perspective with hierarchical cultures are alternative. In Table 8.1, we summarize the characteristics of Serendipitous Organizations. We encourage you to look at the differences in comparison to Social Change Organizations in Chapter 6, Table 6.1 in order to begin to determine for yourself their similarities and differences.

Table 8.1
Characteristics of Serendipitous Organizations

Characteristics	Serendipitous Organizations
Values	To provide avenues for both nondominant and dominant opinions, doctrines, and practices so that inclusion is maximized
Mission and Philosophy	To use the best knowledge available to enhance and achieve the highest social order
Organizational Structure	To allow structure to emerge so that the learning process is facilitated, and to use less bureaucratic, flatter structures whenever possible to facilitate a network of relationships
Programs and Services	To develop educational and human service programs that assist participants in understanding complex issues by increasing consciousness to the degree that understanding leads to more meaningful living

The collaboration and connection goals of Serendipitous Organizations extends to their approach with clients who are seen as collaborators in services designed to fit individual needs, challenges, and gifts. Inclusiveness extends to volunteers and staff. There is fluidity in the service delivery picture that is context embedded and informed, so that roles and structures respond to the needs as they emerge and in ways determined by consensus. The precise role of the leader and the precise design of service delivery, as well as the expected job of staff and volunteers, will emerge and change as understanding about the complexity of the issues at hand emerges within the organization.

Because of this attention to complexity, Serendipitous Organizations will tend to be smaller in size and structural complexity in order to assure the necessary processing of information from internal and external sources. Funding sources may also be less grand. Certainly, appropriate funders supportive of connection and collaboration goals will be comfortable with **emergent planning** (Netting, O'Connor, & Fauri, 2008), with measurement focused on process more than, or as well as, the change product (Netting, O'Connor, & Fauri, 2007).

Change is not intended to alter basic social or service structures, but to help people understand and find meaning to improve their situations within existing structures. The Serendipitous Organization exemplifies in many ways the **learning organization** as described by Peter Senge (1990): "At the heart of the learning organization is a shift of mind from seeing ourselves as separate from the world to connected to the world, from seeing problems as caused by someone or something 'out there' to seeing how our own actions create the problems we experience. A learning organization is a place where people are continually discovering how they create their reality. And how they can change it" (pp. 12–13). Therefore, the environment in which the organization operates is viewed by Serendipitous Organizations as a set of forces to be understood as much as possible so that social order can be reestablished through incremental change that comes from learning. How this happens while maintaining connection and collaboration goals will be explored in detail in what follows.

ROLES AND RELATIONSHIPS WITH AND WITHIN SERENDIPITOUS ORGANIZATIONS

Given the interpretive and regulation perspectives that guide Serendipitous Organizations, Table 8.2 provides a summary of some of the ways in which roles and relationships develop in Serendipitous Organizations. The framework has been seen in previous practice chapters, but a few concepts as well as goals have been changed here to reflect a different orientation.

Table 8.2
Roles and Relationships With and Within Serendipitous Organizations

Type of Relationship	Purpose
Contextual Relationships	To try to understand the complexity of the environment and to use this understanding to set a meaningful context
Relationships with Funders	To obtain any funding that will support the organization's search for knowledge, understanding, and meaning
Relationships with Participant Populations and Referral Sources	To include participants, referral sources, staff, and others in a collaborative process so that programs will be as respectful of diversity as possible
Internal Organizational Roles and Relationships:	
• Managing (Facilitating)	To establish a participatory, relationship-focused approach to management and leadership in which dialogue is freely exchanged in as collaborative and civil a manner as possible
• Communicating	To develop open communication in which the voices of participants, volunteers, and staff are equally heard and respected, and to engage in direct exchanges in which consensus is the goal among diverse participants
• Recognizing Staff Expectations	To hire multicultural staff who respect differences, can tolerate process, and are dedicated to self-awareness and ongoing development

Organization–Environment Relationships

We will examine the Serendipitous Organization's context-dominated view of the external environment, and the internal roles and relationships, elaborating particularly on funding and clients. It is beyond the scope of this text to extend our discussion of environment to include an investigation of cross-cultural differences of the contexts in which Serendipitous Organizations might be located. For some organizational types considered here, context is irrelevant, but for Serendipitous Organizations, explicit responsiveness to cultural expectations is a predictable aspect of organizational survival. For those who are interested in exploring important aspects of process/goal orientation and degrees of emotional expressiveness of the major cultures of the world and their impact on expectations for organizations, we recommend Gannon's (2004) *Understanding Global Cultures: Metaphorical Journeys Through 28 Nations, Clusters of Nations, and Continents*. Those working in Serendipitous Organizations will surely need the information provided.

Contextual Relationships The Interpretive Organization recognizes the importance of the environment as part of the broader context in which it operates. There is an appreciation of and a need for information from diverse opinions, perspectives, and values of the sociopolitical environment to influence the organization for the enactment of meaningful practice. Rather than trying to ignore or control the environment, as Traditional Organizations attempt to do, Serendipitous Organizations welcome the diversity of opinions represented by environmental forces and recognize that the environment has everything to do with their structuring for success. Rather than engendering conflict within the environment, as do radical structuralists, the Serendipitous Organization seeks to be inclusive and to encourage participation from diverse groups and individuals, while at the same time managing conflict as consensus emerges about the structure and focus of the organization.

In the Serendipitous Organization, the environment is a critically important backdrop against which the organization assesses its daily work. For interpretivism, context is everything. It is within context that the Serendipitous Organization creates a consensual clan culture and makes sense out of processes, problems, and issues of concern. The environment, then, serves as a resource for new information and knowledge that assists with organizational meaning making for direction taking. As new information and knowledge are gained, the organization is open to considering new ways of thinking and structures for the work process. Serendipitous Organizations are not fearful of environmental turbulence and change, for this is just reflective of the highly subjective nature of their work context. But unlike Social Change Organizations, they are not bent on embracing conflict to influence structural change. Environmental information in the form of conflict, then, is more grist for the mill in understanding complex situations, and not necessarily something to be seized on with the intent of making broad-scale change. The Serendipitous Organization is more likely to organize a hearing about an issue than participate in the planning of a march about the same issue.

Relationships With Funders   Serendipitous Organizations may have trouble developing and maintaining a stable funding base with traditional funding sources because they can be seen as process focused, and as nonresponsive to the pace required by many funding sources. This is generally true, because the quest for meaning cannot be rushed. Their predisposition to understand everything holistically, carried to an extreme, may become tedious and tiresome to funding sources. Funders that seek clearly defined outcomes and definitive deadlines will not appreciate interpretive, always emerging work efforts, sometimes rejecting this type of organization as not well organized or well run.

However, for funding sources devoted to generating new knowledge, and not quite as focused on immediate product, a Serendipitous Organization can be a dream come true. For the funding source interested in creative expression and free thinking, or understanding new or old problems in new ways, the Serendipitous Organization can be a perfect match. It can also be a match for funding sources interested in culturally competent responses to thorny problems. Then, the Serendipitous Organization, with its great care about appropriate emergence based on respectful consensus through attention to process aimed at understanding and then solving problems, will be enthusiastically supported.

Wilkerson (1988) found that funding can be "whimsical," given rapidly changing societal themes (p. 124). When new problems arise in which there has been no research done or in which there is little information on the topic, and when the problem becomes politically "hot," a Serendipitous Organization may actually be created to generate knowledge and understanding about the subject. The whimsy that Wilkerson identified can occur when understanding has advanced and funding is then diverted to other hot topics. The smart Serendipitous Organization will have a group of creative people who can explore diverse issues and will be able to convince other funding sources to continue to fund them as collaborators as new issues emerge. If the funding source is seeking creative understandings about social problems and/or collaborating with service recipients, the Serendipitous Organization will be a good resource.

Relationships With Participant Populations and Referral Sources   Because Serendipitous Organizations are based on principles of inclusiveness and collaboration, staff members in these organizations view clients and referral sources as colleagues and collaborators. A mutual, consensus-building approach will be used in which various community stakeholders, including service recipients, participate on equal footing with persons who are employed by the agency. Client populations served by Serendipitous Organizations will represent diverse groups. These organizations will provide services to persons not always served by traditional agencies and may call their clients *participants* to emphasize the inclusive nature of their work.

Even though Social Change Organizations include various stakeholders in their processes, there is a big difference between that approach and the interpretive approach to organization. Whereas radical structuralism embraces, even encourages, conflict, interpretivism seeks consensus through less conflict-oriented means. When conflict does occur, interpretivism seeks to turn the conflict dialogic in order to increase the intensity of a collaborative effort toward understanding, not toward revolutionary change.

In summary, Serendipitous Organizations view all aspects of the environment, including funders, collaborating agencies, and clients, as resources and constituencies representing diverse interests. Funding is far less certain than it is for Traditional Organizations. Because the process of organizing and service providing is fluid, the funding is often short lived and tends to be a continual struggle. Survival is not assured, and environmental forces are constantly being scanned for resources. Clients may not be called *clients* at all, because clients imply that professionals do something *for*, when in the Serendipitous Organization, doing *with* is the goal. This view of the resource environment sets a context for examining the organization's internal structure.

Internal Organizational Roles and Relationships

Just as Serendipitous Organizations are attentive to and inclusive of their external environment, so, too, are they concerned with the internal environment of the organization, its operation and program practices. In the previous chapter, you were exposed to the theories guiding decision making about structure and practices. Here, we will investigate how those theories, in combination with the strategic management theories introduced in Chapter 2, create the context for organization practice with goals of connection and collaboration.

Managing   As Mintzberg, Ahlstrand, and Lampel (1998) suggest, schools of management attentive to the communal connections among members are congruent with Serendipitous Organizations. Whether guided by the Cognitive School, with its interest in the mental processes or cognitive mapping that goes into strategic decision making, or by the Learning

School, which asserts that managers and the collective learn over time what is correct, as in management by change, or by the Cultural School, with its attention to the cultural aspect of strategies, management within a more collaborative organization will not have the same "feel" as management within a more bureaucratic, hierarchical structure. Here managers manage *for* difference instead of managing to *control* difference. Though managers may be as specialized and educated as their more functionalist counterparts, what is rewarded within the Serendipitous Organization requires that managers conduct their business very differently. In fact, *management* may be a misnomer in this alternative agency, just as it was for those managing from radical structuralism. Whereas Social Change Organizations typically call their managers *leaders* and *organizers*, Serendipitous Organizations likely use terms such as *coordinators*, *facilitators*, or *team leaders*.

Leadership is exercised, but this leadership is of a facilitative and connected nature. There is a strong standard of civility and respect among organizational members. For example, coordinators will still need to make hard decisions that govern employees' lives inside the organization, but they will make special efforts to make sure that employees understand the process and the results and feel that they have been sufficiently involved in the decision-making process. Senge (1990) referred to this type of leadership as *building a shared vision:* "The practice of shared vision involves the skills of unearthing shared 'pictures of the future' that foster genuine commitment and enrollment rather than compliance. In mastering this discipline, leaders learn the counter productiveness of trying to dictate a vision, no matter how heartfelt" (p. 9).

Interpretive managers attend to the meaning of the work and the organization. They are attuned to the affective dimension of the work life. They respond to the individual human needs of employees beyond the bounds of the organization. Recently in the in the popular press in places like *Newsweek* and *Working Women* there has been a focus on women changing the culture of the workplace. Most women leaders indicate that when management asks what people want and it is given to them, they stay as productive members of the organization. This means that more than merely "official" business will be conducted within the Serendipitous Organization as long as it does not inhibit the work of the organization. This also means that the boundaries between management and workers as well as between real life and work life can become blurred, just as it was in the Orange County case. There, as in most Serendipitous Organizations, we saw a more intimate culture rather than a more traditional organization. This intimacy suggests that organizational norms include expectations that there will be connections among employees and more engagement in one another's lives. Box 8.2 provides a list of characteristics of interpretive leaders who would be most attuned to a Serendipitous Organization.

Box 8.2

CHARACTERISTICS OF SERENDIPITOUS LEADERS

- Is comfortable with ambiguity, uncertainty, and new and emerging ideas
- Thinks hearing all perspectives is important
- Sees the status quo and order as something worth establishing
- Truly appreciates diversity
- Has a high tolerance for differing opinions
- Is predisposed toward creativity
- Has a strong curiosity and thinks critically
- Is satisfied with spending time on understanding and meaning-making activities, without having to use what is learned to make broad-scale change
- Is willing to fully participate in organizational life
- Enjoys people and has strong interpersonal skills
- Has the ability to play with others; is a team player
- Desires to be a lifelong learner
- Has the ability to examine situations from many different directions and is willing to be persuaded to change his or her mind
- Has a high tolerance for process and delayed closure
- Respects people for their strengths and is open to hearing their ideas

---

Communicating Organizational goals are based on consensus, where all participants are expected to have a voice and an appropriate influence regarding the organization. This does not necessarily mean that all will have equal voice. It does mean that all voices are respected for their standpoint vis-à-vis the organization. Given the value of communication across stakeholding groups, the goals and processes of the Serendipitous Organization are relativist. What should happen or what should be constructed as goals will depend on all the unique dimensions of the organization in its context. There is a pragmatic attention to what works for now.

If there are lines of communication within the Serendipitous Organization, they will be loose and fuzzy. Rigid structures in which individuals have to communicate along chains of command do not fit. In fact, communication that freely occurs among all participants serves the organization's purpose of listening to multiple perspectives and of learning from others. In the Orange State Prevention Organization, Jane and Myra took roles as they were needed, without worrying about power and authority. These were pragmatic decisions about what was needed at the time.

Since the focus is informal and pragmatic, Serendipitous Organizations will tend to be constructed as collaboratives or collectives and will rely heavily on groupings and teams or teamwork to accomplish their business. These groupings will be fluid depending on the need, similar to the Orange State example. Serendipitous Organizations, while influenced by the laws and policies that have been derived from a more functionalist perspective regarding such things as equal opportunity hiring practices, board composition, and ownership, will choose a looser approach to decision making and governance to guide hiring, firing, training, and motivating workers. Rules will govern how these processes work, but these rules will always be open to interpretation and discussion by everyone in the organization. Rather than being closely tethered to a policy manual, the organization assumes that *flexibility* is the way to keep employees over the long term. The standard for communication and practice is emergence. What the content of that emergence will be changes with time and circumstance.

Recognizing Staff Expectations   Staff with a preference for personal connection would be congruent with a Serendipitous Organization. Deep-felt connections to others, along with interest in activities built on relationships, also have interpretive assumptions about organizational settings. Abiding interest in gaining deep understanding and sensemaking needs are also congruent. Staff with an attention to the world of possibilities, deep concern for others, and general curiosity would also comfortably fit within the clan culture of a Serendipitous Organization.

Given its preferences for connectedness, many aspects of the Serendipitous Organization are congruent with Myers-Briggs personality types with feeling and judging preferences. Rules and procedures are acceptable only when they make sense for the current situation and the current needs and resources of the context. Alternative decisions should be acceptable given different situations and contexts. What rules do exist should be developed in collaboration with all those responsible for their implementation in order for the rules to have meaning and to be fair.

Mindless paperwork done in isolation merely because accountability requires it will be a challenge for all in Serendipitous Organizations because of the preference for meaningfulness and collaborative connections in the work environment. Attention to the affective dimension of the work environment and the management of personnel will be essential to staff work satisfaction and tenure within a Serendipitous Organization.

Those with an interpretive approach to organizational and work expectations will not necessarily follow those in authority without question. Instead, they will require an understanding of directives and their consequences, thus making it appear that they question authority. More than that, they require collaboration for their comfort in organizational life. They like working with others.

To be congruent with the clan culture and to assure match between personality types and organizational expectations in the interpretive perspective, skills and expertise for the requirements of the work activity are important. Respect for competence will be present, but work in teams where strengths are combined to overcome a variety of weaknesses will be preferred over independence, specialization, and separate work assignments. Division of labor will have less meaning, and there will be an expectation that each person's voice will be heard and considered in management decisions regarding staffing, directing, coordinating, and other organizational activities. Connections with the work at hand on all levels will be accepted as the way to accomplish more productivity, more quality, and more satisfaction. Pay is less important than a collaborative work culture for those with interpretive expectations for organizations.

STANDARDS OF PRACTICE WITHIN SERENDIPITOUS ORGANIZATIONS

Language of Practice in Serendipitous Organizations

The interpretive perspective assumes no such thing as a "best" way of conducting organizational assessment and diagnosis to achieve the best or ideal change. Instead, there is a pragmatic expectation that constructing what will work to solve problems can occur through consensus within the organizational community. The idea is that all involved start from where they are. The challenge of assessment and problem analysis here is to identify all starting points and then enter into a conversation about how to cope with the situation at hand. Therefore, from the interpretive perspective, assessment and analysis consist not so much in finding the best plan for change, but rather in creating the opportunity for meaningful change. Through conversation, participants come to greater clarity about the situation as the possibilities and planning emerge. With that, synergy develops.

In previous chapters, we introduced practice language used in Traditional and Social Change Organizations to describe organization practice. In Table 8.3, we compare the use of language for practice in each type organization thus far.

Assessment is a common term used across the three organizational types. In fact, we have just used this term in the previous section to examine the variables encountered in organizational life. Note that *problem analysis*

Table 8.3
Practice Language Differences Across Three Organization Types

Traditional Organization	Social Change Organization	Serendipitous Organization
Assessment	Assessment	Assessment
Diagnosis	Problem Analysis	Understanding
Planning	Organizing	Collaborating
Incremental Change	Collective Transformational Change	Sense Making

is typically used in Social Change Organizations, even though the use of *diagnosis* (with a medical connotation) is still very prevalent in Traditional Organizations. However, problem analysis takes a much different turn in Serendipitous Organizations because the process of analyzing is so central to the organization's philosophy. Since Serendipitous Organizations may be less prone to label situations, we use the term *understanding* to describe the process used to fully analyze a situation. *Collaborating* is a more interpretive term than *planning* or *organizing*, and *sense making* is interpretive language that implies a very different way of looking at organizational processes and products as meaningful. We will use this language to guide our exploration of what it is like to practice in a Serendipitous Organization.

No matter in what type of organization one practices, there will be times when something needs to change. When change agents attempt to alter something in the Serendipitous Organization, they will typically take on the challenge with the same standard of civility and collaboration that they use in their daily work. Civility and respect toward colleagues are established principles in the clan culture. This is essential because of the frustration that generally accrues in an emergent change process where no one knows for sure what should be done until the process and the product of the change action are evaluated. We now turn to the *nonrational approach* to assessment, understanding, collaborating, and sense making needed to assure emergent planning sensitive to context and multiple perspectives.

ASSESSING SITUATIONS

In the Serendipitous Organization, assessment is an ongoing process that is viewed as only one snapshot in time. Since the organization is always evolving, reassessment must be a continual process, for what is believed to be true about the organization one day can be different tomorrow. The culture of the organization is committed to hearing the voices of all participants and when new information arises, adjustments may be made if everyone thinks that it is a good idea. There is flexibility, fluidity, and a natural evolutionary process going on within these organizations. Since the changes being made are not radical or revolutionary, the status quo is maintained, but minor, incremental adjustments and accommodations are a natural, continuous occurrence. No rules are carved in stone, because there are no absolutes.

Members of a Serendipitous Organization find assessing organizational culture to be very congruent with the philosophy of the organization. In fact, as we have already seen, organizational culture theories are congruent with the assumptions of the Interpretive Paradigm. So to understand the organization from this perspective is to look at the elements identified by organizational culture theorists to guide one's assessment. Elements for dealing with the larger environment are *mission and strategy, goals, means, measurement,* and *correction.* These elements could be framed in questions that would guide one's understanding of the organization:

- How does the organization develop shared understandings of the mission and the tasks to be done?
- How does the organization's core mission contribute to consensus around goals?
- How are goals attained in this organization?
- What criteria are used to measure goal achievement?
- What repair or remedial strategies are used to make adjustments when goals are not achieved? (Schein, 1992, p. 52).

Similarly, questions pertaining to internal integration of the organization's culture follow:

- What common language and conceptual categories are used?
- Who is a part and who is not a part of this organization?
- How do members get, maintain, and lose power in this organization?
- How are appropriate peer relationships defined?
- What is valued and what is not valued in this organization?
- How do members make unexplainable situations meaningful? (Schein, 1992, p. 66).

Finally, one's organizational assessment could include a look at the levels of culture:

- What are the artifacts of this organization (e.g., physical space, group output, artistic expressions, products, members' behaviors, etc.)?
- What values are espoused within this organization?
- What are the underlying assumptions within this organization?
- Do the artifacts and values fit with the underlying assumptions?

Assessing the Serendipitous Organization, then, requires attention to elements not always valued or even seen as very important in traditional organizations.

Having assessed the organization's culture, it will be helpful to examine the implications of this culture for the use of assessment within the organization's programs. For example, in Traditional and Social Change organizations, assessment of clients, organizations, and communities requires systematic quantitative data collection that can be easily translated into numbers and analyzed statistically. The Serendipitous Organization's subjective nature values very different types of assessment tools and strategies. Since Serendipitous Organizations typically focus on complex problems and issues in contexts that are not well understood, the use of qualitative assessment procedures will be highly valued because they provide depth and flexibility. Tools may not be available that focus on the problems addressed in Serendipitous Organizations because context is considered to be everything; thus standardization or the use of established instruments are viewed as barriers when in-depth responses are desired. If the context is essential to understanding the problem, then a tool that has been shaped to capture generalizable variables will not be able to capture the unique situation at hand. Tools emerge from the context and the experience. Instead of a standardized instrument to guide the work, questions are asked of participants the answers to which *they* think are important to know. Therefore, the results are informative to the participants in the questioning, because the answers are to their own questions.

UNDERSTANDING PROBLEMS

In the Serendipitous Organization, problem analysis is much more difficult than it would be in Traditional and Social Change organizations because of the belief that nothing is static, but always in process. While organizations with objectivist perspectives focus on universal truths, and champions of that position guard against goal displacement, Serendipitous Organizations are prone to switch goals if that is group consensus. Therefore, analyzing the problem in a Serendipitous Organization requires a great deal of patience and a real dedication to diversity. However, colleagues will be ready participants in analyzing an organizational problem since feeling–judging personality types naturally engage in ongoing dialogue and analysis. If a problem arises in a Serendipitous Organization, one will have no trouble finding willing colleagues to participate in the collaborative process of analyzing the situation.

The difficulty encountered by practitioners in Serendipitous Organizations is that problem analysis can take a long time. Since the clan culture tolerates ongoing collaboration and dialogue, people may enjoy the process of trying to understand all the nuances of an organizational problem so much that nobody gets around to doing anything about it. The process-oriented nature of these organizations, which value examining every possibility, can actually make achieving consensus difficult. A prime example is a university faculty. Working with faculty members is often described as "herding cats," with persons who are very functionalist in their orientation frustrated with the amount of effort it takes to get to any decision. However, if one looked at universities as a prime site of interpretivists, then one could relax and realize that the assumptions valued by faculty members do not make for efficiency. In fact, the value placed on careful analysis of every issue is one to be admired in this setting, because complex issues are being treated in complex ways.

Programmatically, Serendipitous Organizations must at least temporarily settle on certain opportunities or problems in order to do their work. However, their programs will be highly creative and the curiosity of staff will likely produce some findings formerly unanticipated. Breakthroughs are likely to occur in Serendipitous Organizations because staff members are open to new and unexpected possibilities. The responsiveness of emergent planning gives rise to serendipitous results (Netting, O'Connor, & Fauri, 2008). How often have stories of major findings been reported as accidents when in fact they were the coming together of previously disconnected items in a new way? To the Serendipitous Organization this is hardly an accident—it is the nature of subjective reality and emerging designs for practice.

Collaborating

Whereas planning and organizing are trademarks of Traditional and Social Change organizations, *collaborating* is the term often heard in the hallways of Serendipitous Organizations. According to Hess and Mullen (1996), "to collaborate is to labor together" (p. 5). Wheatley and Kellner-Rogers (1996) frame collaboration differently—as actually playing together, since they view life as creative and "intent on discovering what's possible" (p. 20). Regardless of how one frames collaborative process, it has been the subject of much dialogue in recent years (Ede & Lunsford, 1990; Foreman, 1992; Jacobsen, 1998; O'Connor & Netting, 1999). Macduff and Netting (2000) defined the **collaborative process** as when "two or more persons work and play together to achieve some result or create some product in which they are jointly invested, about which they care enough to pool their strengths" (p. 48). These persons may be from the same or different fields, disciplines, and/or professions. In Serendipitous Organizations, practitioners, clients, volunteers, and others dialogue so that whatever is decided will be based on the strengths of multiple perspectives. That was how the Orange State Organization began, grew, and continues to survive. Connecting multiple players can result in demystifying the process so that professionals and clients alike contribute to cogenerative learning (Greenwood & Levin, 1998).

Because collaboration is the hallmark of Serendipitous Organizations, if one wants a change in this type of organization, then one must be prepared to work with others in the change process. Bulldozing a change through (even if one has authority) or imposing one's moral stance on another are not well received in Serendipitous Organizations. The norm and expected behavior must be steeped in a willingness to listen to all sides of an issue and to be prepared to change one's own view given persuasive evidence of an alternative. In other words, the problem one may have originally defined may be reconstructed a number of times in the collaboration process since the heart of this organization is to fully understand the concerns expressed.

Similarly, when one develops programs within this organization, methods used in working with others will be highly collaborative, typically involving persons from diverse perspectives, backgrounds, and professions. Teamwork, particularly true interdisciplinary teaming, is likely to be used in Serendipitous Organizations. Programs will be designed to be highly inclusive of consumers so that their voices and opinions are genuinely respected and heard.

SENSE MAKING

Phrases like "this makes sense" or "that is meaningful" are appropriate to use in Serendipitous Organizations. While Traditional Organizations seek efficient interventions and Social Change Organizations are bent on social transformation, Serendipitous Organizations are dedicated to discovery in order to make sense of situations. Therefore, if one collaborates on change in this type of organization, one must work with others to be sure the change makes sense to all involved. This takes time. As theorists note, this generally means that sense making will not occur in a linear fashion. In fact, as Weick (1995) notes, sense making may be retrospective and plausibility may take precedence over accuracy. In other words, people have to feel comfortable with the change, mull it over, rethink their original positions, and pay particular attention to the social cues. One can expect one's proposed change to be studied in depth with multiple opinions offered along the way. We have often seen interpretive sensemaking processes occurring in functionalist organizations and the fit is deadly. Functionalists get frustrated, tired, angry, and even obstinate in these emerging situations, where interpretivists are merely trying to participate and understand in order to own the process. When functionalists say things like, "I don't have any idea what just happened in there," or "I would have never guessed that that decision would result from this meeting," they have typically been engaged in an interpretive, emergent process and didn't like it because it lacked control.

Just as sense making forms the process by which practice in a Serendipitous Organization occurs, it also forms the nucleus of how congruent programs work. After assessing, understanding, and collaborating, these programs are designed to engage consumers with staff in a joint process of making sense of difficult situations, finding meaning in their lives, or working toward a more in-depth understanding of their conditions so plans for change can emerge. If one believes, as interpretivists do, that self-actualization involves sense making and understanding, one could argue that their programs meet higher order needs, moving beyond survival to self-actualization. These programs are certainly empowering for all involved. In the Orange State case, not only the participants but also the volunteers and the paid staff learned and grew as a result of the types of change efforts that were designed and enacted there.

Because Serendipitous Organizations do not hold to positivist goals about objective knowledge or truth, plans must be held tentatively, keeping alternative approaches alive as possibilities. A current example of this idea is the parallel planning now in vogue in public child welfare. If the plan for a child placed out of the home is to return the child home, then all service efforts are designed to overcome the problems that led to the child's removal. But at the same time, other planning for adoptive placement is also being undertaken, just in case the family cannot reclaim their child. The idea is that the best interest of the child should be served and both ways might work, so both plans should be evolved. Similar to this example, where children, families (biological, foster, and adoptive), workers, and other service personnel must participate, all participants in interpretive work need to be engaged in constructing the reality of the desired change. The ethics involved in assessing, understanding, collaborating, and sense making for change are meant to design changes so that all stakeholders are given a fair chance. That chance is assured because information is continually inputted to the process and changes are made as a result. The quality of the process protects the quality of the product. The measure of success becomes: Was the problem as constructed solved as desired without oppressing one another?

Table 8.4 provides an overview of practice characteristics in Serendipitous Organizations and provides a summary of the discussion in Part III. You can use this as a way to determine whether organizations with which you are familiar support interpretive organization practice.

PRODUCING PRODUCTS AND OUTCOMES

Serendipitous Organizations are more focused on process than they are on products. However, this does not mean that they do not produce products and even outcomes, only that they value the means taken to achieve them as much as they do the ends achieved. The products and outcomes in Serendipitous Organizations are different from those in Traditional and Social Change organizations, and are often viewed with some disdain by their colleagues in these other paradigms. For example, a valued product for a Serendipitous Organization would be a narrative analysis that uses critical thinking and multiple perspectives to fully articulate an understanding of a highly complex problem. This report would likely present options and their implications, rather than the recommendations for a specific way of solving the defined problem preferred by a functionalist or

Table 8.4
Practice Characteristics in Serendipitous Organizations

Practice Element	Characteristics
Assessment	Attention to hearing multiple perspectives from diverse groups and individuals is critical to information gathering.
	Collecting word data is as important as collecting numeric data.
	Use of open-ended questions and emerging instruments is useful, given the need to develop deep understandings in context.
	Reassessment is a continual and ongoing process.
Understanding	Subjective needs assessment data are shared with all constituencies.
	Analysis is viewed as a broadening process, with efforts made to avoid premature narrowing down of what is known.
Collaborating	Involvement of all parties is highly valued.
	Collaborative process is seen as meaningful in itself.
	Hearing all perspectives and views is encouraged.
	Consensus building is the goal.
Sense Making	Sense making may occur at any level, but the primary focus is typically at the individual and organizational levels.
	Change-from-within tactics (collaboration and campaign) rather than contest (conflict) are preferred.
	The goal is to make changes that become the new status quo and are owned by everyone.

radical structuralist. Another product might be a pilot project that allows for emergent planning (Netting, O'Connor, & Fauri, 2008). For example, in the Orange County State Child Abuse Prevention Agency, programs evolved and even changed in a seamless manner, benefiting from what was learned in the piloting process and changing as needed, according to what was learned in their implementation.

Similarly, outcomes for human service programs delivered in Serendipitous Organizations are often seen as too soft, temporary, difficult to measure, or merely reflecting how people feel, rather than what they can do differently as a result of program intervention. For example, a battered women's shelter may seek to empower women by raising their consciousness and enhancing their feelings of self-worth. Viewed as a meaningful outcome by interpretivists, functionalists would ask, "but what about the needed skills to get women into the societal mainstream?" Radical structuralists would retort, "but what about *changing* the societal structures that oppress women?" In other words, interpretive outcomes are often viewed as being only immediate outcomes from which intermediate and ultimate outcomes must emerge.

Yet the products and outcomes of Serendipitous Organizations are highly thoughtful, time-consuming endeavors that contribute to meaning in the lives of all participants. One danger in the Serendipitous Organization is that staff will be so engaged in meaning making that client outcomes become secondary. We have witnessed Serendipitous Organizations in which the staff felt so good about being a part of a supportive clan culture that it was difficult to distinguish *whose* needs the staff members were there to serve, their own or their clients'.

IMPLICATIONS FOR PRACTICE IN SERENDIPITOUS ORGANIZATIONS

The interpretive perspective offers more value congruence than conflicts for helping professionals. At the same time that it is professionally congruent, this approach also presents many challenges for the organizational leader who is charged with the responsibility of managing the organization, its employees, and its services with as much efficiency as efficacy. This perspective provides an ability to start where the individual is, but it also limits an ability to know for sure that what is being planned or implemented is "right." In fact, most plans are so emergent that it is difficult to fully articulate them until they have been enacted (see Netting, O'Connor, & Fauri, 2008 for a full discussion of the alternative form of planning congruent with Serendipitous Organization goals).

A great challenge in the contemporary context is that outcome measures have limited meaning in an interpretive perspective. Outcomes, while important, are only a small part of the complex picture in Serendipitous Organizations. The focus on outcomes reduces important complexities in this approach. Of interest is what the clients think as much as what they do, even while other stakeholders are being considered. This perspective operationalizes the notion of *person-in-environment*. What is ethical and effective depends on the various elements of the person within a specific context. In the interpretive frame of reference, the determination of an acceptable level of professional performance and client outcomes will ever remain a work in progress. The determination of what is ethical and effective within the Serendipitous Organization will depend on the time and context of individual decisions, which makes effectiveness measurement quite a challenge. This is because the service that should be delivered and what can be determined to be socially just must be context dependent and, therefore, unique to the situations of all involved. Measures of connection and collaboration could be taken during the processes, but the products would be unique to the situation. The same is true regarding the assurance of dignity and worth of the person, the importance of human relationships, integrity, and competence. Each must be assiduously determined within the time and context of the situation, which absolutely requires well-honed critical thinking skills of all within the organization.

The assumptions of Serendipitous Organizations are also congruent with attention to diversity and multiculturalism. In fact, this perspective can help to articulate what constitutes multicultural practice because it forces attention to, and respect for, multiple voices. The approach to organizing will not be simple. The answer will not be clear, but the process will result in the complexity necessary for real recognition of diversity without oppression. It also assures that the organization will never be stuck in political correctness, because there will never be certainty about what the best approach to diversity and multiculturalism should be. This suggests a difficult challenge, fraught with frustration and other surprising issues, but the *relativist* stance of interpretivism as actualized in Serendipitous Organizations allows for pragmatic modification whenever necessary. When the challenge appears too difficult to guarantee consideration of all of the voices of the myriad perspectives, something can change.

Professional ethics from this relativist perspective will be difficult to determine. However, in exchange for lack of certainty, there is great flexibility to probe for deep understandings of all perspectives and an opportunity for powerful targeting of organizational activities. Women and minorities who are represented in both the service providing and the service receiving populations will be less disadvantaged in Serendipitous Organizations than in several other organizational perspectives due to the access provided and required for the presence and consideration of all voices.

CONCLUSION

The Serendipitous Organization is committed to discovery and understanding. This sets up the expectation that discovery of a generalizable truth is not possible, nor does the understanding process result in a final truth. Change will occur as new persons interact intersubjectively within these organizations, and that is to be expected and valued. When the unexpected happens somewhere in the process, then the assumption is that this is how the world works now. Staff members comfortable within Serendipitous Organizations live well with ambiguity; they do not assume that anyone is in control—there are only fleeting images of being in control for the time being.

What the organizational leader gains from interpretivist assumptions, the clan culture, and the congruent schools of management is a commitment from colleagues to work through the process of change and to continue to work in teaming relationships with one another. The leader recognizes that there will be pressures from more traditional funding sources or other agencies to use standardized approaches and tools to aid in response to the call for productivity. Yet, productivity is defined very differently in Serendipitous Organizations, for sense making and meaning making are seen as valuable in themselves. Emergent plans are also valued as they are empowering to all participants. Persons who want more concrete products may view these soft, nonlinear "outcomes" with disdain.

When adopting Serendipitous Organizations' connection and collaboration goals for assessment, understanding, collaborating, and sense making, the organizational leader and worker gains a view of what is unique to the organization and its members in the organizational environment. Subtle influences regarding processes are captured in the data collection for decision making. This is because there is room for consideration of the more qualitative, affective, intuitive aspects of organizational life.

For the organization leader, a serendipitous organizational perspective and accompanying theories offer great help in assessment, understanding, collaborating, and sense making in attending to the special opportunities and challenges provided by that which is different from the norm. Further, there is room for the chaotic and the unexpected, which seem to permeate today's organizational life. The uncontrolled or uncontrollable presence, often attributed to incompetence in the dominant world, is seen in Serendipitous Organizations as normal chaos in contemporary organizations. This leaves space for much creativity.

We now turn to the fourth and final type of organization—the Entrepreneurial Organization—having the least well-defined approach. You will soon see that this perspective on organizing has some assumptions in common with interpretivism, but when it comes to the way in which change is viewed, the Entrepreneurial Organization, steeped in a radical humanist perspective, parts company with the Serendipitous Organization.

DISCUSSION QUESTIONS

1. Why is an emergent approach to change so valued in Serendipitous Organization practice? What paradigmatic and cultural assumptions support it? What benefits are gained by engaging in emergent planning? What might be potential problems?

2. Where is advocacy in Serendipitous Organization practice? What types of tactics are most congruent with the type of change most appreciated in this organization?

3. Given the preferred structure and management style in Serendipitous Organizations, what are the challenges and opportunities for your own practice? How would working in a Serendipitous Organization fit with your comfort zone?

4. Review the characteristics of Serendipitous Organizations in Table 8.1. Where are the potential strengths and challenges for you as a practitioner in this type of organization? Are there other characteristics that you would add to this table? If so, what would they be, and why would you add them?

5. Characterize the roles and relationships that are expected in a Serendipitous Organization. How do these fit with the practice standards and expectations related to managing and being managed in this type organization? Reflect on what the meaning of all this might be for you as a developing practitioner. (This reflection could become part of a regular journaling exercise.)

6. As a practitioner in a Serendipitous Organization, what would you expect the challenges and opportunities might be in relationship to the environment in which a Serendipitous Organization operates? What would you assume the standards and expectations to be vis-à-vis the environment?

7. In reviewing the expectations regarding assessment, understanding, collaborating, and sense making in a Serendipitous Organization, what do you foresee as the strengths and challenges where the organization is engaged in a multicultural environment? What might be social justice issues and opportunities?

8. From the standpoint of a professional practitioner in a Serendipitous Organization, what are the costs and benefits of the preferred manner of evaluation of practice and performance within the organization? What are the challenges where words and meaning are markers for evaluation over numbers and statistics?

9. Going back to the Orange State Child Abuse Prevention Agency case example at the beginning of Part III, use the content in this chapter to conduct an organizational analysis, being especially attentive to structure and standards of practice. What insights are gained from your analysis?

INDIVIDUAL
EMPOWERMENT

I N PART IV, we look more at practices than at structures in Entrepreneurial
Organizations that identify with goals of individual liberation through
individual empowerment. Structures, like theories, represent particular challenges to organizations having individual empowerment goals
since any attempts at uniformity or discipline limit individual freedom.
The liberatory challenges presented by organizing goals seeking to be
congruent with a radical humanist perspective will be the focus of
Chapter 9 in this final part of the text. Chapter 10 is designed to help
the reader to understand standards of behavior and practice in individual
empowerment organizations. The entrepreneurial flavor that constitutes fit
within this perspective is investigated. In Chapters 9 and 10, we reveal the
paradoxical nature of practicing in an organization that is so individualistic
that its goal is to empower individuals and respect difference at all costs.
Starting with the *radical humanist* paradigmatic perspective and moving to
the *adhocracy culture*, attention in this part of the text will be given to the
values, preferences, and decision-making strategies that are congruent
with organizations with *individual liberation* goals.

In Chapter 9, we discuss theories derived from the assumption that
individual empowerment of transformation is ultimately important. Comparisons are made with other radical change interests in order to highlight
how individual empowerment organizations are tied to *power and politics
theories, critical theory,* certain branches of *feminist theory,* and *postmodern
theory,* as are organizations whose goals are larger scale transformative
change. An *antiadministration* approach to theory is introduced to illustrate
the degree of difference between this perspective and the other approaches
to organizations already covered.

Additional discussion of the differences in theoretical emphasis among
organizational perspectives is designed to illustrate just how far apart
traditional and radical change organizations are in their thinking and
theorizing. The emerging nature of postmodern theory related to individual empowerment forms a provocative backdrop against which to explore

the nature and consequences of organizations determined to liberate and empower individuals. The chapter closes with the consideration that this type of organization could become a viable organizational model for true incorporation of global perspectives in the future. Also explored will be the costs and benefits of cultural humility within this organizational perspective.

Continuing the use of the lens of strategic management and the roles of managers and leaders within this approach, the issues of organizing without organizational structures that might confine the individual are considered in Chapter 10. The idea of information as structure for organizing is introduced as a potential means of allowing unlimited change possibilities and the free release of the human spirit. Conflict in these types of organizations is also examined for its potential for transformation. Although we consider practice in this final type of organization (the hardest to describe and comprehend), we think the perspective introduces the reader to many possibilities for future human service practice, particularly in view of how technological advances are shaping organizational and service expectations.

We offer this perspective as the final consideration of multiple perspectives on organizing and practicing with the hope that the critical thinking skills, the growing self-awareness, and the increased understanding of the need for ethnic competence in practice might allow the reader to engage in an even-handed examination of the potential of practice in such a developing, alternative perspective. As an aid in moving away from that which is typically seen in human service agencies, end-of-chapter discussion questions focus on the challenges of transforming individuals within highly flexible organizational boundaries or within organizations having no traditional boundaries or structure.

To begin the investigation of organizations that are essentially against most accepted forms of organizing by virtue of the goal of individual empowerment, we offer the following case example. In the next two chapters, you will see in detail the paradoxical nature of organizational structure and behavior when goals are more individual than communal.

I HELP

Five years ago, Jackson left his last traditional job in a human service agency. For the whole time since he graduated with a Masters in Social Work he kept running into limits in his service delivery experience that never made sense to him. He should have expected this, given that the program he had attended was focused on the concept of radical social work and progressive change. Before he had entered his graduate program, he had already been labeled as someone who questioned authority, and he was at home in a master's program devoted to radical change. He loved his school experience and he loved the idea of making changes in individual lives. He never expected to have so much trouble trying to do so until he hit the "real world" of practice.

Because he came to social work without much practice experience in human services, it was difficult for him to find a job that was congruent with his concept of social work that would allow him to engage in individual advocacy in the most radical sense. At first, he thought it was lack of experience, but then it became clear that the job he had envisioned just did not exist. He took a job as a case manager, thinking that in some direct way he could engage in individual advocacy with his case management clients. Almost the first day, he was crosswise with administration because he wanted to provide services that were not mandated by the program plan or the funding source. It went on like that for months, until both he and his supervisor agreed to disagree and he left.

Several similar experiences both in the public and nonprofit sector followed, until he began to wonder if he really was cut out to be a social worker working in the margins between the individual client and society. He hated the constraints that seemed to be applied wherever he was trying to tackle oppression. He saw excuses being made by others for not doing what he considered to be the right thing. He was determined to do the work differently, and in preparation for that he studied for and received a clinical license. Now he could be an independent practitioner—but how, and with whom, and who would pay for his efforts?

One way that Jackson had been managing his frustration at work was to become involved in computer technology in his off hours. Over the years, he became quite adept and was particularly interested in how significant, intimate connections were being made in cyberspace. He thought of all this as his hobby, until one day it struck him that he had all the tools to do the work that he had been wanting to do all along. He had the license; he had the technology; all he needed was to develop a web page and advertise his availability to help individuals via web-based bio-psycho-social-spiritual interventions. He studied the literature about intervention strategies that seemed to be effective for individual empowerment and found great compatibility with pro-liberation psychology, which recognized that breaking out of psychological or political oppression requires *both* psychological as well as social change. He developed the *I HELP* web page, and developed a description of what he hoped to do—*join with potential users to deal with oppression in a contextual way, working toward goals of personal empowerment*. Then, he waited. Two things happened: (1) Likeminded helpers from all over the world made contact, wanting to join up with him; and (2) busy people, most of whom could speak English, were making outreach from all over the world at all times of the day and night. He had apparently attracted service users as well as therapists, a community of persons who were dedicated to recognizing that change must occur for individuals in order for the world to change.

He had linked a diverse group of co-learners, all seeking ways to overcome oppression, dialoguing together, and working toward individual empowerment. Some of the first e-mails Jackson received were particularly revealing in that themes kept emerging, such as "I want to seek a higher level of consciousness," "I know there are ways to reach a better order of being, but I need the skills to get there," "I don't want to become a member of anything or work as a group, but I desperately am seeking ways to benefit from what others know so I can empower myself to make change in the world," "Empowerment is very individualistic, but if each of us can be empowered in his or her own way, then there is hope for the future," and "I've tried all the traditional approaches to therapy where the therapist is an expert and I'm a client. It doesn't work for me to be depersonalized by an expert and become prescribed and predetermined."

Almost before Jackson knew it, there was a cadre of service providers and those seeking help from all over the world connected through I HELP. There were religious counselors, yogis, physical therapists, social workers, and art therapists all delivering services via the Internet in their own way. Each represented a different profession, even though some had similar training. He really did not know much about their professional status, but he thought that some had licenses. In fact, some advertised their educational background and their accreditation, while others focused their personal pages on designs and information that captured their particular vision of helping. The Web linked all of them through I HELP. Jackson knew that some did their work via mandalas. Others did exercise and breathing. Some offered prayer, while others engaged in narrative therapy via biographies.

Jackson personally preferred the chat aspect of the Web, which allowed him to have real-time, purposeful conversations with his users. He was very careful never to refer to anyone as a *client*. It had been drilled into him in his social work program that *client* implied a one-down status because that made Jackson an "expert." The individuals who sought his services were *service users* and he called himself a *facilitator* rather than a *therapist*. *Therapy* was too tied to traditional interventions that were anything but empowering.

Facilitation meant that he was a helpful guide, but the will and ability to become empowered was within the individual with whom he worked. He recognized that he was learning as much as were the users, making this a co-learning process.

Jackson knew only about his own users, but assumed that others in the network encountered the same sorts of individuals and groups. Some users paid for the service directly; others had certain arrangements with insurance sources that allowed them to get reimbursement. On several occasions, Jackson bartered with users, especially those who lived in distant, interesting locations and who had access to the types of arts and crafts that he loved. The payment process was quite a challenge—so much so, that Jackson decided to sell advertising space on his page. He was particular about whom he contracted with, but somehow he felt he needed to balance his own financial needs with those of his service users. He had enough users that he averaged about five hours of work roughly five days a week; but he was unsure about what his hourly wage was. He paid attention to that only when his bank account didn't look right. What he loved was the fact that he could provide facilitation whenever and wherever he wanted. Recently, he spent a good two hours with a service user in cyberspace while he sat on the beach at Key West. It was great! He was sure that he was doing his best, most creative work ever. He felt energized and fulfilled. He was truly free and self-actualized. From conversations on the Net, he knew the others mostly felt the same; but sometimes he wondered about what sort of ethical responsibility he had regarding the other practitioners who had become linked through I HELP.

CHAPTER 9

Entrepreneurial Organizations

E ARLIER, WE INTRODUCED the Radical Humanist Paradigm and Entrepreneurial Organizations. In this chapter, we deepen our original
description by focusing on the aspects that inform the structure of an
organization intent on individual empowerment. We begin by examining
themes found in radical humanist thinking and the assumptions that flow
from this paradigm, resulting in the individual liberation goals of what we
are calling Entrepreneurial Organizations. Following this paradigmatic
grounding, the major organizational theories that may fit within this
perspective are identified. Notice that we say *may fit*, because a radical
humanist perspective actually takes an antitheoretical approach to knowledge building in its rejection of traditional structures and processes for
knowing. We close the chapter with a critical analysis of the perspective
and its implications, so that the reader is left with a good picture of what is
gained and what is given up when approaching organizations from a
radical humanist worldview. We then transition to Chapter 10, which
focuses on the culture and behavioral expectations that shape standards for
practice when organizing to achieve individual liberation goals.

At this stage in the history of organizational development, there probably is no "pure" radical humanist organization, though more and more
organizations may be moving in that direction. So think of this discussion
as detailing the Entrepreneurial Organization prototype. As with organizations based in assumptions from other paradigms, Entrepreneurial
Organizations may have members that operate under different assumptions. At this phase in the development of the I HELP web-based organization, Jackson must be assuming that all the therapists who have
connected with him are operating from the same set of expectations about
independence and entrepreneurship or they would not have joined his
effort. Jackson really knows only about his users' expectations. However,
at this point, four and a half years into the experience, no one has
demanded a different structure or association because those who are
associated have perfect freedom to act as needed. In his mind, the
practitioners who have joined him have done so out of choice, based

on their recognition of a personal need. To him, this is very different from his experiences elsewhere, where he and probably everybody else joined the organization out of need to make money with the hope of some choice in the process. Most of the time, he felt that he was left without choices, which made him operate almost always paradoxically—holding to his own goals and preferences while doing what he was told to do. In a couple of situations since the start of I HELP, he has encountered paradoxes with insurance companies when differing assumptions collided about service delivery. In those cases, he and his user figured another way to pay for services rendered.

Regarding paradoxes, the most likely scenario for paradoxical experiences is at the paradigmatic, not the organizational, level, because few Entrepreneurial Organizations would attract employees with other than radical humanist worldviews. Rather, employees holding radical humanist assumptions will find themselves in organizations based on other paradigmatic assumptions and will face paradoxical challenges regarding performance, just as Jackson did before he decided to branch out on his own. Because it was so difficult to live in paradox within a Traditional Organization, he chose to risk life outside of traditional social work, rather than conform to expectations.

At the conclusion of this chapter, it is our hope that the reader will understand why radical humanist assumptions about organizational goals will fundamentally collide with functionalist or traditional goals. It will also be clear that both Entrepreneurial Organizations and Social Change

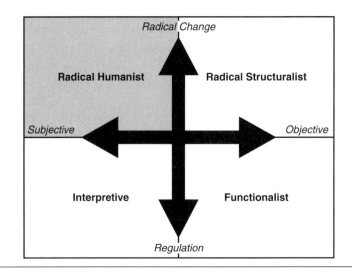

Figure 9.1 Burrell and Morgan's Paradigmatic Framework. *Source:* Adapted from Burrell and Morgan (1979). *Sociological paradigms and organizational analysis.* Aldershot, England: Ashgate. Figure 3.1, p. 22. Used by permission.

Organizations seek transformational change, but differ in how they go about it. Similarly, Entrepreneurial Organizations have subjectivism in common with Serendipitous Organizations, but these organizations part company in how they approach change.

RADICAL HUMANIST THEMES

The most radical approaches to understanding organizations are based on the assumptions of the Radical Humanist Paradigm. It is from this perspective that the most experimental (and some would say most outlandish) efforts are undertaken to reconcile the challenges and the opportunities of modern technology and an emerging world economy into a manageable work life in a complex social structure. Readers interested in looking at the existential challenges currently facing many people may wish to read *The Geography of Nowhere: Finding One's Self in the Post Modern World*, by Gary Eberle (1994). Eberle discusses the changes that have occurred from earlier times when myths and symbols allowed individuals to locate themselves in time and space without reliable reference points like God, church, society, or a sense of self. To manage, he calls for the development of a higher consciousness informed by spirituality.

It is from the radical humanist perspective that the study of organizations is most likely to take on a metaphysical aspect much in keeping with Eberle (1994). Similarly, Mullaly (2007) sees radical humanism as "predicated on the belief that before social transformation can occur, personal transformation must take place" (p. 289). It is also from this perspective that the impact on and the role of the individual in organizational life takes center stage. Sharing with the interpretive perspective, there is recognition that useful study of organizations must be a mix of the rational, the serendipitous, and the intuitive as individuals make sense of the processes and the accepted practices of organizational life. Though the assumptions of radical humanism also require a certain degree of rigor to produce acceptable results, there is an explicit recognition of multiple ways of knowing and understanding. The artistic, the spiritual, and the *other* are included as viable sources of knowledge about organizational life. What an individual feels, senses, or intuits is acceptable information from which to work. From this perspective, *all* the ways the human instrument processes and creates knowing are recognized—they are mechanisms that allow individual consciousness to reach its full potential.

Interestingly and most paradoxically, this recognition of multiple ways of knowing including the spiritual and artistic may have brought the philosophy of science full circle. The natural sciences evolved as a way to refute, overcome, or otherwise eliminate "lesser" ways of knowing the world. The early empiricists chose hard facts over the "magical thinking" of religion, art, and philosophy to build a sensible world. Now, radical humanism returns to pre–Vienna Circle scholarly thinking in ways that accept all sensible sources as potentially rigorous ways of knowing, especially from a subjectivist, individualistic standpoint. For those wishing to read more about the history and politics of philosophy of science, see Diesing (1991).

In radical humanism, objectivity is not expected, but instead the full use of intuition, tacit knowledge, and the insights derived from them are desired dimensions of rigorous knowledge building. Instead of generalization, *individual consciousness raising* is the expected result of inquiry. The true measure of an acceptable level of rigor is where the individual, as a result of the organizational inquiry process, is released from the constraints that hamper personal human development related to the area being investigated. Individual change must be associated with organizational inquiry guided by this perspective in order for the research to reach its expected standard of quality. Personal transformation is the goal of research.

This very different way into understanding organizational behavior and organizational structure presents interesting opportunities to explore the unexplored in organizational life, but its differences present great challenges in a traditional scientific community. At this point, it might be questionable based on traditional standards whether I HELP is really an organization. Uniform variables regarding the architecture of the organization are absent, just as uniform information about what is *done* within the network of information that constitutes the organization is impossible to capture in any uniform way. I HELP presents many unknowns. Hopefully, at the completion of this chapter, the degrees of opportunities and challenges for organizational work from this perspective should be clear.

To accomplish this, we will look in more detail at the assumptions undergirding this perspective. We will also explore the liberty and individualism themes that are important to an Entrepreneurial Organization. The challenges involved in the developing concept of the virtual organization such as I HELP will also be of interest in this part of the text.

ASSUMPTIONS OF THE RADICAL HUMANIST PARADIGM

Radical humanism sees reality as the result of individual consciousness. Reality is created due to active individual participation in the construction of social reality. The assumption is that there exist no universal laws. Instead, there is the unique and the particular, so that knowledge becomes soft, subjective, and even spiritual. Knowledge to be knowledge must be experienced. Therefore, it is believed that human nature is free and proactive. Humans have a central role in the creation of reality. They are self-directing and self-correcting.

Box 9.1

SUBJECTIVISM: DEFINING TERMS

Nominalism (in the mind)
Antipositivism (soft, subjective, must be experienced)
Voluntarism (people create their environments)
Ideographic (analyze subjective accounts that one generates by "getting inside" situations of everyday life)

Source: Adapted from Burrell and Morgan (1979). *Sociological paradigms and organizational analysis.* Aldershot, England: Ashgate. Figure 1.1, p. 3. Used by permission.

Box 9.1 reintroduces the concept of *subjectivism* one last time. Recall that *interpretivism* accepts subjectivism as well.

A subjectivist perspective was elaborated in Chapter 7. In brief, radical humanism is subjectivist because the perspective does not abide a universalism in which there is "one best way." Multiple truths are viewed as arising from within people. Radical humanism is open to alternative ways of thinking, believing that what is considered a best way today may no longer be a best way tomorrow, and that what is good for one person may not be good for another person.

Radical humanism and interpretivism part company in how change is viewed. It is within this change perspective that the association between radical *humanism* and radical *structuralism* is most apparent. Both are change oriented, not at the incremental level but at the transformational level. Box 9.2 summarizes the radical change concerns both perspectives hold.

Individualism and what is necessary to reach personal potential is a central notion in radical humanism. Personal self-interest and involvement

---

Box 9.2

CONCERNS OF THE RADICAL CHANGE PERSPECTIVE

1. Radical change
2. Structural conflict
3. Modes of domination
4. Contradiction
5. Emancipation
6. Deprivation
7. Potentiality

Source: Adapted from Burrell and Morgan (1979). *Sociological paradigms and organizational analysis.* Aldershot, England: Ashgate. Table 2.2, p. 18. Used by permission.

in the types of organizational change necessary to assure personal actualization are important. The expectation of radical change, based on critical analysis for personal gains, represents a challenge to traditional views about organizations and organizational behavior. This alternative perspective questions the basic foundation on which classical organizing is built. It rejects the idea that organizing into a structure that subsumes the individual's choices and prerogatives creates something greater or better. This perspective also presents a challenge for research in organizations where structure and control of results is expected at all levels of organizational life. Here the individually tailored, unique responses are the basis for measuring success.

Because this perspective honors individual autonomy above all else, aggregate research becomes irrelevant. What is important is a very personal view of organizing and structuring for results that have personal, more than organizational, meaning. Jackson and his users are an excellent example of this. However, the degree of difficulty presented by these aspects, as well as the opportunities that this perspective represents, will become clear as we take a thorough look at all of the assumptions of radical humanism. Taken altogether, the assumptions of this paradigm are summarized in Box 9.3. As you read about the theories highlighted in this chapter, Box 9.3 may be a useful reminder of their underlying assumptions.

Given its subjectivist perspective, the Radical Humanist Paradigm does not limit knowledge building to just operationalizable, empirical data. Philosophy, history, arts, and social practices are also seen to be basic to knowledge building (Guba, 1990). The perspective becomes radicalized by means of its association with radical, transformative change. The focus of

---

Box 9.3

ASSUMPTIONS OF THE RADICAL HUMANIST PARADIGM

From the Subjectivist Perspective

1. Social reality exists primarily in the human mind.
2. Knowledge about social reality is soft, subjective, and natural.
3. People can be proactive in creating their own realities.
4. Given that individuals create, change, and interpret the world, qualitative approaches to understanding are useful.

From the Radical Change Perspective

5. Society is characterized by deep-seated structural conflict, modes of domination, and even contradiction.
6. Knowledge for change and action should be the goal.
7. Conflict, rather than consensus, is important.

Source: Adapted from Burrell and Morgan (1979), Chapter 1.

organizational research from this perspective is structural conflict and modes of domination that hamper the individual. The goal is to uncover contradictions and in doing so to provide avenues for individual emancipation (an emancipation that is much more active and less consensus based than what was seen in the Interpretive Paradigm). Of interest to radical humanism is understanding of particularized deprivation and oppression in order to allow for individual consciousness raising and empowerment. This means that "regardless of the individual approach used, it must not de-contextualize human activity or treat it in a de-socialized or a historical way" (Mullaly, 2007, p. 292). It is assumed that with an understanding of the forces and processes in modes of personal domination, individual potentiality can be uncovered and tapped to effect changes that result in true personal fulfillment in organizational life.

Unlike radical structuralism, which seeks changes moving the organization closer to universal goals and principles, radical humanism seeks change so that individuals can be emancipated from personal experiences of domination. From this perspective, a major instrument of domination is suspected to be traditional organizational structures, rules, and procedures. Jackson would certainly agree with this and we assume that the other practitioners associated with I HELP would as well. Since there are no universal goals and truths in the perspective, the premise of this type of emancipation is that each person may come to different conclusions about reality. I HELP should help users to imagine how this translates into organization practice—everyone has a different construction of organizational reality. Because of this and the inherent need to assure individual self-interest, conflict over competing realities may be ongoing, but seems to have been overcome in cyberspace. Unlike radical structuralism, in the radical humanist perspective there is no demand to move toward collective change or to mobilize groups. Each member of I HELP is helping in whatever way he or she sees fit. Change and mobilization occur in radical humanism for individuals. The perspective holds just as passionate a position as that seen in radical structuralism because fundamental changes, either structural and/or interpersonal, are just as urgent since individual oppression cannot be tolerated.

Organizational research from this perspective is actually an invitation to discourse. There is no imposition of authoritative interpretations about the phenomenon under investigation. Instead, the effort is to create reflexive interpretation where language and personal reality are connected. Since the basic assumption of the paradigm is that language constructs the social, this perspective is also characterized by skepticism about truth claims. "Truth" becomes relative to the language and context that constructs it, so no construction is privileged over another. This makes judgment difficult. However, because of the belief in the potentiality of human consciousness, the focus is on individual perception about language and individual conceptual insight that can result from various sources, including individual intuition.

Also because of the trust in and focus on the individual, this perspective can be against institutions that reflect or require sameness and seek consensus. This perspective rejects uniform rules and procedures, including standardization of any kind, such as dress codes or anything that constrains or impedes individuality and, perhaps, individual potentiality. Theories or approaches that are considered part of this paradigm are constructed to deny privilege and power in bureaucracy. Radical humanism believes authority over the individual robs the individual of liberty, and liberty of the individual is the desired state within organizations. Keeping these assumptions in mind, we now turn to the emerging theories that have developed within the Radical Humanist Paradigm and are related to the shaping of Entrepreneurial Organizations.

ENREPRENEURIAL ORGANIZATION THEORIES SUPPORTING INDIVIDUAL EMPOWERMENT GOALS

Included in this theoretical consideration of Entrepreneurial Organizations are three basic themes. The first theme is the importance and possibilities of the individual and self-creation. The second theme is the call to freedom to create the self as one chooses. The third theme is that Traditional Organizations manifest various modes of social domination and, therefore, are oppressive entities working against individual liberty. These themes are grounded in subjectivist assumptions that value difference, combined with assumptions about the importance of transformational change or departure from structures that limit due to their oppression. Anything that adds discipline limits and, therefore, oppresses.

Some of what is presented in the following assumes that self-creation and freedom are possible only through conflict. For example, later in this chapter you will see that Morgan (1997) uses the metaphor of "The Ugly Face" to describe organizations as instruments of domination in which multiple oppressions occur. When the organization is seen as an instrument of domination, conflict is inevitable. Other theorists see subjective radical change as being more poetic or playful, "exploring possibilities of meaning in a world which is also all the time exploring possibilities" (Wheatley & Kellner-Rogers, 1996, p. 49). Some radical humanist theorists focus more on conflict and others focus more on play; both coexist in this paradigm. While traditional ways of thinking might imply that conflict and play cannot coexist, radical humanism might explore how, through the juxtaposition of intense conflict and the joy of play, people can find themselves and, thus, be transformed.

Radical humanist theories are revolutionary. Living with ambiguity, dealing with paradox, and even questioning the entire concept of organization are relevant here. There are no universals or grand theories in radical humanism. In a way, radical humanism reacts against all of the other paradigms on issues of principle. Functionalism and radical structuralism are viewed as attempting to place or force their agendas on others. The assumptions held about the "best" way, that there are "best" approaches and universal truths, are antithetical to radical humanism. Although interpretivism is open to subjectivity, its inertia or incremental-ism is incompatible with radical humanism. Being open to subjectivity and difference represents congruence. However, individual change goals rep-resent a departure in that there is no room for satisfaction with the status quo in radical humanist thinking.

In previous chapters, we used Shafritz, Ott, and Lang (2005) as a resource to identify major perspectives in organizational theory. In this chapter, we focus primarily on theories within four of the groupings that we introduced in Chapter 5 on radical structuralism:

1. Power and politics theories
2. Feminist theories
3. Critical theories
4. Postmodern theories

Since radical humanism seeks change, power and politics theories are relevant here. Because the postmodernist critical stance tends to focus on oppression and domination, it has had a tremendous influence on radical humanism. However, it is important to understand that there are different schools of critical thought within each of these theoretical categories. Theorists coming from a radical humanist perspective will be focused on subjectivism and individualized oppression, which differs from theo-rists coming from a more radical structuralist, objectivist orientation that calls for universal or class-based changes directed toward a more just society.

POWER AND POLITICS THEORIES

When we discussed radical structuralism, we introduced the concept of power and the emergence of two voices—the critical and the rational voices. Radical humanism is influenced by the critical voice that emanates from the work of the early Marx and Weber, and does not relate in any way to the rational voice that sees power as a threat that must be controlled. Radical humanism seeks to understand, use, or oppose power so that individuals can be liberated. Theoretical understandings from writers on power and politics are used, but in different ways than are seen in radical structuralism. Whereas radical structuralism uses power and politics theories to organize collectives or classes of people for social change, radical humanism sees organizing for social change as an attempt to oppress groups of people with different, but still oppressive sets of truths. The alternative, "liberating" truth replaces established truths with new and potentially oppressive truths. Radical humanism is antifunctionalist and antistructuralist, objecting to those who have new truths, believing that, though they may be different, the alternative universal agenda still serves to oppress. Instead, radical humanism is open to many ways of going about individually based change. Group organizing is acceptable only within the context of and with an eye toward individual freedom.

In short, radical humanism may not even support the formation of organizations with agreed-on goals because individuals may not be free to self-determine in their work life. The story of how I HELP came to be is an example of this thinking. When Entrepreneurial Organizations based on radical humanism are formed, it is not with the intent to corral or control people; it is with the intent of liberating people to achieve their highest potential.

Power and politics theorists with radical humanist perspectives do not assume that the organization's primary purpose is to accomplish organizational goals. There is a rejection of the idea that organizational goals are determined and designed by those in charge. Also rejected is the primacy of organizational measurement of effectiveness and efficiency without regard to personal issues. When traditional effectiveness and efficiency measures are applied, personal needs are constrained in favor of organizational needs—a stance antithetical to radical humanism.

There is also rejection of the notion that power is vested in formal authority. Instead, an alternative complex system of individuals and coalitions with interests, benefits, values, perspectives, and perceptions is recognized, acting in competition for organizational resources and in conflict to acquire personal or professional influence. There is recognition that behaviors and decisions are not rational, but the result of personal or political influence. Use of influence is necessary for successful competition and conflict at the individual level.

Morgan's metaphor of "The Ugly Face" fits well within the radical humanist power and politics school of thought. Morgan contends that tracing the development of this metaphor takes one back to ancient peoples. For example, he refers to organizing to build the pyramids and the great sacrifices of human life that accompanied the achievement of these large constructions. For some organizational theorists, this paradox of organizational achievement paired with exploitation of individuals has been a continual feature of organizational life throughout the centuries. *Overcoming* the pursuit of the goals of a few through the labor of many as one mode of social domination has been a critical focus of radical theorists such as Marx, Weber, and Michels.

Weber was concerned with the role of bureaucracy as a form of social domination. For Weber, "the process of bureaucratization presented a very great threat to the freedom of the human spirit and the values of liberal democracy, because those in control have a means of subordinating . . . " (Morgan, 1997, pp. 304–305). In radical humanist power and politics, the process of *rationalization*, giving reasons for limit setting in an organization, is understood as oppressive. Similarly, Michels, a French sociologist, coined the phrase "iron law of oligarchy" to describe how groups of people are controlled by the desires of formal leaders. His studies of supposedly democratic organizations revealed that democracy was little more than window dressing. Michels' ideas, combined with Weber's, resonated with the works of Marx (before Engels' influence), who focused on domination and oppression of the less powerful and ways to achieve individual liberation from this domination. In more recent years, radical theorists attempting to understand domination have built on these ideas, continuing to explore the multiple processes of domination and exploitation (Morgan, 1997). For example, Hearn and Parkin (1987) focus on organizations as multiple oppressors, emphasizing the complexity of domination modes and the depth of exploitation often perpetrated in organizations.

Understanding of power and politics creates the infrastructure of the critical voice in radical humanism. We now turn to feminist theories and critical theories to deepen the understanding of power and oppression in Entrepreneurial Organizations.

FEMINIST THEORIES

In previous chapters, we recognized that there are many different types of feminist theories (Calás & Smircich, 1996). Depending on the assumptions held by various theorists, feminist theories can fall within any of the four paradigmatic perspectives. Feminist theories that assume a radical humanist perspective are what Calás and Smircich (1996) call *third world/(post) colonial theorizations*. This type of feminist theory goes beyond Western thought, questioning the dichotomy of male/female and any generalizations about gender and gender relations. Third-world theorists "hold in common a fundamental suspicion of 'gender' as a stable and sufficient analytical lens that can be applied unproblematically across cultures and histories" (Calás & Smircich, 1996, p. 238). Recognizing the subjectivity of terms and the oppressive nature of Western thought, theorists in this tradition even question themselves and others who attempt to deconstruct Western concepts. They argue that the deconstructive process itself is value laden due to the danger of replacing one dominant construction with another that is equally oppressive.

Third-world/(post) colonial theories raise many questions that illustrate some of the problems faced by radical humanism. How does one move from being part of the dominant culture in a way that does not force the replacement of one way of thinking with another? How does one challenge traditional assumptions without simply replacing them with new assumptions that, in being accepted, will become the oppressive, traditional assumptions of tomorrow? How does one respect difference to the point of recognizing individuality, rather than creating a romantic, abstract view of the diversity found in emerging nations and perspectives? How does an organization exist allowing those differences without having to organize or control them?

Feminist theories, then, have had an influence on Entrepreneurial Organizations but not because of traditional Western feminism. As scholars from around the world publish their work on women-in-development in Western publications, the third-world/(post) colonial approaches to feminist theories are emerging here in the United States in greater detail. Work examining international nongovernmental organizations (INGOs) in emerging nations is a space where this type of feminist thinking is beginning to appear (Calás & Smircich, 1996). In the next chapter, we will show the degree to which this scholarship has influenced the conceptualization of standards for practice in the Entrepreneurial Organization. Third-world/(post) colonial feminist theory asserts that **subjugated knowledge,** that knowledge held by the powerless individual and not respected by the powerful, must be allowed voice in order to fundamentally transform the ways of organizing worldwide.

CRITICAL THEORIES

As with some types of feminist theory, the more individualized perspectives of critical theories fit comfortably in the Radical Humanist Paradigm. These more subjectivist critical theorists find fertile ground for criticism of management and organizations based on what they see as a decline in the effectiveness of and disillusionment with modern assumptions about organizations and their practices. They also participate in the attack on the modernist (positivist or functionalist) tradition. They criticize the individual or personal negative consequences of the size of organizations, the rapid implementation of communication and technology, globalization, the nature of work, and turbulence in the marketplace, among other aspects of current organizational life.

Critical theorists see a crisis in organizations. Rejecting much of the current organizational discussion that no one can control or be controlled, the critical theorist taking a radical humanist perspective rejects the current situation on the basis of personal costs. They assert that the current state of organizations is unacceptable for humanity. The option is a shift in organizational thinking and behavior in order to be attentive to power consequences and individual needs. For them, more attention must be given to employees or modern organizations are doomed (Alvesson & Deetz, 1996).

Many of the early radical humanist critical theorists (see, for example, Benson, 1977; Burrell & Morgan, 1979; Deetz & Kersten, 1983; Fischer & Sirianni, 1984) began their discourse with a criticism of organizational cultural theories that attempt to engineer (or reengineer) personal/professional values. The alternative provided by them was a focus on collaboration in order to achieve organizational goals. More recent theorists (see, Alvesson, 1993; Willmott, 1993) see new social conditions with important individual impact. These conditions require a different approach to analysis providing for a different comprehension in order to achieve significant changes in the way people organize. Many call for organic, adhocratic organizations (Parker, 1993; Thompson, 1993) as a way to overcome the personal exploitation, repression, and unfairness of modern organizations.

Following a central notion of power, the radical humanist critical theorists investigate exploitation, repression, unfairness, asymmetrical power, distorted communication, and false consciousness. Attention to false consciousness about power and the results of power is important because of the radical humanist assumption that there are power relationships in knowledge creation. What gets declared as "acceptable" knowledge in organizations is due to the power of those determining the questions and interpreting the results. This is why radical humanism takes the position that traditional research on organizations asks the wrong questions and attempts answers using the wrong methods. For radical humanism, functionalist findings about "truth" lead to false understandings of individual realities.

The critical theorists move closer to personal experience in organizations. Their attention is on the *intersubjective*, the interconnections among those who people organizations and how people, realities, and social relations are constructed under conditions of power and conflict. The goal is to encounter and then deconstruct and, thus, eliminate the contradictions and suppression of conflict that exist in the dominant discourse. The attempt is to identify that which prevents honest personal expression of needs and thoughts in organizational life. The goal in the process is to open the personal intellectual space for autonomy through reason (Alvesson & Deetz, 1996). Work from this perspective highlights the negative implications of arbitrary authority and the subordination by technological rationality that protects only the dominant group interest to the detriment of the individual's personhood. Through I HELP, Jackson turned his back on this use of technology and developed an approach to protect the personhood of both the practitioner and the person being helped. He did this recognizing that the needs of the powerful organization must be superseded by the needs of the people who comprise the organization. He believes he is highlighting personal needs as

I HELP is moving toward achieving its intent—to allow those wishing to do so to help individuals in need.

Critical theories focus on current social and organizational conditions and seek to uncover the costs of modernity that technology cannot fix. In fact, from this perspective, technology may participate in some of the problem creation. These theorists want to eliminate the mistaken or false consciousness that is attached to the myth of modernism, the myth that what is modern is by definition better, producing better results for the individual. For them, an identification of false consciousness can begin a personal and organizational reconstruction of understanding of the current reality that allows inclusion of multiple considerations from all stakeholders. Multiple points of view serve to overcome systematic distortions in communication that occur as a result of the domination of one perspective. In the process, this reconstruction offers an understanding and critique of domination so that the degree to which the individual is an active participant in his or her own subjugation is made clear—recognition of false consciousness. It is assumed that from this new consciousness a more moral and, therefore, enlightened discourse will ensue, where all organizational participants will provide equal contribution to the future of a changed organization offering more liberty and freedom for all to reach their potential.

In the Radical Humanist Paradigm, critical theorists seek discourse so that all voices can be heard and so that individual perspectives can be articulated and respected. This tenet allows individual discourse wherein participants move to self-transform beyond the constrictions of dominant systems, including the organization in which they operate. The belief is that competent, thinking individuals will become smarter about the situations illuminated in the discourse in order to come to their own personal conclusions free from subtle or not-so-subtle pressures to take a particular position. The discourse process, by its nature, supports variation in ways of coming to understanding and determining the personal consequence of that understanding. Individualism and individual liberation is the driving force in this type of action guided by critical theory. Collective thought or action is not of interest. Personal enlightenment and transformation is.

Radical humanist critical theorists are very explicit about the purpose of their research—to make organizations communities of authentic dialogue among empowered individuals rather than instruments of personal domination (Handler, 1990). As you will see in the next section, these theorists have greatly influenced postmodern organizational theory development.

Postmodern Theories

As with critical theories, the more subjectivist aspects of postmodernism also fit comfortably within radical humanism. However, as we emphasized in our earlier discussion of postmodernism from the radical structuralist perspective, remember that there is no clear consensus about exactly what constitutes postmodern theory (Hassard & Parker, 1993). Postmodern theorists from this paradigm are reacting to cultural changes by deconstructing organizational orthodoxy. Just because "we have always done it this way" or because it is the "rule" is no reason to reject revisiting practices and procedures. New situations (or even well-known old situations) must be investigated for their consequences to the individual. Currently, the radical humanist postmodern focus is on the individual experience of participating in the Information Age and maintaining personal and professional boundaries when confronted by the anarchy, fragmentation, and inconsistencies in organizations and society. The approach rejects the unidimensional relation between forms of representation such as words and images and the objective world in favor of "the rules grounded in practices which precede subjectivity" (Power, 1992, p. 111). All postmodern theorists recognize subjectivity, but radical humanists reach out to embrace it to the point of individual personalization over all else.

Most postmodernists recognize that the traditional social and economic structures that have evolved since the Industrial Revolution are now fragmented. What has developed is a diverse, almost indefinable network, held together by information technology and postmodernist sensibility (Lash & Urry, 1987). This has created a sense of unease for organizations as they are forced to abandon the modern and become what some have called actors in a play (Lyotard & Thibaud, 1985). The basis of the play, or just "play" is language. Language becomes the game of organizing. The language, like the game, is in flux. In fact, meaning is constantly slipping so that it is never stabilized into unchanging, predictable terms. Understand that this is a general postmodern position. The focus becomes radical humanist in orientation when personal experience with language is central. The meaning of words seems to change from day to day, so sometimes it is even difficult to know what you mean. What is the consequence of a personal understanding of the message? What does that have to do with a person's role to be "played" in an organization? What are the personal consequences of learning the language, learning the rules?

For postmodern radical humanism theorists, it is through the language game that the various discourses emanate. It is through language and discourse that actual critical analysis becomes possible. It is critical analysis that allows the central notions of postmodern subjectivist thought to appear—absent false consciousness.

This critical stance allows organizational members to be suspicious about intellectual assumptions (Lawson, 1985) and to engage in **reflexivity,** which is the ability of the human mind to turn back on itself and know that it is knowing (Platt, 1989). This process allows deconstruction to occur, thus allowing the reflexive individual to identify the real (for them), the language, and the universe divorced from language. It is from this self-reflection that the person becomes cognizant of the "games" being enacted and the personal consequences of those games. With this information, then, the person is prepared to change the language, the communication patterns, and the game in favor of his or her own empowerment. Jackson, in his experience with a Traditional Organization, became empowered only when he and his supervisor agreed to disagree—and he left the organization because the language and the game would not change.

A postmodern approach to the individual within organization suggests that knowledge cannot be characterized with any prestige, nor can it be separated from everyday life. Knowledge, then, is "more or less" knowledge, interesting to the individual—and no more. For the individual within organizational life, the expectation of linear "progress" or even the progress narrative is rejected. Linearity precludes many voices, so linear progress is rejected in order to allow for the possibility of multiple alternative voices in the discourse. Further, there is no assumption of rationality in the discourse in order to capture the wisdom and power of the nonrational and the surprise of the irrational. (See Netting, O'Connor, & Fauri, 2008 for more discussion of rational, nonrational, and irrational thinking.)

In postmodern thought, once an individual recognizes that his or her own perceptions of the situation within the organization have merit, that in fact they are just as meritorious as any other perspective, personal permission to enter the conversation is likely. Once in the conversation, because it is a very personal one, individual progress related to the object of focus will occur simply because energy is directed in that way. But the expectation of linear achievement of goals is eliminated because there is no *if–then* linearity in the conversation or work process. Results emerge almost serendipitously as a result of the multiple perspectives, honest conversations, and the consciousness raising that has ensued.

Raising suppressed voices is important to postmodernist theorists holding a radical humanist perspective. Finding ways to demarginalize these voices is critically important in order to achieve individual transformational change. Farmer (1998) suggests that there are three aspects of demarginalizing what is unconscious in organizations. First, administrators have to accept that the unconscious is an important aspect of organizational life that has been trivialized by rational thinkers. Psychological considerations are not peripheral, but are very much tied to what happens in organizations. They help one understand why things happen. Second, once the unconscious is recognized, it is important to actually accept the interpretations that emerge from repressed thoughts. Third, the oppressive mechanisms within the organization that keep the unconscious suppressed must be dismantled. "Because language and speech are intersubjective, so the unconscious is transpersonal" (Farmer, 1998, p. 69).

Because of the paradigmatic assumptions, the radical humanist post-modernist is really unconcerned about theory construction at the institutional level. In fact, large-scale theory is rejected as not useful. Instead, the focus is on individual hunches and structures to understand power. What is important is the individual's perception about how to become personally empowered. Coordinated action guided by theory is important only when guiding individuals to personal empowerment. Managers no longer control fate. Power is in social interdependence that is unique to each organizational relationship held by each person. This is the transpersonal aspect of understanding, devoid of theories that bind the organization to prescribed avenues of analysis and performance.

Postmodernists challenge the concept of grand narratives; history becomes individual histories, and professionals represent only their own construction of what they should do in their discipline, much like Jackson and the others have done. The concept of a professional is called into question and the privileged position of persons in positions of authority for whatever reason is questioned. Organizationally, managers, administrators, and persons with formal power fall off their pedestals and are subject to scrutiny. No longer do the cloaks of professionalism or disciplinary lines allow one to hide behind illusions of expertise. There is no more of "do it my way because I know what is best." Diversity becomes relevant with all the differences that this implies. As with I HELP, the assumption is the more the information from more standpoints, the richer the potential even in the chaos and cacophony of opinions. Strengths are based in individuals rather than in what are assumed to be silos of oppressive professionalism.

Anti-administration Because postmodernists reject established notions about organizations, it is important to consider what would happen if one tried to view an organization from a different, nonrational perspective. Anti-administration approaches are such examples. Just as rational approaches attempt to prescribe how one might begin to perform administratively in an organization using rational thought and linear decision making, antiadministration begins to develop circular or nonrational strategies for organizing. *Anti-administration* is the most complete current description about what a nonrational Entrepreneurial Organization might be like.

Antiadministration is the embodiment of the rejection of bureaucratic technology and technocratic rationality seen in most postmodern thought (see Arendt, 1998; Heidegger, 1977; Marcuse, 1991; Oakeshott, 1962). It demonstrates the same antipathy to bureaucracy as postmodernism, but it differs in its solution in organizations. The solution is a type of self-conscious practice that is hoped to produce relevance for all stakeholders in the organization. Those taking an antiadministration view see facts as social constructs such that the facts are changing as the context changes. In recognizing the complexity of current organizations, this position calls for a serious exploration of bureaucracy, its internal functioning, and relationships to other societal features.

From this position it is also necessary to explore the place and functioning of this complexity in the lives of individuals as *bio-psycho-socio-spiritual* entities (Farmer, 1999, p. 304). The human side of the organizational enterprise must take central stage in the discourse. With this attention to the individual humanity in organization comes recognition that the societal/contextual considerations must include the political, legal, economic, psychological, sociological, biological, cultural, and spiritual. There is no simple way to grapple with the personal and organizational together; they must be considered together. Understanding and managing this complexity requires a personal self-consciousness of those within organization built on assumptions of contingency (planning for the chance or possible event), plurality (there is no single dominant answer or truth), and arbitrariness (meaning depends on the roles and relationships in the context). In other words, personal understanding of organization requires assumptions that anything might happen because anything might be true because everything depends on everything else.

Through antiadministration, there is recognition not only that bureaucracy is not possible, but also that it is not desirable. In its antipathy toward bureaucracy, an antiadministrative goal is avoidance of marginalization. It is against hierarchy because hierarchy serves to marginalize participants. Anti-administration holds an emphasis on achieving human liberty with demarginalized groups, types of reason or cognitive styles, and language. Giving preference to certain groups (or types of thought or certain languages) marginalizes not only the preferred group but all others as well. This same marginalization happens against alternative ways of thinking, ways of communication, or ways of capturing meaning or getting to "truth."

The alternative to bureaucracy is a type of play that allows the use of reflexive (reflective) language. Play results in a playful framing and reframing of the situation where multiple perspectives are entertained. *What-ifs* are considered in what might be understood as a constant brainstorming process, so that not just the scientific answer gets precedence, but also the aesthetic aspects of imagination come from the margins into the organizational investigation and analysis. The organization becomes antiadministration to the degree that measures of organizational success other than efficiency are considered. This opens the opportunity for social justice, liberation, and the public good to become part of the consideration of organizational quality. Farmer (1999) calls this a process of *transcending self-interest* (p. 316).

Anti-administration offers an alternative to hierarchy and bureaucracy[1] by suggesting a more interpretive process of organizing that promotes and

---

1. We are indebted to Jon Singletary for bringing anti-administration to our attention.

values understanding in organizations in a way that all are equal even though their positions differ. This change in the way of organizing is based on dialogue where knowledge is seen as valuable/true for those who recognize it as such. Mullaly (2007) points out the importance of dialogical relationships as those "wherein *all participants in the dialogue are equals,* wherein each learns from the other and teaches the other" (p. 317). In the I HELP case, dialogical relationships developed in a virtual environment, surprising Jackson in their intensity through ongoing online chats from people all over the world.

In antiadministration, there is a shared commitment to the work and a shared commitment to create shared language. The idea is to facilitate an engagement in the organizing process by all stakeholders who know that the process is always changing, but is essential to the effort and to personal self-actualization. The shared commitment to the work seems enough to organize in cyberspace. It does not seem that shared language is necessary there, because of the technology. In a more time-and-space-defined organizational arena, the process of organizing /including would need to be built on care and respect, where participants are humble, hopeful, and trusting that all will contribute to the search for possibilities in the organization. This requires comfort with multiplicity, with conflict, and with the creation of many options to select for the next stage of the organization. Through the search for options, it is hoped that liberation and empowerment of all will be achieved.

The practice of antiadministration (Farmer, 1995, 1998, 1999) is based on several simple principles. First, there should be hesitancy in decision making. Work should be tentative, slow, intentional, interpersonal, and adaptive. This means no "quick-and-dirty" and no "quick fixes." It should be skeptical with a real resistance to finding a final, true answer. If it feels like the "right" answer, try the opposite alternative as well. Work should be collaborative in that decision making should connect all stakeholders in a tentative process. It should be incremental with an enthusiastic engagement of "muddling through," including much recycling and various iterations to a contingent finding. This decision should be full of "it depends" so that the value of the interaction of all stakeholders and all perspectives is respected over efficient, quick action.

The process should be based on **alterity,** which moves knowing the *other* at a distance to a real relationship with the *other*. Alterity removes objective engagement with others in the organization and replaces objectivity with real, subjective, intimate, personal connections. The stakeholders in an antiadministration framework overcome distance by valuing each individual's self-identity. The *other* is different, but not distant. In this difference, meaning making is promoted so that what different people bring to the organization can really be part of the process. Difference presents opportunity for personal growth. Growth happens as all stakeholders are compelled to understand and find meaning in the difference. No discourse, no way of being, thinking, or doing takes precedence over another. So difference is the medium of the discussion, rather than being marginalized through a dominant discourse regarding the way it *is* or *should be*.

Finally, the practice of antiadministration counts on imagination over instrumental rationality for the work. Instead of deductive, linear thinking that limits options, this approach calls for a spontaneous, open, creative, uncertain, ambiguous, reflexive stance. Divergent thinking is preferred over convergent thinking. This makes room for play, games, dance, and song and the creation of different metaphors for work and organizations. A kind of divergence, developed without a need for consensus, along with an embracing of conflict, is what makes this approach radical humanist. Games are encouraged to exist in the sense that the rules for the organizational structure and organizational behavior are expected to be made up as needed. Each who wishes to play is included; no person is seen to be the first or best authority; each game is different; each time there is a need, a different person may go first or take the lead in creating the structure and the rules of operation. If a volunteer has the best idea about how to help clients to access service, test the idea by trying to recruit recipients and if it works, no one will see this as inappropriate or surprising. A volunteer had an idea that worked; now let's use it until it does not work anymore. This type of playfulness should generate options, alternatives, and ideas that

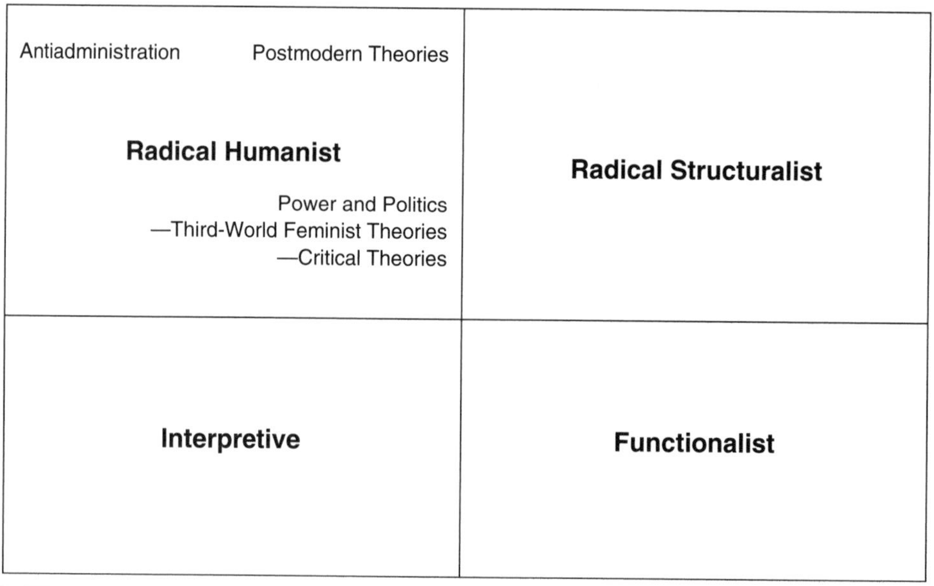

Antiadministration Postmodern Theories **Radical Humanist** Power and Politics —Third-World Feminist Theories —Critical Theories	**Radical Structuralist**
Interpretive	**Functionalist**

Figure 9.2   Organizational Theories Within the Radical Humanist Paradigm.

have not yet been imagined to respond to the as-yet inexperienced in postmodern organizations. Instead of the familiar organizational chart with its many symbols of hierarchy and power, the antiadministration organizational design might more closely resemble a tic-tac-toe game, where players and places change depending on the perceived need.

Figure 9.2 shows the theories discussed in this chapter and their placement within the Radical Humanist Paradigm. Notice that their placement is a reflection of commonalities with assumptions from neighboring paradigms.

COSTS AND BENEFITS

The Radical Humanist Perspective and Its Theories

The greatest costs and the greatest benefits of this perspective come from its position against traditional theoretical frameworks and the assumptions on which they are built. Radical humanism makes every idea worthy of consideration, but also makes it very difficult to test ideas using any commonly agreed-on standard or manner of testing. Having a perspective tied so heavily to different personalities who determine what has merit makes any judgment according to commonly agreed-on standards impossible. The only thing that can be measured is whether the individuals participating in the process are more aware of the elements and complexity of the focus of their inquiry. Are they smarter for having participated? Are they more able to effect changes in desired directions? Are they more free? Can they more easily reach their human potential? The challenge is to determine when one knows the answers to these very fundamental questions, knowing that the answers (and even the relevant questions) will change as participants and contexts change.

This perspective and the theories within it give no certainty as to appropriate action. Everything, from the structure to whatever is contained within it, must depend on the context and the people involved inside or outside of the context. Everything matters, but the way to articulate the scope and depth of importance entirely depends on the individual and his or her conscious use of self in relation to information and knowledge building. Radical humanism and the theories within this perspective really do describe a geography of *nowhere* that gets *somewhere* only through individual initiative.

Mullaly (2007) provides a helpful commentary on the controversy among radical practitioners about radical humanism and radical structuralism and which must come first. There are some radicals who believe that transforming society has to start in radical humanism, for without first empowering individuals, no collective movements can be formed. Others see social transformation as a ticket to individual empowerment, with personal change coming forth as a result of large-scale societal change and individuals having an opportunity to fully find themselves separate from the movement. Yet others, as in the women's movement, see both approaches happening simultaneously in a dialectical process. In sum, there is no agreement about how to enact the perspective and its theories— it all depends.

ENTREPRENEURIAL ORGANIZATIONS WITH INDIVIDUAL EMPOWERMENT GOALS

From a philosophical perspective, does this consciousness and liberty mean more satisfaction in the work environment and more personal happiness? At some level many of the postmodern thinkers would hope that this is the result of all the desired conscious analysis, but perhaps satisfaction and happiness are not natural by-products of empowerment. From a metaphysical perspective, what is needed for consciousness raising in order to escape the constraints of structural limits may not produce happiness. Instead, what may be produced is a transcendent empowerment regarding the full role of the individual in organization and society. This requires taking personal power and personal responsibility for the context of work and assuring that the context is structured to support all human potential. This sounds to us like very hard work and work that may require commitment and responsibility beyond what is normally found in one's work life.

Perhaps this also means that the separation between work and the rest of life becomes less definable. For those who enjoy the challenges of the work organization, this may be a pleasant, seamless existence. For those who need real boundaries between work and the rest of life, the demands of work from a radical humanist perspective may be too costly and too intrusive.

Clearly, the critical and analytic demands of thoughtful life within organizations working from the radical humanist perspective could be exhausting to some. In addition, the antipositivistic and antideterministic stance of the paradigm will be a source of great discomfort for those who really prefer work from the assumption of an immutable truth and a determined human existence. A wish for certainty and a rejection of subjectivity will cause some to reject out of hand both the uncontrolled nature of the Entrepreneurial Organizational process and the nongeneralizable, insiders' views of organizational reality. Since those taking a traditional view of knowledge and organizing see nothing rigorous or useful in the radical humanist view, much criticism will accrue from traditional researchers, administrators, or leaders. What might be worse, no criticism will be forthcoming from them because what is produced from this perspective is not seen to be even worthy of critical assessment.

There will probably be great criticism of the preferred qualitative aspects of radical humanist research designs and ways of organizing. Because other ways of knowing, including art and religion, can be brought to the inquiry process and product, many, especially more traditional funders, will question the scientific worth of the research or organizing effort. Many will reject the results seen in structure change or new knowledge as irrelevant.

However, the philosophical perspective of radical humanism creates an adequate space for play. Playing with ideas about organizations, how they do work and should work in the future and how human nature fits into this work, is absolutely possible here. The power of ideas and the power of people shift in such ways that all can benefit from the exchange of ideas. Ideas (more than experience, expertise, or history) present powerful propellants for action. Granted, there is little control of the research or work, and there exists much need to trust and respect others in the emergence of processes and products. But individuals committed to achieving the goals of the organization of which they are members will have a great chance of recognizing and being recognized for the contributions made. This makes experiencing organizing and the organization profoundly unlike what is found in many organizational structures today. It may be the opening to actual multicultural organizing in human services.

CONCLUSION

The theories touched on in this chapter have one thing in common: They question everything. Theorists holding radical humanist assumptions are reacting against dominant ways of thinking that oppress individuals in countless ways. This *anti*-stance poses somewhat of a dilemma in that some feminist, critical, and postmodern theorists are too quickly written off by persons from other paradigms for railing against *what is* rather than offering viable options for how things could work differently. But that is just the point. Determining what is a viable option is a judgment call and is usually based on what dominant thinkers believe to be acceptable. It is little wonder that dialogue stops and stalemate ensues when alternative thinkers want each individual to have a space for his or her own personal approach to organizing work life. Unfortunately, at this stage of the development of this paradigm, even the concept of antiadministration implies *what it is not*, rather than what it is.

The Radical Humanist Paradigm and Entrepreneurial Organizations are foreign to current forms of organizational life in the United States beyond cyberspace. It may be the rare person who can comprehend what it would be like to practice in an organization that espouses a completely different set of assumptions and values than have been previously encountered for centuries in North American organizational life. However, we contend that the vast majority of people in the Western world understand radical humanism more than they know.

The focus on individualism over the collective good, the right to free speech, and a host of other factors taken for granted in our society fit quite well with radical humanist thought. If radical humanists are individualists, then the individualism in American society would seem to fit within this paradigm. However, most people were schooled to accept as "truth" that organizations are collections of people who come together for a purpose and work toward common goals. Therefore, individualism within organizations historically has been defined as a problem or as a nonrational act, appropriate for one's personal life but something to give up (at least partially) in one's organizational life. Ironically, radical humanism and Entrepreneurial Organizations would suggest that individualism within organizations is actually a desirable condition. Not only would bringing one's sense of self into an organization be a way to strengthen the organization, but it would be compatible with the way in which employees have been socialized to seek individual self-fulfillment. Certainly Entrepreneurial Organizations offer provocative possibilities, possibilities currently being tested in some cutting-edge high-tech organizations.

Next, we examine the behaviors and practices congruent with an Entrepreneurial Organization through a more complete look at the *adhocracy culture*, which is also congruent with the Radical Humanist Paradigm. It is time to see how the theories in this chapter can be translated into human service practice in organizations that come from a radical humanist perspective. In doing so, we look at values, preferences, and strategies in organizations with individual empowerment goals.

DISCUSSION QUESTIONS

1. Compare and contrast the major assumptions of the Radical Humanist Paradigm with the goals of the Entrepreneurial Organization. How are they similar or different? What are the costs and benefits of the similarities? Of the differences? Is it really possible to have an Entrepreneurial Organization?

2. Imagine you run a website for those interested in entrepreneurial human service agencies, particularly people wishing to work in that sort of professional environment. Given your analysis regarding costs and benefits of this approach to organizing, what "words to the wise" might you give to potential candidates for jobs in these types of organizations? What might you advise them about regarding what to look for in assessing their match with the organization's goals and expectations?

3. Review the theory discussion and compare the similarities and differences between the various aspects of power and politics theories, feminist theories, critical theories, and postmodern theories. How might these theories impede or enhance individual liberation in an

organization? Which of these theories is most congruent with your preferences about structure and behavior in an organization? What would it take for you to thrive in an antiadministration environment?

4. In the beginning of this part of the text, a case example was introduced—I Help. Go back to the case and consider the following questions:

   a. What characteristics of this organization make it an Entrepreneurial Organization? Are there characteristics that are less change oriented than others?

   b. What assumptions did Jackson embed as the founder of this organization? How were these assumptions helpful (or not) to him in carrying out his responsibilities?

   c. As the agency developed, what did members do to insure that it remained focused on an antiadministrative stance?

5. Imagine you are starting a small organization and that you want to be sure the structure of that organization is congruent with its environment. What issues would you need to address if you chose an entrepreneurial structure to be sure that it matched a particular environment? Describe the environment for which an Entrepreneurial Organization is most suited.

6. You are a supervisor or manager in a human service agency. What would make you prefer working in an Entrepreneurial Organization with individual liberation goals? What challenges would you face personally as a leader? Could you be a leader in this type of organization?

7. In the I HELP case example, the founder of the organization has very little control over those associated with him. What are the risks and benefits to professional practice in being associated in such a loose way with a large cadre of professional helpers from different disciplines and cultures?

CHAPTER 10

Practice in Entrepreneurial Organizations

THE MOST RADICAL or postmodern approaches to designing organizations are based on the assumptions of the Radical Humanist Paradigm. However, it is also interesting to note that much of the language in the traditional and popular organizational literature sounds very compatible with radical humanism. Words such as *empowerment*, *transpersonalism*, and *organizational spirit*, and concepts such as *transformational leadership* and *leading with soul* as well as an assortment of other rather spiritual and artistic terms and phrases are sprinkled throughout the current management literature. We caution the reader about such terminology. Often the language of radical humanism is used wittingly or unwittingly to engage employees in organizations that are still based on dominant, traditional modes of thinking. Therefore, one has to be very careful to look beyond the language used and into the behaviors and attitudes within the organization to determine whether indeed this is an Entrepreneurial Organization.

In the Entrepreneurial Organization, there will be a passion for individual transformation. Entrepreneurial Organizations will recognize and respect diversity, but they will also not be satisfied until they have made changes that will fully liberate individuals from oppression. Participants in Entrepreneurial Organizations will not necessarily concern themselves with consensus building, instead embracing conflict and difference in order to individually empower themselves individually. Empowering individuals will take different forms since no two people are alike. Radical humanism does not hold deterministic assumptions about universal principles or values. In fact, those holding this perspective strive for creative innovation that takes people to places where they might not have been before and even where others fear to go. If one seeks comfort in well-defined structures, universal values, and certainty, the Entrepreneurial Organization could well be one's worse nightmare.

Entrepreneurial Organizations will be loose collections of people who are open to individual differences as is seen in the I HELP case example. Rather than coming together for a joint purpose, there might not be consensus about one organizational goal. There may be multiple goals. In fact, organizational goals may be constantly shifting as new ideas emerge, if there are organizational goals at all. Our case example shows a group of practitioners who came together in order to share creative energy, but they probably do not agree on intervention methods, accountability standards, or ethical positions. One might assume that they are in this association because they think that their practice with people in pain is improved because of their association with other service professionals also wishing to provide their own best possible practice, but there might also be myriad other reasons for associating in this way. There might not be exact consciousness about why they connected, but they probably stay because the virtual organization has helped each find ways to increase his or her abilities to be a professional or recipient of services, to self-actuate, to create, and to perform or to do whatever the person desires to be or do.

As another example, the concept of self-help is based in radical humanist assumptions. In an organization dedicated to self-help activities, there is an assumption that every individual will have to determine for himself or herself what is a personal quality-of-life experience. Granted, some of the same methods may be used across people, but each person will have a carefully customized plan for achieving his or her individual desires and growth, with every person changing at his or her own pace and in his or her own unique way. People join self-help groups for very personal reasons, and for their own unique needs. Change in one person's life, even having had a similar experience, will be very different from what other people experience. The Entrepreneurial Organization is an incubator for individual transformation.

At this time in organizational development, few fully formed Entrepreneurial Organizations can be identified. Close to this organizational prototype are the new, fast-paced high-technology organizations with structures that exist only in the minds of their founders and whose employees work wherever and whenever they want, as long as there is electricity and a computer with sufficient capacity. The central notion of information and the need for its free flow defines such organizations. What is not yet clear is how other types of organizations with other types of goals can be constructed within this vision of work.

We think the structure of a loosely affiliated number of social workers who form a private practice group could be an Entrepreneurial Organization if structured within a radical humanist perspective. It could be entrepreneurial if the empowerment of individual therapists to do their own best work with clients is their intent, rather than collaboration and creating community among therapists. Therapists could share the same building, even the same office space, yet rarely see one another. Their basic needs could be handled by a management firm that attends to independent, autonomous individuals who rent space within the facility. Tasks pertaining to mail sorting and delivery, answering phones, and building oversight and management could be a purely contractual arrangement in which individual private agents go about their business without a sense of being part of a community or collective. Similar to artists' studios, where each person rents a space and seeks personal transformation through his or her medium of choice, the individualism of private practice could potentially fit this approach to organizing.

In this chapter, we focus on the content and standards for practice within Entrepreneurial Organizations. We return to the five questions originally introduced in Chapter 4 to guide the reader: (1) What are the cultural values and characteristics of organizations derived from the assumptions of this paradigm? (2) What roles and relationships are congruent with the culture of this type of organization? (3) What are the standards for practice within this type of organization? (4) What are the implications for practice within this type of organization?

CULTURAL VALUES AND CHARACTERISTICS OF ENTREPRENEURIAL ORGANIZATIONS

In Chapter 2, we referred to Cameron and Quinn's (2006) Competing Values Framework. The Entrepreneurial Organization discussed in this chapter is most congruent with the *adhocracy culture*, with its dynamism, creativity, and entrepreneurial spirit. Those within the organization are not afraid to take risks. In fact, what seems risky to outside observers may appear as normal next steps to the innovators within the organization. Commitment to experimentation and innovation, rather than attention to structure and rules, holds the adhocracy culture together. The emphasis is on reaching for the leading or transformational edge that allows growth and uniqueness. Individual initiative and freedom is central to this culture based on differentiation, making the role of management almost unnecessary. Box 10.1 replicates Box 2.9, which provides a reminder of the basic cultural elements that inform an Entrepreneurial Organization.

VALUES IN ENTREPRENEURIAL ORGANIZATIONS

The Entrepreneurial Organization is grounded in *subjectivism*, which takes a *relativist* stance on values. These organizations, following radical humanism, are very open to situational ethics in which choices made in one situation may change in light of new information or a shift in the scenario. Being relativists, radical humanists believe that principles change, that

---

Box 10.1

ENTREPRENEURIAL ORGANIZATIONS

- The *subjective* nature of persons who provide valuable insights, perform significant deeds, and think outside the box is recognized and respected. It is recognized that contributions may not be corralled into a group effort.
- *Flexibility and discretion* are promoted. It is understood that workers will not only be mavericks in their programs but may question or resist most aspects of what they are trying to do.
- Individual contribution is expected with a recognition that individuals are so *differentiated* that they work best on their own without the confines of a program.
- Conflict is expected when *radical change* is being pursued individually. Causes are supported in nontraditional ways.

---

values change with time, that there are multiple truths, and that there are multiple ways of knowing and doing that can lead to useful results.

True consciousness, true understanding of the personal implications of the work and work life, is an important element of entrepreneurial organizational quality standards. All the dimensions in the organization that might constrain individual fulfillment or potential are targets for elimination because of the belief that the best work and the best effects can be achieved when individual organization members are not constrained by anything that might inhibit personal development. Rules and procedures will not be present in any objective way. Instead, decisions about what needs to be done now will be determined by those involved now. Liberty, then, is a central value within the organization. The idea is to transcend structures, bonds, or limits that exist in Traditional Organizations. There is a belief that existing social patterns hamper development, so questioning the status quo is not only expected, but also demanded in order that true liberty for all can be achieved through honest dialogue.

Mission/Philosophy of Entrepreneurial Organizations

The mission of the Entrepreneurial Organization is to establish a platform from which individuals can self-transform within arenas where power and politics do not always support such transformation. There is an assumption that the societal context and its institutions are oppressive. Following radical humanism, members of Entrepreneurial Organizations engage in meaning making and sense making, but they do not stop with this enhanced understanding. Their philosophy is that one will take this new meaning and sense making and use it to make individual changes against personal oppression. There is acceptance that this is not always easy, particularly when one has been oppressed in multiple ways. In human services, this might mean helping a victim of domestic violence recognize her right not to be violated, not through therapy but through discussions with others who have been abusers, victims, and therapists. The goal would be for this woman to find her own way not just to safety but to a sense of power such that she would never allow personal victimization in the future.

Embracing diversity and opening the possibility for mutual engagement requires that organizational members hear multiple views. Members will often be in conflict when views clash. However, the expectation is that conflict is a healthy part of the creative process. Its purpose is for clarity, not to oppress or to "win." Through conflict, clarity is derived and strength for making change can happen. Participants can actually find this creative endeavor playful: "It requires a new way of being in the world. It requires being in the world without fear. Being in the world with play and creativity. Seeking after what's possible. Being willing to learn and to be surprised" (Wheatley & Kellner-Rogers, 1996, p. 5). This playfulness seems counterintuitive, given the serious and incredible oppressions many participants face or have experienced. Part of the organization's philosophy is seeing the nature of what is or has been in a completely different way and pushing for change in as unusual and creative a way as possible. There is a hopeful energy in this work. One can see this same hopeful energy expressed in a slightly different way in the I HELP case example. Each individual professional is imbued with the energy to help. Each has his or her own take on how that helping should be enacted. Rather than engaging in conflictual dialectic about the preferred way to practice, one follows one's personal muse with no strictures on the shape of one's performance.

PREFERRED STRUCTURE IN ENTREPRENEURIAL ORGANIZATIONS

Not being certain that organizations really exist in anything other than a conceptual sense, Entrepreneurial Organizations do not recognize organizational structure as really important. Instead, the process of organizing the work and the perspectives of those who are involved in this organizing are of interest. This informal mode of organizing means that the nature of the organization evolves as new ideas or needs emerge. How things are structured today might change as situations and needs change tomorrow. Although the Entrepreneurial Organization is concerned with how participants feel about the social world of the organization, it is equally concerned with how they use these feelings and meanings to advance the cause of individual change, so the structure may change not for productivity's sake but because personal needs demand it.

Along with the surprisingly rapid development of the high-technology industry and the astonishing changes in everyday life brought about by the Internet, the structure and feel of the Entrepreneurial Organization is just beginning to emerge. At its most understandable in traditional organizational terms, the Entrepreneurial Organization is a loosely coupled entity where information is the organizing element. At its most radical, the Entrepreneurial Organization demonstrates no measurable organizational structure, while at the same time producing a desired product that results from concerted efforts of its members. These organizations may not have the same time-and-space orientation as Traditional Organizations. People do not need to be working at the same time or in the same location in order for organizational goals to be attained. Through the help of telecommunications, members of organizations can maintain their own work rhythms, working while others sleep or working where others play, as long as the desired product is produced or the desired goal is attained. In the I HELP case, a therapeutic service is offered on the Internet. Therapists are located all over the world and the service is available at all times and in all parts of the world. What is being described is the emerging virtual organization, where individuals are connected and organized via information technology—and nothing more.

Whether as a full organization or a unit in a larger organization, a radical humanist approach requires recognition of and choosing to live in the paradoxes of modern life. One of the major paradoxes of the Entrepreneurial Organization is that in the face of complexity this type of organization seeks to think simply about how to organize human activities. Instead of being drawn to more complexity, participants in the Entrepreneurial Organization find more delightful ways of organizing their programs and services. Philosophy, poetics, novels, and spiritual teachings enter the dialogue as means of exploring what can be possible in the new organization. Team meetings might have poetry readings on a subject related to the work as a means of focusing all participants in a useful direction. This would be chosen over the presentation of a recipe for performance presented by those in charge.

At the base of this thinking are new images of organizations and new incentives for the organization of human endeavor. This approach to organization calls for the questioning, if not breaking, of old habits, by investigating and questioning the beliefs about people, life, and the world that underlie them. It is this thinking and the resulting consciousness that is the essential ingredient for the construction of a different understanding of how to organize. If the Entrepreneurial Organization ever becomes the Traditional Organization of the future, it will be totally unrecognizable to those with only traditional organizational experience.

TYPES OF PROGRAMS AND SERVICES IN ENTREPRENEURIAL ORGANIZATIONS

In Chapter 1, we introduced different types of programs and services. Recall that *direct service programs* directly serve clients. *Staff development and training programs* focus on staff, and *support programs* undergird direct service and staff programs. Entrepreneurial Organizations may contain all three types of programs, but they will look very different from the same types of programs offered in other types of organizations.

Programs and services in Entrepreneurial Organizations focus as much on the experience as they would on final results, primarily because nothing is considered "final." The concepts of *end products* or *outcomes* do not translate well in Entrepreneurial Organizations because things continually change, even change itself. More importantly, requiring certain outcomes as a measure of success is in itself a type of oppression. Therefore, entrepreneurial programs and services might not be appreciated by traditionalists who seek control, closure, or finality in their programming.

Programs and services here are designed to be highly flexible, so flexible that they may not be "designed" as we commonly understand the process. Instead, they will be encouraged to emerge. They are intended to incorporate participants in every aspect of their own transformation as much as possible, in order to counter oppression, and to seek customized approaches to change. In this way, two persons will not go through an entrepreneurial program in exactly the same way, nor will they experience exactly the same changes. This is likely the case in traditional programs also, but it is not recognized or accepted or is hidden because achieving client conformity is valued. This nonstandardized way of programming is valued in the Entrepreneurial Organization because it is assumed to enhance growth and development, creating opportunities for unexpected possibilities. To traditionalists, this nonstandardized approach is nonscientific, if not irresponsible and unethical.

Summary Characteristics of Entrepreneurial Organizations

Entrepreneurial Organizations are considered alternative agencies to traditional, functionalist organizations. More than that, because they hold nothing in common, the Entrepreneurial Organization can be conceived as the exact opposite of the traditional, functionalist organization. The entrepreneurial openness to diversity and high desire for change is in opposition to functionalism. If there is an alternative agency that is seen as "on the fringe" by traditional functionalists, it would be the Entrepreneurial Organization. The radical humanist perspective of entrepreneurs would be seen as turning the Traditional Organization upside down because they do not organize in any way that would be understandable from a functionalist perspective. Everything held as true for the functionalist would be questioned by the radical humanist in the Entrepreneurial Organization in the spirit of the earlier discussion of the antiadministration framework.

However, as with interpretivists in Serendipitous Organizations, radical humanists are open to diversity and context. As with radical structuralists in Social Change Organizations, radical humanists are focused on change

Table 10.1
Characteristics of Entrepreneurial Organizations

Characteristics	Entrepreneurial Organization
Values	Runs counter to ideologies related to objectivism (external truth); accepting of alternative opinions and practices, focusing on individual empowerment and social justice
Mission and Philosophy	To seek individual transformation
Organizational Structure	To develop minimal structure so that changes can be easily made in an ongoing manner without impinging on the individuals inside the structure
Programs and Services	To create opportunities for people to grow and develop individually

and are open to conflict. These linkages suggest that the Radical Humanist Paradigm and Entrepreneurial Organizations, though departing fundamentally from traditional ways of doing the business of organizing, still maintain elements in common with paradigms and organization types developed over the last half of the 20th century.

In previous chapters, we presented the characteristics of various types of organizations and we continue that pattern here. Table 10.1 summarizes the characteristics of Entrepreneurial Organizations.

Entrepreneurial Organizations are alternative agencies, but they are so different from other organizations that the very terminology used to describe their characteristics may be a loose fit. For example, the term *client* will rarely be used in these organizations because *client* as a concept implies a power imbalance in which a professional has expertise. In Entrepreneurial Organizations, professional lines are no longer drawn since a radical humanist perspective respects everyone's experience and a "client" is considered the expert in her or his own life. Professionals are not placed on pedestals so that clients can benefit from their insights. Instead, everyone has expertise based on his or her subjective experience and professionals and clients mutually benefit from their respective expertise. *Leadership* is another word that fits uneasily into entrepreneurial language. Here leadership is a shared concept, one in which people take turns as designated leaders, but in which there are no permanent lines drawn between leaders and followers. There is a preference to use each person's competence and strengths as needs emerge. *Service delivery* sits uneasily in the language of this type of organization as well. Service delivery implies that something will be given to someone. In instances of individual transformation, service is not "delivered"; one attains the knowledge or skills to be able to empower oneself. It is not delivered or given to that person; instead the person accesses what is necessary. Similarly, the concept of *size* is somewhat irrelevant since Entrepreneurial

Organizations are not in the business of worrying about size and expansion. Whatever is necessary is what is expected to develop. In other words, when one looks at the concepts typically used to characterize even other alternative agencies, the Entrepreneurial Organization does not fit. It is an alternative to the alternatives!

There are basic underlying assumptions about locus of control and change in an Entrepreneurial Organization. It is designed to seek radical change. Radical change is intended to transform individuals and although individual transformation may lead to broader social change, this is only a residual of personal, individual transformation. Those in Entrepreneurial Organizations, therefore, will not be spending time mobilizing groups of people toward joint goals. When these organizations deal with groups, each member of the group will be expected unapologetically to have or develop his or her own personal agenda.

ROLES AND RELATIONSHIPS WITH AND WITHIN ENTREPRENEURIAL ORGANIZATIONS

Given the radical humanist liberational perspectives that guide Entrepreneurial Organizations, Table 10.2 provides a summary of some of the ways in which roles and relationships develop in Entrepreneurial Organizations.

Table 10.2
Roles and Relationships with and Within Entrepreneurial Organizations

Type of Relationship	Purpose
Task Environment Relationships	To see the environment as a source of invigorating differences and unlimited subjectivities, once liberation from limits is achieved
Relationships with Funders	To seek financial resources that give individuals as much control as possible
Relationships with Client Populations and Referral Sources	To open one's doors to individuals from all walks of life, embracing diversity
Internal Organizational Roles and Relationships:	
• Managing	To alternate and even share leadership roles among members in as informal a way as possible with the goal being individual transformation
• Communicating	To use the latest in information technology to enhance connections among people, while also honoring all methods, means, and media of communication
• Recognizing Staff Expectations	To engage people in a creative process, thus seeking persons who are conscious, self-directed, committed, and comfortable with conflict and ambiguity

By now, the format for this framework should be quite familiar. Please note how the contents of this table differ from other types of organizations with very different goals.

ORGANIZATION–ENVIRONMENT RELATIONSHIPS

As with the other practice chapters, we begin by looking at how Entrepreneurial Organizations view their relationships with the larger environment. We follow this with an examination of the Entrepreneurial Organization's internal roles and relationships with particular attention to funding and clients.

Task Environment Relationships   The Entrepreneurial Organization recognizes the environment as part of the broader context in which it operates. The organization and environment are viewed as mutually influential as diverse opinions, perspectives, and values interact. The Entrepreneurial Organization embraces environmental forces that represent a diversity of opinions, recognizing that diversity can create oppression that stultifies human potential. Those with a radical humanist perspective do not always worry about seeking ways to build consensus among differing opinions. Instead, they are intent on addressing issues of oppression that impact organizational participants so that everyone has a chance to be everything he or she can be.

In fact, the Entrepreneurial Organization is so connected to the environment that its boundaries are typically far more porous than those of organizations with other paradigmatic assumptions. The Entrepreneurial Organization might have participants (clients) that also deliver service or service providers who are also recipients of service. What is important is doing what is necessary to access the resources to reach personal potential, defined differently by everyone associated with the organization. Since diversity is embraced and differences are expected, there is little need to shield the agency against environmental forces or to control what is inevitably uncontrollable. In the I HELP case, this is certainly true. The concept of the environment as a turbulent source of unexpected conditions to be feared is foreign to such an organization. Instead, the environment is exciting and stimulating because it brings unlimited possibilities for liberation. The biggest problem the environment imposes on this type of organization is that there is such an explosion of knowledge that one can never fully attend to the rapid swirl of information amid unlimited possibilities. Thus, there is heavy reliance on discourse and dialectic to gather multiple ideas about meaning and implications of current conditions or individuals managing this in whatever way they can.

Relationships with Funders   Entrepreneurial Organizations may have difficulty developing and maintaining a stable funding base because they are seen as too threatening to the status quo or too "loopy" to be defined and controlled for accountability. Stable funders may appear to participants to have too much power in the organization. Beyond this, though, the creativity and innovation that permeates Entrepreneurial Organizations suggest that traditional ways of thinking about funding do not always fit well here; nor are they necessary. The idea of an organization receiving United Way dollars or government grants and contracts doesn't compute here, because these funding sources would not be able to identify with radical humanist approaches in which outcome measurement is not seen as relevant. Perhaps some private foundations with quirky leaders who are enamored with postmodern thought might consider funding such organizations, but even they might be a little concerned about how to monitor organizational activities for accountability. In our case example, the original developer of the I HELP website, Jackson, is even considering selling advertising to assure service delivery.

Funding, then, for the Entrepreneurial Organization may be as individualistic in orientation as its mission. For example, persons who participate might pay for what they receive in much the same way as in a for-profit business, or someone might sponsor another person by donating money for a scholarship for services. Some might engage in bartering. The Entrepreneurial Organization is a place in which individual entrepreneurs could flourish, if they could also maintain a focus on individual rights and responsibilities. Just as private donations, endowments, personal fees, or other private monies fund innovative, traditional companies, the Entrepreneurial Organization could find its support in those arenas. Consider that Entrepreneurial Organizations fit very well into free market economies where freedom and individualism reign and everyone is encouraged to "do their own thing." In fact, funding patterns in Entrepreneurial Organizations, as in the I HELP case, could make them very much a part of free market enterprise, especially because of the recognition and inclusion of politics in the organizational and individual consciousness.

Relationships with Client Populations and Referral Sources   In the Entrepreneurial Organization, renewed consciousness reveals that organizing is a process rather than an object. The organization is always in the process of organizing rather than staying within some defined picture of what it must be. Therefore, engaging clients and referral sources in the organizing process is critical. Accessing the resources, information, or people to engage in the service process is the role of all organizational participants. This inclusiveness shift in perspective allows a new way of thinking about the stakeholders in the organization so that they become self-organizing.

Clients are not so much clients as they are *members* or *participants*. Members of this type of organization, following radical humanism, will see clients and referral sources as participants in the work of the organization and will be highly inclusive in their approach.

Stakeholders in the Entrepreneurial Organization will be seekers of service or knowledge who emerge from the larger environment. They will be encouraged to represent as much difference as one can imagine. In this organization, participants will not feel they have to conform, but will engage in experiences in which they actually self-transform. Thus, the very concept of referral sources may be difficult to comprehend in the Entrepreneurial Organization, because there might not be other similar organizations available within the community to which to refer participants. There might be instead a loose network of groups and opportunities that look very different from traditional service delivery systems. What is necessary will be constructed by the individuals needing the service, which is a very different approach to human potential development. It grows from within the individuals who have the need instead of being delivered from without, so monetary funding may be less necessary than human resources for human service delivery. In the I HELP case, people found ways to identify needed services on the Internet. In most cases, their own ingenuity, rather than a referral process, netted them assistance from the I HELP website.

In summary, Entrepreneurial Organizations view funding and participants as resources from the environment and recognize that they represent diverse interests. Funding patterns may look very much like those of innovative for-profits that are dependent on private sources of support. Or it might not look like any configuration yet seen in human services. Clients might not be called *clients* at all because clients imply that professionals do something *for* someone in need, where Entrepreneurial Organizations attempt to support individualization and growth among all concerned. This view of the environment sets a context for examining the organization's internal structure (or lack thereof).

Internal Organizational Roles and Relationships

The Entrepreneurial Organization is influenced by frameworks that are grouped under power and politics as well as postmodernist perspectives. These are reflected in the organization's internal operations.

Managing Management is almost a misnomer in the Entrepreneurial Organization. Terms such as *coordinators, facilitators,* or even *team leaders* may better describe these organizational roles. Leadership is completely reconceptualized from traditional notions of leaders and followers. Everyone is considered to carry elements of leadership within Entrepreneurial Organizations. In a sense, everyone is his or her own leader since individualism is so valued.

In Chapter 2, we indicated that Mintzberg, Ahlstrand, and Lampel (1998) identify only one school of strategic management that fits the freewheeling nature of the Entrepreneurial Organization, with its adhocracy culture and individual empowerment goals. The Entrepreneurial School uses intuition, judgment, wisdom, experience, and insight to determine direction and future vision. This management style is malleable, with strategies that emerge as the needed details unfold, and sometimes is more semiconscious and rooted in experience and intuition than in any specific form of strategic thinking. This style may be enacted by the nominal leader, but it is also the practice norm for all participants in the organization.

In the Entrepreneurial Organization, needed structures, patterns of behavior, and processes for accomplishing goals are designed as individuals come to know what they need in order to do their work. Through dialogue among participants, agreement is achieved about what makes sense. Behaviors and relationships, especially related to support and trust built on excellent communication, emerge from the process of doing the work. All this is useful but temporary. The conditions of work are the focus of the designated leader. It is his or her role to assure the support of necessary structures. Freedom, not conformity and compliance, is the vision. Individual responsibility, where people do for themselves what has been done to them in other organizations in the past, becomes the focus of all members of the organization. Think about work teams where each person is secure in his or her own skills and talents and all of the team together have constructed a vision of where they want to go and then go about the business of getting there with what seems from the outside to be unlimited energy and creativity. This is the type of "leaderlessness" seen in the Entrepreneurial Organization. The organization becomes a virtually leaderless organization because all who are part of it are leading it to creative consequences as people are supported for who they really are. This sets up a productive context for both stability and personal discovery.

The concept of personnel policies and procedures is not very important in the Entrepreneurial Organization. Certainly, some guidelines must be established legally for the organization to operate in a predominantly functionalist environment, but these procedures are kept to a minimum. In fact, procedure can be oppressive and every person will have his or her own understanding of what any procedure means. Therefore, basic guidelines exist so that the organization will be able to function in the larger environment, but these will not be the focus of the organization or its members. Keeping things procedurally simple is a must, so that the complexity of understanding and change can be the focus.

In an Entrepreneurial Organization, each individual needs to work at his or her maximum pace or level of creativity. Having said that, management, in fact, has little to manage other than information. This is because few employees are present to be managed and few decisions will rest with any of them alone. The expectation is that all employees within their levels of competence will participate in all portions of the life of the organization. Just as no piece of communication should take precedence over another, so also no privilege is given to a particular individual within any existing organizational structure. The idea that "the buck stops here" has no meaning within the Entrepreneurial Organization, because both the authority and the accountability rest with all who have a stake in the particular organizational undertaking. All are held accountable by all who participate in the organizational dialogue and in organizational life.

In service organizations, rather than having a full-scale Entrepreneurial Organization in the current human service environment, it will be more likely that some of the spirit of the radical humanist perspective will be operationalized in smaller units of an organization by midlevel organizational leaders who can promote and facilitate the vision on a smaller scale, such as at the unit level. At a minimum, this would include instituting a collaborative leadership style noted for collaborative decision making (see O'Connor & Netting, 1999), in which conflict is faced squarely when it arises and even encouraged as an element of creative thinking. It would also mean selection of employees who wish to have a great degree of liberty, autonomy, and individual responsibility within their work lives. It would include employees who are stable enough to agree to disagree.

Box 10.2 provides a list of the characteristics of an entrepreneurial leader. See how these characteristics vary from those of previous organizational types.

Box 10.2

CHARACTERISTICS OF ENTREPRENEURIAL LEADERS

- Is comfortable with ambiguity, uncertainty, and new and emerging ideas
- Thinks that hearing all perspectives is important
- Sees conflict as inevitable when all perspectives are heard
- Truly appreciates and acts on diversity
- Has high tolerance for differing opinions
- Is predisposed toward creativity and innovation
- Has strong curiosity and passion for change
- Is not satisfied with just understanding and meaning making, but is committed to turning what is discovered into action
- Maintains one's sense of individualism within organizational life
- Is self-directed
- Is able to examine situations from many different directions and will argue passionately for a cause
- Has high tolerance for process, as long as radical change is the goal
- Sees self-transformation of individuals as a desired state

Communicating Giving and receiving accurate information at the right time becomes the currency of the Entrepreneurial Organization, whether its structure resembles a traditional, alternative, or virtual configuration. Without the free flow of information, not only will the organization fail to meet its goals, but it will also fail to exist. Information in all its forms becomes the context or the framework of the Entrepreneurial Organization.

The individualized subjective view of the organization, its expectations and its potentiality, must be an important part of this communication. No organization really exists outside the individual consciousness, so presenting that consciousness in some linguistic form is essential for the work of the organization to proceed. The conversation or dialogue could move to dialectic as misconceptions and politics become part of the communication among organization members. Some would say that dialectic and even stronger conflict is inevitable due to the limits currently existing with communication. We think the full potential of the Entrepreneurial Organization will be limited in reaching its more spiritual or holistic goals for organizational members until a transcendent communication modality is developed (perhaps in the form of a *mind meld*, as seen in the original *Star Trek* series—an idealized version of "perfect" communication). This is because individuals have uneven levels of skills in moving intuition into propositional, or word, forms. Individuals have varying levels of consciousness and varying levels of commitment and capacity to reach the existential goals of this type of organization.

Given the openness of the Entrepreneurial Organization, conflict among divergent forces, opinions, ideas, and information is inevitable. Fortunately, radical humanists expect conflict; they feel comfortable with conflict and do not always feel the need to make things right collaboratively. Since conflict is a part of life, there are times when people will simply agree to disagree and go their separate ways within the organization or in the larger environment. When this happens, it is without feeling they must have closure or needing to be sure no one's feelings are hurt. Feelings may be hurt—an inevitable result of embracing subjectivity and change—but consciousness will be raised, which is more important.

Recognizing Staff Expectations For the manager in an Entrepreneurial Organization, responding to staff expectations most likely means identifying the problem and simply getting out of the way as the members of the organization mobilize to take action to right that which is wrong. The challenge is to facilitate a common understanding of the problem and an understanding of that which can be associated with its existence.

Personality types with the Myers-Briggs *feeling–perceiving* characteristics, highly respectful of individual differences and having great comfort with change, fit well within the entrepreneurial, radical, adhocracy perspective of the Entrepreneurial Organization. They have a concern for human potential and uniqueness while also being very open to possibilities. These employees appreciate clever, creative leadership capable of generating hope and potential. Employees with this worldview will be ethical relativists, seeing what is deemed "right" as being imbedded in the context. Multiple experiences with the reality will result in multiple constructions of the reality, its meaning, and what should be done about it. They are comfortable with this.

Managing the consequences of the need to view all experiences and all goals from an individualistic lens will be a challenge. Coming to consensus or at least achieving the appropriate level of consciousness among all stakeholders to the question will require strength of character, great communication skills, and implicit trust in the potential of the individuals involved. The task of creating a culture to support this may be the responsibility of organizational administrators, but all the stakeholders must be helped to share the vision. This may become a challenge when the stakeholders do not share time or space, but in those cases the need for consensus may also be lessened.

If the organization is one with these adhocracy cultural norms, but peopled by individuals who do not share this vision or expectations for organizational life, the challenges for managers and other radical humanists within the organization will be great. Those who approach problem solving more linearly or empirically will question the call to action by those with shared radical humanist visions. Those from a more traditional worldview will find it hard to join the dialectical processes. They will tend to doubt the goals and procedures that result. They may be seen to be obstructionist to the organization and its members. Though teamwork is not necessarily expected in this very individualist view of organization, participation in the organizational dialogue is demanded. Now imagine what it would be like for someone with an entrepreneurial spirit to try to make his way in a traditional organization. The failures to communicate will be almost unending. Remember the trouble Jackson had before founding I HELP. The independence/dependence paradox operant in Entrepreneurial Organizations will probably not make sense to those who do not share a radical humanist vision.

STANDARDS OF PRACTICE WITHIN ENTREPRENEURIAL ORGANIZATIONS

LANGUAGE IN ENTREPRENEURIAL ORGANIZATIONS

The radical humanist perspective assumes no such thing as a "best" way of approaching organizational change. Those in Entrepreneurial Organizations will work to solve problems by engaging multiple persons with diverse views in an effort to understand what the problem is. They are

Table 10.3
Practice Language Differences Across Four Paradigms

Traditional Organization	Radical Change Organization	Serendipitous Organization	Entrepreneurial Organization
Assessment	Assessment	Assessment	Assessment
Diagnosis	Problem Analysis	Understanding	Discovery
Planning	Organizing	Collaborating	Innovating
Incremental Change	Collective Transformational Change	Sense Making	Empowering Individuals Transformation

concerned with moving the process beyond simply understanding and using those understandings to make individual change occur. They welcome contention and conflict, expecting to have intense dialectical interactions as a normal part of a conscious organizational life. Practitioners here are not satisfied with personal incremental change.

In previous chapters, we introduced language used in other approaches to organizing to describe organization practice. In Table 10.3, we show the use of language in organizations built on the assumptions of all four of the paradigms.

Recognizing the degree to which language constructs reality, assessing the Entrepreneurial Organization is somewhat difficult, because there is a tendency to use words like *assessment*, which has a different meaning in each paradigm. We now turn to assessing these organizations with the caveat that special attention to the importance of thinking about terminology and language has just begun. Assessment implies that there are facts to collect and concrete data to gather in order to begin thinking about a situation, even if that assessment represents only a snapshot in time. What follows is a close look at assessment in an Entrepreneurial Organization. The process may not be understood as *assessment* in any of the other paradigms.

ASSESSMENT

For the radical humanist, there is no expectation that assessment will happen in a formalized way using standardized tools. In fact, this process is viewed as only one of an unlimited number of ways to understand a situation, condition, or problem. In fact, standardized tools may be subtle instruments of oppression that hinder individual understanding of the institutional setting because standardized tools ask the questions that those in power want answered, not necessarily what an individual worker needs to know in order to perform. Those in Entrepreneurial Organizations also assume that even after organizational participants have started to take one approach to assessment, it is just as likely that they will change course in the process as they discover other viable approaches. Assessment, then, is an emergent process. To assess from this perspective requires organizational members to be constantly vigilant, open to new possibilities, and keenly aware that what appear to be "flukes" and even mistakes can offer incredible insights. Practitioners here are critical thinkers who are not afraid of ambiguity and ambivalence. Assessment may be a starting point from which stakeholders begin. Where they emerge will be anything but linear in its progression.

In the Entrepreneurial Organization, assessment is a continuous process because the organization is always evolving. Since diverse ideas and opinions are constantly circulating, assessment is tricky business. Nothing stays the same from day to day, even hour to hour. Therefore, practitioners are open to surprise, even playful in their assessing. No idea is too frivolous or trivial to consider in examining a situation within the organization. People are heard to exclaim, "Well, just when I thought I had seen everything!" or "I've never seen that happen before" or "I've never even thought of this that way!" In Entrepreneurial Organizations, these exclamations are not made in fear, but are cries of surprise (and even joy). Unusual and creative thoughts about agency conditions are sought. Since radical individual change is a goal, radical ideas about what is going on and how to proceed are welcomed.

Wheatley and Kellner-Rogers (1996) describe this process of assessment as a form of emergence: "What do we do with surprise? What do we do with a world which cannot be known until it is in the process of discovering itself? It requires constant awareness, being present, being vigilant for the newly visible. We need to notice things we weren't looking for, things we didn't know would be important, influences we hadn't thought of, behaviors we couldn't predict. . . . An emergent world welcomes us in as conscious participants and surprises us with discovery" (p. 75). Consciousness about what is discovered might only occur after the fact, making it difficult to know when assessment has been completed and another stage of planning or practice has begun (Netting, O'Connor, & Fauri, 2008).

Although Wheatley and Kellner-Rogers frame this process as somewhat playful, members of the Entrepreneurial Organization are used to and expect conflict. There is no need to soft pedal or underplay what is discovered in the assessment process even when the processes raise emotional feelings and political eyebrows. Assessing their organization, the entrepreneurial personality may borrow from the differentiators in organizational culture theory, those independent scholars who think that traditional organizational theory and research is uncreative and dull. Recall that some of these scholars are qualitative researchers or people considered on the fringe of organizational research. They focus on topics such as values, symbolism, meaning, and emotion—topics neglected in traditional organizational research. They face conflict head on, believing that a good organizational study must uncover the complexities of deep-rooted conflict, inconsistencies, and differences in interpretation among cultural members in order for the process to have individual and/or organizational transformational merit.

These differentiators, recognizing the benefits of an adhocracy culture, are helpful in guiding the assessment process in an entrepreneurial context. It is understood that there will be as many social constructions of the organization as there are people in that organization. There is attention to differing ways of knowing about the organization. The purpose of assessment is to find out what the situation is so that it can change for the individual. The process is to bring people together to figure out what needs to be worked on, and once there is some sense of what needs to change the discovery process has already begun.

Discovery

Subjectivists engage in discovery with a strong belief in the value of **emergence,** a process in which unexpected ideas and new information will be constantly appearing and interacting with what is already "known." Unexpected understandings (the *aha* experience) result. Emergence takes a much different turn in Entrepreneurial Organizations because the process of discovery is so central to the organization's philosophy of considering multiple subjectivities. There is little narrowing down for problem analysis, because here it is not necessarily assumed there is even a problem to be analyzed. The discovery process could reveal conditions and opportunities that have not yet been defined as problems by the larger society, but merely for individuals (see Netting, O'Connor & Fauri, 2008, for more discussion of this).

Discovery in the Entrepreneurial Organization is a totally inclusive process in which everyone's experience and any knowledge held by anyone about a particular situation are entered into the process. Rather than stopping with analysis and renewed understanding of the situation, participants argue and disagree among themselves in order to come up with ways in which change can occur. The intent of these participants is to remove barriers or constraints that would liberate people to do their work in a more powerful and fulfilling way. Here the understandings that emerge from discovery are pushed hard for transformational change.

If there is a need to sort out why people in the neighborhood are not participating in the activities of the local activity center, discovery will not be limited to asking for answers to this question. Those employed by the agency might be asking themselves this question and, then, out of the various answers that might emerge, the agency might decide to first ask the neighbors around the agency what they think about the service and why people might not want to come. They might also be asked what might get them to go there or whether there might be another way of delivering activities. Former clients would be contacted and asked about their experiences, but also about what they thought the agency ought to do to get other individuals involved. All this information together would be shared with all having a stake in the services in order to determine what might be the ways of being available to all the individuals in the neighborhood as well as assuring that the employees were satisfied with themselves and the services they were rendering.

Innovating

Entrepreneurial personalities are creative. However, one can be creative without fully engaging in radical change. Innovative people are the ones who take creativity and use it for change. Entrepreneurial Organizations depend on creativity *and* innovation. Innovating is the trademark of the Entrepreneurial Organization. When change needs to occur within the organization, those in it seize the opportunity to innovate. Their innovation will be based on what they learned in the processes of assessment and discovery. Innovation will not be sacrificed on the altar of civility among colleagues in these organizations. In fact, engaging in innovative change in Entrepreneurial Organizations will involve contentiousness and playfulness side-by-side, depending on how much conflict the proposed change engenders. Of particular importance will be the desire to think outside the box and then to act accordingly for individual purposes.

In the same neighborhood center, the idea of closing the formalized services and developing moveable activities that could go from block to block might be a consideration resulting from the discovery of why the organization is not serving sufficient clients. This might upset those clients who had continued to value what was offered. It might upset employees who had their pat way of relating to clients. It might offer a nightmare of logistics to those responsible for that aspect of the organization. Feelings might be hurt in the process or people might express their dissatisfaction or fear related to such a radical change; but after many hours of conversation and argument, it becomes clear that each block could be transformed with the neighborliness that might evolve from neighbors interacting with neighbors. Less fear of each other and of the location would be the result of a mobile unit moving from block to block. This is real innovation.

Individual Transformation or Empowerment

Individual transformation is language unique to the Entrepreneurial Organization.

The *transformational process* is one in which subjectivist traits are extremely important as individuals attempt to make sense of what needs to change. In Entrepreneurial Organizations, participants must move beyond current oppressions and find ways to liberate themselves from those restrictions that have hampered their personal evolution. The organization composed of more highly evolved individuals will be changed because its participants will look on it differently, thus causing new cultural norms to emerge. The belief is that consciousness engenders empowerment, and through empowerment, transformational change occurs.

In the neighborhoods mentioned earlier, both the service providers and the participants may be changed as a result of the innovation in service delivery. Neighbors connect with neighbors. Employees may grow to know their neighborhood. People might agree to participate with each other in many ways. Some persons will take responsibility for organizing activities for those who are homebound; others will respect the wishes of those who don't want to be involved but need to overcome social isolation by developing telephone trees. All participants could become less fearful in the neighborhood because they know who is there. Those who looked scary before are now appreciated for what they brought to the life on the block. Individuals who live in this neighborhood begin to feel safer, more empowered, and more in control of their own lives. Individual transformation can occur.

The I HELP case example also presents stories of transformation and empowerment, not just for those receiving services, but also for the providers. Jackson is an excellent example of the liberating force of such an organization. He had experienced years and years of lack of fit between his goals and dreams as a practitioner and the expectations of the organizations in which he practiced. He was thwarted and unappreciated until he constructed a less constraining context for the practice he chose to enact. He is fulfilled because he is able to engage in helping in a way that suits his approach to practice and to life within an organization. He is much happier; he feels more creative and he thinks he is doing better work now than ever before.

In order to summarize the specifics of practice within an Entrepreneurial Organization, Table 10.4 provides an overview of their specific practice characteristics. It should serve as a synopsis for assessing the degree to which an organization is practicing from a radical humanist perspective within an adhocracy culture.

PRODUCING PRODUCTS AND OUTCOMES

Entrepreneurial Organizations are more focused on process than products or outcomes. Therefore, persons in organizations with alternative perspectives and goals may not value the products of these organizations. Yet, the

Table 10.4

Practice Characteristics of Entrepreneurial Organizations

Practice Element	Characteristics
Assessment	Attention to hearing multiple perspectives from diverse groups and persons is critical to information gathering.
	Collection of word data is more important than collecting numeric data because of meaning-making and dialectic possibilities.
	Use of dialectical and honest dialogue is needed to develop deep understandings—hermeneutic circles may be used.
	Reassessment is a central, continual and ongoing process.
	Participants trust emergence in order to evolve to the right questions.
Discovery	Subjective needs assessment data are shared with all constituencies for the purpose of consciousness raising.
	Discovery is viewed as a broadening process, with efforts made to avoid narrowing down of what is known.
Innovating	Involvement of all stakeholders is critical.
	Conflict is faced as inevitable and important to the creative process.
	Honest communication can be playful, contentious or vague because of respect and acceptance of difference.
Individual Transformation/ Empowerment	Transformation occurs for all participants.
	Contest (conflict) tactics are preferred.
	The goal is to liberate individuals.

concepts of radical personal transformation, self-actualization, spiritual wholeness, and an assortment of other related terms signal for many people the ultimate in meaning and growth.

Whereas interpretivists in Serendipitous Organizations may delight in greater meanings and understandings nurtured through intense collaboration, radical humanists in Entrepreneurial Organizations want to take those meanings and understandings and use them to make radical individual or personal change. The radical change that is expected will be individualized, because here there is recognition that every person is unique. Therefore, a self-help group within an Entrepreneurial Organization may take their participants to new ways of living, more centered lives, more spiritually complete lives, more artistic lives, and more balanced lives so that they will become transformers of themselves within the context of the larger environment. To persons who need products that are easy to measure using standardized tools, the work of Entrepreneurial Organizations will seem soft, subjective, and somewhat esoteric, perhaps even a bit crazy.

IMPLICATIONS FOR PRACTICE IN ENTREPRENEURIAL ORGANIZATIONS

For human service professionals who claim to give attention to the individual within his or her context in order to help the individual navigate more effectively, there could be no better fit between these professional claims and the assumptions of the radical humanist perspective. However, regardless of the progressive rhetoric, history would suggest that helping professionals are much more traditional and conservative than many practitioners would like to believe. Therefore, although radical humanism as operationalized in the Entrepreneurial Organization has a great deal of congruence with the values and practice principles of the many helping professionals, the practical consequences of this congruence create problems for the practitioners who may be reactive, rather than proactive, regarding human needs.

The radical demands of this perspective mean that change must come to the individual as a result of the work. This holds the practitioner not only to the standard of helping the individual to help himself or herself, but also to be changed personally as a result of the interaction. This requires a level of introspection and honesty that is rarely found in a profession filled with individuals whose goal is to be seen as a professional expert. Those in an Entrepreneurial Organization do not bow to professional experts. In fact, they question the nature of professional identity and the false dichotomy of expert–client.

However, this perspective gives ample room and guidance for recognizing, respecting, and relishing difference. We see this perspective as the most amenable to a multicultural lens. Unfortunately, because of its very responsiveness to difference and respect for individuality in the construction of meaning and subsequent behaviors, those requiring specific steps to assure good practice will be frustrated by the lack of traditional theoretical guidance. A shift in expectations will be necessary in order to get the most of what the Entrepreneurial Organization has to offer for diversity and complex practice.

This approach to organizing provides the context for more questions than answers, and more discomfort than surety. To be ethical will require serious thought and complex considerations. The ethical relativity that is present here is a relativity that has no functional tether other than the measure of whether transcendent change has occurred as a result of the work. The real measure of ethical performance, then, is emergent, both during and after the process. Because the process is always in process, there is an aspect of "never knowing" that comes with any consideration of social work professional ethics from an entrepreneurial perspective. Further, due to the nature of the assumptions of the radical humanist paradigm, there is no hope that more clarity will emerge as the dimensions of the paradigm develop in the future. Therefore, social work professionals working from this perspective must have astutely developed human instruments to guide their practice. They must practice with those who are similarly evolved in order to assure ethical performance within the organization.

The current practice arena that is constructed of service delivery systems (or nonsystems) responsible for brokered care will be both a particular challenge and an opportunity for practice from this perspective. Barriers can be broken down between organizations when leadership is assumed by those operating from a professional ethical perspective. Practitioner voices in the service context are essential to prepare the way for leaders to exhibit a strong presence in the evolving virtual service organization and other helping services that will be developed and delivered in the future through advanced technological means.

CONCLUSION

The Entrepreneurial Organization is committed to discovery and understanding. Radical humanists want to use new understandings to enact individual, transformational change. They do not believe that there is a best way for change. For them, there is no possibility of a generalizable truth, nor does the understanding process result in a final truth. Change will occur as individuals interact intersubjectively within these organizations, and that is to be expected and valued. When the unexpected happens somewhere in the process, then the assumption is that this is how the world works, unexpectedly and serendipitously in a true adhocracy culture. Those comfortable within an Entrepreneurial Organization live well with ambiguity. There are no assumptions that anyone is in control. There are only fleeting images of being in control, for the time being.

What the organizational leader gains from radical humanist assumptions is a commitment from colleagues to work through the process of change and to continue to work in a passionate manner toward subsequent personal changes. The leader recognizes that pressures from more traditional funding sources or other agencies will be to use standardized approaches and tools to aid in response to the call for productivity. Yet, productivity is defined very differently here, for sense making and meaning making are seen as essential to fundamental personal change. In

Entrepreneurial Organizations, there is a commitment to make meaning and use it to empower individuals in ways never imagined. Persons who want more concrete products or who are fearful of the unknown may view these "outcomes" with disdain.

When adopting this perspective for assessment, discovery, innovating, and individual empowerment, the worker gains a view of what is unique to the organization and its members in the organizational environment. Subtle influences regarding processes are captured in the data collection for decision making. This is true because there is room for consideration of the more qualitative, affective, intuitive aspects of the individual perspective on organizational life. For the organizational leader, this approach and the theories guiding it offer great help in attending to the special opportunities and challenges provided by that which is different from the norm. Further, there is room for the chaotic and the unexpected, which seems to permeate today's organizational life. The presence of chaos and the appearance of the unexpected, often attributed to incompetence in the dominant world, is seen in Entrepreneurial Organizations as normal organizational life, full of unlimited possibilities.

This is the last of a series of chapters that have focused on specific types of organization and approaches to organization practice, the theories derived from them, and the implications in four types of organizations. Now, it is time to face the paradoxes all these differences represent because individuals and organizations from different perspectives interact daily in organizational life. In fact, various approaches operate simultaneously in most organizations having any degree of complexity. The final chapter examines multiparadigmatic practice in diverse, contemporary organizations.

DISCUSSION QUESTIONS

1. Why is emergence so valued in Entrepreneurial Organization practice? What paradigmatic and cultural assumptions support it? What benefits are gained by using emergence to achieve change? What might be potential problems?
2. Where is advocacy in Entrepreneurial Organization practice? What type of tactics might be most congruent with the type of change most appreciated in this organization?
3. Given the preferred structure and management style (or lack of same) in Entrepreneurial Organizations, what are the challenges and opportunities for your own practice, given your comfort zone?
4. Review the characteristics of Entrepreneurial Organizations in Table 10.1. Where are the potential problems and challenges for you as a practitioner in this type of organization? Are there other characteristics that you would add to this table? If so, what would they be and why would you add them?

5. Characterize the roles and relationships that are expected in an Entrepreneurial Organization. How do these fit with the practice standards and expectations related to managing and being managed in this type of organization? Reflect on what the meaning of all this might be for you as a developing practitioner. (This reflection could become part of a regular journaling exercise.)

6. As a practitioner in an Entrepreneurial Organization, what would you expect the challenges and opportunities might be in relationship to the environment in which this type of organization operates? What would you assume the standards and expectations to be vis-à-vis the environment? How important would those be to practitioners within the organization?

7. In reviewing the expectations regarding assessment, discovery, innovating, and empowering individuals' transformation in an Entrepreneurial Organization, what do you foresee as the challenges and opportunities where the organization is engaged in a multicultural environment? What might be social justice issues and opportunities?

8. From the standpoint of a professional practitioner in an Entrepreneurial Organization, what are the costs and benefits of the preferred manner for evaluation of practice and performance within the organization? What are some of the measurement issues in such an individualistic approach to organizing?

9. Going back to the I HELP case example in the beginning of this part of the text, use the content in this chapter to conduct an organizational analysis looking especially at structure and practice standards. What insights are gained from your analysis?

CONCLUSION

CHAPTER 11

Multiparadigmatic Practice

B Y NOW, YOU might know which paradigm you prefer. It is probably the place where you feel most comfortable because of your personality or it may be the one you think best serves your professional goals. Figure 11.1 lays out the four prototypes we have discussed in previous chapters, according to Burrell and Morgan's *four paradigms* and to Cameron and Quinn's *four organizational* cultures. You probably can identify the type of organization and culture within which you would be most comfortable.

We hope that you realize that wherever you land it does not mean that this represents the "best" paradigm or organizational culture, or that one should expect others to prefer the same set of worldview assumptions or cultural values in their work within an organization. When we analyze our own professional growth, we have found that people do not necessarily prefer the same paradigm at every life stage or in every organizational environment. Thus, the central element in multiparadigmatic practice is being aware of one's current paradigmatic standpoint and the expectations of the present organizational perspective and culture in relation to that. Self-awareness requires knowing where one prefers to be and why one feels most comfortable there, just as it is important to understand the assumptions that one finds in the particulars of an organization's practice. Basically what is at issue is being aware of what is necessary to meet organizational goals and expectations. This sets the stage for successful and rewarding organization practice.

We think that knowing one's preferred fit is important for understanding why certain people or events may cause a person to overreact, become angry, or feel threatened or hurt. Individuals have times in organizational life in which they find themselves reacting quickly or feeling strongly about an issue, an event, or an interpersonal interaction. This may not come from profound psychological sources or differing degrees of competence; it may be a competing values clash. Understanding paradigmatic perspectives and competing organizational values is an aid to being aware of why one responds in a particular way and what might be the basis of the reaction.

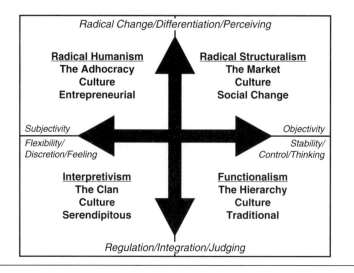

Figure 11.1   Location of the Preferred Organization Practice Context.

This also serves as a source of understanding about why others in the organization are responding in certain other ways. This consciousness is also a window into the paradoxical pulls that are normal in modern organizations.

Given the differing assumptions and values of various approaches to organizational life, a person trying to simultaneously operate within more than one paradigm is a living paradox. To avoid paradox, an alternative could be the ability to sequentially move to different paradigms at different times, depending on the situation or need. This would be the simplest way to manage the complexity of modern organizational practice, going gracefully from one paradigm to the other; but research evidence indicates that it does not happen this way (Cameron & Quinn, 2006; O'Connor, Netting, & Fabelo, in press). It appears that complex organizations operate from all paradigms. Certainly an organization may lean toward a favored prototype based on organizational goals, but practice in the real world seems to require that modern organizations are the essence of paradox. Later in this chapter, we will report our findings about organizational paradox, but first it is important to revisit and compare some important aspects of differing organizations that set the stage for the paradoxes we will describe.

Comparisons are provided so that you might get close to how very different each perspective is in order to extend your understanding of what those differences mean to you. This requires practicing stretches in thinking to assume the perspectives of other paradigms. When it is not your "home" paradigm, effective understanding or action in a "foreign" paradigm requires a great deal of work in translation, much like moving comfortably in another culture or language. Effective action is more difficult, because organizational goals based on assumptions from another paradigm are not as "natural" or familiar; without specific understandings of multiple standards of practice, one may be engaged in what one sees as best practice, but fail because of one's own off-targeted performance expectations.

To manage this challenge, some persons consciously or unconsciously locate their comfort zone paradigm, and then search for an organizational type that is primarily based on those same assumptions. This option may provide great comfort due to goal congruence, but it closes many options for creativity and discovery. If anyone has come to the conclusion that this is the preferred way to manage the complexities touched on in this book, we want to be clear that this is not what we are suggesting. Certainly there will be people who do work in their preferred organizational type; however, with or without paradigmatic match between yourself and your organizational setting, there will always be circumstances requiring cross-paradigm engagement. No matter the organization in which one accepts employment or volunteers, there will be persons or units within that organization or even an entire organizational culture that will embrace a different set of assumptions than yours. Navigating those differences requires *multiparadigmatic practice*.

In this chapter, we begin with a brief overview of organizational themes across all four *paradigms*, and then examine the organizational theories that grow from differing paradigms. We then compare and contrast the four *organizational types*. Finally, and most importantly, we examine empirical evidence about paradigmatic differences and what this means for human service practice.

ORGANIZATIONAL THEMES

The basic themes found within the differing approaches to organizing are paradigmatically and theoretically based, creating important distinctions related to assumptions about how the world works and how one comes to know that world, and also about how to plan, manage, and practice in an organization. Figure 11.2 combines thematic elements that have been introduced before, but we have placed them in a familiar *subjective/objective, regulation/radical change* configuration in order to make paradigmatic comparisons. Both worldviews and derived cultural values combine to create very different perspectives with diverse expectations and differing resultant manifestations of organizational structure and practice.

Traditional Organizations steeped in functionalist assumptions of a static, definable world that can be controlled for predictability is also embedded in the organization's history and traditions of what has worked in the past, choosing to change only when objective, reliable sources suggest mechanisms for change. Change must be undertaken with an

Entrepreneurial Organizations	Social Change Organizations
• The *subjective* nature of persons who provide valuable insights, perform significant deeds, and think outside the box is recognized and respected. It is recognized that contributions may not be corralled into a group effort. • *Flexibility and discretion* are promoted. It is understood that workers not only will be mavericks in their programs but may question or resist most aspects of what they are trying to do. • Individual contribution is expected with recognition that individuals are so *differentiated* that they work best on their own without the confines of a program. • Conflict is expected when *radical change* is being pursued individually. Causes are supported in non-traditional ways.	• The historical significance of social movements, social reform, and advocacy motivates programs to seek external *objective sources of recognized expertise to mobilize/organize change.* • *Differentiation and external focus* are promoted so that programs have the capacity to respond to larger community/societal needs for change. • *Stability and control* of programs is promoted through interrelated duties and/or tasks to be arrived at by focusing on best practice standards in activist activities. • Conflict and competition is expected, building organizational and programmatic structures to recognize competing interest groups in a *market culture.*
Serendipitous Organizations	**Traditional Organizations**
• The capacity of human beings to bring their *subjective* differences together is respected in seeking to continually redesign and develop programs and the organization. • *Integration* is supported so the organization runs smoothly through agreed-upon structure, created by team members and subject to change by consensus as needs shift. • *Flexibility and discretion* to gain consensus, listening to multiple voices, constructing new realities, and allowing programs to emerge permits individuals to finding meaning in their roles. • Coordination rather than management creates *clan culture*, where each has a voice. Hearing all perspectives is a norm in the organization's culture.	• History and tradition are respected as important parts of their programs, seeking external *objective sources of recognized expertise to design and develop programs.* • *Stability and control* are promoted so that programs run smoothly as workers conform to established protocols. • Programs are *integrated* by establishing interrelated duties and tasks to be carried out, assuming these duties and tasks establish best practices. • Well-defined organizational and programmatic structures are created, and are typically *hierarchical*, so lines of authority are clear.

Figure 11.2 Organizational Themes Compared.

expectation of returning to stability and control; thus, incremental rather than transformative change is preferred. Once change is accomplished, all involved are expected to conform unerringly to the established protocols. These protocols identify specific tasks and responsibilities to assure that all are involved in empirically based best ways of practice. Assurances of best practices are achieved through well-defined hierarchical organizational and programmatic structures established to maintain proper authority and accountability. Viewed as "the earliest approach to organizing in the modern era," Cameron and Quinn (2006, p. 37) refer to Traditional Organizations as having *hierarchical cultures*.

Social Change Organizations hold most of the same expectations and norms as Traditional Organizations based on their shared perspectives about the world and how to come to know it. Departure from the traditional comes with radical structuralist assumptions about how knowledge should affect change and how that change should occur. While objective, expert knowledge is used to mobilize change, these organizations' external focus and assumptions about transformational change make sweeping change through social movements, social reform and advocacy as preferred strategies. Though stability and control are enacted through the selection of the best way to achieve fundamental change, conflict and competition, including questioning authority, is expected and encouraged. Seen as "another form of organizing [that] became popular during the late 1960s as organizations faced new competitive challenges," Cameron and Quinn (2006, p. 39) refer to this type of organization as having a *market culture*.

Serendipitous Organizations, based on interpretive, subjectivist assumptions, look at multiple ways of understanding and practicing in organizations with the expectation that through consensus and integration appropriate ways of practice within a specific context will emerge. When the context changes, then flexibility and discretion are expected as all within the organization find a "new normal" for organizational structure and relationships. Individuality within the group is honored as trusted relationships form for consensus about direction and to give meaning to the work. Based on family-like organizations in which "teamwork, employee involvement programs, and corporate commitment to employees" (Cameron & Quinn, 2006, p. 41) became valued in the 1960s and early 1970s, this *clan culture* is consistent with the Serendipitous Organization.

Entrepreneurial Organizations also share the subjectivist perspective, but through a radical humanist lens that assumes that individuality and personal differentiated freedom are the desired vehicles for radical, individualized transformation. Independent, nontraditional action is the standard of practice. Cameron and Quinn (2006) see the *adhocracy culture* as having emerged most recently in response to the need to "foster entrepreneurship, creativity, and activity 'on the cutting edge' " (p. 43). The adhocracy type of culture fits best with the assumptions of an Entrepreneurial Organization.

ORGANIZATIONAL THEORY REVISITED

In previous chapters, we introduced organizational theories that fit within each of the four paradigms and that guide the practice within the different organizational types. Figure 11.3 provides an overview of all these theories and where we have located them within the confines of each paradigmatic perspective. Note that location within the paradigm gives an indication about the "purity" of the theoretical perspective. The purest representatives of each perspective are closer to the outside corners of each quadrant, and those most related to other paradigmatic perspectives are closer to the lines that determine paradigmatic boundaries.

The Functionalist Paradigm contains early organizational theories that dominated the way in which the first organizational developers understood how one led, managed, and worked within organizations. The classical, neoclassical, "modern" structural, and early human relations and systems theorists were functionalist in their assumptions. In fact, organizational theories in the first half of the 1900s were reflective of the assumptions of their time. It was assumed that there were best ways to

Postmodern Theories Antiadministration Postmodern Theories **Radical Humanist** Power and Politics —Third-World Feminist Theories —Critical Theories	Postmodern Theories Power and Politics —Radical Feminist Theories —Critical Theories **Radical Structuralist** Systems Theories (morphogenic, factional, and catastrophic analogies) Population Ecology and Transorganizational Theories
Organization Culture Diffusionists **Interpretive** Organizational Culture Integrationists Organizational Culture Revolutionary Vanguard Sensemaking Theory	Systems Theories (Mechanistic and Organismic Analogies) Human Relations Theories **Functionalist** "Modern" Structural Theories Neoclassical Theories Classical Theories

Figure 11.3 Organizational Theories Within the Four Paradigms.

structure organizations and if one could find that best way, then accepted truths about division of labor, human interaction, systems functioning, and a host of other traits would prevail. Since most of these theories were based on a closed-systems perspective, one did not have to consider the larger environmental context of the organization. One could focus instead on determining how to structure and work within the organization, ignoring environmental forces such as power and politics. In the early days of the Industrial Revolution, when the modern organization was developing, this thinking was sufficient to guide organizational decision makers in solving the problems at hand, because this approach to the structuring of factories had impressive impacts.

Even when open-systems theories became the dominant way of viewing organizations, some theoreticians continued to guard the organization from the consideration of environmental forces, as witnessed by mechanical and organismic analogies. These systems theorists understood the environment as a force that worked against maintaining the organization's equilibrium. They believed the environment could be bounded and controlled as part of the perfect structure.

As the need was recognized, there were also open-systems analogies that embraced the interaction between organizations and their environments and viewed the environment as providing opportunities. These latter ways of theorizing about organizations as in morphogenic, factional, and catastrophic analogies not only considered the existence of conflict, but in some cases, actually embraced it as a useful way to change larger structures. With organizations developing and becoming more sophisticated and complex, more complex thinking was necessary to respond to the needs of the times. Radical structuralist systems theorists began to see conflict as inevitable. Systems were constantly changing; there was turbulence among diverse groups within and outside systems; and this was not necessarily something to be avoided. Instead of believing that systems always sought equilibrium and it was only the environment that was turbulent, these newer theorists did not need to reduce conflict; the dynamics within organizations served as an incubator for change. This position opened thinking for power and politics theorists to also articulate the assumptions of radical structuralists by acknowledging these powerful dynamics and multiple constituencies within organizations and their environments.

The theories that emerge from both the Functionalist and Radical Structuralist paradigms have something very important in common—*objectivism*. Objectivism accepts definite, concrete truths. People may disagree about what those truths are, but the goal of both paradigms is to identify or convince others of the superiority of the universal truths one embraces. The theories in these two paradigms, then, are based on a desire to point organizations and their managers toward the best way to achieve goals and the best structures to keep the organization focused. For the functionalists, that way is the established standard of the status quo. For radical structuralists, it is the *new* best way that is a morally superior approach able to recognize the voices of oppressed persons so that oppression can cease through radical, fundamental change.

Based on the challenge of managing difference within systems, theorists became unleashed, expanding their boundaries regarding theory. Open-systems theory established the consideration of the importance of context for organizations, and contingency theory cemented the recognition that the best way for planning and structuring within an organization will depend on what is happening both inside and outside of the organization. Organizational ecology brought research precision to the organizational decision-making enterprise.

But, then, theorizing began to get complicated, because those using the system, contingency, and population ecology theories to guide their work in organizations started branching out beyond a unitary perspective to answer the challenges of a rapidly changing organizational environment. Now, looking back, it is clear that these theories began taking the standpoint of a variety of paradigms, while still remaining connected to a particular theory label. For this reason, clarity about the assumptions underlying the research and decision making that result is essential in order to judge the usefulness and rigor of the research process and product for application in a particular organization. If, for example, systems theory is used interpretively, then generalizability beyond the current time and context is a virtual impossibility. If a manager requires answers that go across time and locality, then that manager will be frustrated by what open-systems, contingency, or population ecology theories can produce from an interpretive standpoint. If, however, these theories are used to provide a deep understanding of current environmental considerations from a more radical structuralist perspective in order to suggest survival strategies for now and not beyond, then the product will be very useful for the manager.

All this change in theoretical thinking or the emergence of new schools of organizational thought did not mean that early theories were thrown out. In fact, sometimes researchers coming from different assumptions used elements of earlier theories to rethink organizations. Recognition increased about just how complex organizations are and how difficult it is to understand them. Postmodern theorists, working in reaction to theoretical history, influenced all the alternative views of organizations in various ways, beginning with the radical structuralist and moving to the more subjectivist interpretivist and radical humanist. *Complex, diverse, multicultural, pluralistic,* and many other terms began to be used in describing organizations. These were terms that assumed difference, something traditional organizational theorists had been less inclined to recognize.

It is logical that the next phase of organizational theory development would introduce schools of thought such as sense making and organizational culture. Early theorists in this interpretive tradition were viewed as countercultural, somewhat interesting, but not in line with previous schools of organizational thought. Something important was happening regarding understanding organizations. The interpretivist perspective began to have influence in the direction of more traditional thinkers. The Search for Excellence movement revealed nuances in how leaders influenced culture. Popular, traditional management literature adopted new, softer language referring to organizations as "dancing giants" and using terms such as *empowerment* and *leading with the spirit*. The floodgates were open and the interpretive language penetrated even the Traditional Organization. The problem this created was that even though interpretive language was increasingly used in Traditional Organizations, basic, underlying assumptions had not changed. Understanding deep assumptions in organizations became even more essential, because what was done and how one talked about it began to seem like parallel processes fraught with potential for mistakes, misunderstandings, and bad feelings.

Bad feelings may in fact be the basis of the most modern theoretical developments from the Radical Humanist Paradigm. Theories here seek to unhinge, implode, or otherwise decommission traditional ways of doing business in organizations. Starting with the deconstruction of the postmodernists and moving through the consciousness-raising efforts of the critical theorists who are listening to women's and minority voices, and assessing power and politics that disenfranchise, ideas are developing to again rethink the way people organize to achieve goals. Antiadministration is the most recent example developed as a way to honor and enhance the payoff of difference.

Take a moment to think about the challenges that might develop if there was a unit guided by interpretive principles of collaboration and consensus housed in a Traditional Organization with expectations of hierarchical control. What sorts of predictable paradoxes can you imagine? Now assume that you have an employee guided by radical humanist assumptions working within a Social Change Organization. Though transformational goals are held from both perspectives, what might be the challenges both to the employee and the employee's manager?

Just as we covered the theoretical perspective regarding how organizations are structured and work, we also presented various perspectives on the management of those doing the work of the organization. Figure 11.4 again distributes the various schools of management theory or thought according to the paradigmatic perspectives.

Now that you are well versed in the various theories undergirding organization practice, it should not be difficult to see the relationships between the various theories and the management schools. Shared

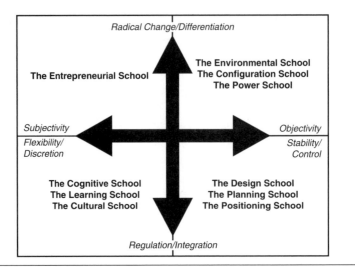

Figure 11.4 Schools of Management Thought Placed Within Multiple Frameworks. *Source:* Mintzberg, Ahlstrand, and Lampe (1998).

assumptions and worldviews should be clear so that it should not be difficult to see why certain perspectives on management are also congruent with organizational theories. We leave it to you to draw some of the links as well as the distinctions in preparation for a closer comparison of organizational goals and characteristics. Try, for example, to imagine the challenges that would result if a manager were guided by the assumptions and expectations of the Learning School while working in a Traditional Organization. What might be the paradoxes if a manager assumed the practices of the Power School where the organization embraced more interpretive assumptions?

COMPARING AND CONTRASTING ORGANIZATIONAL GOALS AND CHARACTERISTICS

GOALS

The exercises and questions posed in the Discussion sections of the previous chapters should have helped to clarify that just as the paradigmatic perspective influences worldview and preferred organizational culture, different organizational goals are paradigmatically and culturally congruent, and the lack of these types of congruence also engenders paradoxes. Actually, the differing expectations regarding organizational structure and performance may be made most clear at the organizational goal level. Figure 11.5 repeats the four organizational goals built on differing paradigmatic, theoretical, and values assumptions.

Given the differences in how goals are operationalized in each type of organization, Table 11.1 provides a comparison of the derivative values,

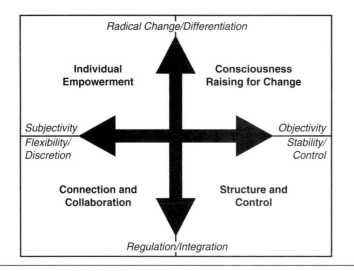

Figure 11.5 Organizational Goals Within Multiple Frameworks.

mission and philosophy, organizational structure, and programs and services across organizational types. Clearly, the practitioner in each perspective must be able to accomplish very different activities toward differing goals, depending on the underlying assumptions and values that drive the mission and philosophy of the organization. Differing practice expectations are derived from all the dimensions of the contradictory perspectives that we have already addressed, and are also guided by different theories for structuring and managing organizations. In the next section, continue to think about what happens when the individual worker, the manager, or a unit or program fail to share the overarching goals of the organization in which the work is expected to occur.

Traditional Organizations hold goals of stability and control. They are incrementalists that think that people must be helped to adapt, adjust, and be accommodating to the larger society in order to function in it. Their programs will not look toward large-scale reformation, but rather just small changes within the individual or society. Social Change Organizations aspire to establish consciousness raising for change. They see no usefulness in accommodation to the status quo, preferring a strategy that forces fundamental changes in institutional or societal structures in order to meet group needs. Serendipitous Organizations seek connection and collaboration, and they work at achieving incremental change through understanding, believing that with consciousness raising and collaboration, opportunities for change will emerge. Further, all will be better off because change will be the result of consensus. Entrepreneurial Organizations are after individual empowerment. They focus on individual resistance to adaptation, adjustment, and accommodation. Societal structures

Table 11.1

Comparing Characteristics of Four Organizational Types

Characteristics	Traditional Organizations	Social Change Organizations	Serendipitous Organizations	Entrepreneurial Organizations
Values	To operationalize dominant opinions, doctrines, and practices, focusing on efficiency and effectiveness	To provide avenues for nondominant opinions, doctrines, and practices	To provide avenues for both nondominant and dominant opinions, doctrines, and practices so that inclusion is maximized	Runs counter to ideologies related to objectivism (external truth); accepting of alternative opinions and practices, focusing on individual empowerment and social justice
Mission and Philosophy	To use the best knowledge available to enhance and achieve the highest social order	To use the best knowledge available to enhance and achieve the highest social change for the common good	To use the best knowledge available to enhance and achieve the highest social order	To seek individual transformation
Organizational Structure	To establish clear relationships between organizational members and among units within the organization, and to be part of service delivery structures that are established by agency staff and protocols that have been used over the years	To allow structure to emerge so that the organization's cause is best facilitated, and to use less bureaucratic, flatter structures whenever possible	To allow structure to emerge so that the learning process is facilitated, and to use less bureaucratic, flatter structures whenever possible to facilitate a network of relationships	To develop minimal structure so that changes can be easily made in an ongoing manner without impinging on the individuals inside the structure
Programs and Services	To use incremental or gradual change to alter people's status so that they can function best within society	To develop advocacy-based programs and services designed to change oppressive structures and empower people	To develop educational and human service programs that assist participants in understanding complex issues by increasing consciousness to the degree that understanding leads to more meaningful living	To create opportunities for people to grow and develop individually

338

should be forced to change in order to meet individual needs, but if individual accommodations are not certain, the individual can be helped to transcend the limits of society in order to achieve a much more evolved state.

How Programs Differ

Given these differing goals, programming across organizations will be planned and delivered very differently, even when the programs focus on the same population group or social problem. A good example of how these differences in program philosophy get operationalized in practice would be through the creation of an English-language program for recent immigrants. A Traditional Organization would design the program for participants to acquire language and cultural skills as quickly as possible in order to replace old practices and languages. Assimilation would be the goal. A Social Change Organization would see the traditional program as merely a band-aid measure, possibly designed to deny one's culture of origin and to get immigrants to disappear into the melting pot. As an alternative, their language program would first seek to organize immigrants to stand up for their language rights. While English as a second language might be desirable, the primary goal of services would be to form a collective in which the participants in the program could become empowered as a group and recognized as a viable community.

A Serendipitous Organization might develop a language program that would educate staff to become multicultural and multilingual. The program goal would be to understand the subtleties of language and the meaning attached to words so that the staff could better collaborate with recent immigrants from the immigrants' perspectives. From the staff perspective, cultural sensitivity and higher-order cultural competence would be the aim. English-language acquisition would emerge from this educational process, but the service would be a consciousness-raising experience for all involved, one in which all participants were learners. An Entrepreneurial Organization would focus on the individual immigrant and his or her empowerment, even resisting the learning of English and certainly never encouraging the loss of one's first language in the process of socialization to this country. This organization would create programs that were highly individualistic and customized to the needs of the individual immigrant rather than lumping recent immigrants into a collective category.

We began this book with a chapter on the diverse organizational landscape. There we introduced three types of programs often planned for and/or provided in organizations dedicated to human needs: direct service, staff development and training, and support. Having read the English-language example above, we hope that the reader recognizes that these programs will look different under the auspices of different organizational types with differing overall goals.

In the Traditional Organization, direct service programs will be highly organized and designed with outcome measurement in mind. Given its predisposition to maintain the status quo, the Traditional Organization will usually not attempt to solve societal-wide, large-scale problems, focusing instead on meeting immediate human needs. Staff development and training programs may be heavily focused on training for specific skills, such as filling out forms accurately or following established practice protocols. Support programs, such as advocacy efforts, will be primarily focused on case or client advocacy, which might emphasize the importance of getting a client his or her benefits. Can you see how a practitioner with more radical goals might have trouble following practice expectations here?

In the Social Change Organization, direct service programs will also be highly organized and outcome-focused, but identified outcomes will be more radical or far-reaching than those of a Traditional Organization. Beyond meeting immediate client needs, larger scale programs designed to bring about community or even societal changes are expected. Staff development and training programs may be designed to assist volunteers, paraprofessionals, staff, and consumers, first in understanding the "problem(s)" and then in community organizing, campaign development, and mobilizing resources. Those in Social Change Organizations may look at traditional programs with disdain, indicating that they are not concerned enough with change on a broader scale and that their programs are just band-aids. In fact, support programs such as advocacy efforts may actually be the defining programs of many Social Change Organizations, since their emphasis is on collective change. Think about the practitioner who is more comfortable with slow, well-managed incremental change being expected to perform according to standards in a Social Change Organizations. Where would the paradoxes be?

In the Serendipitous Organization, direct service programs will be much more subjective or affective, focusing on the importance of clients and staff relationships and in understanding themselves and others. These programs may be very reflective, thoughtful, and insightful, viewing all parties as co-learners in the process of collaborative program implementation. Staff development and training programs in these organizations may focus on the development of critical thinking skills, learning new collective human service approaches and methods such as cooperative decision making, and emphasizing staff development over training. Staff development for improved personal and professional development will be a signature program for this type of organization, but the goal of this development is connection and relationship building for greater understanding. Those in Serendipitous Organizations will look with some antipathy at those in Traditional Organizations who seem more concerned about training for precision than for meaning. They will also look at those in Social Change Organizations as somewhat obsessed with change to the exclusion of understanding. Therefore, support programs in a Serendipitous Organization may take the form of research or educational units designed to enhance the efforts of members who want to fully understand the context and concepts of problems. What would be the challenges for the manager or employee who believes in more action orientation aimed at changing the status quo?

In the Entrepreneurial Organization, direct service programs are typically constructed as self-help or empowerment programs, seeking to create opportunities for individuals to grow and develop beyond where they are now. Staff development and training may be provided, but on a very individualistic basis, such as encouraging organizational members to seek their own sources of new knowledge across a range of disciplines. Since everyone's learning is unique, there will be little desire to corral people into training events. Self-paced learning is preferred and now very possible in the virtual training platforms of cyberspace. But regardless of the medium, developing a mechanism for individual, lifelong learning is preferred. To this end, support programs may be loosely established to offer participants opportunities to identify and secure what they need to move toward individual empowerment through their own "learning to speak to power." Essentially, the programs of the Entrepreneurial Organization are nontraditional in every aspect, with the goal to free the human spirit to achieve a higher level of being. The entrepreneur may mock the rigid, protocol-oriented, rule-bound programs developed by traditional practitioners as being irrelevant for human development. They could scoff at the Social Change Organization's need to form collective goals in their change efforts for lack of attention to the individual. They would push interpretivists in Serendipitous Organizations to use their new understandings to effect change, particularly at the individual level.

Organizations in all four paradigms may have all types of programs (direct service, staff development and training, and support), but they will differ in how they are designed and what will be emphasized. They will differ regarding what programs are preferred or even seen as useful and relevant. Also, regardless of paradigm, some organizations will devote themselves to only one program and be highly specialized; others will not. For example, a Traditional Organization might be a government-planning agency dedicated to the planning of human service programs that serves as a pass-through for funding to provider organizations, with no efforts in advocacy and few expectations regarding staff development. A Social Change Organization might be a social movement organization or a grassroots organization, dedicated to programming in a highly specialized, cause-oriented fashion that would require approximately equal attention to programs, staff development, and advocacy. A Serendipitous Organization might be a research institute on social problems that finds depth and understanding about the very problems other agencies will try to resolve. In this organization, there would be no real direct service, but attention to staff development and advocacy by way of dissemination of findings would be central to their collaborative efforts. An Entrepreneurial Organization could be a self-improvement organization, running groups and retreats that focus on spiritual growth. Programming and staff enrichment would be central, with little effort expended in the direction of advocacy as it is commonly defined. The point is that the preferred manner of intervention will be guided by the worldview and assumptions that the organization has about the "best" way to solve individual and societal problems related to their particular organizational goals.

The differences in programs sometimes vary within the same organization, with each programmatic unit having its own subculture within the larger organizational culture. This complex interplay of subcultures requires the practitioner to fully appreciate the roles and relationships that engage the external environment as well as the inner workings of the organization itself. This situation is a classic example of an organizational design destined to create a lived experience of organizational paradox. Try to identify where those paradoxes might accrue.

COMPARING AND CONTRASTING ROLES AND RELATIONSHIPS

ENVIRONMENT

Adding to an already complex picture, the four types of organizations differentially engage their task environments. For the Traditional Organization, the environment is an uncertain and turbulent sea of forces to be controlled as much as possible, whereas the Social Change Organization seeks to seize or create that uncertainty and within the chaos mobilize diverse forces for change. Both organizations attempt to control environmental forces, but in different ways: For the functionalist it is control to maintain order; for the radical structuralist it is to create chaos within which major change becomes possible. The Serendipitous Organization wants to understand environmental complexity, seeing this complexity as a way to achieve higher understanding, meaning and, thus, potential unexplored resources. Without the environmental context, there would be no meaning about the problem or how to solve it. The Entrepreneurial Organization goes beyond understanding context and sees the environment as a source of invigorating differences into which the human spirit can soar to new heights if escape from environmental limits is achieved.

Think about the implications for practice posed by these four views of an organization's environment. Traditional practitioners may be fearful of an uncontrolled environment, almost shielding themselves and their organizations from uncertain forces. Maintaining calm within the organization, feeling that the organization is a refuge from the storm, and making peace within the organization may take precedence. Social change practitioners may actually bring environmental influences into the organization, challenging themselves and others to harness those forces for change against the status quo. Persons in Serendipitous Organizations preferring collaboration and consensus will be content to process the nuances of environmental context, seeking new ideas and perspectives with an eye to the importance of what they are learning and what it all might mean for the organization. Entrepreneurs likely agree with their social change colleagues on the importance of environmental forces, but they will use these forces in very different ways. While social change practitioners will seek collective change, spurred by environmental opportunities, entrepreneurs will seek individual transformation without regard and sometimes in resistance to the collective.

Funding Relationships

Critical components of the human service organization's environment are current and potential funding sources. Traditional Organizations seek to obtain funding that flows from long-established, multiple sources. Stability and predictability are desired. Traditional Organizations and their funding sources develop close relationships, and it is expected that funders actually influence the agency's direction or its programming. Traditional Organizations of any size will tend not to put all their financial eggs in one basket if they can help it, unlike alternative agencies that might feel fortunate even to locate a funding source for their cause.

As an alternative agency, the Social Change Organization often has trouble developing and maintaining a stable funding base because it embraces controversial, even unpopular causes. Unless there are funding sources in the larger environment that agree with their mission, these organizations may operate on a shoestring budget, with continuing questions about their long-term survival. Similarly, Serendipitous Organizations might have trouble developing and maintaining a stable funding base, but for different reasons. Even if their causes are less controversial, their predisposition to understand everything holistically, carried to an extreme, may become tedious and tiresome to funding sources, especially since it is the rare funding source that is interested in the details of process over product. Entrepreneurial Organizations also might have difficulty developing and maintaining a stable funding base. The creativity and innovation that permeates Entrepreneurial Organizations suggest that traditional ways of thinking about funding do not always fit well here; nor are they necessary. Here, the old rules about fundraising do not apply.

Relationships with funders may depend on compatibility between worldviews held by funding sources and those of the human service organizations. Stable funders that are seeking incremental change, for example, may appear to entrepreneurial or social change leaders to have too much power in the organization and to be too conservative in their influence. If the Social Change Organization is successful in raising the public consciousness, then the novelty of its cause may attract temporary funding interests. However, because of the fickle nature of funding streams, working in a Social Change Organization could mean that one's job (along with the funding) disappears as suddenly as it appeared if soft monies are not continued or if another cause catches the eye of funders. The volatility of funding, then, is an ongoing issue for agencies that assume a radical or even alternative orientation. Working in them may feel very much like a rollercoaster ride—invigorating yet somewhat risky and uncertain.

Funders that seek clearly defined outcomes and definitive deadlines will not appreciate interpretive, always emerging work efforts, sometimes rejecting a Serendipitous Organization as not well organized or well run. However, for funding sources devoted to generating new knowledge, and not quite as focused on immediate product, a Serendipitous Organization can be a positive match. If the funding source is seeking creative understandings about social problems and/or collaborating with service recipients, the Serendipitous Organization will be a good resource. Whatever the funding source, policies and regulations that accompany the receiving of funds will become part of the environmental forces that must constantly be considered in the relationship. Think here about what happens in the mismatch between the intent of the organization and the expectations of the funding source. Might it ever reach the level of ethical dilemma?

RELATIONSHIPS WITH CLIENTS

Depending on how specialized an organization is, the numbers and characteristics of clients will vary, as will the organization's attitudes toward and relationships with them. Since human service organizations exist to do something for the betterment of clients, it might be helpful to revisit the four case examples that were introduced in the four part openers, focusing on how clients differed in each of the organizational types.

The Washington County Office on Aging case example, presented in Part I, is an Area Agency on Aging designed to plan for and provide services for older persons. Funded by the Older Americans Act and other public dollars, this nonprofit office is replicated in multiple counties within the state through formalized procedures and protocols. Its clients are viewed as the older generation of Americans who have contributed to the community and who have multiple potential needs for chronic care issues that deserve a response. There are established mechanisms for these senior members of society to have their voices heard in a cyclical needs-assessment process that results in the development of a plan. There are assumptions that elders deserve service; that activities should be provided through senior centers; and that incremental planning should include a consumer voice to some extent. Relationships with clients are supportive and perhaps a little paternalistic and protective as people age in place within their communities.

Compare the Washington County Office on Aging's relationships with clients to those of the Consumer-Directed Advocacy Agency, as presented in Part II. This Social Change Organization doesn't like the word *client* and uses the word *consumer* to describe its constituents. The disabilities community is composed of a very proactive group that fights together for legislative change with the assistance of the organization. The director is seen as both consumer and leader and the methods used in promoting structural change mobilize consumers to join a cause. Consumers actually take on the provider system and demand adjustments to the gaps in services they have identified. There is a joining of forces among agency staff, volunteers, and consumers, who are all considered valuable partners in the quest for change. There is nothing passive about the relationship this organization has with its consumers, and conflict is expected and embraced in the process of getting things done. Paternalism and protection are unacceptable.

A third case example was provided in Part III, in the Orange State Child Abuse Prevention Agency. Unlike the public mandate that established the Area Agency on Aging, but similar to the establishment of the Consumer-Directed Advocacy Agency, this organization was established by consumers. But there is a huge difference in how the founders grew the organizational culture, not as a radical change agency but as a safe, inclusive haven for defenseless children (and later, their families). This agency is built on relationships among participants, in which listening to all voices, processing all issues, and providing care and attention are paramount. Maintaining respectful relationships with participants is utterly ingrained in the organization so that staff and volunteer roles are so intertwined that it is possible to find an ongoing mixing and phasing of roles. Clients are viewed as *participants*, and coming to a consensus among all parties is important to the agency's operation.

Finally, the case example provided in Part IV reveals the I HELP agency, although it is more a virtual reality than an "agency" in the traditional sense. Jackson attracted a cadre of therapists from all over the world to join an Internet-connected approach to providing services. Because all of these therapists provide different things, their relationships with clients (users of service) do not conform to any particular way of doing business. In fact, their relationships are highly individualistic and empowering. There is trust and respect here just as in the child abuse prevention agency, but it is operationalized differently and has very different results. There is another similarity in that in the service process here, the providers of service are being empowered as well, so that the distinction between helper and service user blurs, but in ways that are different from those of the child abuse agency seen in Part III. In the child abuse agency, the recipient may become the provider of service at some point or vice versa. Here, boundaries blur in the process, so that those roles become insignificant.

Internal Organizational Roles and Relationships

Within a human service organization, certain functions have to be performed that involve an assortment of roles and relationships. In previous chapters, we identified three of those functions as managing, communicating, and staffing. Cameron and Quinn (2006) are particularly helpful in identifying how these functions may look different in each of the four cultures they identify.

In a Traditional Organization with a hierarchical culture, Cameron and Quinn identify three managerial competencies: managing *acculturation, managing the control system,* and *managing coordination* (2006, p. 121). Managing acculturation requires clear communication skills in helping staff adjust to what is expected of them in the organization's culture. Since certain expectations will be in place, usually in the form of handbooks and personnel manuals, the acculturation process is facilitated by institutionalized procedures, rules, and guidelines. Managing the control system means careful supervision and oversight to be certain that processes and procedures are followed as intended, and managing coordination requires overseeing how information is processed and decision making occurs within organizational units and with external units. For example, in the Washington County Office on Aging, consistency and protocol requires rational managing, attention to consistent communication, and staff compliance. What are the paradoxes that emerge if an employee, manager, or unit sees other goals less related to control?

In a Social Change Organization with a market culture, Cameron and Quinn identify three different managerial competencies: *managing competitiveness, energizing employees,* and *managing customer service* (2006, p. 121). Managing competiveness is tied to an aggressive approach to making things happen, a challenging of the status quo in order to become something different and better. This type of aggressive approach in the Social Change Organization requires an energized workforce, dedicated to making change happen and led by persons who have a sense of vision. Involving consumers requires engaging them in full participation, with a special focus on including participants who are not always reached by traditional human service organizations. For example, in the Consumer-Directed Advocacy Agency, consumers participated in all aspects of the organization and worked together for structural change. What happens if an employee, manager, or unit wants less aggression and more intimacy?

In Serendipitous Organizations with a clan culture, Cameron and Quinn identify three additional competencies for managers: *managing teams, managing interpersonal relationships,* and *managing the development of others* (2006, p. 120). The inclusiveness of the clan culture demands that teams must be high functioning and cohesive, drawing in the voices and perspectives of anyone who will be touched by the agency. In addition, interpersonal relationships must be supportive and enduring so that a smooth operation can maintain a consensual (and evolving) status quo. In order to do this, communication is essential, as well as attention to the development of others so that organizational and personal growth can occur. The Orange State Child Abuse Prevention Agency provides an example of how teamwork, interpersonal relationships, and the care and nurturance of others were the practices that formed the culture of this organization. What happens in this culture when an employee or manager resists processing for consensus and just wants to be told what to do by someone in charge?

The Entrepreneurial Organization that has an adhocracy culture has other different competencies for managers: *managing innovation, managing the future,* and *managing continuous improvement* (Cameron & Quinn, 2006, p. 121). Here, there is nothing as important as facilitating innovation and pushing individuals to be creative and to generate new ideas. Managing in this type of culture requires articulating a clear vision of the future and pushing toward its achievement in an individually empowering way. Given the nature of this type of organization, the changing future context will bring unprecedented possibilities and continuous improvement; thus individuals must be flexible and poised for the unexpected. The I HELP organization is a good example of this type of managerial context, in which the word *facilitation* is probably more appropriate than any traditional views of management. What challenges do you envision as a new worker in this individualistic setting?

Given the differing roles and relationships in the four organizational types, Table 11.2 provides a summary overview, comparing each type. Keep in mind that we are discussing *ideal* types and forms of roles. The real world of practice is never so tidy. However, from this ideal we hope that the paradoxical challenges that come from the messiness will become more understandable. Being aware of different approaches to understanding roles and relationships is a beginning step to recognizing what can happen when they are mixed and matched.

Table 11.2

Comparing the Purpose of Roles and Relationships Across Four Organizational Types

Type of Relationship	Traditional Organizations	Social Change Organizations	Serendipitous Organizations	Entrepreneurial Organizations
Task Environment Relationships	To recognize that the environment is uncertain and turbulent, and to do whatever possible to control environmental forces	To recognize environmental uncertainty as an opportunity to interact with and mobilize diverse forces to benefit the organization's cause.	To try to understand the complexity of the environment and to use this understanding to set a meaningful context	To see the environment as a source of invigorating differences and unlimited subjectivities, once liberation from limits is achieved
Relationships With Funders	To obtain funding that flows from long-established and multiple sources	To obtain any funding that will support the organization's cause	To obtain any funding that will support the organization's search for knowledge, understanding, and meaning	To seek financial resources that give individuals as much control as possible
Relationships With Client Populations and Referral Sources	To fund, plan, or deliver socially acceptable programs to socially acceptable clients in need	To advocate with, rather than for, consumers and to encourage the development of programs that have full community participation	To include participants, referral sources, staff, and others in a collaborative process so that programs will be as respectful of diversity as possible	To open one's doors to individuals from all walks of life, embracing diversity
Internal Organizational Roles and Relationships: • Managing	To designate administrators and supervisors within a defined structure and to work toward consensus (agreement) so that tasks can be logically addressed; value hierarchical communication and decision making	To establish a participatory, inclusive approach to management and leadership in which dialogue and debate are freely exchanged	To establish a participatory, relationship-focused approach to management and leadership in which dialogue is freely exchanged in as collaborative and civil a manner as possible	To alternate and even share leadership roles among members in as informal a way as possible with the goal being individual transformation

348

• Communicating	To develop established protocols, such as organizational charts and information systems, so that expectations about communication are clear	To develop open communication in which the voices of clients, volunteers, and staff are equally heard, and to engage in face-to-face exchanges in which conflict is accepted as part of the dialectical process	To develop open communication in which voices of participants, volunteers, and staff are equally heard and respected, and to engage in direct exchanges in which consensus is the goal among diverse participants	To use the latest in information technology to enhance connections among people, while also honoring all methods, means, and mediums of communication
• Recognizing Staff Expectations	To hire persons who will work in the most efficient and effective manner	To hire persons who will embrace the cause and who have advocacy skills	To hire multicultural staff who respect differences, can tolerate process, and who are dedicated to self-awareness and ongoing development	To engage people in a creative process, thus seeking persons who are conscious, self-directed, committed, and comfortable with conflict and ambiguity

Leadership

It is the effective organizational leader who can quickly identify what is expected in the work environment and compare that to what is needed to meet human needs. The leader is also self-aware enough to understand what kind of stretching will be necessary personally and professionally to meet the expectations in a particular organizational context. Table 11.3 provides a comparative view of the role of the leader in human service organizations in the different paradigms.

Each role represents a personality and skill package interaction. Think about which you prefer. Then think about the other three paradigms and the characteristics within those perspectives. How do you think you could work with persons from other paradigms? Meeting persons where they are is a basic tenet of direct service, but it is also basic to organization practice in which you may have to meet entire organizational cultures or units that hold assumptions different from your own. The point of this analysis is answering the question, "Can another way of proceeding based on another perspective better serve our social work goals and values?" Our challenge to you is not to forsake who you are, but to learn to be multiparadigmatic or multicultural in your approach. Leaders are conscious of their preferences and they are able to cross boundaries to work with others who do not share their preferences. They do this in order to accomplish needed organizational goals. Multiparadigmatic practice now makes it impossible and unacceptable to say, "This is who I am. Take it or leave it."

STRENGTHS AND CHALLENGES

With each way of approaching organizations and their practices, some things are gained and others are lost. Here are just a few of the most obvious considerations.

The Traditional Organization favors the status quo and stability over the chaos and uncertainty of change, but in doing so sometimes misses opportunities to make real societal differences. Attention is generally given to the collective or average information, overlooking the individual or the unique and missing opportunities to make individual differences.

Focusing on the greatest good for the greatest number, Social Change Organizations tend to take an in-your-face approach to problem identification and solution at a class-based level. The tensions created with this approach will create *ahas* in certain segments of the population, but will be threatening or distasteful to those who do not appreciate or cannot comfortably engage in confrontation. This might lose potential collaborators and certainly might represent cultural insensitivity in certain sectors of society. While focusing on large-scale change, like the Traditional

Table 11.3

Comparing Leadership in Four Organizational Types

Traditional Leader	Social Change Leader	Serendipitous Leader	Entrepreneurial Leader
Is comfortable with clearly defined rules, procedures, and directions	Questions existing rules, procedures, and directions	Comfortable with ambiguity, uncertainty, and new and emerging ideas	Is comfortable with ambiguity, uncertainty, and new and emerging ideas
Seeks consensus among colleagues	Actively engages in conflict	Thinks hearing all perspectives is important	Thinks that hearing all perspectives is important
Sees conflict as something to be reduced	Can incite conflict when necessary	Sees the status quo and order as something worth establishing	Sees conflict as inevitable when all perspectives are heard
Truly appreciates collegiality and mutual respect for organizational goals	Is comfortable with dialectical interaction	Truly appreciates diversity	Truly appreciates and acts on diversity
Is comfortable with maintaining the status quo	Is thick skinned, able to deal with insults	Has a high tolerance for differing opinions	Has high tolerance for differing opinions
Likes concrete, measurable artifacts	Is cause or mission driven	Is predisposed toward creativity	Is predisposed toward creativity and innovation
Works toward identifying best practices, best ways of doing the work	Makes no distinction between personal and work life (sees what one does as a higher calling)	Has a strong curiosity and thinks critically	Has strong curiosity and passion for change
Likes having maximum control at work	Makes radical change as needed	Satisfied with spending time on understanding, meaning making type activities, without having to use what is learned to make broad scale change	Is not satisfied with just understanding and meaning making, but is committed to turning what is discovered into action

(Continued)

Table 11.3
(Continued)

Traditional Leader	Social Change Leader	Serendipitous Leader	Entrepreneurial Leader
Is viewed by others as "rational" under stress	Believes passionately in what one does	Willing to fully participate in organizational life	Maintains one's sense of individualism within organizational life
Tolerates process but sees outcomes as most important	Can be aggressively assertive when necessary	Enjoys people and has strong interpersonal skills	Is self-directed
Is able to separate personal from professional life, believing in the importance of clear boundaries	Is invigorated and challenged by taking on "the system"	Has the ability to play with others; is a team player	Is able to examine situations from many different directions and will argue passionately for a cause
Follows the rules	Can support cause with factual information	Desires to be a lifelong learner	Has high tolerance for process, as long as radical change is the goal
Makes incremental change as needed	Believes there are higher truths to be pursued	Has the ability to examine situations from many different directions and is willing to be persuaded to change one's mind	Sees self-transformation of individuals as a desired state
		Has a high tolerance for process and delayed closure	
		Respects people for their strengths and is open to hearing their ideas	

Organization, the Social Change Organization overlooks the unique needs and abilities of the individual in favor of mass issues and actions, potentially leaving the individual behind. Sometimes their work in overcoming oppression creates alternative forms of oppression.

The Serendipitous Organization is so engrossed in the effort to understand multiple perspectives and multiple connections in any given problem, that change efforts may be overlooked in favor of further investigation. Though deep individual meaning is addressed and collaborative efforts are encouraged, so much attention may be paid to the relational process that product may not appear in a timely fashion. When products *do* appear, statements such as "additional study is needed" usually accompany them, because almost everything is held tentatively so that whatever is discovered in the process really is not expected to apply anywhere else than in that particular context.

Finally, at the Entrepreneurial Organization, while it is helping members and service recipients to identify and overcome the powerful institutional and societal influences that serve to impede growth, its *anti* position may also serve to impede joint action with others holding other perspectives toward a common good. Narcissism rather than empowerment may be central to practice. In addition, with the rejection of traditional ways and means of organizing, nothing but personal "navel gazing" may be accomplished. The change that is spurred may be so individualistic that a sense of the community is lost and success is impossible to replicate.

We leave it to you seriously to consider the challenges that might accumulate as a result of the kinds of mixing and matching of people, programs, and organizations that are seen quite frequently in human services. What will be the result for the practitioners and the clients of having a serendipitous program mounted in a traditional, hierarchical organization? What will happen when an entrepreneur goes to work for a Social Change Organization? How can a Traditional Organization house a social change program dedicated to structural change when a funding source disagrees with its aggressiveness? What will be the clashes of expectations? What will be the challenges in mixing different standards of practice? There are so many combinations and permutations of how people, programs, and organizations might represent different paradigms that it makes the mind spin; however, be reminded that this actually represents current practice in human services.

In a prototypical world, organizations might fall within specific paradigms with distinctively defined cultures. A practitioner might have leadership characteristics associated with one paradigm, and be always consistent in behavior and attitudes. Programs would be distinctive subcultures, fitting within distinctive organizational cultures. Finding a fit between the practitioner, program, and organization would be like putting square pegs in square holes. The world would make sense in what seem a fairly boring, nondiverse, simple way.

But the world of human service practice is anything but boring and simplistic. In fact, practitioners of today cannot afford to be bound to one paradigm. People are too diverse and problems too complicated, and too much information and too many creative opportunities are available outside one paradigm. Human potential and organizational potential rests within each perspective. Risks and challenges also abound within each. Our research suggests that consciously or unconsciously, organizational practitioners recognize that there are good and useful ideas for effective practice in each approach. How we manage the inherent paradox of being in more than one set of assumptions, expectations, and ways of doing business at one time is probably the paramount challenge in postmodern organization practice.

The following section demonstrates how human service practitioners are managing this complexity. We offer this information in order to normalize the experience of paradox and extend your thinking about multiparadigmatic practice. We do so because we believe it is the role of the multiparadigmatic practitioner to unlock the potential of paradoxical practice and to manage the attendant risk through critical analysis of what will work best in each situation.

OUR HUMAN SERVICE ORGANIZATION RESEARCH

In one aspect of our research, we asked 200 field instructors about how they perceived their organizations in light of the four types described in this book. We used the characteristics identified in Table 11.1 and the roles and relationships in Table 11.2 to develop a series of randomized statements describing the various dimensions of the four prototype organizations (O'Connor, Netting, & Fabelo, forthcoming). Please see the appendix for the most recent version of the instrument.

These human service professionals overwhelmingly revealed that their agencies straddle more than one paradigm, and in fact have dimensions of all four paradigms. Because the assumptions of each paradigm are opposite to one another, to simultaneously hold views from different paradigms means living in a multidimensional paradox. Just as the Competing Values Framework (Cameron & Quinn, 2006) spells paradoxical practice in which organizations face dilemmas in which equally important (and opposite) values are held, our study supported this contention for the human service agencies we studied.

For anyone familiar with human service practice, this is not a surprising set of findings. In fact, the findings underscore what has long been known about human service organizations. For many years, persons who study organizations have recognized the ambiguity under which human service organizations perform their work (see, for example, Hasenfeld, 2000). Our study underscores the multidimensionality of this ambiguity (O'Connor, Netting, & Fabelo, forthcoming).

Top Characteristics Reflect Paradox

As a whole, leaders in the field agencies we studied saw their organizations as highly functionalist, Traditional Organizations. But they also held selected characteristics from other paradigms as equally present. For example, statements about clients from Entrepreneurial, Traditional, and Serendipitous organizations were all present. Interestingly, this placed cultures in which respondents confirmed that their organization opened "its doors to individuals from all walks of life, embracing individual diversity" (most highly ranked across all variables by all respondents) close to "This organization provides socially acceptable programs to socially acceptable clients in need." The paradox encountered by opening one's doors to all clients, juxtaposed with taking in those clients who were seen as "socially acceptable," is as intriguing as it is paradoxical. Clients from all walks of life may not always be seen as deserving or "socially acceptable" by larger communities and societies, and even funding sources. Yet, this reflected the cultures of those human service organizations that attempted to be open to wide diversity in whom they serve, even in the face of serving those clients who were viewed as "worthy" by persons with power (O'Connor, Netting, & Fabelo, forthcoming).

Statements about staff from three different paradigms or cultures were also within the most likely characteristics. The traditional characteristic focused on efficient, effective staff, whereas the social change characteristic focused on hiring cause-oriented persons with strong advocacy skills. The serendipitous statement about staffing focused on multicultural staff who respect differences, can tolerate process, and who are dedicated to self-awareness and ongoing development. As with clients, this multidimensional aspect of these agencies' cultures means that multidimensional staff are sought who are able to focus on traditional service provision, also having strong skills in changing the tradition, all the while respecting differences. Balancing efficiency and effectiveness with deep understandings of differences requires multiskilled staff who can work in highly ambiguous environments. Again, this is not a surprise to persons working in human service organizations, but our study supported the complexity of staffing and the skills necessary in these types of agencies (O'Connor, Netting, & Fabelo, forthcoming).

Two types of communication were seen as characteristic of the agencies we studied. Traditional patterns of communication complete with established protocols were joined by a serendipitous type of communication that raised the voices of all parties and sought consensus toward a goal. It is likely that the former reflects formal communication processes and that coexisting is an informal communication process as well. Thus, within the same set of organizations is the desire for established protocols, complete with organizational charts and clear relationships, while concurrently recognizing that open communication is sought in which every perspective is heard. This open interpretive communication may be the espoused culture, but one wonders whether traditional protocols might sometimes hamper consensus building. This might underscore the use of an informal communication system within these organizations and its importance, even in the face of increasing formality as reflected in the high ranking given to a traditional functionalist structure (O'Connor, Netting, & Fabelo, forthcoming).

Of the possibilities given, the most often marked of the mission/philosophy characteristics was an entrepreneurial statement: "In this organization, individuals are encouraged to use any and all sources of knowledge for their own transformation." This statement is probably the most revealing of anything we found, because it is the only mission/philosophy statement across the four paradigms that is so highly ranked. This highly transformative statement of mission/philosophy emphasizes individualism and transformative change, when other highly ranked variables such as staff, clients, structure, communication, product, policies, and funding were traditional. Paradigmatically, Traditional Organizations and Entrepreneurial Organizations are diametrically opposite to one another in the Burrell and Morgan framework. The hierarchical culture is more structured, formalized, product oriented, and traditional. The adhocracy culture leans toward antiadministration and antistructure, leaving room for radical transformation of the individual while rejecting anything that engenders discipline or control. Philosophically, these organizations may have transformative goals or mission statements, but in the carrying out of what they do on a daily basis it appears that they may not be transformative at all. Rather they are heavily rule governed, hierarchical, and bureaucratic. Perhaps it is a wish of these respondents that a transformative vision be held, even in the face of less-than-radical change. Holding onto a culture that espouses transformational change may keep the dream alive, when incremental practice is the rule in daily operations. In essence, the language of transformation may not always be enacted by the organization's practice (O'Connor, Netting, & Fabelo, forthcoming).

CULTURES APPEAR TO BE DIFFERENT

An ongoing debate on how public and private organizations are different has occurred over the years, with a growing recognition that roles are often so blurred across sectors that human service organizations are as likely to be quasi-public or quasi-nongovernmental as they are to be ideal types. We are not going to debate those issues here. However, our study did reveal that as a group, public agencies significantly differed from private (both nonprofit and for-profit agencies) in how respondents viewed their cultures. Both types of cultures were multidimensional, reflecting dimensions of multiple paradigms, but they differed in their tendencies (O'Connor, Netting, & Fabelo, forthcoming).

When we examined responses from public and private agencies, there were significant differences. Of particular importance is that these agencies are more likely to be different in paradigms that are seen as alternative to Traditional Organizations (Serendipitous, Entrepreneurial, and Social Change). Private sector agencies often claim to be "alternative" to Traditional Organizations, and public agencies are often portrayed as more functionalist in their cultures. Therefore, it was not surprising to see that they differ significantly in how they view themselves. The primary consideration here was that both sets of organizations were multidimensional, but they were multidimensional in different emphases. Being a part of a public agency did not necessarily mean that one lived in less paradox. It was just a *different* paradox from that of a private agency. Multidimensional practice was across the board; but its complexion (at least in these field agencies) differed (O'Connor, Netting, & Fabelo, forthcoming).

In this study, younger agencies tended to be more alternative in their cultures than older agencies. The dimensions on which they significantly varied were very much in line with the thinking that newer agencies were founded to meet unmet needs and reflect a more alternative approach to how they view the world. Because these are the dimensions on which younger agencies vary from older ones the most, taken together they formed an incredibly interesting story. They were interpretive in how they set their goals, chose their clients, managed their operations, defined problems, and developed their policies. Their focus was on differences, participation, free exchange, diversity, interaction, harmony, and transformation. From both radical humanist and radical structuralist perspectives, change is so much a part of these younger agencies that it defines their culture, as opposed to more established organizations. Radical dimensions included not only their mission and goals, but their structure, programs, policies, leadership, and even whom they targeted for funding. Change was the basic theme that ran throughout these significant differences (O'Connor, Netting, & Fabelo, forthcoming).

One might ask if the older agencies in our study were once like these younger agencies, embracing alternative culture and change. Obviously, we do not know, given this onetime snapshot of field agencies as they currently exist. However, the question begs for future research that examines agencies from a longitudinal perspective. As they mature, do these younger alternative agencies morph into more Traditional Organizations in the next generation, becoming more functionalist in their multidimensionality? This appears to be what Cameron and Quinn witnessed in their studies of for-profit organizations. From our data, this is impossible to tell, but what we do know from these data is that younger agencies were decidedly different in their alternative dimensions than were older, more established organizations in this sample (O'Connor, Netting, & Fabelo, forthcoming). We are currently involved in research with human service agencies that are more than 100 years old. It is our hope that our work uncovering their history will also allow us to trace changes in assumptions, goals, and expectations over time.

A MORE RECENT USE OF THE ORGANIZATION ASSESSMENT INSTRUMENT

Based on the intriguing findings from field agencies, recently a more focused project allowed us to compare the current perspectives of a 100+-year-old nonprofit agency with a public social service agency with about a 75-year history. In this case, the idea was to look at management and employee perspectives from three standpoints: views of the ideal organization, the work unit in which most time was spent, and the overall organization. Of interest first was whether the multiparadigmatic and, thus, paradoxical approach to organizing was present. Second was whether there were significant differences between an older nonprofit and an older public agency. Finally, we were interested in the differences between the units of analysis, as well as what differences there might be between employees who were highly satisfied with their work environment and those who were not.

Again, the findings indicate distribution across the paradigms; that distribution includes participants' ideal vision of organization, their work units, and their organization.[2] This represents a paradoxical profile, where the ideal profile almost always is greater than that of the unit or organization. Our findings suggest that participants in their ideal are even more interested in paradoxical practice. Figure 11.6 gives an overall distribution across the paradigms by the units of analysis.

When looking at the profiles in relationship to overall participant satisfaction with their work environment, it appears that as organizational satisfaction decreases, the unit and the organizational profiles move farther from the ideal. In addition, we found evidence of the buffering potential of the work unit (Thompson, 1967). As overall satisfaction decreases, the location of the unit and organization profiles change, moving the organizational profile further from the ideal. The unit, then, becomes closer to the ideal. However, as unit satisfaction decreases, the location of the unit profile changes. In these cases, the organization appears to be the buffering agent between the unit and the ideal.

---

2. We are grateful to Humberto Fabelo and Abigail Wyche who have joined us in the development and testing of the instrument.

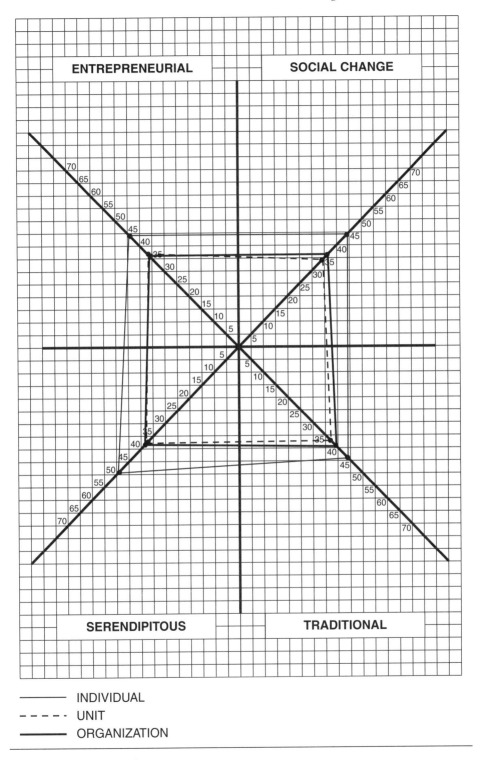

Figure 11.6 Overall Distribution by Units of Analysis.

Though there were differences between the unit and organizational perspectives among the administrators participating in this project, there were no statistical differences between their ideal organizational distributions among the perspectives, and there was statistical significance between their ideals and the most dissatisfied participants. This suggests that the instrument can be useful not only as an overall assessment tool, but also as a planning tool. In Figure 11.7, one administrator's profiles are provided.

Notice the difference between this and the distribution of the overall findings. This administrator finds the organization and the unit much more traditional than the ideal. It is clear, however, that the work unit is also acting as a buffer between the organization and the ideal. This administrator sees the ideal organization as both more serendipitous and more geared to social change. By knowing this positioning in relationship to both the workers who are currently satisfied and those who are not, this administrator is able to identify the areas in which there may be resistance to change as a move is made from more traditional goals to those that are more geared to collaboration and social change.

In the situation where the instrument was used as a planning tool, all managers completed the questionnaire (attached as Appendix: Organization Assessment). Their results were graphed and compared with that of the administrator. Where there were major differences, the management team discussed those differences in preparation for moving in the direction of desired change. The differences in their personal ideals about the organization (the only unit of analysis where major differences existed among team members) served as a basis for clarification of differences and for understanding when those differences might serve as barriers to the change process. The tool helped them not only to understand the paradoxical nature of their practice within their organization, but also to preview where some of the bumps might emerge as the organization's culture, structure, and practice norms were changed.

PRACTICE IMPLICATIONS

The Burrell and Morgan framework is a conceptual contribution, but when it appeared it had not been empirically tested (Burrell, 1996). Subsequently, our work revealed that the agencies sampled do not fit within one particular paradigm or worldview, but hold competing assumptions simultaneously. Rather than identifying agencies with predispositions for congruent cultures, we were able to document opposing worldviews being held simultaneously (O'Connor, Netting, & Fabelo, forthcoming). This reinforced what Cameron and Quinn found in testing their Competing Values Framework. Burrell and Morgan indicate that this creates paradox, as do Cameron and Quinn. Our empirical work may help explain why

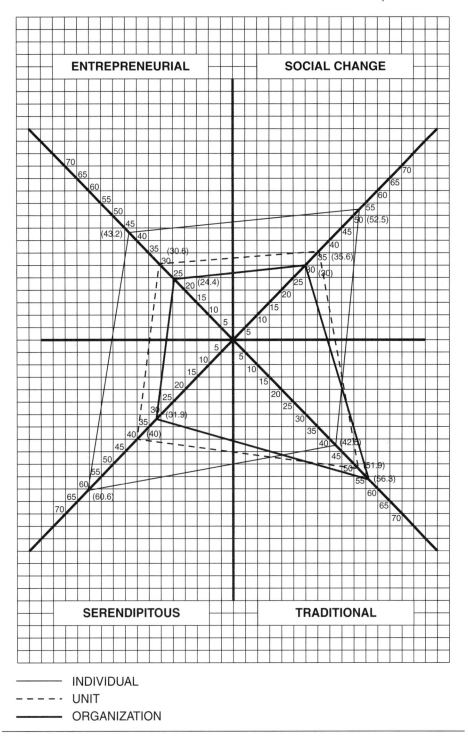

Figure 11.7 Example of Plotted Results of One Participant's Organizational Assessment.

there are so many seemingly unexplained discontinuities in practice settings.

Our findings are consistent with those of other researchers (Cameron & Quinn, 2006; Jaskyte & Dressler, 2005) who contend that organizational culture is not always congruent. Although other researchers have not used the Burrell and Morgan framework, our findings indicate that the Organization Assessment tool, based on their framework, is useful in assessing cultural assumptions and identifying incongruence. The mapping of survey results appears to provide a particularly transparent manner of demonstrating these. The tool we have developed is included in the appendix to this volume along with a score sheet and instructions on how to plot the scores. The tool is intended to be used in assessing units or programs within organizations as well as the organization itself. It can also be helpful as a planning tool.

We offer the tool to human services management and leadership in order to identify the basis of differences among employees, thus increasing understanding of why competing assumptions in different areas of the organization result in paradoxical situations. In addition, being able to plot an organization's fit within the Burrell and Morgan framework allows employees within an organization to see just how much their organization may straddle the various views of the standards for structure and practice within organizations. Having a graphical representation of an organization's fit within the framework also has the potential to create an *aha* experience for students in field placements and employees who are aware that they are working in paradox, but have not been able to see the big picture of just what the resulting ambiguity is all about. For example, an organization that is predominately in a Functionalist Paradigm may find itself generally aligned with traditional funding sources, but the rub comes when they advocate for social change. Seeing just how much the organization straddles the line between being a Traditional Organization and a Social Change Organization may provide clues as to how much tension employees are encountering.

The tool can also be useful in overall organizational assessment, especially if all stakeholders within the same organization complete the assessment. Averages of their ratings and mapping could reflect their pooled vision of what characterizes the organization. Individual perspectives and mapping would also be informative. In large organizations, with subcultures that may reflect different paradigmatic assumptions, the tool could be useful as a mechanism for making different perspectives visible. A program unit nested within a larger organization may have to work under different assumptions than its host. This could be the case when social workers are hosted in a large health-care system or public agency. Being able to identify and assess paradoxes encountered through the use of this survey instrument could provide the impetus for communication about what could now be understood as clashes in worldviews rather than incompetence or resistance. This reframing of difficulties along any of the dimensions identified in the instrument may lead to more respectful and innovative ways to address them.

Paradoxes and discontinuities are ever-present aspects of the complexities of social work practice. Recognizing that human service agencies represent different emphases, yet all are functioning multidimensionally, may somewhat normalize the ambiguity faced in human service practice. This may help educators prepare their students for practice in agencies where these challenges are the norm. In addition, knowing how an organization is perceived by others may be helpful in recognizing some of the inherent paradoxes faced, rather than individuals assuming that there is a logically coherent culture that they just do not understand. This multiparadigmatic tool is intended to aid the professional in understanding personal preferences or ideals in combination with work unit expectations set in the context of organizational norms. Being able to establish what dimensions are dominant within an organization should allow the professional to assess his or her fit within that organization and how to approach change within respective cultures.

We offer our tool, based on an integration of the material in this text, as a beginning step toward recognizing the existence of multiparadigmatic practice and the paradoxes that are created. We think it is in the paradox caused by crossing the borders into other paradigms that there is hope. Our hope comes from the potential of joining the forces of difference to confront what until now have appeared to be intractable social problems at the local, national, and international levels.

CONCLUSION

We wish you well as you begin your great adventure into leadership in organizational practice. We hope that this book has given you some resources to construct a career of taking advantage of opportunities, recognizing risks, and embracing the advantages of difference. Have the courage to take your place and think differently about how to organize human service activities. Explore the possibilities of new designs and arrangements, but don't forget to continue to examine your beliefs, because it is at the belief level that true change originates. Enjoy a lively adventure!

Organization Assessment

I N THE NEXT several pages is an assessment tool that is intended to serve as a framework for the analysis of various important dimensions of organizational life. Conceptually it is closely related to the ideas contained in this text. The tool continues to be in a developmental stage, so the psychometric properties are unavailable for those hoping to administer the tool as part of rigorous research efforts. Instead it is offered as yet another framework to help the practitioner to make sense of their own (and others') positions in organizational life.

What follows is a three part tool that looks at one's personal ideal about what an organization should be; an assessment of one's work unit; and an assessment of the overall organizational context. Included is a score sheet for each section and a grid that allows the plotting of all three perspectives.

Organization Assessment

DIRECTIONS

The following series of questions look at your perceptions of the organization in which you work. You will be asked to answer the questions from three perspectives: 1) your view of the ideal organization; 2) your view of the work unit in which you spend the most time; and 3) the overall organization in which you are employed.

Place scores on the score sheet for the number listed in each blank on the questionnaire. Add the scores in each section for each paradigm. Then plot the scores to see what type organization is dominant.

(Continued)

---

1. PERSONAL PERSPECTIVE

With regard to your ideal notions of how an organization should be, please indicate the extent to which you agree or disagree with each of the following statements by placing the appropriate number beside each statement. Please answer all questions to the best of your ability according to the 7 point scale below.

1	2	3	4	5	6	7
None of the Time	Very Rarely	A Little of the Time	Some of the Time	A Good Part of the Time	Most of the Time	All of the Time

1. _____ In an organization, inclusion should be valued, so that both non-dominant and dominant opinions, doctrines and practices are all accepted.

2. _____ An organization should seek open communication in which the voices of clients, volunteers and staff are equally heard and respected, and in which consensus among diverse perspectives is the goal.

3. _____ In an organization, it should be important to hire persons who will embrace the organization's cause and who have strong advocacy skills.

4. _____ An organization should open its' doors to individuals from all walks of life, embracing individual diversity.

5. _____ An organization should seek open communication in which the voices of clients, volunteers and staff are equally heard, and in which conflict is acceptable, as long as it moves participants toward collective change.

6. _____ An organization should view environmental uncertainty as an opportunity to interact with and mobilize diverse forces to benefit the organization's cause.

7. _____ In an organization, there should be a well established structure, in which clear relationships between organizational members and among units are specified.

8. _____ An organization should have well established protocols such as organizational charts and information systems designed to clearly communicate expectations.

9. _____ An organization should advocate with, rather than for, consumers and develop programs that have full community participation.

10. _____ In an organization, there should be a participatory, relationship-focused approach to management and leadership in which dialogue is freely exchanged in as collaborative and civil a manner as possible.

11. _____ An organization should provide socially acceptable programs to socially acceptable clients in need.

12. _____ In an organization, advocacy-based programs and services should be designed to change oppressive structures and to empower groups of people.

13. _____ An organization should target funding sources that will support the organization's search for knowledge, understanding, and meaning.

14. _____ An organization should view the environment as uncertain and try to control it.

15. _____ In an organization, individuals should be encouraged to use any and all sources of knowledge for their own transformation.

16. _____ An organization should target multiple and well-established funding sources.

17. _____ Structure in an organization should change to whatever is necessary in order to facilitate large scale change.

18. _____ In an organization, any and all sources of knowledge should be used to enhance awareness, provide meaningful information and recognize complexity at all levels of society.

19. _____ An organization should seek liberation from boundaries that limit its' relationship with the larger environment, welcoming diverse thinking that will move its members toward individual transformation.

20. _____ In an organization, there should be a participatory, inclusive approach to management and leadership in which disagreements are freely aired.

21. _____ An organization should target funding sources that support cause-oriented advocacy efforts.

22. _____ In an organization, members should alternate and even share leadership in as informal a way as possible with the goal being individual transformation rather than collective agreement.

23. _____ Minimal structure should occur within an organization and should even be discouraged so that individuals can do what they need to do in order to be as independent as possible.

24. _____ In an organization all methods, means and mediums of communication should be acceptable in pushing individuals toward self transformation.

25. _____ Non-dominant opinions, doctrines, and practices should be valued in an organization.

26. _____ In an organization, it should be important to hire persons who are creative, self directed, and individualistic.

27. _____ In an organization, programs and services should be intended to create opportunities for people to grow and transform as individuals.

28. _____ An organization should respect diversity and include clients, referral sources, staff and others in a collaborative process.

29. _____ In an organization, it should be important to hire persons who will work in the most efficient and effective manner.

30. _____ Dominant opinions, doctrines, and practices should be valued in an organization.

31. _____ In an organization, it should be important to hire multicultural staff who respect differences, can tolerate process, and who are dedicated to self awareness and ongoing development.

32. _____ An organization should try to understand the meaningful context of the environment.

33. _____ Inspiring ultimate self determination and uniqueness should be valued in an organization.

34. _____ In an organization, programs and services should use education and consciousness-raising to assist participants in understanding and making sense out of complex situations.

35. _____ In an organization, structure should be allowed to emerge so that the learning process is best facilitated, using less bureaucratic, flatter structures whenever possible to facilitate a network of relationships.

36. _____ Programs and services within an organization should use incremental or gradual change to alter people's status so that they can function best within society.

(Continued)

37. _____ In an organization, the best knowledge available should be used to maintain the status quo.
38. _____ In an organization, the best knowledge available should be used so that social change and reform can be used to push toward the common good.
39. _____ An organization should target funding sources that encourage individual liberation and transformation.
40. _____ In an organization, administrators and supervisors should work within a defined and ordered structure so that tasks can be logically completed.

2. WORK UNIT PERSPECTIVE

From the perspective of your assigned work unit, please indicate the extent to which you agree or disagree with each of the following statements by placing the appropriate number beside each statement. Please answer all questions to the best of your ability according to the 7 point scale below.

1	2	3	4	5	6	7
None of the Time	Very Rarely	A Little of the Time	Some of the Time	A Good Part of the Time	Most of the Time	All of the Time

41. _____ This work unit values including everyone's perspective. All opinions, doctrines and practices, whether popular or unpopular, are accepted.
42. _____ This work unit seeks open communication in which the voices of clients, volunteers and staff are equally heard and respected. Reaching a consensus among diverse perspectives is the goal.
43. _____ In this work unit, it is important to hire persons who will embrace the organization's cause and who have strong advocacy skills.
44. _____ This work unit open its' doors to individuals from all walks of life, embracing individual diversity.
45. _____ This work unit seeks open communication in which the voices of clients, volunteers and staff are equally heard. Here, conflict is acceptable as long as it moves participants toward group change.
46. _____ This work unit views uncertainty in the community environment as an opportunity to interact with and mobilize diverse forces to benefit the organization's cause.
47. _____ In this work unit, there is a well established structure, in which the relationships between organizational members and among units are clearly defined.
48. _____ This work unit has well established protocols such as organizational charts and information systems designed to clearly communicate expectations.
49. _____ This work unit advocates with, rather than for, consumers and develop programs that have full community participation.
50. _____ In this work unit, the manager builds relationships with everyone and encourages them to participate in decision-making, by holding free and open conversations with all unit members.
51. _____ This work unit provides socially acceptable programs to socially acceptable clients in need.

52. _____ In this work unit, advocacy-based programs and services are designed to change oppressive institutions and to empower groups of people.

53. _____ This work unit targets funding sources that will support the organization's search for knowledge, understanding, and meaning.

54. _____ This work unit views the community environment as uncertain and tries to control it.

55. _____ In this work unit, individuals are encouraged to use any and all sources of knowledge for their own transformation.

56. _____ This work unit targets multiple and well-established funding sources.

57. _____ Structure in this work unit is likely to change to whatever is necessary in order to facilitate large scale change.

58. _____ In this work unit, any and all sources of knowledge and information are used to do the work., so that enhance awareness, provide meaningful information and recognize complexity at all levels of society.

59. _____ This work unit seeks to eliminate boundaries that limit its relationship to the community environment, welcoming diverse thinking that will move its members toward individual transformation.

60. _____ In this work unit, there is a participatory, inclusive approach to management and leadership in which disagreements are freely aired.

61. _____ This work unit targets funding sources that support cause-oriented advocacy efforts.

62. _____ In this work unit, members alternate and even share leadership in as informal a way as possible with the goal being individual transformation rather than collective agreement.

63. _____ Minimal structure occurs within this work unit, or structure is even discouraged, so that individuals can be as independent as possible.

64. _____ In this work unit all methods, means and mediums of communication are acceptable in pushing individuals toward self transformation.

65. _____ Unpopular opinions, doctrines, and practices are valued in this work unit.

66. _____ In this work unit, it is important to hire persons who are creative, self directed, and individualistic.

67. _____ In this work unit, programs and services are intended to create opportunities for people to grow and transform as individuals.

68. _____ This work unit respects diversity and include clients, referral sources, staff and others in a collaborative process.

69. _____ In this work unit, it is important to hire persons who will work in the most efficient and effective manner.

70. _____ Only dominant opinions, doctrines, and practices are valued in this work unit.

71. _____ In this work unit, it is important to hire multicultural staff who respect differences, can tolerate it when staff need to process, and who are dedicated to self awareness and ongoing development.

72. _____ This work unit tries to understand the meaningfulness of its community environment.

73. _____ Inspiring ultimate self determination and uniqueness is valued in this work unit.

(Continued)

74. _____ In this work unit, programs and services use education and consciousness-raising to assist participants in understanding and making sense out of complex situations.

75. _____ In this work unit, structure is allowed to emerge so that the learning process is best facilitated, using less bureaucratic structures whenever possible to facilitate a network of relationships.

76. _____ Programs and services within this work unit use gradual change strategies with clients so that they can function best within society.

77. _____ In this work unit, the best knowledge available is used to maintain the status quo.

78. _____ In this work unit, the best knowledge available is used so that social change and reform can be used to push toward the common good.

79. _____ This work unit targets funding sources that encourage individual liberation and transformation.

80. _____ In this work unit, administrators and supervisors work within a defined and ordered structure so that tasks can be logically completed.

3. ORGANIZATIONAL PERSPECTIVE

From the perspective of the overall organization, please indicate the extent to which you agree or disagree with each of the following statements by placing the appropriate number beside each statement. Please answer all questions to the best of your ability according to the 7 point scale below.

1	2	3	4	5	6	7
None of the Time	Very Rarely	A Little of the Time	Some of the Time	A Good Part of the Time	Most of the Time	All of the Time

81. _____ In this organization, inclusion is valued, so that both non-dominant and dominant opinions, doctrines and practices are all accepted.

82. _____ This organization seeks open communication in which the voices of clients, volunteers and staff are equally heard and respected, and in which consensus among diverse perspectives is the goal.

83. _____ In this organization, it is important to hire persons who will embrace the organization's cause and who have strong advocacy skills.

84. _____ This organization open its' doors to individuals from all walks of life, embracing individual diversity.

85. _____ This organization seeks open communication in which the voices of clients, volunteers and staff are equally heard, and in which conflict is acceptable, as long as it moves participants toward collective change.

86. _____ This organization views environmental uncertainty as an opportunity to interact with and mobilize diverse forces to benefit the organization's cause.

87. _____ In this organization, there is a well established structure, in which clear relationships between organizational members and among units are specified.

88. _____ This organization has well established protocols such as organizational charts and information systems designed to clearly communicate expectations.

89. _____ This organization advocates with, rather than for, consumers and develop programs that have full community participation.

90. _____ In this organization, there is a participatory, relationship-focused approach to management and leadership in which dialogue is freely exchanged in as collaborative and civil a manner as possible.

91. _____ This organization provides socially acceptable programs to socially acceptable clients in need.

92. _____ In this organization, advocacy-based programs and services are designed to change oppressive structures and to empower groups of people.

93. _____ This organization targets funding sources that will support the organization's search for knowledge, understanding, and meaning.

94. _____ This organization views the environment as uncertain and tries to control it.

95. _____ In this organization, individuals are encouraged to use any and all sources of knowledge for their own transformation.

96. _____ This organization targets multiple and well-established funding sources.

97. _____ Structure in this organization changes to whatever is necessary in order to facilitate large scale change.

98. _____ In this organization, any and all sources of knowledge are used to enhance awareness, provide meaningful information and recognize complexity at all levels of society.

99. _____ This organization seeks liberation from boundaries that limit its relationship with the larger environment, welcoming diverse thinking that will move its members toward individual transformation.

100. _____ In this organization, there is a participatory, inclusive approach to management and leadership in which disagreements are freely aired.

101. _____ This organization targets funding sources that support cause-oriented advocacy efforts.

102. _____ In this organization, members alternate and even share leadership in as informal a way as possible with the goal being individual transformation rather than collective agreement.

103. _____ Minimal structure occurs within this organization and is even discouraged so that individuals can do what they need to do in order to be as independent as possible.

104. _____ In this organization all methods, means and mediums of communication are acceptable in pushing individuals toward self transformation.

105. _____ Non-dominant opinions, doctrines, and practices are valued in this organization.

106. _____ In this organization, it is important to hire persons who are creative, self directed, and individualistic.

107. _____ In this organization, programs and services are intended to create opportunities for people to grow and transform as individuals.

108. _____ This organization respects diversity and include clients, referral sources, staff and others in a collaborative process.

109. _____ In this organization, it is important to hire persons who will work in the most efficient and effective manner.

110. _____ Dominant opinions, doctrines, and practices are valued in this organization.

111. _____ In this organization, it is important to hire multicultural staff who respect differences, can tolerate process, and who are dedicated to self awareness and ongoing development.

(Continued)

112. _____ This organization tries to understand the meaningful context of the environment.
113. _____ Inspiring ultimate self determination and uniqueness is valued in this organization.
114. _____ In this organization, programs and services use education and consciousness-raising to assist participants in understanding and making sense out of complex situations.
115. _____ In this organization, structure is allowed to emerge so that the learning process is best facilitated, using less bureaucratic, flatter structures whenever possible to facilitate a network of relationships.
116. _____ Programs and services within this organization use incremental or gradual change to alter people's status so that they can function best within society.
117. _____ In this organization, the best knowledge available is used to maintain the status quo.
118. _____ In this organization, the best knowledge available is used so that social change and reform can be used to push toward the common good.
119. _____ This organization targets funding sources that encourage individual liberation and transformation.
120. _____ In this organization, administrators and supervisors work within a defined and ordered structure so that tasks can be logically completed.

Organization Assessment Score Sheet

PERSONAL PERSPECTIVE

Scores

Traditional Organization	Social Change Organization	Serendipitous Organization	Entrepreneurial Organization
7. ___	3. ___	1. ___	4. ___
8. ___	5. ___	2. ___	15. ___
11. ___	6. ___	10. ___	19. ___
14. ___	9. ___	13. ___	22. ___
16. ___	12. ___	18. ___	23. ___
29. ___	17. ___	28. ___	24. ___
30. ___	20. ___	31. ___	26. ___
36. ___	21. ___	32. ___	27. ___
37. ___	25. ___	34. ___	33. ___
40. ___	38. ___	35. ___	39. ___
T ___ Total	SC ___ Total	S ___ Total	E ___ Total

WORK UNIT PERSPECTIVE

Scores

Traditional Organization	Social Change Organization	Serendipitous Organization	Entrepreneurial Organization
47. ___	43. ___	41. ___	44. ___
48. ___	45. ___	42. ___	55. ___
51. ___	46. ___	50. ___	59. ___
54. ___	49. ___	53. ___	62. ___
56. ___	52. ___	58. ___	63. ___
69. ___	57. ___	68. ___	64. ___
70. ___	60. ___	71. ___	66. ___
76. ___	61. ___	72. ___	67. ___
77. ___	65. ___	74. ___	73. ___
80. ___	78. ___	75. ___	79. ___
T ___ Total	SC ___ Total	S ___ Total	E ___ Total

ORGANIZATIONAL PERSPECTIVE

Score

Traditional Organization	Social Change Organization	Serendipitous Organization	Entrepreneurial Organization
87. ___	83. ___	81. ___	84. ___
88. ___	85. ___	82. ___	95. ___
91. ___	86. ___	90. ___	99. ___
94. ___	89. ___	93. ___	102. ___
96. ___	92. ___	98. ___	103. ___
109. ___	97. ___	108. ___	104. ___
110. ___	100. ___	111. ___	106. ___
116. ___	101. ___	112. ___	107. ___
117. ___	105. ___	114. ___	113. ___
120. ___	118. ___	115. ___	119. ___
T ___ Total	SC ___ Total	S ___ Total	E ___ Total

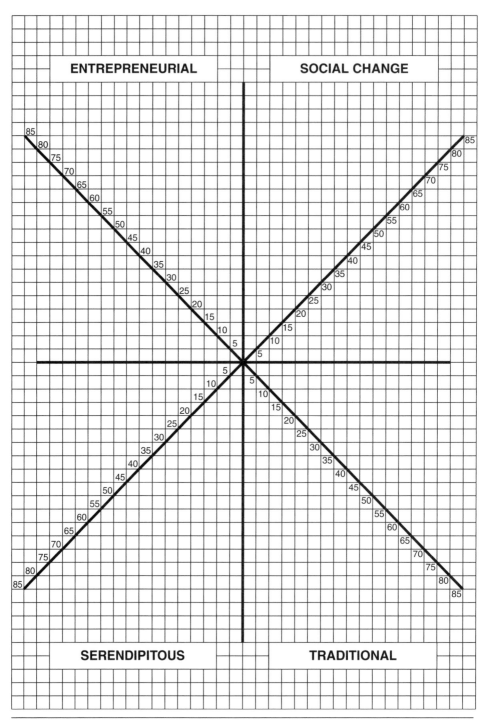

Figure A.1 Organization Assessment Graph.

Glossary

ABSOLUTISTS: Persons who believe that basic principles do not change and that there are overriding universal values that will withstand the test of time and are in fact *God given*.

ADHOCRACY CULTURE: A dynamic, entrepreneurial, and creative place to work in which people take risks in taking initiatives and in respecting individuality (Cameron & Quinn, 2006).

ADVOCACY: "The exclusive and mutual representation of a client(s) or a cause in a forum attempting to systematically influence decision making in an unjust or unresponsive system(s)" (Schneider & Lester, 2001, p. 65).

AFFILIATIONS: Formal and informal connections made by organizations with other groups that are aligned with their values or ideology. These connections add to the cultural identity of the organization and to their public visibility.

ALTERITY: The process of moving from knowing the *other* at a distance to developing a real relationship with the *other*.

ANTIPOSITIVISM: The view that knowledge about reality is soft, subjective, and natural.

ASSESSMENT: A process in which a person or group gathers information about a service, program, or organization. How wide the net is cast will depend on the purpose of the assessment. Some assessments may gather information on a single agency program, whereas others may examine an entire organization. The type of data collected and the method of collection will also depend on the reason one is undertaking an assessment.

BOUNDED RATIONALITY: A concept that recognizes that no matter how much information individuals collect, or how logical they are, they will always have to make decisions within limits.

CASE OR CLIENT ADVOCACY: Assuring that "services provided to clients are both relevant to the problem and available within the community" (Schneider & Lester, 2001, p. 152).

CAUSE ADVOCACY: "Promoting changes in policies and practices affecting all persons in a certain group or class, for example, the disabled, welfare recipients, elderly immigrants, or battered women" (Schneider & Lester, 2001, p. 196).

CLAN CULTURE: A very friendly place to work in which employees see themselves as extended family and in which teamwork, participation, and consensus are prized (Cameron & Quinn, 2006).

COLLABORATIVE PROCESS: Where "two or more persons work and play together to achieve some result or create some product in which they are jointly invested, about which they care enough to pool their strengths" (Macduff & Netting, 2000, p. 48).

COMPETING VALUES: A matrix developed by Cameron and Quinn (2006) in which opposite values intersect to demonstrate how values compete with one another in forming four differing organizational cultures.

CONSTRAINT: Something an organization cannot control, but with which the organization must contend.

CONTINGENCY: Something an organization has a chance of either changing or negotiating.

COOPTATION: Including alternative perspectives in decision-making processes in order to control opposition. The intention is to lure or persuade the opposition to join or accept the perspective.

CRITICAL THINKING: "Involves a careful appraisal of claims, a fair-minded consideration of alternative views, and a willingness to change your mind in light of evidence that refutes a cherished position" (Gibbs & Gambrill, 1996, p. 23).

CULTURAL FIT: "The degree of alignment between two or more cultural configurations" (Cox, 1994, p. 170).

DECONSTRUCTION: To take apart as a way of demonstrating just how artificial values, norms, and knowledge are. The exercise of deconstruction also reveals how the concept of rationality is socially constructed. What seems reasonable depends on the historical moment.

DENSITY DEPENDENCE: The number of organizations in the population.

DETERMINISM: The belief that reality shapes action and perception.

DIAGNOSIS: Occurs when data are understood and translated into information, so that problems and needs are labeled and analyzed.

DIVERSITY: Differences that represent fundamental and instrumental variations. Organization diversity includes elements like structure, type, affiliation, and location. Group diversity includes gender, race, nationality, sexual orientation, culture, and discipline. Individuals also reflect diversity within groups, including differences represented and covered by the Americans with Disabilities Act or the Age Discrimination Act. These multiple, and often overlapping, aspects of diversity are related to organizational behaviors and outcomes.

EMERGENCE: A process in which unexpected ideas and new information will be constantly appearing and interacting with what is already known.

EMERGENT PLANNING: Alternative approach to program planning using emergent logic. Based on assumptions of interpretive planning, consists of several predictable dimensions, the specific content of which cannot be known in advance: engagement, discovery, sense making, and unfolding (Netting, O'Connor, & Fauri, 2008).

EMIC: Proving an insider's perspective.

ENTREPRENEURIAL ORGANIZATION: A workplace that tends to be on the cutting edge of new developments and structures with people who may think and act nontraditionally.

EPISTEMOLOGY: Assumptions related to what can be known and how researchers can be expected to come to know it.

ETHNIC AGENCY: An organization affiliated with a particular ethnic group, having the following characteristics: (1) serving primarily ethnic clients; (2) predominately staffed by persons who have the same ethnicity as the clients served; (3) having a majority of its board from the ethnic group served; (4) having an ethnic community and/or ethnic power structure to support it; (5) integrating ethnic content into its programs; (6) desiring to strengthen the family as a primary goal; and (7) maintaining an ideology that promotes ethnic identity and participation in the decision-making process (Jenkins, 1980).

ETIC: Providing an outsider's perspective.

EXTROVERSION: A characteristic of personality in which one draws one's energy from association with others.

FALSE CONSCIOUSNESS: A set of values strongly held by dominant (and sometimes subordinate) interests that are believed to be in error.

FEDERATION: An umbrella organization under which a number of agencies join together. Federations hold some centralized power, with the central unit making resource and other decisions for its members.

FEELING: A personality characteristic in which one prefers to make decisions by trusting one's emotions rather than one's cognitions.

FEMINIST ORGANIZATION: Agencies defined as meeting "any of the following criteria: (a) has a feminist ideology; (b) has feminist guiding values; (c) has feminist goals; (d) produces feminist outcomes; (e) was founded during the women's movement as part of the women's movement (including one or more of its submovements, e.g., the feminist self-help health movement [or] the violence against women movement)" (Martin, 1990, p. 815).

FLEXIBILITY AND DISCRETION: A value proposed by Cameron and Quinn (2006) in their Competing Values Framework that is the opposite of stability and control, which sits at the other end of the continuum.

FOR-PROFIT AGENCIES: Businesses that are part of the commercial or market economy. They pay taxes, have boards of directors who generally are compensated, and may have investors or stockholders who can benefit financially from the organization's profits.

FRAMEWORK: A supporting and flexible structure that guides conceptual thinking and allows the user to manage complex information; a type of heuristic.

FRANCHISE: Organizations that conform to a particular approach to doing business with permission from a national or regional group. Although nonprofit agencies might not think of themselves as franchises, there are numerous long-established exemplars, including Goodwill Industries, Planned Parenthood, Prevent Child Abuse America, and the Alzheimer's Association.

FUNCTIONALIST PARADIGM: A perspective that assumes the social world is composed of relatively concrete empirical artifacts and relationships that can be identified, studied, and measured through approaches derived from the natural sciences.

GANTT CHART: Bar graphs illustrating who is supposed to do what task at what time. Originally developed during World War I by H. L. Gantt to track ammunition.

GENERAL ENVIRONMENT: Organizations, groups, and individuals in a larger environment with which the organization does not have a direct relationship.

GLASS CEILING: When the upper reaches of an organization are visible, but not attainable.

GRASSROOTS ASSOCIATIONS (GAs): One type of voluntary association that is focused on the local community. Smith defines GAs as "locally based, significantly autonomous, volunteer-run, formal nonprofit groups that manifest significant voluntary altruism as a group; they use the associational form of organization and thus have an official membership of volunteers who perform all or nearly all of the work done in and by the nonprofits" (1999, p. 443).

HIERARCHY CULTURE: A very traditional, formal work setting in which formal rules and policies provide direction and control for employees (Cameron & Quinn, 2006).

HOMEOSTASIS: In systems theory, a state of balance in which every part is working together and is integrating with the whole.

HOST ORGANIZATIONS: Large agencies that deliver human services or employ human service workers as part of what they do, but whose primary purpose is not the delivery of human services.

HEURISTICS: A framework that allows for a reduction of information in order to process meaning.

IDIOGRAPHIC: Descriptions or interpretations that are unique to the individual, which capture what is individually distinctive.

INTERORGANIZATIONAL RELATIONSHIPS: Those situations in which more than one organization works in some way with others, thus cutting across formal organizational boundaries.

INTERPRETIVE PARADIGM: A perspective informed by a concern to understand the world as it is at the level of subjective experience, within the realm of individual consciousness and subjectivity, and from the frame of reference of the participant, as opposed to the observer of action. It sees the social world as an emergent social process that is created by the individuals concerned. Reality is little more than a network of assumptions and intersubjectively shared meanings that hold only as meaning is shared.

INTERVENTION: Action taken to change an organization or an organizational unit. Individuals, groups, and communities can also be the change target.

INTERVENTIONIST: Controlling.

INTROVERSION: A personality characteristic in which one draws one's energy from internal reflection.

INTUITION: A personality characteristic in which one prefers to take in information by seeing patterns and trusting inspiration (focusing inward).

JUDGING: A personality characteristic that appreciates order and sticking to a plan, trying to avoid the stresses of sudden or rapid change.

LEADERSHIP: An attitude about responsibilities in an organization based on professional skills and a set of values that compel an individual to act. Leadership may come from any organizational member, regardless of the formal authority and power structure in that organization.

LEARNING ORGANIZATION: An organizational environment where people are continually discovering how they create their reality and how they can change it (Senge, 1990, p 13).

MARKET CULTURE: A results-oriented, competitive setting in which the major concern is getting the job done and being productive (Cameron & Quinn, 2006).

MANAGING DIVERSITY: Planning and implementing organizational systems and practices to manage people so that the potential advantages of diversity are maximized while minimizing its potential disadvantages.

MECHANISTIC ORGANIZATIONS: Organizations that are highly traditional in terms of hierarchy, formal rules and regulations, communication, and decision making. This type of organization is particularly useful in producing inanimate products (Burns & Stalker, 1961).

METAPHORS: Using one element of experience to explain another. An example would be comparing organizations to machines.

MINORITY PRACTICE: "The art and science of developing a helping relationship with an individual, family, group, and/or community whose distinctive physical or cultural characteristics and discriminatory experiences require approaches that are sensitive to ethnic or cultural environments" (Lum, 1992, p. 6).

MORPHOGENESIS: A change in structure.

MORPHOSTASIS: Structure maintaining.

MULTICULTURAL ORGANIZATION: Agencies in which the majority of organizational participants hold distinctly different group affiliations of cultural significance. Multicultural organizations can be diverse in four ways: in the clients they serve, the staff and volunteers they use, their own corporate culture and subcultures, and how they vary from other agencies.

MULTIPARADIGMATIC PRACTICE: Being able to identify assumptions-in-use within an organization and then use one's critical thinking and practice skills to move in and out of different ways of thinking (paradigms).

NEW LEADERSHIP APPROACH: Leaders are viewed as creators of vision, culture, and strategy. They are often called *transformational* or *transactional* leaders.

NOMINALISM: The belief that human reality exists within the mind.

NOMOTHETIC: The view that natural science methods can be applied to the study and understanding of social reality.

NONGOVERNMENTAL ORGANIZATION (NGO): An organization typically formed at the grassroots level to address a community need; not mandated by government.

NONPROFIT ORGANIZATIONS: Agencies referred to as *nongovernmental, third sector, voluntary, charitable,* or *tax exempt.* They have uncompensated, voluntary boards of directors who cannot benefit financially from the organization's profits. Any profit made must be reinvested in the organization. Nonprofit voluntary agencies are more bureaucratically structured than voluntary associations and are "governed by an elected board of directors, employing professional or volunteer staff to provide continuing social service to a continuing clientele in the community" (Kramer, 1981, p. 9).

OBJECTIVIST PERSPECTIVE: The view that people are shaped by reality as products of their environment and that knowledge is hard and concrete.

ONTOLOGY: Perspective on the nature of reality. Is it above and beyond individual knowledge or is it based on individual consciousness without regard to the outside world.

ORGANIC ORGANIZATIONS: Organizations that function in highly changeable environments, requiring staff who can make decisions quickly in adapting to change (Burns & Stalker, 1961).

ORGANIZATION: "Social unit[s] with some particular purpose" (Shafritz, Ott, & Lang, 2005, p. 1).

ORGANIZATION PRACTICE: Working and surviving in organizational arenas and making changes that address the needs of multiple stakeholders and constituencies reflecting a strong grounding in professional values, critical thinking, and self-awareness.

ORGANIZATIONAL CULTURE: "A pattern of shared basic assumptions that the group learned as it solved its problems of external adaptation and internal integration, that has worked well enough to be considered valid and, therefore, to be taught to new members as the correct way to perceive, think, an feel in relation to those problems" (Schein, 1992, p. 12).

ORGANIZATIONAL OUTFLANKING: A process used by those in dominance to gain consent and subordination of organizational members; can be seen as a type of cooptation.

ORGANIZATIONAL TRANSFORMATION: Implies a "profound reformulation of not only the organization's mission, structure, and management, but also fundamental changes in the basic social, political, and cultural aspects of the organization" (Leifer, 1989, p. 900).

ORGANIZED ANARCHIES: Describes the confused power present in large organizations (such as universities) based on ambiguity of power, purpose, experience, and what constitutes success; differing from Entrepreneurial Organizations in structure and intent.

PARADIGM: The general organizing principles governing perceptions, including beliefs, values, and techniques that describe what exists, where to look, and what the person can expect to discover (Ritzer, 1980).

PARADOX: Created in an organization when it is attempting to work from two very different sets of assumptions that contradict one another; holding seemingly contradictory perspectives, opinions, and interpretations, or two different things as true at the same time.

PERCEIVING: A personality characteristic in which a person thrives on spontaneity and feels energized when pressures mount.

PERCEIVED NEEDS: Those needs that have not yet come to the attention of service providers, but that are identified by persons in need. They remain invisible and ignored in the planning of services.

PLANNED CHANGE: A process of deliberately identifying a problem and, using linear logic, analyzing its causes, carefully determining a strategy to alter the situation according to predetermined outcomes.

PLANNING: Preparing to resolve problems and address organizational needs. Can be rational or interpretive, using prescriptive or emergent approaches.

POPULATION DYNAMICS: Reflects the idea that as new organizations are founded, resources are often more difficult to obtain since these sets of organizations typically depend on (and compete for) similar funding sources.

POSITIVISM: The assumption that knowledge about social reality is hard and concrete.

POWER: The ability to get things done by influencing others.

PRACTICE ARENAS: Communities, organizations, and small task groups in which and through which human services are planned and delivered.

PRESCRIPTIVE: Describing what strategies and tactics to use in advance, with the assumption that there is a best way to approach the situation.

PRIVATE AGENCIES: A broad category of organizations, including those that are called *nonprofit* and *for-profit*.

PROGRAMS: Structural containers for long-term commitments, services, and/or activities designed to directly or indirectly address human needs; a set of activities designed to fulfill a social purpose (Netting, O'Connor, & Fauri, 2008). *Direct service programs* focus on clients. *Staff development and training programs* target staff, the intention being that because staff will have additional knowledge and skills they will be able to do better direct service provision. *Support programs* are designed to assist direct service or staff development and training programs.

PROVIDER AGENCIES: Organizations that hire practitioners in direct practice roles to implement programs through the provision of services. Sometimes they are referred to simply as *providers*.

PUBLIC OR GOVERNMENTAL AGENCIES: Organizations mandated by law at some level of government, established through a local, state, or federal system with the purpose of that agency contained in legal statutes. Examples of public agencies are local, state, or federal departments of human or social services, health, education, and aging.

PUBLIC INTEREST ADVOCACY: Involves having the opportunity to take part in the civic process in service of communal good.

RADICAL CHANGE: Based on assumptions that focus on deep-seated structural conflict, modes of domination, and even contradiction.

RADICAL HUMANIST PARADIGM: A highly individualist perspective that respects differences and engages conflict in the interest of individual transformation or liberation.

RADICAL STRUCTURALIST PARADIGM: A perspective that assumes the social world is composed of relatively concrete empirical artifacts and relationships that can be identified, studied, and measured through approaches derived from the natural sciences. The results of this study and measurement should be used to fundamentally transform conditions for oppressed populations.

REALISM: The assumption that reality is above and beyond individual knowledge.

REFLEXIVITY: The ability of the human mind to turn back on itself and, therefore, know that it is knowing.

REGULATION PERSPECTIVE: Held by persons who embrace the status quo, and seek consensus rather than focusing on conflict; assumes that society is characterized by social order and equilibrium.

RELATIVISTS: Persons who believe there are multiple truths because "ethical standards depend on cultural practices, political climate, contemporary norms and moral standards, and other contextual considerations" (Reamer, 1995, p. 48).

RELIGIOUS AFFILIATES: Social service organizations that publicly acknowledge a relationship with a religious group or faith community. Typically, they are separately incorporated as nonprofit organizations and have names like Lutheran Social Ministries, Catholic Charities, and United Methodist Homes.

SATISFICING: Occurs when decision makers recognize that they will never know everything that it is possible to know about any situation, but they make a decision anyway, mostly using bounded rationality.

SELF-AWARENESS: In an organizational setting, being aware of the interpersonal patterns and perceptions of self and others as key in understanding organizational behavior.

Sensing: A personality characteristic in which one prefers to take in information by experiencing the situation (focusing outward, rather than inward).

Serendipitous Organization: A work setting in which a great deal of attention is paid to the people side of the enterprise, not just to understand human needs and wants in order to create conditions for greater productivity, but to establish quality networks of relationships for improved practice.

Service: A specific intervention, a combination of which may comprise a program. For example, a service could be counseling or distributing mobile meals. Both are human services for they directly impact clients.

Sex Role Spillover: Carrying socially defined gender-based roles into the workplace.

Situational Ethics: "Right" choices made in one situation are not assumed to hold in other circumstances. What is considered morally or ethically appropriate may change in light of new information or a shift in scenarios.

Situational Leadership: This occurs when the fit between leader and follower has to be carefully assessed and then style is adapted accordingly.

Social Action: A philosophical approach to change; a collective effort in the face of opposition to promote a cause or make a progressive change (Hardcastle, Wenocur, & Powers, 2004).

Social Change Organization: Exists for the purpose of radically altering the status quo with the goal of consciousness raising for transformative change.

Social Entrepreneurs: Persons who use their own expertise, social and political connections, and sometimes their own money to leverage action toward positive change in tackling social problems.

Solopsism: The assertion that there exists no independent reality outside of the mind.

Stability and Control: A value proposed by Cameron and Quinn (2006) in their Competing Values Framework that is the opposite of flexibility and discretion, which sits at the other end of the continuum.

Subjectivist Perspective: Assumes that social reality exists primarily in the human consciousness (a product of one's mind).

Subjugated Knowledge: Knowledge held by the powerless and not respected by the powerful.

Task Environment: Those organizations, groups, and individuals with which an organization has active relationships in order to enact their responsibilities.

Theory X: The assumptions held by managers that it is human nature to hate work and to avoid it whenever possible. Therefore, coercion, control, discipline, and direction are essential if employees are expected to work toward organizational goals.

Theory Y: The assumptions held by managers that it is human nature for employees to take control and personal responsibility for their work. Therefore, one can assume that employees will be self-directed and motivated.

Theory Z: The assumptions held by managers that participation by all employees in all decision-making processes will make for a consensually based, family-like organization in which everyone is committed to the work at hand.

Thinking: A personality characteristic in which one prefers to make decisions in an intellectual manner (focusing inward and cognitively, rather than outward and emotionally).

Traditional Organization: Seeks to operate like a well-calibrated machine, based on the belief that the best work is produced when things are ordered and predictable. The goal is structure and control.

Transformation: Involves fundamental structural change and is more concerned with a vision of a greater society than with either individual rights or public interest advocacy; seen as a process by which people come to understand their own internal spirit and strength in order to develop alternative visions of their community.

Transformative Community Practice: Seeks to change: (1) how individuals see themselves, developing deeper understanding of who they are and what they can accomplish; (2) how they see themselves in relationship to others in the community, building a collective identity and sense of common purpose and efficacy; and (3) how people outside the community view the community and its people (O'Donnell & Karanja, 2000, pp. 75–76).

True Consciousness: Occurs when individuals' knowledge transforms their awareness so that empowerment results.

Umbrella Associations: "Nonprofit associations whose members are themselves nonprofit organizations." It is estimated that one out of every five nonprofit organizations belongs to an umbrella association (Young, 2001, p. 290).

Verstehen: A concept used by Gadamer to describe the results of hermeneutics, which should be agreement or *understanding* through critical controlled interpretation.

Virtual Organizations: Contemporary organizations that transcend geography, connected by technological innovation.

Voluntary Associations: Membership organizations in which persons come together for a specific purpose. They may be highly formalized or informal/grassroots oriented.

Voluntarism: The belief that people can be proactive in creating their own realities.

References

Acker, J. (1990). Hierarchies, jobs, bodies: A theory of gendered organizations. *Gender and Society, 4*(2), 139–158.

Acker, J. (1994). The gender regime of Swedish banks. *Scandinavian Journal of Management, 10*(2), 117–130.

Alinsky, S. (1969). *Reveille for radicals.* NY: Vintage.

Allen, R. W., & Porter, L. W. (1983). *Organizational influence processes.* Glenview, IL: Scott, Foresman.

Alvesson, M. (1993). *Cultural perspectives on organizations.* Cambridge: Cambridge University Press.

Alvesson, M., & Deetz, S. (1996). Critical theory and postmodernism approaches to organizational studies. In S. R. Clegg, C. Hardy, & W. R. Nord (Eds.), *Handbook of organization studies* (pp. 191–213). London: Sage.

Andrews, K. R. (1987). *The concept of corporate strategy.* Homewood, IL: Irwin.

Angus, I. (1992). The politics of common sense: Articulation theory and critical communication studies. In S. Deetz (Ed.), *Communication Yearbook 15* (pp. 535–570). Newbury Park, CA: Sage.

Ansoff, H. I. (1965). *Corporate strategy.* New York: McGraw-Hill.

Arendt, H. (1998). *The human condition.* Chicago: University of Chicago Press.

Argyris, C. (1970). *Intervention theory and method.* Reading, MA: Addison-Wesley.

Auslander, G. K. (1996). Outcome evaluation in host organizations: A research agenda. *Administration in Social Work, 20*(2), 15–27.

Austin, M. J., & Solomon, J. R. (2000). *Managing the planning process.* In R. J. Patti (Ed.), *The handbook of social welfare management* (pp. 341–359). Thousand Oaks, CA: Sage.

Bailey, D., & Koney, K. M. (2000). *Creating and maintaining strategic alliances: From affiliations to consolidations.* Thousand Oaks, CA: Sage.

Bailey, R., & Brake, M. (Eds.). (1975). *Radical social work.* London: Edward Arnold.

Baldridge, J. V. (1971). *Power and conflict in the university.* New York: Wiley.

Bales, F. (1954). In conference. *Harvard Business Review, 32*(2), 44–50.

Bargal, D. (2000). The manager as leader. In R. Patti (Ed.), *The handbook of social welfare management* (pp. 303–319). Thousand Oaks, CA: Sage.

Barker, R. L. (1999). *The social work dictionary.* Washington, DC: The National Association of Social Workers.

Barnard, C. I. (1938, 1968). *The functions of the executive.* Cambridge, MA: Harvard University Press.

Becker, H. S., Greer, B., Hughes, E. C., & Stauss, A. L. (1961). *The boys in white: Student culture in medical school.* Chicago: University of Chicago.

Beechey, V., & Donald, J. (1985). *Subjectivity and social relations.* Philadelphia: Opa University Press, Milton Keynes.

Bennis, W. G. (1966). *Changing organizations.* New York: McGraw-Hill.

Bennis, W. G., & Slater, P. E. (1968). *The temporary society.* New York: Harper & Row.

Bennis, W. G., Berkowitz, N., Affinito, M., & Malone, M. (1958). Authority, power and the ability to influence. *Human Relations, 11*(2), 143–56.

Benson, J. K. (1977). The interorganizational network as a political economy. *Administrative Science Quarterly, 20.*

Berger, P. L., & Luckman, T. (1967). *Social construction of reality.* Garden City, NY: Doubleday Anchor.

Bertalanffy, L. von. (1951). General systems theory: A new approach to unity of science. *Human Biology, 23,* 303–361.

Billis, D. (1993). *Organizing public and voluntary agencies.* London: Routledge.

Blake, R. R., & Mouton, J. S. (1978). *The new managerial grid.* Houston: Gulf Publishing.

Blau, P. M., & Scott, W. R. (1962). *Formal organizations.* San Francisco: Chandler.

Bogner, W. C., & Thomas, H. (1993). The role of competitive groups in strategy formulation: A dynamic integration of two competing models. *Journal of Management Studies, 30*(1), 51–67.

Bolman, L. G., & Deal, T. D. (1991). *Reframing organizations: Artistry, choice, and leadership.* San Francisco: Jossey-Bass.

Bolman, L. G., & Deal, T. D. (1997). *Reframing organizations: Artistry, choice, and leadership* (2nd ed.). San Francisco: Jossey-Bass.

Bolman, L. G., & Deal, T. D. (2003). *Reframing organizations: Artistry, choice, and leadership.* San Francisco: John Wiley & Sons.

Bordt, R. L. (1997). How alternative ideas become institutions: The case of feminist collectives. *Nonprofit and Voluntary Sector Quarterly, 26*(2), 132–155.

Bornstein, D. (2004). *How to change the world: Social Entrepreneurs and the power of new ideas.* Oxford: Oxford University Press.

Bourdieu, P. (1977). *Outline of a theory of practice.* Cambridge: Cambridge University Press.

Bowers, D., & Seashore, S. (1966). Predicting organizational effectiveness with a four-factor theory of leadership. *Administrative Science Quarterly, 11,* 238–263.

Brager, G., & Holloway, S. (1978). *Changing human service organizations: Politics and practice.* New York: Free Press.

Braybrooke, D., & Lindblom, C. E. (1963). *A strategy of decisions.* New York: Free Press.

Briggs Myers, I., & Myers, P. (1995). *Gifts differing: Understanding personality type* (2nd ed.). Palo Alto, CA: Davies-Black Publishing.

Brilliant, E. L. (2000). Women's gain: Fund-raising and fund allocation as an evolving social movement strategy. *Nonprofit and Voluntary Sector Quarterly, 39,* 554–570.

Brinton, C. (1938). *The anatomy of revolution.* New York: Vintage Books.

Brown, L. D., & Moore, M. H. (2001). Accountability, strategy and international nongovermental organizations. *Nonprofit and Voluntary Sector Quarterly, 30*(3), 569–587.

Burns, J. (1978). *Leadership.* New York: Harper and Row.

Burns, T., & Stalker, G. M. (1961). *The management of innovation.* London: Tavistock Publications.

Burrell, G. (1996). Normal science, paradigms, metaphors, discourses and genealogies of analysis. In S. R. Clegg, C. Hardy, & W. R. Nord (Eds.), *Handbook of organization studies* (pp. 642–658). London: Sage.

Burrell, G., & Morgan, G. (1979). *Sociological paradigms and organisational analysis.* London: Heineman.

Calás, M. B., & Smircich, L. (1996). From 'the woman's' point of view: Feminist approaches to organization studies. In S. R. Clegg, C. Hardy, & W. R. Nord (Eds.), *Handbook of organization studies* (pp. 218–257). London: Sage.

Cameron, K. S., & Quinn, R. E. (1999). *Diagnosing and changing organizational culture based on the competing values framework.* Reading, MA: Addison-Wesley.

Cameron, K. S., & Quinn, R. E. (2006). *Diagnosing and changing organizational culture* (rev. ed.). San Francisco: Jossey-Bass.

Chandler, A. D. (1962). *Strategies and structure: Chapters in the history of the industrial enterprise.* Cambridge, MA: MIT Press.

Clausewitz, C. von. (1968). *On war.* New York: Penguin Books.

Clegg, S. R., Hardy, C., & Nord, W. R. (1996). *Handbook of organization studies.* London: Sage.

Cnaan, R. A. (1999). *The newer deal: Social work and religion in partnership.* New York: Columbia University Press.

Cnaan, R. A. (2002). *The invisible caring hand: American congregations and the provision of welfare.* New York: New York University Press.

Cohen, M. D., & March, J. G. (1974). *Leadership and ambiguity: The American college president.* New York: McGraw-Hill.

Collins, P. H. (1990). *Black feminist thought.* New York: Routledge.

Cooper, R., & Burrell, G. (1988). Modernism, post-modernism, and organizational analysis: An introduction. *Organization Studies, 9,* 99–112.

Cortes, M. (1998). Counting latino nonprofits: A new strategy for finding data. *Nonprofit and Voluntary Sector Quarterly, 27,* 437–458.

Cox, T., Jr. (1994). *Cultural diversity in organizations: Theory, research & practice.* San Francisco: Berrett-Koehler.

Dalton, M. (1950, June). Conflicts between staff and line managerial officers. *American Sociological Review,* 342–352.

Daly, A. (Ed.). (1998). *Workplace diversity issues and perspectives.* Washington, DC: National Association of Social Workers.

Davies, R. (1975). *Women and work.* London: Arrow.

Deetz, S., & Kersten, A. (1983). Critical models of interpretative research. In L. Putnam & M. Pacanowsky (Eds.), *Communication and organizations.* Beverly Hills: Sage.

Devore, W., & Schlesinger, E. G. (1991). *Ethnic-sensitive social work practice* (3rd ed.). New York: Macmillan.

Diesing, P. (1991). *How does social science work? Reflections on practice.* Pittsburgh: University of Pittsburgh.

Dreyfus, H., & Rabinow, P. (1983). *Michel Foucault: Beyond structuralism and hermeneutics* (2nd ed.). Chicago: University of Chicago Press.

Drucker, P. F. (1954). *The practice of management*. New York: Harper.

Drucker, P. F. (1988). The coming of the new organization. *Harvard Business Review (January–February)*, 45–53.

Eberle, G. (1994). *The geography of nowhere: Finding one's self in the postmodern world*. Kansas City, MO: Sheed & Ward.

Ede, L., & Lunsford, A. (1990). *Singular texts: Plural authors: Perspectives on collaborative writing*. Carbondale, IL: Southern Illinois University Press.

Edwards, J. (1977). Strategy formulation as a stylistic process. *International Studies of Management and Organizations, 7*(2), 13–17.

Ellor, J. W., Netting, F. E., & Thibault, J. M. (1999). *Religious and spiritual aspects of human service practice*. Columbia, SC: University of South Carolina Press.

Ennis, R. H. (1989). Critical thinking and subject specificity: Clarification and needed research. *Educational Researcher, 18*(3), 4–10.

Etzioni, A. (1975). *Comparative analysis of complex organizations: On power, involvement, and their correlates*. New York: Free Press.

Ezell, M., & Patti, R. J. (1990). State human service agencies: Structure and organization. *Social Service Review, 64*, 23–45.

Falck, H. S. (1988). *Social work membership perspective*. New York: Springer.

Farazmand, A. (Ed.). (1994). *Modern organizations: Administrative theory in contemporary society*. Westport, CT: Praeger.

Farmer, J. D. (1995). *The language of public administration: Bureaucracy, modernity and postmodernity*. Tuscaloosa: University of Alabama Press.

Farmer, J. D. (Ed.). (1998). *Papers on the art of anti-administration*. Burke, VA: Chatelaine Press.

Farmer, J. D. (1999). Public administration discourse: A matter of style? *Administration & Society, 31*(3), 299–320.

Fay, B. (1996). *Contemporary philosophy of social science*. Oxford: Blackwell.

Fayol, H. (1916, 1949). *General and industrial management* (C. Storrs, Trans.). London: Pitman. (Original work published 1916).

Featherstone, M. (Ed.). (1988). *Postmodernism*. Newbury Park: Sage.

Fellin, P. (1995). *The community and the social worker* (2nd ed.). Itasca, IL: F. E. Peacock.

Fenby, B. (1991). Feminist theory, critical theory, and management's romance with the technical. *Affilia, 6*(1), 20–37.

Ferree, M. M., & Martin, P. Y. (1995). *Feminist organizations: Harvest of the new women's movement*. Philadelphia: Temple University.

Festinger, L. A. (1957). *Theory of cognitive dissonance*. New York: Harper & Row.

Fiedler, F. E. (1967). *A theory of leadership effectiveness*. New York: McGraw-Hill.

Firsirotu, M. (1985). *Strategic turnaround as cultural revolution* (Doctoral dissertation, McGill University, Faculty of Management, Montreal).

Fischer, F., & Sirianni, C. (Eds.). (1984). *Critical studies in organization and bureaucracy*. Philadelphia: Temple University Press.

Flexner, A. (1915). Is social work a profession? *Proceedings of the Forty-second National Conference of Charities, Second Corrections* (pp. 576–590) Fort Wayne, IN: Fort Wayne Printing Co.

Follett, M. P. (1926). The giving of orders. In G. Lindzey (Ed.), *Handbook of social psychology, vol. 2: Special fields and applications* (pp. 1104–1123). Reading, MA: Addison-Wesley.

Foreman, J. (1992). *New visions of collaborative writing.* Hanover, NH: Boynton/Cook.

Foreman, K. (1999). Evolving global structures and the challenges facing international relief and development organizations. *Nonprofit Voluntary Sector Quarterly, 28,* 178–197.

Fox, C., & Miller, H. (1995). *Postmodern public administration: Toward discourse.* Thousand Oaks, CA: Sage.

French, J., & Raven, B. (1959). The bases of social power. In D. P. Cartwright (Ed.), *Studies in social power* (pp. 150–167). Ann Arbor, MI: Institute for Social Research, University of Michigan.

Frost, P. J. (1980). Toward a racial framework for practicing organization science. *Academy of Management Review, 5,* 501–507.

Galper, J. (1976). Introduction to radical theory and practice in social work education: Social polity. *Journal of Education in Social Work, 12,* 3–9.

Gannon, M. J. (2004). *Understanding global cultures: Metaphorical journeys through 28 nations, clusters of nations, and continents* (3rd ed.). Thousand Oaks, CA: Sage.

Gherardi, S. (1995). *Gender, symbolism and organizational cultures.* London: Sage.

Gibbs, L., & Gambrill, E. (1996). *Critical thinking for social workers: A workbook.* Thousand Oaks, CA: Pine Forge Press.

Giddens, A. (1987). *Central problems in social theory.* London: Macmillan.

Gilbelman, M., & Kraft, S. (1996). Advocacy as a core agency program: Planning considerations for voluntary human service agencies. *Administration in Social Work, 20*(4), 43–59.

Glisson, C. (2007). Assessing and changing organizational culture and climate for effective services. *Research on Social Work Practice, 17*(6), 736–747.

Goldstein, E. G. (1995). *Ego psychology and social work practice* (2nd ed.). New York: Free Press.

Greenwood, D. J., & Levin, M. (1998). *Introduction to action research: Social research for social change.* Thousand Oaks, CA: Sage.

Guba, E. (Ed.). (1990). *The paradigm dialog.* Newbury Park, CA: Sage.

Gulick, L. (1937). Notes on the theory of organization. In L. Gulick & L. Urwick (Eds.), *Papers on the science of administration* (pp. 3–13). New York: Institute of Public Administration.

Gutek, B. A., & Cohen, A. (1982). Sex ratios, sex role spillover, and sex at work: A comparison of men's and women's experiences. *Human Relations, 40*(2), 97–115.

Gutierrez, L. M., & Lewis, E. A. (1999). *Empowering women of color.* New York: Columbia University Press.

Habermas, J. (1971). *Knowledge and human interests* (J. Shapiro, Trans.). London: Heinemann.

Habermas, J. (1984). *The theory of communicative action, vol. 1: Reason and the rationalization of society.* (T. McCarthy, Trans.). Boston: Beacon.

Hagen, S. (1995). *How the world can be the way it is: An inquiry for the new millennium into science, philosophy and perception.* Wheaton, Il: Quest Books.

Handler, J. F. (1990). *Law and the search for community.* Philadelphia: University of Pennsylvania Press.

Handy, F., Kassam, M., Feeney, S., & Ranade, B. (2006). *Grass-roots NGOs by women for women: The driving force of development in India.* New Delhi, India: Sage.

Hannan, M. T., & Freeman, J. (1977). The population ecology of organizations. *American Journal of Sociology, 82*(5), 149–164.

Hansmann, H. B. (1981). Reforming nonprofit corporation law. *University of Pennsylvania Law Review, 129*(3), 500–563.

Hardcastle, D. A., Wenocur, S., & Powers, P. R. (2004). *Community practice: Theories and skills for social workers* (2nd ed.). New York: Oxford University Press.

Hardy, C., & Clegg, S. R. (1996). Some dare call it power. In S. R. Clegg, C. Hardy, & W. R. Nord (Eds.), *Handbook of organization studies* (pp. 622–641). London: Sage.

Harper, K. V., & Lantz, J. (1996). *Cross-cultural practice: Social work with diverse populations.* Chicago: Lyceum.

Harris, M. (1998). Doing it their way: Organizational challenges for voluntary associations. *Nonprofit and Voluntary Sector Quarterly, 27,* 144–158.

Harrison, M. I. (1994). *Diagnosing organizations: Methods, models, and processes* (2nd ed.). Thousand Oaks, CA: Sage.

Harrison, M. I., & Shirom, A. (1999). *Organizational diagnosis and assessment: Bridging theory and practice.* Thousand Oaks, CA: Sage.

Hasenfeld, Y. (1983). *Human service organizations.* Englewood Cliffs, NJ: Prentice-Hall.

Hasenfeld, Y. (2000). Social welfare administration and organizational theory. In R. Patti (Ed.), *The handbook of social welfare management* (pp. 89–112). Thousand Oaks, CA: Sage.

Hassard, J., & Parker, M. (Eds.). (1993). *Postmodernism and organizations.* London: Sage.

Hatch, M. J., & Cunliffe, A. L. (2006). *Modern, symbolic, and postmodern perspectives* (2nd ed.). New York: Oxford University Press.

Hearn, J., & Parkin, P. W. (1987). *"Sex" at "work": The power and paradox of organization sexuality.* New York: St. Martin's Press.

Heidegger, M. (1977). *The question concerning technology and other essays.* New York: Harper & Row.

Henderson, B. D. (1979). *Henderson on corporate strategy.* Cambridge, MA: Abt Books.

Hepworth, D., Rooney, R., Rooney, G. D., Strom-Gottfried, K., & Larsen, J. (2006). *Direct social work practice: Theory and skills* (7th ed.). Pacific Grove, CA: Brooks/Cole.

Hersey, P., & Blanchard, K. H. (1977). *Management of organizational behavior: Utilizing human resources* (3rd ed.). Englewood Cliffs, NJ: Prentice-Hall.

Herzberg, F. (1966). *Work and the nature of man.* Cleveland: World Publishing.

Hess, P. M., & Mullen, E. J. (Eds.). (1996). *Practitioner-researcher partnerships: Building knowledge from, in, and for practice.* Washington, DC: National Association of Social Workers Press.

Heydebrand, W. V. (Ed.). (1973). *Comparative organizations: The results of empirical research.* Englewood Cliffs, NJ: Prentice-Hall.

Hirsh, S. (1992). *MBTI team building program: Team members' guide.* Palo Alto, CA: Consulting Psychologists Press.

Hutchinson, J. G. (1967). *Organizations: Theory and classical concepts.* New York: Holt, Rinehart & Winston.

Hyde, C. (1992). The ideational system of social movement agencies: An examination of feminist health centers. In Y. Hasenfeld (Ed.), *Human services as complex organizations* (pp. 121–144). Newbury Park, CA: Sage.

Hyde, C. (2000). The hybrid nonprofit: An examination of feminist social movement organizations. *Journal of Community Practice, 8*(4), 45–67.

Iannello, K. P. (1992). *Decisions without hierarchy: Feminist intervention in organization theory and practice.* New York: Routledge.

Iglehart, A. P., & Becerra, R. M. (1995). *Social services and the ethnic community.* Boston: Allyn & Bacon.

Jacobsen, W. (1998). Defining the quality of practitioner researcher. *Adult Education Quarterly, 48*(3), 125–138.

Jaques, E. (1951). *The changing culture of the factory.* London: Tavistock Institute.

Jaques, E. (1990, January–February). In praise of hierarchy. *Harvard Business Review,* 127–133.

Jaskyte, K., & Dressler, W. W. (2005). Organizational culture and innovation n nonprofit human service organizations. *Administration in Social Work, 29*(2), 23–41.

Jenkins, S. (1980). The ethnic agency defined. *Social Service Review, 54,* 249–261.

Johnson, G. (1992). Managing strategic change: Strategy, culture and action. *Long Range Planning, 25*(10), 28–36.

Kanter, R. M. (1977). *Men and women of the corporation.* New York: Basic Books.

Kanter, R. M. (1979). Power failure in management circuits. *Harvard Business Review, 57,* 65–75.

Kanter, R. M. (1987). Power failure in management circuits. In J. M. Shafritz & J. S. Ott (Eds.), *Classics of organizational theory* (pp. 349–363). Chicago: Dorsey Press.

Kanter, R. M. (1989). *When giants learn to dance.* New York: Simon & Schuster.

Katz, D., & Kahn, R. (1966). *The social psychology of organizations.* New York: Wiley.

Kaufman, H. (1960). *The forest ranger.* Baltimore: Johns Hopkins University Press.

Kellner, D. (1998). Postmodernist as social therapy: Some challenges and problems. *Theory, Culture and Society, 5*(2–3), 239–269.

Kelly, R. M. (1991). *The gendered economy: Work, careers, and success.* Newbury Park, CA: Sage.

Kettner, P. M., Daley, J. M., & Nichols, A. W. (1985). *Initiating change in organizations and communities: A macro practice model.* Monterey, CA: Brooks/Cole.

Kettner, P. M., Moroney, R. M., & Martin, L. L. (2008). *Designing and managing programs: An effectiveness-based approach* (3rd ed.). Thousand Oaks, CA: Sage.

Kets de Vries, M. F. R. (1985, November–December). The dark side of entrepreneurship. *Harvard Business Review,* 160–167.

Kiechel, W., III. (1984, May). Sniping at strategic planning. *Planning Review,* 8–11.

Kikert, W. (1993). Complexity, governance, and dynamics: Conceptual explorations of public network management. In J. Kooiman (Ed.), *Modern governance: New government-society interactions* (pp. 191–204). London: Sage.

Kilmann, R. H., Saxton, M. J., Serpa, R., & Associates. (1985). *Gaining control of corporate culture.* San Francisco: Jossey-Bass.

Kirk, S. A., Siporin, M., & Kutchins, H. (1989). The prognosis for social work diagnosis. *Social Casework, 70,* 295–307.

Knights, D., & Willmott, H. (1989). Power and subjectivity work: From degradation to subjugation in social relations. *Sociology, 23,* 535–538.

Koen, S. (1984). *Feminist workplaces: Alternative models for the organization of work* (Doctoral dissertation, Union for Experimenting Colleges University of Michigan Dissertation Information Service).

Kondrat, M. E. (1999). Who is the "self" in self-aware: Professional self-awareness from a critical theory perspective. *Social Service Review, 73,* 451–477.

Koontz, H. (1961). The management theory jungle. *Academy of Management Journal, 4,* 174–188.

Koroloff, N. M., & Briggs, H. E. (1996). The life cycle of family advocacy organizations. *Administration in Social Work, 20*(4), 23–42.

Kramer, R. M. (1981). *Voluntary agencies in the welfare state.* Berkeley: University of California Press.

Kravetz, D. (2004). *Tales from the trenches: Politics and practice in feminist service organizations.* Dallas: University Press of America.

Kroeger, O., & Thuesen, J. M. (1988). *Type talk.* New York: Dell.

Lapierre, R. (1980). *Le changement strategique: Un Reve en Quete de Reel* (Doctoral management policy course paper, McGill University).

Lash, S., & Urry, J. (1987). *The end of organized capitalism.* London: Polity.

Laudan, L. (1996). *Beyond positivism and relativism: Theory, method and evidence.* Boulder, Co: Westview Press.

Lawler, E., Nadler, D., & Cammann, C. (Eds.). (1980). *Organizational assessment.* New York: Wiley.

Lawrence, G. (1993). *People types and tiger stripes* (3rd ed.). Gainesville, FL: Center for Applications of Psychological Type.

Lawrence-Lightfoot, S. (1999). *Respect: An exploration.* Cambridge, MA: Perseus Books.

Lawson, H. (1985). *Reflexivity: The postmodern predicament.* London: Hutchinson.

Lechich, A. J. (2000). Home care in jeopardy. *Care Management Journals, 2,* 128–131.

Leifer, R. (1989). Understanding organizational transformation using a dissipative structure model. *Human Relations, 42*(10), 899–916.

Levy, B. S. (1994). *The empowerment tradition in American social work.* New York: Columbia University Press.

Lewis, D. (2002). Organization and management in the third sector: Toward a cross-cultural research agenda. *Nonprofit Management and Leadership, 13*(1), 67–83.

Lewis, J. A., Packard, T., Lewis, M. D., & Souflee, R. (2001). *Management of human service programs* (3rd ed.). Pacific Grove, CA: Brooks/Cole.

Likert, R. (1961). *New patterns of management.* New York: McGraw-Hill.

Lincoln, Y., & Guba, E. (1985). *Naturalistic inquiry.* Beverly Hills: Sage.

Lindenberg, M. (1999). Declining state capacity, voluntarism, and the globalization of the not-for-profit sector. *Nonprofit and Voluntary Sector Quarterly, 28,* 147–167.

Linstead, S. (1993). Deconstruction in the study of organizations. In J. Hassard & M. Parker (Eds.), *Postmodernism and organizations* (pp. 49–70). London: Sage.

Lohmann, R. A. (1989). And lettuce is non-animal: Toward a positive economics of nonprofit action. *Nonprofit and Voluntary Sector Quarterly, 18,* 367–383.

Louis, M. R. (1980). Surprise and sense making: What newcomers experience in entering unfamiliar organizational settings. *Administrative Science Quarterly*, 25(2), 226–251.

Lugones, M. C., & Spelman, E. V. (1983). Have we got a theory for you!: Feminist theory, cultural imperialism and the demand for "the woman's voice." *Women's Studies International Forum*, 6(6), 573–581.

Lum, D. (1992). *Social work practice and people of color: A process-stage approach* (4th ed.). Pacific Grove, CA: Brooks/Cole.

Lune, H. (2002). Weathering the storm: Nonprofit organization survival strategies in a hostile climate. *Nonprofit and Voluntary Sector Quarterly*, 31(4), 463–483.

Lyotard, J. F., & Thibaud, J. L. (1985). *Just gaming*. Manchester, UK: Manchester University Press.

Macduff, N., & Netting, F. E. (2000). Lessons learned from a practitioner–academician collaboration. *Nonprofit Voluntary Sector Quarterly*, 29, 46–60.

MacMillan, I. C. (1978). *Strategy formulation: Political concepts*. St Paul: West.

Mann, M. (1986). *The sources of social power, vol. 1: A history of power from the beginning to A.D. 1760*. Cambridge: Cambridge University Press.

Mannheim, K. (1936). *Ideology and utopian* (L. Wirth & E. Shils, Trans.). New York: International Library of Psychology, Philosophy of Scientific Method.

Marcuse, H. (1991). *One-dimensional man: Studies in the ideology of advanced industrial society*. Boston: Beacon.

Margolis, H. (1993). *Paradigms and barriers: How habits of the mind govern scientific belief*. Chicago: University of Chicago Press.

Martin, C. (1997). *Looking at type: The fundamentals*. Gainesville, FL: Center for the Applications of Psychological Types.

Martin, J. (2002). *Organizational culture: Mapping the terrain*. Thousand Oaks, CA: Sage.

Martin, J., & Frost, P. (1996). Organization culture war games: Struggle for intellectual dominance. In S. R. Clegg, C. Hardy, & W. R. Nord (Eds.), *Handbook of Organization Studies* (pp. 598–621). London: Sage.

Martin, L. L. (2000). The environmental context of social welfare administration. In R. J. Patti (Ed.), *The handbook of social welfare administration* (pp. 55–67). Thousand Oaks, CA: Sage.

Martin, P. Y. (1990). Rethinking feminist organizations. *Gender & Society*, 4(2), 182–206.

Martin, P. Y., & O'Connor, G. G. (1989). *The social environment: Open systems applications*. New York: Longman.

Maslow, A. H. (1943). A theory of human motivation. *Psychological Review*, 50, 370–396.

Mayo, G. E. (1933). *The human problems of an industrial civilization*. Boston, MA: Harvard Business School, Division of Research.

McGregor, D. M. (1957). The human side of enterprise. *Management Review*, 46, 22–28, 88–92.

McGregor, D. M. (1960). *The human side of enterprise*. New York: McGraw-Hill.

Merton, R. K. (1952). Bureaucratic structure and personality. In R. K. Merton, A. P. Gray, B. Hockey, & H. C. Selvin, (Eds.), *Reader in bureaucracy* (pp. 261–372). Glencoe, IL: Free Press.

Metzendorf, D. (2005). *The evolution of feminist organizations*. Lanham, MD: University Press of America.

Metzendorf, D., & Cnaan, R. A. (1992). Volunteers in feminist organizations. *Nonprofit Management & Leadership, 2*(3), 255–269.

Miller, J. (2001). Social workers as diagnosticians. In K. J. Bentley (Ed.), *Social work practice in mental health*. Pacific Grove, CA: Brooks/Cole.

Millman, M., & Kanter, K. (Eds.). (1975). *Another voice: Feminist perspectives on social life and social sciences*. Garden City, NJ: Doubleday.

Minkoff, D. C. (2002). The emergence of hybrid organizational forms: Combining identity-based service provision and political action. *Nonprofit and Voluntary Sector Quarterly, 31*(3), 377–401.

Mintzberg, H. (1979). *The structuring of organizations: A synthesis of the research*. Englewood Cliffs, NJ: Prentice Hall.

Mintzberg, H., Ahlstrand, B., & Lampel, J. (1998). *Strategy safari a guided tour through the wilds of strategic management*. New York: Free Press.

Mintzberg, H., & McHugh, H. (1985). Strategy formation in an adhocracy. *Administrative Science Quarterly, 30*, 160–197.

Mizruchi, M. S., & Galaskievicz, J. (1993). Networks of organizational relations. *Sociological Methods and Research, 22*, 46–70.

Mondros, J. B., & Wilson, S. M. (1994). *Organizing for power and empowerment*. New York: Columbia University Press.

Morgan, G. (1986). *Images of organization*. Newbury Park, CA: Sage.

Morgan, G. (1997). *Images of organization* (2nd ed.). Thousand Oaks, CA: Sage.

Morgan, G. (2007). *Images of organization* (rev. ed.). Thousand Oaks, CA: Sage.

Morris, R., & Lescohier, I. H. (1978). Service integration: Real versus illusory solutions to welfare dilemmas. In R. C. Sarri & Y. Hasenfeld (Eds.), *The management of human services*. New York: Columbia University Press.

Münsterberg, H. (1922). *Hugo Münsterberg: His life and work*. New York: Appleton.

Mullaly, B. (2007). *The new structural social work* (3rd ed.). New York: Oxford.

Myers, I. B. (1998). *Introduction to type: A guide to understanding your results on the Myers-Briggs type indicator* (6th ed.). Palo Alto, CA: Consulting Psychologist Press.

Myers, K., & Kirby, L. (1994). *Introduction to type: Dynamics and development, exploring the next level of type*. Palo Alto, CA: Consulting Psychologists Press.

Nelson, R. R., & Winter, S. G. (1982). *An evolutionary theory of economic change*. Boston: Harvard University Press.

Netting, F. E, Kettner, P. M., & McMurtry, S. L. (2008). *Social work macro practice* (4th ed.). Boston: Allyn & Bacon.

Netting, F. E., & O'Connor, M. K. (2003). *Organization practice*. Boston: Allyn & Bacon

Netting, F. E., & O'Connor, M. K. (2005, Winter). Lady boards of managers: Subjugated legacies of governance and administration. *Affilia, 20*(4), 448–464.

Netting, F. E., & O'Connor, M. K. (2008). Recognizing the need for evidence-based macro practices in organizational and community settings. In M. Roberts-DeGennaro (Ed.), Paradigm of Evidence-Based Macro Practice [Special issue]. *Journal of Evidence-Based Social Work, 5*(3-4), 473–496.

Netting, F. E., O'Connor, M. K., & Fauri, D. (2007). Planning transformative programs: Challenges for advocates in translating change processes into effectiveness measures. *Administration in Social Work, 31*(4), 59–81.

Netting, F. E., O'Connor, M. K., & Fauri, D. P. (2008). *Comparative approaches to program planning.* Hoboken, NJ: Wiley.

Netting, F. E., O'Connor, M. K., & Singletary, J. (2007). Finding homes for their dreams: Strategies founders and program initiators use to position faith-based programs. *Families in Society, 8*, 19–29.

Netting, F. E., O'Connor, M. K., & Yancey, G. (2006). Belief systems in faith-based human service programs. *Journal of Religion and Spirituality in Social Work, 23*(3/4), 261–286.

Nyden, P., Figert, A., Shibley, M., & Burrows, D. (1997). *Building community: Social science in action.* Thousand Oaks, CA: Pine Forge Press.

Oakeshott, M. J. (1962). *Rationalism in politics and other essays.* New York: Basic Books.

O'Connor, M. K., & Netting, F. E. (1999). Teaching students about collaborative approaches to organizational change. *Affilia, 14*(3), 315–328.

O'Connor, M. K, Netting, F. E., & Fabelo, H. E. (in press). A multi-paradigmatic survey of field agencies. *Administration in Social Work.*

O'Donnell, S. M., & Karanja. S. T. (2000). Transformative community practice: Building a model for developing extremely low income African American communities. *Journal of Community Practice, 7*(3), 67–84.

Odendahl, T., & O'Neil, M. (Eds.). (1994). *Women and power in the nonprofit sector.* San Francisco: Jossey-Bass.

Oster, S. M. (1992). Nonprofit organizations as franchise operations. *Nonprofit Management & Leadership, 2*(3), 223–238.

Ouchi, W. G. (1981). *Theory Z.* Reading, MA: Addison-Wesley.

Oxford University Press Staff. (2000). *Oxford dictionary of American usage and style.* New York: Berkley Publishing Group.

Parker, M. (1992). Post-modern and organizations or postmodern organization theory? *Organization Studies, 13*(1), 1–17.

Parker, M. (1993). Life after Jean-Francois. In J. Hassard & M. Parker (Eds.), *Postmoderism and organizations* (pp. 204–212). London: Sage.

Parsons, T. (1956). Suggestions for a sociological approach to the theory of organizations. *Administrative Science Quarterly, 1*, 63–85.

Paul, R. W. (1993). *Critical thinking: What every person needs to know to survive in a rapidly changing world.* XX: Foundation for Critical Thinking.

Paul, R. W., & Elder, L. (2002). *Critical thinking: Tools for taking charge of your professional and personal life.* Upper Saddle River, NJ: Financial Times/Prentice Hall.

Peters, T. J., & Waterman, R. H., Jr. (1982). *In search of excellence.* New York: Harper & Row.

Pettigrew, A. M. (1985). *The awakening giant: Continuity and change in Imperial Chemical Industries.* Oxford: Basil Blackwell.

Pfeffer, J. (1981). *Power in organizations.* Marshfield, MA: Pitman Publishing.

Pinchot, G., III (1985). *Intrapreneuring.* New York: Harper & Row.

Piven, F. F., & Cloward, R. A. (1971). *Regulating the poor: The functions of public welfare.* New York: Pantheon Books.

Platt, R. (1989). Reflexivity, recursion, and social life: Elements for a postmodern sociology. *Sociological Review, 37*(4), 636–667.

Porter, M. E. (1980). *Competitive strategy: Techniques for analyzing industries and competitors.* New York: Free Press.

Power, M. (1992). *Modernism, postmodernism, and organization.* In J. Hassard & D. Pym (Eds.), *The theory and philosophy of organizations: Critical issues and new perspectives.* London: Routledge & Kegan Paul.

Preston, M. S. (2005). Child welfare management training: Towards a pedagogically sound curriculum. *Administration in Social Work, 29*(4), 89–111.

Quinn, R. E., Faerman, S. R., Thompson, M. P., & McGrath, M. R. (2003). *Becoming a master manager: A competency framework* (3rd ed). New York: John Wiley & Sons.

Rauch, J. B. (Ed.). (1993). *Assessment: A sourcebook for social work practice.* Milwaukee, WI: Families International, Inc.

Reamer, F. G. (1995). *Social work values and ethics.* New York: Columbia University Press.

Reddin, W. J. (1970). *Managerial effectiveness.* New York: McGraw-Hill.

Reed, M. (1993). Organizations and modernity: Continuity and discontinuity in organization theory. In H. Hassard & M. Parker (Eds.), *Postmodernism and organizations* (pp. 163–182). Newbury Park, CA: Sage.

Reed, M. (1996). Organizational theorizing: A historically contested terrain. In S. R. Clegg, C. Hardy, & W. R. Nord (Eds.), *Handbook of organization studies* (pp. 31–56). London: Sage.

Reger, R. K., & Huff, A. S. (1993). Strategic groups: A cognitive perspective. *Strategic Management Journal, 14*, 103–124.

Resnick, H., & Patti, R. J. (1980). *Change from within: Humanizing social welfare organizations.* Philadelphia: Temple University Press.

Richmond, M. (1917). *Social diagnosis.* New York: Russell Sage Foundation.

Ritzer, G. (1980). *Sociology: A multiple paradigm science* (rev. ed.). Boston: Allyn & Bacon.

Rodwell, M. K. (1987). Naturalistic inquiry: An alternative model for social work assessment. *Social Service Review, 6*, 231–246.

Rodwell, M. K. (1998). *Social work constructivist research.* New York: Garland Publishers.

Roethlisberger, F. J., & Dickson, W. J. (1939). *Management and the worker.* Cambridge, MA: Harvard University Press.

Rogers, R. E. (1975). *Organizational theory.* Boston: Allyn & Bacon.

Rothman, J. (2007). Multi modes of intervention at the macro level. *Journal of Community Practice, 15*(4), 11–40.

Rothman, J., Erlich, J. E., & Tropman, J. E., (Eds.). (2008). *Strategies for community intervention* (6th ed.). Belmont, CA: Brooks/Cole.

Ruggiero, V. R. (2001). *Thinking critically about ethical issues* (5th ed.). Boston: McGraw-Hill.

Sackman, S. A. (1993). *Cultural knowledge in organizations: Exploring the collective mind.* Newbury Park, CA: Sage.

Sarrazin, J. (1977/1978, Fall/Winter). Decentralized planning in a large French company: An interpretive study. *International Studies of Management and Organization*, 37–59.

Schein, E. H. (1985). *Organizational culture and leadership.* San Francisco: Jossey-Bass.

Schein, E. H. (1989). Reassessing the "divine rights" of managers. *Sloan Management Review, 30*(2), 63–68.

Schein, E. H. (1992). *Organizational culture and leadership* (2nd ed.). San Francisco: Jossey- Bass.

Schneider, R. L., & Lester, L. (2001). *Social work advocacy.* Belmont, CA: Brooks/Cole.

Scott, W. G. (1961). Organization theory: An overview and an appraisal. *Academy of Management Journal, 4,* 7–26.

Scott, W. G., & Mitchell, T. R. (1972). *Organization theory: A structural and behavioral analysis* (rev. ed.). Chicago: Dorsey Press.

Seashore, S., Lawler, E., Mirvis, P., & Cammann, C. (Eds.). (1983). *Assessing organizational change.* New York: Wiley.

Selznick, P. (1948). Foundations of the theory of organization. *American Sociological Review, 13,* 25–35.

Selznick, P. (1957). *Leadership in administration: A sociological interpretation.* Evanston, IL: Row, Peterson.

Senge, P. M. (1990). *The fifth discipline: The art and practice of the learning organization.* New York: Doubleday.

Shafritz, J. M., & Ott, J. S. (1987). *Classics of organization theory* (2nd ed.). Chicago: Dorsey.

Shafritz, J. M., & Ott, J. S. (2001). *Classics of organization theory* (5th ed.). Fort Worth, TX: Harcourt College Publishers.

Shafritz, J. M., Ott, J. S., & Lang, Y. S. (2005). *Classics of organization theory* (6th ed.). Belmont, CA: Thomson Wadsworth.

Simon, H. A. (1946). The proverbs of administration. *Public Administration Review, 6,* 53–67.

Simon, H. A. (1947). *Administrative behavior.* New York: Macmillan.

Simon, H. A. (1957). *Administrative behavior.* New York: Macmillan.

Smircich, L., & Calás, M. (1987). Organizational culture: A critical assessment. In F. Jablin, L. Putnam, K. Roberts, & L. Porter (Eds.), *Handbook of organizational communications* (pp. 228–263). Newbury Park, CA: Sage.

Smith, A. (1776). Of the division of labour. In *An inquiry into the nature and causes of the wealth of nations* (pp. 5–15). (Printed for W. Strahan and T. Cadell in the Strand, London).

Smith, D. H. (1999). The effective grassroots association, pt. 1: Organizational factors that produce internal impact. *Nonprofit Management and Leadership, 9*(4), 443–456.

Starbuck, W. H., & Milliken, F. J. (1988). Executives' perceptual filters: What they notice and how they make sense. In D. C. Hambrick (Ed.) *The executive effect: Concepts and methods for studying top managers* (pp. 35–65). Greenwich, CT: NAI.

Steiner, G. A. (1969). *Top management planning.* New York: Macmillan.

Stogdill, R. M., & Coons, A. E. (1957). *Leader behavior: Its description and measurement.* Columbus: Ohio University Press.

Tannebaum, R., & Schmidt, W. H. (1958). How to choose a leadership pattern. *Harvard Business Review, 36,* 95–101.

Taylor, F. W. (1911, 1947). *Scientific management.* New York: Harper & Row.

Taylor, F. W. (1916). The principles of scientific management. *Bulletin of the Taylor Society.* (An abstract of an address given by Dr. Taylor before the Cleveland Advertising Club, March 3, 1915.)

Thayer, F. E. (1981). *An end to hierarchy and competition: Administration in the post-affluent world* (2nd ed.). New York: New Viewpoints.

Thompson, J. D. (1967). *Organizations in action.* New York: McGraw-Hill.

Thompson, P. (1993). Postmodernism: Fatal distraction. In J. Hassard & M. Parker (Eds.), *Postmodernism and organizations* (pp. 183–203). Newbury Park, CA: Sage.

Tieger, P., & Barron-Tieger, B. (1992). *Do what you are: Discover the perfect career for you through the secrets of personality type.* Boston: Little, Brown.

Toffler, A. (1970). *Future shock.* New York: Random House.

Toynbee, A. J. (1957). *Study of history. Abridgement of vols. I–X.* New York: Oxford University Press.

Tuominen, M. (1991). Caring for-profit: The social, economic, and political significance of for-profit child care. *Social Service Review, 65,* 450–467.

Turner, F. J. (1994). *Social work treatment: Interlocking theoretical approaches* (4th ed.). New York: Free Press.

Turner, J. H. (1987). Toward a sociological theory of motivation. *American Sociological Review, 52,* 15–27.

Van Maanen, J. (Ed.). (1979). *Qualitative methodology.* Newbury Park, CA: Sage.

Van Maanen, J. (Ed.). (1983). *Qualitative methodology.* Newbury Park, CA: Sage.

Van Maanen, J., Dabbs, J. M., Jr., & Faulkner, R. R. (Eds.). (1982). *Varieties of qualitative research.* Newbury Park, CA: Sage.

Vibert, C. (2004). *Theories of macro organizational behavior.* Armonk, NY: M. E. Sharpe.

Walker, A. H., & Lorsch, J. W. (1968). Organizational choice: Product vs. function. *Harvard Business Review, 46,* 129–138.

Weber, M. (1922). Bureaucracy. In H. Gerth & C. W. Mills (Eds.), *Max Weber: Essays in sociology.* Oxford, UK: Oxford University Press.

Weber, M. (1946). *From Max Weber: Essays in sociology* (H. H. Gerth & C. W. Mills,Trans.). New York: Oxford University Press.

Weber, M. (1947a). *The methodology of social sciences.* Glencoe, IL: Free Press.

Weber, M. (1947b). *The theory of social and economic organization* (A. M. Henderson & T. Parsons, Trans.). New York: Macmillan. (First published in 1924.)

Weick, K. E. (1995). *Sensemaking in organizations.* Thousand Oaks, CA: Sage.

Weiner, M. E. (1990). Trans-organizational management: The new frontier for social work administrators. *Administration in Social Work, 14*(4), 11–27.

Wiener, N. (1948). *Cybernetics: Or control of communication in the animal and the machine.* Cambridge, MA: MIT.

Westley, F., & Mintzberg, H. (1989). Visionary leadership and strategic management. *Strategic Management Journal, 10,* 17–32.

Wheatley, M. J., & Kellner-Rogers, M. (1996). *A simpler way.* San Francisco: Berrett-Koehler.

Whyte, W. H., Jr. (1956). *The organization man.* New York: Simon & Schuster.

Wilkerson, A. E. (1988). Epilogue. In F. D. Perlmutter (Ed.), *Alternative social agencies: Administrative strategies* (pp. 119–128). New York: Haworth Press.

Williams, R. (1977). *Marxism and literature*. Oxford: Oxford University Press.

Willmott, H. (1993). Strength is ignorance; slavery is freedom: Managing culture in modern organizations. *Journal of Management Studies, 30*(4), 515–552.

Wilson, F. (1996). Research note. Organizational theory: Blind and deaf to gender. *Organizational Studies, 17*, 825–842.

Wineburg, B. (2001). *A limited partnership: The politics of religion, welfare, and social service*. New York: Columbia University Press.

Wolff, J. (1977). Women in organizations. In S. Clegg & D. Dunkerley (Eds.), *Critical issues in organizations* (pp. 7–20). London: Routledge & Kegan Paul.

Wood, R. L. (2002). *Faith in action: Religion, race, and democratic organizing in America*. Chicago: University of Chicago Press.

Woods, M. E., & Hollis, F. (2000). *Casework: A psychosocial therapy* (5th ed.). Boston: McGraw Hill.

Wuthnow, R. (2004). *Saving America? Faith-based services and the future of civil society*. Princeton, NJ: Princeton University Press.

Young, D. R. (2001). Organizational identity and the structure of nonprofit umbrella associations. *Nonprofit Management & Leadership, 11*, 289–304.

Yunus, M. (2003). *Banker to the poor: Micro-lending and the battle against world poverty*. New York: Public Affairs.

Yunus, M. (2007). *Creating a world without poverty: Social business and the future of capitalism*. New York: Public Affairs.

Zald, M. (1970). Political economy: A framework for comparative analysis. In Zald, M. (Ed.), *Power in organizations* (pp. 221–261). Nashville: Vanderbilt University Press.

Zald, M. N., & Berger, M. A. (1978). Social movements in organizations: Coup d'etat, insurgency, and mass movements. *American Journal of Sociology, 84*(4), 823–861.

AUTHOR INDEX

A

Acker, J., 230
Ahlstrand, B., xi, 69–71, 73, 75, 77, 139, 194, 250, 311, 336
Alinsky, S., 201
Allen, R. W., 166
Alvesson, M., 160, 171, 172, 285
Andrews, K. R., 70
Angus, I., 157
Ansoff, H. I., 71
Arendt, H., 289
Argyris, C., 103
Auslander, G. K., 20
Austin, M. J., 137

B

Bailey, D., 15
Bailey, R., 201
Baldridge, J. V., 165
Bales, F., 27
Bargal, D., 27, 28
Barker, R. L., 135
Barnard, C. I., 100
Barron-Tieger, B., 26, 69
Becerra, R. M., 142
Becker, H. S., 221
Beechey, V., 170
Bennis, W. G., 108, 165
Benson, J. K., 171, 285

Berger, M. A., 73
Berger, P. L., 221
Bertalanffy, L. von, 108
Billis, D., 14
Blake, R. R., 27, 28
Blanchard, K. H., 28
Blau, P. M., 105, 107
Bogner, W. C., 75
Bolman, L. G., 23, 27, 73, 106, 221
Bordt, R. L., 21, 201
Bornstein, D., 12
Bourdieu, P., 170
Bowers, D., 27
Brager, G., 29, 34, 122
Brake, M., 201
Braybrooke, D., 75
Briggs, H. E., 21
Briggs Myers, I., 83
Brilliant, E. L., 175, 191
Brinton, C., 74
Brown, L. D., 15
Burns, J., 28
Burns, T., 107, 379, 380
Burrell, G., x, xi, 46–56, 58, 83, 92, 94, 95, 109–111, 113, 154, 158, 159, 161, 172, 182, 214, 217, 218, 274, 277, 278, 285, 360
Burrows, D., 200

C

Calás, M., 172
Calás, M. B., 169, 170, 229, 283, 284
Cameron, K. S., x, xi, 58–62, 180, 241, 301, 328, 331, 346, 347, 362, 375, 376, 378, 379
Cammann, C., 135
Chandler, A. D., 70
Clausewitz, C. von, 72
Clegg, S. R., 165, 166, 168
Cloward, R. A., 201
Cnaan, R. A., 17, 18
Cohen, A., 169
Cohen, M. D., 166
Collins, P. H., 230
Coons, A. E., 27
Cooper, R., 172
Cortes, M., 18
Cox, T., Jr., 25, 36, 376
Cunliffe, A. L., 23, 24

D

Dabbs, J. M., Jr., 220
Daley, J. M., 29, 34
Dalton, M., 101
Daly, A., 22
Davies, R., 229
Deal, T. D., 23, 27, 73, 106, 221
Deetz, S., 160, 171, 172, 285
Devore, W., 36
Dickson, W. J., 229
Diesing, P., 276
Donald, J., 170
Dressler, W. W., 362
Dreyfus, H., 170
Drucker, P. F., 108

E

Eberle, G., 275

Ede, L., 258
Edwards, J., 76
Elder, L., 30, 37
Ellor, J. W., 17
Ennis, R. H., 30
Etzioni, A., 105, 106
Ezell, M., 10

F

Faberlo, H. E., 56, 57, 328, 354–358, 360
Faerman, S. R., 20
Falck, H. S., 32
Farazmand, A., 23
Farmer, J. D., 55, 288, 290, 291
Faulkner, R. R., 220
Fauri, D., 205, 246
Fauri, D. P., 7, 8, 246, 258, 261, 262, 288, 316, 317, 377, 381
Fay, B., 46
Fayol, H., 97
Featherstone, M., 173
Feeney, S., 201
Fellin, P., 17
Fenby, B., 200
Ferree, M. M., 201
Festinger, L. A., 229
Fiedler, F. E., 28
Figert, A., 200
Firsirotu, M., 74
Fischer, F., 171, 285
Flexner, A., 134
Follett, M. P., 103
Foreman, J., 16, 258
Fox, C., 26
Freeman, J., 73
French, J., 165
Frost, P., 220, 222, 223
Frost, P. J., 171

G

Galaskievicz, J., 164
Galper, J., 201
Gambrill, E., 30, 376
Gannon, M. J., 248
Gherardi, S., 230
Gibbs, L., 30, 376
Giddens, A., 170
Glisson, C., 58
Goldstein, E. G., 135
Greenwood, D. J., 258
Greer, B., 221
Guba, E., 46, 234, 278
Gulick, L., 123, 130
Gutek, B. A., 169
Gutierrez, L. M., 185, 194

H

Habermas, J., 170
Hagen, S., 46
Handler, J. F., 172, 286
Handy, F., 201
Hannan, M. T., 73
Hansmann, H. B., 11
Hardcastle, D. A., 184, 383
Hardy, C., 165, 166, 168
Harper, K. V., 36
Harris, M., 15
Harrison, M. I., 135
Hasenfeld, Y., 42, 43, 141, 163,
    168, 171, 172
Hassard, J., 26, 173, 287
Hatch, M. J., 23, 24
Hearn, J., 229, 283
Heidegger, M., 289
Henderson, B. D., 72
Hepworth, D., 32, 135
Hersey, P., 28
Herzberg, F., 103
Hess, P. M., 258

Heydebrand, W. V., 105
Hirsh, S., 26, 69
Hollis, F., 135
Holloway, S., 29, 34, 122
Huff, A. S., 75
Hughes, E. C., 221
Hutchinson, J. G., 23,
    25, 27
Hyde, C., 18, 164, 201

I

Iannello, K. P., 164
Iglehart, A. P., 142

J

Jacobsen, W., 258
Jaques, E., 108, 221
Jaskyte, K., 362
Jenkins, S., 17, 377
Johnson, G., 76

K

Kahn, R., 109
Kanter, K., 169
Kanter, R. M., 169
Karanja, S. T., 188, 191, 384
Kassam, M., 201
Katz, D., 108, 109
Kaufman, H., 221
Kellner, D., 173
Kellner-Rogers, M., 258, 280,
    303, 316
Kelly, R. M., 115, 229
Kersten, A., 171, 285
Kets de Vries, M. F. R., 77
Kettner, P. M., 29, 34, 99, 137, 139,
    140, 199
Kiechel, W., III, 75
Kikert, W., 164
Kilmann, R. H., 227

Kirby, L., 26
Kirk, S. A., 134, 135
Knights, D., 173
Koen, S., 170
Kondrat, M. E., 33, 34
Koney, K. M., 15
Koontz, H., 23
Koroloff, N. M., 21
Kramer, R. M., 14, 380
Kravetz, D., 201
Kroeger, O., 30
Kutchins, H., 134, 135

L

Lampel, J., xi, 69–71, 73, 75, 77, 139, 194, 250, 311, 336
Lang, Y. S., 3, 23, 24, 96, 99–102, 105, 160, 167, 168, 220, 227, 281, 380
Lantz, J., 36
Lapierre, R., 75
Larsen, J., 32, 135
Lash, S., 287
Laudan, L., 46
Lawler, E., 135
Lawrence, G., 26, 69
Lawrence-Lightfoot, S., 37
Lawson, H., 287
Lechich, A. J., 129
Leifer, R., 190, 381
Lescohier, I. H., 164
Lester, L., 122, 375
Levin, M., 258
Levy, B. S., 200
Lewis, D., 20
Lewis, E. A., 185, 194
Lewis, J. A., 27, 137
Lewis, M. D., 27, 137
Likert, R., 27
Lincoln, Y., 234
Lindblom, C. E., 75

Lindenberg, M., 15
Linstead, S., 173
Lohmann, R. A., 11
Lorsch, J. W., 105, 107
Louis, M. R., 223, 224, 230
Luckman, T., 221
Lugones, M. C., 230
Lum, D., 36, 379
Lune, H., 21
Lunsford, A., 258
Lyotard, J. F., 287

M

Macduff, N., 258, 376
McGrath, M. R., 20
McGregor, D. M., 27, 103
McHugh, H., 75
MacMillan, I. C., 73
McMurtry, S. L., 29, 99, 137, 139
Mann, M., 166
Mannheim, K., 170
March, J. G., 166
Marcuse, H., 289
Margolis, H., 46
Martin, C., 26
Martin, J., 220–223
Martin, L. L., 128, 140, 199
Martin, P. Y., 18, 50, 52, 53, 109–112, 161, 162, 170, 201, 377
Maslow, A. H., 103
Mayo, G. E., 103
Merton, R. K., 115
Metzendorf, D., 18, 201
Miller, H., 26
Miller, J., 134, 135
Milliken, F. J., 231
Millman, M., 169
Minkoff, D. C., 20
Mintzberg, H., xi, 69–77, 107, 130, 139, 194, 250, 311, 336

Mirvis, P., 135
Mitchell, T. R., 23
Mizruchi, M. S., 164
Mondros, J. B., 200
Moore, M. H., 15
Morgan, G., x, xi, 23, 24, 46–56, 58, 83, 92, 94, 95, 99, 109–111, 113, 154, 158, 159, 161, 182, 214, 217, 218, 230, 231, 274, 277, 278, 280, 283, 285
Moroney, R. M., 140, 199
Morris, R., 164
Mouton, J. S., 27, 28
Mullaly, B., 275, 279, 291, 293
Mullen, E. J., 258
Münsterberg, H., 103
Myers, I. B., xi, 25, 26, 63–65
Myers, K., 26
Myers, P., 83

N
Nadler, D., 135
Nelson, R. R., 75
Netting, F. E., 7, 8, 17, 20, 22, 29, 43, 56, 57, 77, 99, 137, 139, 193, 205, 246, 258, 261, 262, 288, 312, 316, 317, 328, 354–358, 360, 376, 377, 381
Nichols, A. W., 29, 34
Nord, W. R., 166
Nyden, P., 200

O
Oakeshott, M. J., 289
O'Connor, G. G., 50, 52, 53, 109–112, 161, 162
O'Connor, M. K., 7, 8, 17, 20, 22, 43, 56, 57, 77, 193, 205, 246, 258, 261, 262, 288, 312, 316, 317, 328, 354–358, 360, 377, 381
Odendahl, T., 201

O'Donnell, S. M., 188, 191, 384
O'Neil, M., 201
Oster, S. M., 19
Ott, J. S., 3, 23, 24, 96, 97, 99–102, 105, 160, 167, 168, 220, 222, 227, 281, 380
Ouchi, W. G., 223, 235
Oxford University Press Staff, 134, 135

P
Packard, T., 27, 137
Parker, M., 26, 173, 285, 287
Parkin, P. W., 229, 283
Parsons, T., 101
Patti, R. J., 10, 29, 34, 35, 83, 122
Paul, R. W., 30, 31, 37
Peters, T. J., 223, 235
Pettigrew, A. M., 76
Pfeffer, J., 27, 165
Pinchot, G., III, 77
Piven, F. F., 201
Platt, R., 287
Porter, L. W., 166
Porter, M. E., 72
Power, M., 287
Powers, P. R., 184, 383
Preston, M. S., 20

Q
Quinn, R. E., x, xi, 20, 58–62, 180, 241, 301, 328, 331, 346, 347, 362, 375, 376, 378, 379

R
Rabinow, P., 170
Ranade, B., 201
Rauch, J. B., 135
Raven, B., 165
Reamer, F. G., 382

Reddin, W. J., 28
Reed, M., 101, 104, 112, 234
Reger, R. K., 75
Resnick, H., 29, 34, 35,
    83, 122
Richmond, M., 134
Ritzer, G., 45
Rodwell, M. K., 134, 234
Roethlisberger, F. J., 229
Rogers, R. E., 99
Rooney, G. D., 32, 135
Rooney, R., 32, 135
Rothman, J., 183, 201
Ruggiero, V. R., 30

S
Sackman, S. A., 231
Sarrazin, J., 73
Schein, E. H., 31, 44, 223, 224–226,
    256, 380
Schlesinger, E. G., 36
Schmidt, W. H., 27
Schneider, R. L., 122, 375
Scott, W. G., 23
Scott, W. R., 105, 107
Seashore, S., 27, 135
Selznick, P., 70, 101
Senge, P. M., 246, 251, 379
Shafritz, J. M., 3, 23, 24, 96, 97,
    99–102, 105, 160, 167, 168, 220,
    222, 227, 281, 380
Shibley, M., 200
Shirom, A., 135
Simon, H. A., 75, 100, 108
Singletary, J., 77, 193
Siporin, M., 134, 135
Sirianni, C., 171, 285
Slater, P. E., 108
Smircich, L., 169, 172, 170, 229,
    283, 284

Smith, A., 97, 123
Smith, D. H., 16, 378
Solomon, J. R., 137
Souflee, R., 27, 137
Spelman, E. V., 230
Stalker, G. M., 107, 379, 380
Starbuck, W. H., 231
Stauss, A. L., 221
Steiner, G. A., 71
Stogdill, R. M., 27
Strom-Gottfried, K., 32, 135

T
Tannebaum, R., 27
Taylor, F. W., 98, 122, 123
Thayer, F. E., 108
Thibaud, J. L., 287
Thibault, J. M., 17
Thomas, H., 75
Thompson, J. D., 107, 109, 127,
    165, 189, 358
Thompson, M. P., 20
Thompson, P., 234, 285
Thuesen, J. M., 30
Tieger, P., 26, 69
Toffler, A., 108
Toynbee, A. J., 74
Tuominen, M., 12
Turner, F. J., 135, 232

U
Urry, J., 287

V
Van Maanen, J., 220
Vibert, C., 93, 96, 113

W
Walker, A. H., 105, 107
Waterman, R. H., Jr., 223, 235

Weber, M., 53, 98, 99, 130
Weick, K. E., 231, 232, 259
Weiner, M. E., 164
Wenocur, S., 184, 383
Westley, F., 77
Wheatley, M. J., 258, 280, 303, 316
Whyte, W. H., Jr., 101, 221
Wiener, N., 108
Wilkerson, A. E., 191, 193, 194, 249
Williams, R., 170
Willmott, H., 171, 173, 285
Wilson, F., 164
Wilson, S. M., 200
Wineburg, B., 17

Winter, S. G., 75
Wolff, J., 169
Wood, R. L., 17
Woods, M. E., 135
Wuthnow, R., 17

Y
Yancey, G., 17
Young, D. R., 15, 384
Yunus, M., 13

Z
Zald, M., 168
Zald, M. N., 73

SUBJECT INDEX

A

AAHSA, *see* American Association of Homes and Services for the Aged

AARP, *see* American Association of Retired Persons

Absolutism:
ethical, 141–142, 202–203
in Social Change Organizations, 181, 182
in Traditional Organizations, 121, 123

Absolutists, 48

"Acceptable" knowledge, 285

Acquisitions, 15

Action model, 201

Adaptation, external, 225

Adhocracy culture, 60–62, 331. *See also* Radical Humanist Paradigm
in Entrepreneurial Organizations, 301, 314
mission/philosophy in, 356
school of management related to, 77–78

Administration:
anti-administration, 289–292
defining/measuring objectives of, 100
science of, 97–98

Administrative advocacy, 184

Advocacy:
administrative, 184
case (client), 122–123, 183, 240
cause, 154, 184
legislative, 184
as means of influence, 183
public interest, 184
and radical structuralism, 172
by Serendipitous Organizations, 240
in Social Change Organizations, 183–184, 186

Affiliations, 13–15, 17. *See also* Organizational relationships

Age Discrimination Act, 25

Age of agency, culture and, 357–358

Alienation, 164

Alinsky, Saul, 193

Allegiances, *see* Organizational relationships

Alliances, 187. *See also* Organizational relationships

Alterity, 291–292

Alternative organizations:
Entrepreneurial Organizations, 305
feminist, 169–170
funding for, 191

Alternative organizations:
  (*Continued*)
  in postmodern theory, 334
  private agencies as, 357
  Serendipitous Organizations,
    245
Alvesson, M., 171–172
The Alzheimer's Association, 16, 21
Americans with Disabilities Act, 25
American Association of Homes
    and Services for the Aged
    (AAHSA), 15, 21
American Association of Retired
    Persons (AARP), 14, 187–188
American Red Cross YMCA, 21
Analogies of social systems,
    109–112, 190
Anarchies, organized, 166
Anti-administration, 289–292, 335
Antideterminism, 294
Anti-organization theory, 55
Antipositivism, 47, 216
  defined, 217, 277
  in Entrepreneurial Organizations,
    294
Applied psychology, 102–103
Artifacts, in organizational culture,
    226
Assessment, 8, 135–136
  defined, 135
  diagnosis vs., 134, 135
  of effectiveness, 42
  in Entrepreneurial Organizations,
    315–317
  nonrational approach to, 255–257
  of organizational life, 365–374
  in Serendipitous Organizations,
    254–257
  in Social Change Organizations,
    198–199

  in Traditional Organizations,
    136–138
Associations, 14–16, 21. *See also*
    Organizational relationships
  umbrella, 15
  voluntary, 14–15
Assumptions:
  about employees, 25–27
  about managers and leaders,
    27–28
  about organizations, 22–25
  clashes of, 29, 31, 32
  of classical organization theories,
    97
  of comfort zone paradigm, 329
  in critical thinking, 30–32
  in diverse view of the world, 45
  in Entrepreneurial Organizations,
    273
  of Functionalist Paradigm, 51,
    93–95, 97
  of Interpretive Paradigm, 53, 54,
    216–219
  and multiparadigmatic thinking,
    57
  in organizational culture,
    226–227
  of paradigms, 46, 55–57
  of Radical Humanist Paradigm,
    56, 276–280
  of Radical Structuralist Paradigm,
    52, 157–159
  of Serendipitous Organizations,
    263
  shared, 31, 224
  in Social Change Organizations,
    188
  of structural theoretical
    perspective, 106
  of systems theories, 113

as theories-in-use, 43–44
in Traditional Organizations, 335
Autocratic leaders, 27
Autonomy:
  managerial, 106
  in Radical Humanist Perspective, 278
Awareness, in Serendipitous Organizations, 240

B

Barnard, Chester, 100
Becerra, R. M., 142
Behaviorism, 102–103
Best practices, in Traditional Organizations, 126
Biases, self-awareness of, 36
Bio-psycho-socio-spiritual nature of individuals, 290
Black Panthers, 193
Bounded rationality, 100
Briggs, Katharine Cook, 26
Brilliant, E. L., 175
Budgeting, in Traditional Organizations, 124
Bureaucracy:
  and anti-administration concept, 289–290
  efficiency maximized by, 115
  elements congruent with social work, 142
  ideal type of, 98–99
  play as alternative to, 290
  as social domination, 283
  as structural theory, 114
  in Traditional Organizations, 123, 130
Bureaucratic personality, 115
Burns, T., 107
Burrell, G., 46–56

Burrell and Morgan paradigmatic framework, 46–56, 360. *See also individual paradigms*
  with Competing Values, 61
  Functionalist Paradigm, 50–51, 92
  Interpretive Paradigm, 53–54, 214
  with Myers-Briggs behavioral dimensions, 65
  with organizational goals, 79
  and Organization Assessment tool, 362
  Radical Humanist Paradigm, 54–56, 274
  Radical Structuralist Paradigm, 51–52, 154
  regulation–radical change continuum, 48–50
  with schools of management thought, 70
  subjectivist–objectivist continuum, 46–48

C

Calás, M. B., 229
Cameron, K. S., 58–62, 346–347
Case (client) advocacy, 122–123, 183, 240
Catastrophic analogy of social systems, 109, 110, 161, 162
Catastrophic change, 182
Catholic Charities, 21
Cause advocacy, 154, 184
Centers for New Horizons, 191
Change, 42
  collective transformational, 198
  in Entrepreneurial Organizations, 307
  incremental, 126, 337
  innovative, 318

Change (*Continued*)
  in Interpretive Paradigm, 217, 218
  in morphogenic systems, 190
  planned, 122, 136
  in Radical Humanist Paradigm,
    279
  radicalized planned, 183
  in Serendipitous Organizations,
    217, 243, 248
  in Social Change Organizations,
    184, 188. *See also* Social Change
    Organizations
  through consciousness raising,
    147, 335, 337
  in Traditional Organizations, 86,
    122, 124, 126
Chaos, in multicultural
  organizations, 44
Chaos theory, 113
Charismatic leadership, 193–194
Charitable organizations, 11
Child Welfare League of America
  (CWLA), 14, 15, 21, 240
Church affiliates, 17
Church agencies, 17
Church-related agencies, 17
Clan culture, 60–62, 331. *See also*
    Interpretive Paradigm
  schools of management related
    to, 75–77
  in Serendipitous Organizations,
    241, 243, 248
Classics of Organizational Theory
    (Shafritz, Ott, and Lang),
    227–228
Classical organization theories, 23, 24,
    96–99, 102
Clients:
  new programs or services
    meeting needs of, 9

  relationships with, *see* Client
    relationships; Consumer
    relationships; Participant
    relationships
  socially-acceptable, 129–130, 355
Client advocacy, *see* Case advocacy
Client-centered services/therapy,
    53, 119
Client relationships:
  in multiparadigmatic practice,
    344–346
  in Traditional Organizations,
    129–130, 348
Coalitions, 15. *See also*
    Organizational relationships
Cognitive dissonance theory, 229
Cognitive School, 75, 250
Collaboration:
  in Entrepreneurial Organizations,
    285, 312
  nonrational approach to, 255–257
  in Serendipitous Organizations,
    235, 240–241, 246, 255, 258–259,
    337
  theories supporting, 219–233
Collaborative organization, 56
Collaborative process, 258
Collective transformational change,
    198
Comfort zone paradigm, 329
Communal connections, 75
Communication, 37. *See also*
    Language
  dialectical process for, 186
  in Entrepreneurial Organizations,
    313, 349
  in human service practice,
    355–356
  in Serendipitous Organizations,
    252–253, 349

in Social Change Organizations, 192, 194, 195, 349
in Traditional Organizations, 131–132, 349
Communities:
ideological, 17–19, 21
as practice arenas, 5
Community practice:
Functionalist Paradigm in, 51
transformative, 188
Competing values framework, 57–63, 241
Complexity:
in Entrepreneurial School, 77
in postmodern theories, 290, 334
in Serendipitous Organizations, 262
in Traditional Organizations, 125–126
Confidence, in Social Change Organizations, 195
Configuration School, 74, 194
Conflict, 104–105
in competing values framework, 57–58
in critical theories, 170–171
in Entrepreneurial Organizations, 303, 313, 316–317
in morphogenic systems, 190
in postmodern theories, 172
in Serendipitous Organizations, 249
in Social Change Organizations, 201–202
in Traditional Organizations, 137–138
Conflict theory, 52
Connection:
in Serendipitous Organizations, 235, 240–241, 246, 337

in Social Change Organizations, 195
theories supporting, 219–233
Consciousness:
false, 181, 285, 286
in Social Change Organizations, 194, 195
true, 144, 145, 181–182, 302
Consciousness raising, 147, 335. *See also* Social Change Organizations
goals for, 175–176
in problem analysis, 200
in radical humanism, 276
theories supporting, 159–174
Consensus building:
for adapting externally, 225
in Entrepreneurial Organizations, 299
political process of, 10
in Serendipitous Organizations, 250
in Traditional Organizations, 122
Consolidations, 15
Consortia, 15
Constraints, 5
Consumer-Directed Advocacy Agency case study, 149–152, 345. *See also* Social Change Organizations
Consumer relationships, in Social Change Organizations, 192, 348
Contextual awareness, 34, 35
Contextual relationships, in Serendipitous Organizations, 248–249
Contingencies, 5

Contingency approach, 28
Contingency theory, 113, 334
Contingency view of management, 73–74
Contradictions, in Social Change Organizations, 160
Control, 85
  in competing values framework, 58, 59
  organizational coordination and control concept, 106
  in Traditional Organizations, 85, 337. *See also* Traditional Organizations
Convergent thinking, 292
Cooptation, 101
Coordination, 106
Corporate culture, 223. *See also* Organizational culture(s)
Corporations, 12
Correction, gaining consensus on, 225
Costs and benefits:
  in Entrepreneurial Organizations, 293–295
  in Serendipitous Organizations, 234–235
  in Social Change Organizations, 174–176
  in Traditional Organizations, 114–116
Crises:
  in current organizations, 284–285
  in Social Change Organizations, 160
Critical reflectivity, 34, 35, 156, 157
Critical theories, 23
  in Entrepreneurial Organizations, 284–286

in Social Change Organizations, 168, 170–172
Critical thinking, 30–32, 34–37
  about organizations, 29
  assumptions in, 30–32
  in multicultural organizations, 34–37
  tasks in, 30, 31
Critical voice, 165, 166, 281
Cross-cultural competence, 36
Cultural fit, 36
Cultural School, 76, 251
Cultural values and characteristics:
  of Entrepreneurial Organizations, 301–307
  of Serendipitous Organizations, 241–247
  of Social Change Organizations, 180–188
  of Traditional Organizations, 120–126
Cultures. *See also* Organizational culture(s)
  group/subgroup, 35–36
  national, 7
Curiosity, 37
CWLA, *see* Child Welfare League of America
Cybernetics (N. Wiener), 108

D
Dalton, Melville, 101
Danone, 13
Decision making:
  in anti-administration, 291
  assumptions underlying, 334
  depoliticization of, 112
  Simon's concepts of, 100–101
Decision theory school of thought, 27

Deconstruction, 172–173, 335
Deetz, S., 171–172
Demarginalizing suppressed
  voices, 288
Democratic leaders, 27
Density dependence, 163
Design School, 70–71, 131, 139
Determinism, 48
  defined, 158
  in Functionalist Paradigm, 94
Diagnosis:
  assessment vs., 134, 135
  definitions of, 134–136
  social, 134
  and Social Change Organizations,
    197
  in Traditional Organizations,
    138–139
Dialectical communication/
  conversation, 37
  in Entrepreneurial Organizations,
    313
  in Social Change Organizations,
    192
Dialectical process:
  in Entrepreneurial Organizations,
    314
  in Social Change Organizations,
    156, 186
Dialogue, 37, 311
Differentiators, 228–229,
    316–317
Direct practice:
  Functionalist Paradigm in,
    50, 51
  and Radical Structuralist
    Paradigm, 52
Direct service programs, 8
  across different types of
    organizations, 339–342

  in Entrepreneurial Organizations,
    304–305
  in Serendipitous Organizations,
    244–245
  in Social Change Organizations,
    185, 199
  in Traditional Organizations, 123
Discontinuities, 363
Discovery, in Entrepreneurial
  Organizations, 317–318
Discretion, in competing values
  framework, 58, 59
Divergent thinking, 292
Diversity, 21
  among employees, 26–27
  in Entrepreneurial Organizations,
    303
  within groups, 25
  honoring, 25
  management view of,
    26–27
  organizational, 25
  in postmodern theories, 334
  Serendipitous Organizations'
    acceptance of, 243, 263
  staff and client, 25
Division of labor and work,
    123
Documentation, in Traditional
  Organization, 133
Domination, 160
  bureaucracy as, 283
  in critical theories, 172
  in feminist theory, 168
  in postmodern theories, 173
Drucker, Peter, 108

E
EAPs (employee assistance
  programs), 21

Eberle, Gary, 275
Effectiveness:
  measures of, 42
  in Serendipitous Organizations,
    262
  as Traditional Organization goal,
    121
Effectiveness-based planning
    model, 140–141
Efficiency:
  maximized by bureaucracy,
    115
  in Traditional Organizations,
    121, 132
Emergence:
  in Entrepreneurial Organizations,
    316, 317
  value of, 317
Emergent planning, 246, 258
Emic perspective, 243
Empirical school of thought, 27
Employees. *See also* Staff
    expectations
  assumptions about, 25–27
  performance expectations for, 68
  self-government of, 164
  social needs of, 102
Employee assistance programs
    (EAPs), 21
Empowerment, 37
  in Entrepreneurial Organizations,
    293–295, 299, 318–319, 337
  from individual transformation,
    319
  in Radical Structuralist Paradigm,
    155
  in Social Change Organizations,
    186, 195, 200–201
  theories supporting, 280–292
  use of term, 119

Enactment, in sense making, 232
Entrepreneurial Organizations,
    267–268, 273–276, 295–296,
    299–301, 322–323.
    See also Radical Humanist
    Paradigm
  assessment in, 315–317
  and assumptions of radical
    humanist paradigm, 276–280
  communication in, 349
  costs and benefits in,
    293–295
  critical theories in, 284–286
  cultural values and
    characteristics of, 301–307,
    338
  discovery in, 317–318
  environment in, 342, 343
  feminist theories in, 283–284
  funding relationships in, 343,
    348
  goals and personal preferences in,
    81, 82, 337
  I HELP case study, 268–271
  implications for practice in,
    321–322
  individual empowerment goals
    in, 293–295
  individual transformation or
    empowerment in, 318–319
  innovation in, 318
  internal organizational roles and
    relationships in, 310–314,
    348–349
  language in, 314–315
  leaders in, 341–342
  management in, 348
  managerial competencies in,
    347
  mission/philosophy of, 302–303

organization-environment relationships in, 308–310

participant relationships in, 345–346, 348

postmodern theories in, 286–292

power and politics theories in, 281–283

preferred structure in, 303–304

producing products and outcomes in, 319–321

program goals in, 339

as prototype, 273

radical humanist themes in, 275–276

referral sources in, 309–310, 348

roles and relationships with and within, 307–314, 348–349

staff expectations in, 349

standards of practice within, 314–321

strengths of and challenges for, 353

task environment relationships in, 348

themes of, 330–331

theories supporting individual empowerment goals in, 280–292

types of programs and services in, 304–305, 341, 342

Entrepreneurial School, 77–78, 311

Environments:
general, 109
interaction of organization and, 101, 109. *See also* Organization-environment relationships
multicultural, 35
in multiparadigmatic practice, 342–343
social, 105–106
sociopolitical, 42
task, 109
turbulent, 5–6

Environmental School, 73–74, 194

Epistemology, functionalist, 93

Ethics:
in Entrepreneurial Organizations, 321–322
in Serendipitous Organizations, 260, 262, 263
situational, 242

Ethical absolutism, 141–142, 202–203

Ethical relativity, 321–322

Ethnic agencies, 17–18

Ethnic-sensitive competence, 36

Etic perspective, 243

Extracted cues, in sense making, 232

Extroversion, 26

F

Fabelo, H. E., 354–358

Factional analogy of social systems, 109, 110, 161, 162

Faith-based agencies, 17

Faith communities, 17

False consciousness, 181, 285, 286

Fayol, Henri, 97–98

Federations, 15, 16. *See also* Organizational relationships

Feeling:
as Myers-Briggs characteristic, 64, 65
thinking vs., 26

Feeling-judging (FJ) dimension (Myers-Briggs), 64, 65, 67
Feeling-perceiving (FP) dimension (Myers-Briggs), 64, 65, 68, 313–314
Feminist organizations, 18
Feminist social movement organizations (FSMOs), 18
Feminist theories:
 branches of, 168–169
 in Entrepreneurial Organizations, 283–284
 radical, 168–170
 and sense-making theories, 229–230
 and Social Change Organizations, 168, 201
 third world/(post) colonial, 283–284
FJ dimension, *see* Feeling-judging dimension
Flexibility:
 in competing values framework, 58, 59
 in Entrepreneurial Organizations, 305
 in Serendipitous Organizations, 253
Follett, Mary Parker, 103
Formal organizations, 6
 basis of authority in, 165
 Traditional, 123, 132
For-profit organizations, 10, 12. *See also* Social entrepreneurs
FP dimension, *see* Feeling-perceiving dimension
Fragmentation, 164
Frameworks, 41–83
 competing values, 57–63
 defined, 44

 integrated, 78–82
 multiparadigmatic, 45–57
 Myers-Briggs, 63–69
 and organizational theories, 41–44
 strategic management, 69–78
Franchises, 19, 21
FSMOs (feminist social movement organizations), 18
Functionalist Paradigm, 50–51
 assumptions of, 93–95
 criticism of, 114
 and interpretivism, 217
 organizational theories in, 332–334
 personality types in, 65–66
 postmodern theorists in, 174
 schools of management related to, 70–73
 theories within, 114–115
 in Traditional Organizations, 92–93, 123
 usurpation of interpretive concept in, 227–228
Funding relationships:
 in Entrepreneurial Organizations, 309, 348
 in multiparadigmatic practice, 343–344
 in Serendipitous Organizations, 249, 348
 in Social Change Organizations, 187, 190–191, 348
 in Traditional Organizations, 128–129, 348

G
GAs (grassroots associations), 16
Games, in anti-administration, 292

Gannon, M. J., 248
Gantt, H. L., 98
Gantt charts, 98
General environments, 109
The Geography of Nowhere
(G. Eberle), 275
Gerontological Society of America
(GSA), 239
Gestalt therapy, 53
Gherardi, S., 230
Glass ceiling, 143
Global organizations, 7
Goals:
in Entrepreneurial Organizations,
81, 82, 282, 300
gaining consensus on, 225
of human service organizations,
42
for individual empowerment,
293–295
integrated framework built on,
78–82
in multiparadigmatic practice,
336–342
in organizational life, 105
in Planning School of
management, 71
in power and politics theories,
167–168
in programs across practices,
339–342
in Serendipitous Organizations,
81, 252
in Social Change Organizations,
79, 80
in Traditional Organizations,
79, 80
Goodwill Industries, 19
Government agencies, *see* Public
agencies

Grassroots associations (GAs), 16
Groups:
cultures of, 35–36
diversity within, 25
in Entrepreneurial Organizations,
307
passivity of, 166
as practice arenas, 5
in Radical Humanist Paradigm,
282
GSA (Gerontological Society of
America), 239
Gulick, Luther, 98, 99

H
Habitat for Humanity International,
16
Habitual distortions, 32
Hasenfeld, Y., 42–43, 354
Hawthorne plant, Western Electric
Company, 102, 103
Herzberg, G., 103
Heuristics, 45
Hierarchical cultures, 56, 59–62, 331.
See also Functionalist Paradigm
mission/philosophy in, 356
schools of management related
to, 70–73
Traditional, 123, 130
Homeostasis, 112
Hospice organizations, 240–241
Hospitals, social services in, 21
Host relationships, 19–21
Human behavior school of thought,
27
Human relations/organizational
behavioral theory, 101–104, 116
Human Relations School, 102
Human resource/organizational
behavior theory, 23, 24, 27

Human service organizations:
  connecting organizational
    theories and, 41–44
  forthcoming research on,
    354–361
  unique characteristics of, 42–43
Human service outcomes, 141
Human service work, 5
  delivery systems for, 6
  diversity of perspectives in, 7
  formalization of delivery, 6
  privatization of, 12
Humility, 37

I
Identity, in sense making, 232
Ideographic perspectives, 47, 217,
    277
Ideological communities, 17–19, 21
Ideological critiques, 172
I HELP case study, 268–271,
    345–346. See also
    Entrepreneurial Organizations
Images of Organization (G. Morgan),
    23–24
Images of Organization (G. Morgan),
    230–231
Implications for practice:
  in Entrepreneurial Organizations,
    321–322
  from multiparadigmatic research,
    360, 362–363
  in Serendipitous Organizations,
    262–263
  in Social Change Organizations,
    202–203
  in Traditional Organizations,
    141–143
Inclusion, in Serendipitous
    Organizations, 248

Incremental change, 126, 337
Independent consultants, 5
Indirect service programs, 8
Individualism, 277, 278, 286
Individual transformation,
    318–319
Industrial psychology, 102–103
Informal organizations, 6
  basis of authority in, 165
  Serendipitous Organizations as,
    244
Inglehart, A. P., 142
INGOs, see International
    nongovernmental
    organizations
Innovation, 77, 301, 318
In Praise of Hierarchy (E. Jaques), 108
In Search of Excellence (T. J. Peters
    and R. H. Waterman, Jr.), 223
Institutional theory, 113
Integrated frameworks, 56–57,
    78–82
Integrationist perspective, 223–228
Intellectual humility, 37
Interfaith Alliance, 182
Internal organizational roles and
    relationships:
  in Entrepreneurial Organizations,
    310–314, 347–349
  in multiparadigmatic practice,
    346–347
  in Serendipitous Organizations,
    250–254, 347–349
  in Social Change Organizations,
    193–197, 346–349
  in Traditional Organizations,
    130–134, 346, 348–349
Internal structure, 105–106
Internal uncertainties and
    turbulence, 5–6

International nongovernmental organizations (INGOs), 15–16, 284
Interorganizational relationships, 15
Interpretive Paradigm, 53–54
  assumptions of, 216–219
  differentiation in, 228–229
  in evolution of organizational theories, 335
  integrationism in, 223–228
  organizational theories in, 234, 332
  personality types in, 67
  schools of management related to, 75–77
  in Serendipitous Organizations, 214–216
  theories in, 219–220
  value engineering in, 222–223
Interpretive theories, 23
Interpretivism, 216
Intersubjective experiences, 285
Interventions. *See also* Services
  organizations as object of, 5
  planned change, 122
  in Social Change Organizations, 183, 198, 200–202
  in Traditional Organizations, 122, 139–141
Interventionist organizations, 156
Introversion, 26
Intuition:
  in radical humanism, 276
  sensing vs., 26

J
Jaques, Elliott, 108
Joint ventures, 15
Judging:

feeling-judging dimension, 64, 65, 67
  as Myers-Briggs characteristic, 64, 65
  perceiving vs., 26
  thinking-judging dimension, 64–66

K
Kanter, R. M., 169
Kellner-Rogers, M., 316
Kettner, P. M., 140
Knowing, multiple ways of, 275–276
Knowledge:
  "acceptable," 285
  postmodern view of, 288
  subjugated, 284
Knowledge building:
  in Interpretive Paradigm, 215–216
  in radical humanism, 276
Ku Klux Klan, 182

L
Lang, Y. S., 220, 227–228
Language:
  in anti-administration, 290–291
  differences across organization types, 254
  differences across paradigms, 315
  in Entrepreneurial Organizations, 306, 314–315
  in evolution of organizational theory, 335
  of organizational culture, 221
  in postmodern theories, 287
  of radical humanism, 299
  in Radical Humanist Paradigm, 279
  in research process, 215, 234
  in sense making, 233

Language: (*Continued*)
   in Serendipitous Organizations, 250, 251, 254–255
   in Social Change Organizations, 192, 197–198
   in Traditional Organizations, 119, 134–136, 335
Latino Nonprofit Women's Shelter, 21
Leaders and leadership, 29–37
   approaches to understanding, 27–28
   assumptions about, 27–28
   autocratic vs. democratic, 27
   charismatic, 193–194
   critical thinking skills for, 30–32, 34–37
   defined, 29
   in Entrepreneurial Organizations, 306, 310–312, 341–342
   in Entrepreneurial School, 77
   in multicultural organizations, 34–37
   in multiparadigmatic practice, 350–352
   as professional responsibility of practitioners, 29
   self-awareness in, 32–37
   in Serendipitous Organizations, 241, 246, 251–252, 263–264, 341–342
   in Social Change Organizations, 193–195, 341–342
   in Traditional Organizations, 131, 132, 341–342
Leadership skills, 29
Learning organizations, 246–247
Learning School, 75–76, 250–251
Legislative advocacy, 184
Liberal feminist theories, 168–169, 174, 229

Liberty, 302
Life experiences, 33
Linkages, *see* Organizational relationships
Locus of control:
   in Entrepreneurial Organizations, 307
   in Social Change Organizations, 188
Louis, M. R., 230

M
McGregor, Douglas, 103
Management:
   in Entrepreneurial Organizations, 310–312, 347, 348
   of formal and informal power, 165
   POSDCORB functions of, 99
   scientific, 98, 116
   in Serendipitous Organizations, 250–252, 347, 348
   in Social Change Organizations, 193–194, 346–348
   symbolic, 221–222
   in Traditional Organizations, 130–131, 346, 348
Management by objectives (MBO), 142
The Management of Innovation (T. Burns and G. M. Stalker), 107
Management styles, 27–28
Management theories, 23–24. *See also* Frameworks
   of Fayol, 97
   models of, 27
Managers:
   assumptions about, 27–28
   network allegiances of, 164
Managerial autonomy, 106

Managing diversity, 25
Marginalization, 290
Market culture, 60–62, 73–75, 331.
    See also Radical Structuralist
    Paradigm
Martin, L. L., 140
Martin, P. Y., 112
Marx, Karl, 165
Maslow, Abraham, 103
Master plans, 7
Mathematical school of thought, 27
Mayo, Elton, 102, 103
MBO (management by objectives),
    142
Means to attain goals, gaining
    consensus on, 225
Measurement:
    gaining consensus on, 225
    in Traditional Organizations, 86,
        122, 137
Mechanical analogy of social
    systems, 109–112
Mechanistic approaches, 99
Mechanistic organizations, 107
Media, in postmodern theories, 173
Mediterranean Marxism, 52
Mergers, 15
Metaphors, 23–24, 99, 109, 230–231
Military family assistance
    programs, 21
Mind meld, 313
Minority practice, 36
Mintzberg, H., 107
Mission/philosophy:
    across types of organizations, 356
    of Entrepreneurial Organizations,
        302–303
    gaining consensus on, 225
    of Serendipitous Organizations,
        243

of Social Change Organizations,
    182–184
of Traditional Organizations,
    122–123
"Modern" structural organization
    theory, 23, 24
    based on Functionalist Paradigm,
        50
    in Traditional Organizations,
        104–108
Moral values, 42
Morgan, G., 23–24, 46–56, 99,
    230–231
Moroney, R. M., 140
Morphogenic analogy of social
    systems, 109, 110, 161, 162,
    190
Morphostasis, 162
Motivation, 103
Multiculturalism:
    in Entrepreneurial Organizations,
        321
    in postmodern theories, 334
    Serendipitous Organizations'
        acceptance of, 243, 263
Multicultural practice, 57
    critical thinking and self-
        awareness in, 34–37
    degree of chaos and uncertainty
        in, 44
Multiparadigmatic framework,
    45–57
    basic assumptions of paradigms,
        46, 55–57
    Functionalist Paradigm, 50–51
    Interpretive Paradigm, 53–54
    Radical Humanist Paradigm,
        54–55
    Radical Structuralist Paradigm,
        51–52

Multiparadigmatic framework
(*Continued*)
   regulation/radical change
     continuum, 48–50
   subjectivist–objectivist
     continuum, 46–48
Multiparadigmatic practice,
   327–363
   challenge of, 329
   defined, 58
   environmental differences in,
     342–343
   funding relationships in,
     343–344
   goals and characteristics in,
     336–342
   in human service organization
     research, 354–361
   internal organizational roles and
     relationships in, 346–347
   leadership in, 350–352
   organizational themes in,
     329–331
   and organizational theory,
     332–336
   paradoxes in, 328
   practice implications of research
     on, 360, 362–363
   programming differences in,
     339–342
   relationships with clients in,
     344–346
   roles and relationships in,
     342–352
   strengths and challenges in, 350,
     353–354
Multiparadigmatic thinking, 57
Münsterberg, Hugo, 103
Myers, Isabel Briggs, 26
Myers-Briggs test, 25–26
   and clashes of personality types,
     68–69
   dimensions in, 63–65
   extroversion-introversion
     continuum, 63
   feeling-judging dimension, 64, 65,
     67
   feeling-perceiving dimension, 64,
     65, 68
   as framework, 63–69
   management use of, 26
   sensing-intuition continuum, 63
   thinking-judging dimension,
     64–66
   thinking-perceiving dimension,
     64–67
   uses of, 69

N
Narrative therapy, 53
National Association of Social
   Workers (NASW), 14, 15, 21
National Citizens Coalition on
   Nursing Home Reform
   (NCCNHR), 188
National cultures, mutual
   sensitivity and competence
   across, 7
NCCNHR (National Citizens
   Coalition on Nursing Home
   Reform), 188
Needs, 103, 199
Needs assessments, in Social
   Change Organizations, 198–199
Neoclassical organization theory,
   23, 24, 99–101
Netting, F. E., 354–358
Networks, 15, 164
Newcomers, transitions for, 223
New leadership approach, 28

NGOs, *see* Nongovernmental organizations
Nominalism, 47, 217, 277
Nomothetic stance, 48
 defined, 158
 in Functionalist Paradigm, 94
Nongovernmental organizations (NGOs), 11, 15–16
Nonprofit organizations, 10–12. *See also* Social entrepreneurs
 defining, 11
 for-profit agencies created by, 12
 governmental programs used by, 11–12
 grassroots associations as, 16
 with religious affiliations, 17
 streams of thinking about, 21
 umbrella associations of, 15
Nonrational approach, 255
Norms of rationality, 109

O
Objectivism, 57–58, 333
 in Functionalist Paradigm, 50, 93, 94
 and Radical Structuralist Paradigm, 51, 159
 terms defining, 157, 158
O'Connor, G. G., 112
O'Connor, M. K., 354–358
Ongoing events, in sense making, 232
Open-systems theory, 165, 333, 334
Operational school of thought, 27
Orange State Child Abuse Prevention Agency case study, 208–211, 345. *See also* Serendipitous Organizations
Order, in Serendipitous Organizations, 217, 244

Organic organizations, 107
Organismic analogy of social systems, 109–112
Organizations. *See also specific types, e.g.:* Traditional Organizations
 affiliations among, *see* Organizational relationships
 assumptions about, 22–25
 as collections of programs/ services, 8–9
 defined, 3
 employment expectations of, 4
 evolution of, 7
 feminist, 169–170
 formal vs. informal, 6
 for-profit, 12
 global, 7
 master plans for, 7
 mechanistic, 107
 nonprofit, 11–12
 as practice arenas, 5
 private agencies, 10–13
 public agencies, 9–10
 social businesses, 13
 social entrepreneurs, 12–13
 support-only, 4–5, 8
 as systems, 6
 uncertain, turbulent environments of, 5–6
 virtual, 4
Organizational behavior theory, *see* Human relations/ organizational behavioral theory; Human resource/ organizational behavior theory
Organizational coordination and control, 106
Organizational culture(s), 5, 61, 62. *See also* Cultural values and characteristics

Organizational culture(s)
(*Continued*)
adhocracy, 60–62, 77–78
assumptions in, 226–227
changing, 58
clan, 60–62, 75–77
clash in, 7
defining, 224
in Entrepreneurial Organizations,
81, 82
in evolution of organizational
theory, 335
as form of collective cognition, 76
functionalist/hierarchical, 70–73
hierarchy, 59–62, 70–73
interaction of group/subgroup
cultures and, 35–36
interpretivist/clannish, 75–77
levels of, 226
market, 60–62, 73–75
in public vs. private agencies,
356–357
radical humanist/adhocractic,
77–78
radical structuralist/market-
oriented, 73–75
in Serendipitous Organizations,
81
shared assumptions in, 31
in Social Change Organizations, 80
in Traditional Organizations, 79
in younger vs. older agencies,
357–358
Organizational Culture and Leadership
(Edgar Schein), 223–224
Organizational culture theory, 23,
24, 220–229, 244
Organizational ecology, 334
Organizational economics theory,
23

Organizational life:
important dimensions of, 105
meaning dimension of, 220. *See
also* Organizational culture
theory
Organizational outflanking, 166–
167
Organizational outputs, 141
Organizational relationships, 13–21.
See also Organization-
environment relationships
associations, 14–16, 21
franchises, 19, 21
host relationships, 19–21
ideological communities, 17–19,
21
Organizational theories, 22–25, 27.
See also specific theories
across types of organizations,
332–336
connecting human service
organizations and, 41–44
cross-fertilization of, 108
in Entrepreneurial Organizations,
280–292
in Functional Paradigm, 50, 51
in Interpretive Paradigm, 53, 54,
234
and multiparadigmatic practice,
332–336
in Radical Humanist Paradigm,
55
in Radical Structuralist Paradigm,
52
in Serendipitous Organizations,
219–233
in Social Change Organizations,
159–174
in Traditional Organizations,
96–114

Organizational transformation, 190
Organization Assessment tool,
    365–374
  graph used in, 374
  in recent research, 358–363
  score sheet for, 373
Organization-environment
    relationships:
  in Entrepreneurial Organizations,
    308–310
  in Social Change Organizations,
    189–192
  theories of, *see* Theories
  in Traditional Organizations,
    127–130
Organization practice:
  arenas of, 5–6
  assessment/reassessment in, 8
  defined, 3
  organizational theories of, 22
Organized anarchies, 166
Organizing interventions, in Social
    Change Organizations, 200–202
Ott, J. S., 220, 227–228
Outcomes:
  in Entrepreneurial Organizations,
    305, 319–321
  human service, 141
  in Serendipitous Organizations,
    242–243, 260–262
  in Social Change Organizations,
    202
  in Traditional Organizations, 124,
    141
Outflanking, organizational,
    166–167
Outputs:
  organizational, 141
  social vs. physical determinants
    of, 102

P
Paradigms, 45
  defined, 45
  Functionalist, 50–51
  Interpretive, 53–54
  organizational theories across,
    332–336
  Radical Humanist, 54–55
  Radical Structuralist, 51–52
Paradigmatic perspectives:
  combined with cultural
    frameworks, 78
  at different levels of an
    organization, 56
  as frameworks, 45
Paradoxes, 62, 363
  in Entrepreneurial Organizations,
    282, 304
  in human service practice,
    354–355
  from incompatible perspectives,
    56
  in multiparadigmatic practice,
    328
  from operating in more than one
    paradigm, 328
  in public vs. private agencies,
    357
  in Serendipitous Organizations,
    213
  in Social Change Organizations,
    153, 154
  in Traditional Organizations,
    119–120
Parallel planning, 260
Parish social work programs, 21
Parsons, Talcott, 101, 112
Participant relationships:
  in Entrepreneurial Organizations,
    309–310, 346, 348

Participant relationships:
(*Continued*)
in Serendipitous Organizations,
242–243, 249–250, 348
Passivity of groups, 166
Perceived needs, 199
Perceiving:
feeling-perceiving dimension, 64,
65, 68
judging vs., 26
as Myers-Briggs characteristic, 64,
65
thinking-perceiving dimension,
64–67
Personal behavior, 32
Personal biases, 32
Personal history, 33
Personality preferences, dimensions
of, 26
Personality types. *See also* Myers-
Briggs test
bureaucratic, 115
in Entrepreneurial Organizations,
313–314
and functionalism/hierarchy
culture, 71–73
functionalist, 133
interaction of skills and, 350
and interpretivism/clan culture,
76–77
and radical humanism/
adhocracy culture, 77–78
and radical structuralism/market
culture, 74–75
in Serendipitous Organizations,
253
in Social Change Organizations,
196–197
in Traditional Organizations,
133–134

Personal preferences:
in Entrepreneurial Organizations,
81, 82
integrated frameworks built on,
78–82
in Serendipitous Organizations,
81
in Social Change Organizations,
79, 80
in Traditional Organizations, 79,
80
Personal reactions, congruence of
reality and, 33
Personal Responsibility and Work
Opportunity Reconciliation Act
(1996), 17
Personal style, 33
Person-in-environment concept,
262
Peters, T. J., 223
Philosophy, organizational, *see*
Mission/philosophy
Plans, organizational, 7
Planned change, 122, 136, 183
Planned Parenthood, 19
Planning:
defined, 136
emergent, 246, 258
parallel, 260
radical structuralist view of,
197–198
social, 197
in Traditional Organization,
139–141
Planning School, 71–72, 131, 139
Plausibility, in sense making, 232
Play:
as alternative to bureaucracy,
290

in Entrepreneurial Organizations, 303

Pluralism, in postmodern theories, 334

Political economy, 168

Political theory, 27. *See also* Power and politics theories

Population dynamics, 163

Population ecology theory, 113, 163–165, 334

POSDCORB management functions, 99

Positioning School, 72–73, 131, 139

Positivism, 48
  defined, 158
  in Functionalist Paradigm, 50, 92–94
  in Radical Structuralist Paradigm, 155

Postmodern theories:
  development and use of, 334
  in Entrepreneurial Organizations, 286–292
  in Social Change Organizations, 172–173

Post-positivists, 50

Power:
  defined, 167
  in liberal feminist theory, 169
  in postmodern theories, 173
  radical humanist view of, 281–282
  in Social Change Organizations, 192
  sources of, 165–166
  as tool for domination, 168
  types of, 165

Power and politics theories, 23, 24, 44, 335
  development and use of, 333

in Entrepreneurial Organizations, 281–283
  in Social Change Organizations, 165–168

Power School, 73, 194

Practice arenas, 5–6. *See also specific types of organizations*
  community practice, 51, 188
  direct practice, 50–52
  implications of organizational structure for, *see* Implications for practice
  standards for, *see* Standards of practice

Pre-conscious awareness, 33–35

Preferred structure:
  in Entrepreneurial Organizations, 303–304
  in Serendipitous Organizations, 244
  in Social Change Organizations, 184–185
  in Traditional Organizations, 123

Prejudices, self-awareness of, 36

Prescriptive management, 131

Prevent Child Abuse, 16

Prevent Child Abuse America, 21

Private agencies, 10–13, 356–357

Problem definition and analysis:
  in Serendipitous Organizations, 255, 257–258
  in Social Change Organizations, 199–200
  in Traditional Organizations, 138–139

Problem identification and solution skills, 29

Problem solving, critical thinking in, 30

Problem-solving casework, 53
Products:
  in Entrepreneurial Organizations,
    319–321
  in Serendipitous Organizations,
    260–262
  in Social Change Organizations,
    202
  in Traditional Organizations,
    141
Professionalization, 106
Programs, 8–9
  client-centered, 119
  defined, 8
  differing goals in, 339–342
  in Entrepreneurial Organizations,
    304–305
  in multiparadigmatic practice,
    339–342
  as multiple services, 9
  in Serendipitous Organizations,
    244–245, 259–260
  in Social Change Organizations,
    185–186
  in Traditional Organizations,
    123–124
Provider agencies, 9
Public agencies, 9–10, 356–357
Public interest advocacy, 184

Q
Quinn, R. E., 58–62, 346–347

R
Radical change perspective, 49
  concerns of, 158, 277
  in Entrepreneurial Organizations,
    307, 318, 320–321
  in Radical Humanist Paradigm,
    54, 278

  and Radical Structuralist
    Paradigm, 51, 158, 159
Radical feminist theory, 168–170
Radical Humanist Paradigm,
    54–55
  assumptions of, 276–280
  basis of developments from, 335
  differentiators aligned with, 228–
    229
  in Entrepreneurial Organizations,
    267, 273, 275–276
  organizational theories in, 332,
    335
  personality types in, 68
  postmoderism in, 172
  Radical Structuralist Paradigm
    vs., 277, 279
  revolutionary nature of, 280–281
  school of management related to,
    77–78
  theories in, 292–295
Radicalized planned change, 183
Radical organizational theory, 52
Radical Structuralist Paradigm,
    51–52
  assumptions of, 157–159
  organizational theories in, 332–
    334
  personality types in, 66–67
  postmodern theorists in, 173
  Radical Humanist Paradigm vs.,
    277, 279
  schools of management related
    to, 73–75
  in Social Change Organizations,
    153–157
  theories in, 174–175
Rationality:
  in critical theories, 171–172
  in Functionalist Paradigm, 94

in "modern" structural organization theory, 104
norms of, 109
Rationalization, 283
Rational system theory, 27
Rational voice, 165, 166, 281
Realism, 57–58, 158
Reality:
  congruence of personal reactions and, 33
  in Functionalist Paradigm, 93, 94
  as social construction, 55
  socially constructed, 221
  subjectivist perspective on, 216–217
Reductionism, in Traditional Organizations, 139
Referral sources:
  in Entrepreneurial Organizations, 309–310, 348
  in Serendipitous Organizations, 249–250, 348
  in Social Change Organizations, 192, 348
  in Traditional Organizations, 129–130, 348
Reflective/analytic listening, 30
Reflective awareness, 34, 35
Reflexive awareness (reflexivity), 34, 35, 287–288
Reform, through changes in organizational culture, 227–228
Regulation perspective, 49
  in Functionalist Paradigm, 50, 94, 95
  in Interpretive Paradigm, 53, 217–218
  in Serendipitous Organizations, 245

Regulation–radical change continuum, 48–50, 58
Relationships:
  as core human service activities, 42
  interorganizational, 15
  organizational, *see* Organizational relationships
Relativism:
  in Entrepreneurial Organizations, 301, 302
  in Serendipitous Organizations, 263
Relativists, 47
Relativity, ethical, 321–322
Religious affiliates, 17
Religious Right, 182
Research:
  assumptions underlying, 334
  in Entrepreneurial Organizations, 316–317
  on human service organizations, 354–361
  in Interpretive Paradigm, 214–215
  interpretive perspective on, 234
  from radical humanist perspective, 276, 279, 285, 294
Resource dependence theory, 113
Respect, 36–37
Responsibilities of leaders, 29
Retrospection, in sense making, 232
Revolutionary vanguards (culture theorists), 221–222
Risk, in Entrepreneurial Organizations, 301
Roles and relationships:
  in Entrepreneurial Organizations, 307–314, 348–349
  internal, *see* Internal organizational roles and relationships

Roles and relationships: (*Continued*)
  multiparadigmatic practice,
    342–352
  in Serendipitous Organizations,
    247–254, 348–349
  in Social Change Organizations,
    189–197, 348–349
  in Traditional Organizations,
    127–134, 348–349
Rothman, J., 183
Russian social theory, 52

S
Safety, 37
Satisficing decisions, 100
Schein, Edgar, 223–227
Schneider, Mitch, 193
Schools of organizational/
    management thought, 27, 334
  Cognitive, 75, 250
  Configuration, 74, 194
  Cultural, 76, 251
  decision theory, 27
  Design, 70–71, 131, 139
  empirical, 27
  Entrepreneurial, 77–78, 311
  Environmental, 73–74, 194
  human behavior, 27
  Human Relations, 102
  Learning, 75–76, 250–251
  mathematical, 27
  operational, 27
  paradigmatic perspectives of,
    336
  Planning, 71–72, 131, 139
  Postioning, 72–73
  Power, 73, 194
  social systems, 27
School social work services, 21
Scientific management, 98, 116

Search for Excellence movement,
  335
Sectarian agencies, 17
Self-awareness, 32–37
  in choice of organization, 327
  in multicultural organizations,
    34–37
  types of, 33–35
Self-help, 300
Self-help groups, 320–321
Self-respect, 36–37
Selznick, Phillip, 101
Senge, Peter, 246–247
Sense making, 7
  in Entrepreneurial Organizations,
    302
  in evolution of organizational
    theory, 335
  invention in, 231–232
  nonrational approach to, 255–257
  properties of, 232
  in Serendipitous Organizations,
    259–260
Sense-making theory, 24, 44
  feminist theories in, 229–230
  mental processes in, 230–231
  in Serendipitous Organizations,
    229–233, 244
Sensing, intuition vs., 26
Sensitivity, ethnic and cultural, 36
Serendipitous Organizations,
    207–208, 213–214, 235, 239–241,
    263–264. *See also* Interpretive
    Paradigm
  assessment of situations in,
    255–257
  assumptions of Interpretive
    Paradigm, 216–219
  collaboration in, 258–259
  communication in, 349

costs and benefits in, 234–235

cultural values and characteristics of, 241–247, 338

environment in, 342, 343

funding relationships in, 343, 344, 348

goals and personal preferences in, 81, 337

implications for practice in, 262–263

internal organizational roles and relationships in, 250–254, 348–349

interpretive themes in, 214–216

language in, 254–255

leaders in, 341–342

management in, 348

managerial competencies in, 347

mission/philosophy of, 243

Orange State Child Abuse Prevention Agency case study, 208–211

organizational culture theory in, 220–229

participant relationships in, 345, 348

preferred structure in, 244

producing products and outcomes in, 260–262

program goals in, 339

as prototype, 213

reasons for development of, 239–241

referral sources in, 249–250, 348

roles and relationships with and within, 247–254, 348–349

sense making in, 259–260

sense-making theory in, 229–233

staff expectations in, 349

standards of practice within, 254–262

strengths of and challenges for, 353

task environment relationships in, 348

themes of, 330, 331

theories supporting connection and collaboration goals in, 219–233

types of programs and services in, 244–245, 340–342

understanding problems in, 257–258

Services, 9

client-centered, 119

defined, 9

in Entrepreneurial Organizations, 304–305

in multiparadigmatic practice, 339–342

in Serendipitous Organizations, 244–245, 259–260

in Social Change Organizations, 185–186

in Traditional Organizations, 123–124

Service delivery systems, 6, 42

in Entrepreneurial Organizations, 306

formalization of, 6

interdependent nature of, 11–12

Sex role spillover, 169

Shafritz, J. M., 220, 227–228

Shared assumptions, 31, 224

Shared vision, 251

Simon, Herbert, 100–101

Simple conscious awareness, 34, 35

Situational ethics, 242

Situational leadership, 28

Smircich, L., 229
Smith, Adam, 97, 123
Social action:
    advocacy vs., 184
    in Social Change Organizations, 184
Social businesses, 11, 13
Social Change Organizations, 147–148, 153–154, 176, 203–205. *See also* Radical Structuralist Paradigm
    analysis of problems in, 199–200
    assessment of situations in, 198–199
    and assumptions of radical structuralist paradigm, 157–159
    change in, 337
    communication in, 349
    Consumer-Directed Advocacy Agency case study, 149–152
    consumer relationships in, 192, 345, 348
    costs and benefits in, 174–176
    critical theories in, 170–172
    cultural values and characteristics of, 180–188, 338
    environment in, 342, 343
    funding relationships in, 343, 344, 348
    goals and personal preferences in, 79, 80, 337
    implications for practice in, 202–203
    internal organizational roles and relationships in, 193–197, 348–349
    language in, 197–198
    leaders in, 341–342
    management in, 348
    managerial competencies in, 346–347
    mission/philosophy of, 183–184
    organizational theories in, 335
    organization-environment relationships in, 189–192
    organizing interventions in, 200–202
    population ecology theory in, 163–165
    postmoden theories in, 172–173
    power and politics theories in, 165–168
    preferred structure in, 184–185
    producing products and outcomes in, 202
    program goals in, 339
    as prototype, 153
    radical feminist theory in, 168–170
    radical structuralist themes in, 155–157
    reasons for development of, 179–180
    referral sources in, 192, 348
    roles and relationships with and within, 189–197, 348–349
    staff expectations in, 349
    standards of practice within, 197–202
    strengths of and challenges for, 350, 353
    systems theory in, 161–163
    task environment relationships in, 348
    themes of, 330, 331

theories supporting consciousness-raising goals in, 159–174

types of programs and services in, 185–186, 340–342

Social constructionism, 53

Social constructive awareness, 34, 35

Social constructivism, 53

Social control, 164

Social diagnosis, 134

Social entrepreneurs, 11, 12–13

Social environment, 105–106, 122

Social investors, 13

Socialist feminist theories, 229, 230

Socialization, in sense making, 232

Social justice, in multicultural environments, 35

"Socially acceptable" clients, 129–130, 355

Socially constructed reality, 221

Social planning, 197

Social policies, 10

Social science, perspectives on, 46–48

Social systems analogies, 109–112, 161–163, 190

Social systems school of thought, 27

Society, perspectives on, 48–50

Sociopolitical environment, 42

Solipsism, 55

Solo practitioners, 5

Southern Empowerment Project, 191

Southern Poverty Law Center, 182

Spiritual counseling, 55

Stability:

in competing values framework, 58, 59

in Traditional Organizations, 85, 337

Staff characteristics, across organization types, 355

Staff development and training programs, 8–9

across different types of organizations, 339–342

in Entrepreneurial Organizations, 304–305

in Serendipitous Organizations, 244, 245

in Social Change Organizations, 185

in Traditional Organizations, 123–124

Staff expectations:

in Entrepreneurial Organizations, 313–314, 349

in Serendipitous Organizations, 253–254, 349

in Social Change Organizations, 195–197, 349

in Traditional Organizations, 133–134, 349

Stakeholders, in Entrepreneurial Organizations, 310

Stalker, G. M., 107

Standards of practice:

in Entrepreneurial Organizations, 314–321

in Serendipitous Organizations, 254–262

in Social Change Organizations, 197–202

in Traditional Organizations, 134–141

Status quo:

in critical theories, 170

in Interpretive Paradigm, 217, 218

Status quo: (*Continued*)
  in postmodern theories, 173
  in Serendipitous Organizations, 227, 255
  in Traditional Organizations, 122, 125
Stereotypes, self-awareness of, 36
Strategic choice theory, 113
Strategic management framework, 69–78
  Cognitive School, 75
  Configuration School, 74
  Cultural School, 76
  Design School, 70–71
  Entrepreneurial School, 77–78
  Environmental School, 73–74
  functionalism/hierarchy perspective, 70–73
  interpretivism/clan perspective, 75–77
  Learning School, 75–76
  Planning School, 71–72
  Postioning School, 72–73
  Power School, 73
  radical humanism/adhocracy perspective, 77–78
  radical structuralism/market perspective, 73–75
Strategic planning, 142
Structuralist thinking, 107
Structure. *See also specific types of organizations, e.g.:* Traditional Organizations
  to control human beings, 101–102
  internal, 105–106
  "modern" structural organization theory, 23, 24, 104–108
  preferred, *see* Preferred structure
  Smith's theory of, 97
  task, 105
The Structuring of Organizations (H. Mintzberg), 107
Style approach, 27
Subjectivist–objectivist continuum, 46–48
Subjectivist perspective, 47, 48
  in Interpretive Paradigm, 53, 216, 217
  in Radical Humanist Paradigm, 54
  in Serendipitous Organizations, 242
  terms defining, 216–217, 277
  views of reality in, 216, 217
Subjugated knowledge, 284
Support programs, 9
  across different types of organizations, 339–342
  in Entrepreneurial Organizations, 304–305
  in Serendipitous Organizations, 244, 245
  in Social Change Organizations, 185–186
  in Traditional Organizations, 124
SWOT analysis, 70
Symbolic interactionism, 53
Symbolic management, 221–222
Symbolic theory, 27
Systems, 6–7, 333
Systems theories, 23, 24
  assumptions of, 113
  development and use of, 334
  interaction of environment and organization in, 116
  limitations of, 112
  mechanical vs. organismic approaches in, 109–112

paradigmatic assumptions of,
113
pivotal works on, 108–109
in Social Change Organizations,
161–163

T
Tacit knowledge, in radical
humanism, 276
Task environments, 109
Task environment relationships:
in Entrepreneurial Organizations,
308, 348
in Serendipitous Organizations,
348
in Social Change Organizations,
189–190, 348
in Traditional Organizations, 127,
128, 348
Task structure, in organizational
life, 105
Tax exempt organizations, 11
Taylor, Frederick, 98
Technology:
in critical theories, 171, 286
in postmodern theories, 173
and structure of Entrepreneurial
Organizations, 303–304
Temporary Assistance for Needy
Families, 130
Tennessee Valley Authority, 101
Theories:
accounting for nature of human
services, 43
frameworks vs., 44
functionalist, 92–93
within Functionalist Paradigm,
114–115
hunches and assumptions as,
43–44

in Interpretive Paradigm,
219–220, 234
management, 23–24
organizational, 22–25. See also
Organizational theories
in Radical Humanist Paradigm,
292–295
in Radical Structuralist Paradigm,
174–175
supporting individual
empowerment, 280–292
supporting structure and control
goals, 96–114
Theory X, 103
Theory X managers, 27
Theory Y, 103–104
Theory Y managers, 27
Theory Z, 223, 235
Thinking:
divergent vs. convergent, 292
feeling vs., 26
metaphorical, 231
multiparadigmatic, 57
as Myers-Briggs characteristic, 64,
65
in Radical Humanist Paradigm,
275–276
structuralist, 107
Thinking-judging (TJ) dimension
(Myers-Briggs), 64–66, 133
Thinking-perceiving (TP)
dimension (Myers-Briggs),
64–67, 196
Think tanks, 239, 240
Third sector organizations, 11
Third world/(post) colonial
theories, 283–284
Time-and-motion studies, 98, 122
TJ dimension, see Thinking-judging
dimension

Top down organization, 130
Top up organization, 130
TP dimension, *see* Thinking-
perceiving dimension
Traditional Organizations, 85–86,
91–92, 116–117, 119–120,
143–145. *See also* Functionalist
Paradigm
alliances of, 187
assessment of situations in,
136–138
assumptions in, 335
and assumptions of functionalist
paradigm, 93–95
classical organization theory in,
96–99
client relationships in, 344–345,
348
communication in, 349
costs and benefits in, 114–116
cultural values and
characteristics of, 120–126, 338
diagnosis of problems in,
138–139
environment in, 342–343
functionalist themes in, 92–93
funding relationships in, 343, 348
goals and personal preferences in,
79, 80, 337
human relations/organizational
behavioral theory in, 101–104
implications for practice in,
141–143
incremental change in, 337
internal organizational roles and
relationships in, 130–134,
348–349
language in, 119, 134–136, 335
leaders in, 131, 132, 341–342
management in, 348

managerial competencies in, 346
mission/philosophy of, 122–123
"modern" structural
organization theory in, 104–108
neoclassical organization theory
in, 99–101
organizational theories in, 335
organization-environment
relationships in, 127–130
organization-environment
theories in, 108–114
planning interventions in,
139–141
preferred structure in, 123
producing products and
outcomes in, 141
program goals in, 339
as prototype, 91
referral sources in, 129–130,
348
roles and relationships with and
within, 127–134, 348–349
staff expectations in, 349
standards of practice within,
134–141
strengths of and challenges for,
350
task environment relationships
in, 348
themes of, 339–342
theories supporting structure and
control goals in, 96–114
types of programs and services in,
123–124, 340, 341
Washington County Office on
Aging case study, 86–89
Trait approach, 27
Transactional leaders, 28
Transcendental meditation, 55
Transcending self-interest, 290

Transformation:
  collective, 147. *See also* Social
    Change Organizations
  defined, 184, 188
  in Entrepreneurial Organizations,
    280, 299, 318–319
  individual, 318–319
  organizational, 190
  in Radical Humanist Paradigm,
    275
  in Social Change Organizations,
    156, 179, 183
  through strategic management, 73
Transformational leaders, 28
Transformational process, 319
Transformative community
    practice, 188
Transorganizational theory, 164,
    165
Transpersonal work, 55
True consciousness, 144, 145,
    181–182, 302
Truth(s):
  in Functionalist Paradigm, 94
  in Interpretive Paradigm, 219
  in objectivism, 333
  in Radical Humanist Paradigm,
    279, 282
  in Radical Structural Paradigm,
    182, 188
Turbulence, 5–6
  and evolution of organizational
    theories, 333
  in Serendipitous Organizations,
    248
  in Traditional Organizations, 128

U
"The Ugly Face" metaphor, 280, 282
Umbrella associations, 15

Uncertainties, 5–6
  in Entrepreneurial Organizations,
    294
  internal, 5–6
  in multicultural organizations, 44
  in Traditional Organizations,
    128
Understanding:
  in Interpretive Paradigm, 214
  multiple ways of, 275
  nonrational approach to,
    255–257
  of problems, 257–258
  in Serendipitous Organizations,
    239, 240, 242
Understanding Global Cultures
    (M. J. Gannon), 248
The United Way, 21
Universalism, Interpretive
    Paradigm and, 217

V
Values:
  in Entrepreneurial Organizations,
    301–302
  of human service organizations,
    42
  of leaders, 29
  in organizational culture,
    226, 227
  in Serendipitous Organizations,
    242–243
  in Social Change Organizations,
    181–183
  in Traditional Organizations,
    121–122
Value engineering, 222–223
Verstehen, 53
Vibert, C., 113–114
Virtual organizations, 4, 304

Vision, 29
  in Entrepreneurial Organizations, 311
  shared, 251
Voluntarism, 47, 216, 217, 277
Voluntary associations, 14–16
Voluntary organizations, 11

W
Washington County Office on Aging case study, 86–89, 344–345. *See also* Traditional Organizations
Waterman, R. H., Jr., 223

The Wealth of Nations (Adam Smith), 123
Weber, Max, 98–99, 165, 282, 283
Weick, K. E., 231–233
"Welfare Reform" Act, 17
Wheatley, M. J., 316
White House Office of Faith-based and Community Initiatives, 17
Whyte, W. H., 101
Wiener, N., 108
Wilkerson, A. E., 191, 249
Womanspace, 170
World Vision International, 16
Worthiness, 37